Unsaying the Commonplace

George MacDonald
and the Critique of
Victorian Convention

Edited By
Daniel Gabelman and Amanda B. Vernon

UNSAYING THE COMMONPLACE
George MacDonald
and the Critique of Victorian Convention

Edited by Daniel Gabelman and Amanda B. Vernon

Copyright © 2024 George MacDonald Society

Winged Lion Press
Hamden, CT

All rights reserved. Except in the case of quotations embodied in critical articles or reviews, no part of this book may be reproduced or transmitted in any form or by any means, electronic or mechanical, including photocopying, recording, or by any storage system.

WINGED LION PRESS

ISBN 978-1-935688-44-0

In memoriam
Stephen Prickett (1939–2020)
Colin Manlove (1942–2020)
Rolland Hein (1932–2023)
Pioneers of MacDonald Studies

ABOUT THE COVER

Arthur Hughes' illustration is a depiction of George MacDonald with his daughter, Mary Josephine. "St. George" has apparently slain the dragon through his writing, which is represented by the scroll of paper held in his hand as well as by the ink pen and writing desk emitting what seems to be a divine light. Mary Josephine stands resting her foot on the dragon's snout: a picture of innocent and unconcerned victory. This image first appeared in the periodical *Good Things* (1873), accompanying the poem "My daughter," by William Brighty Rands.

The rose design framing the inner illustration was adapted from a cover of *At the Back of the North Wind* (Blackie, 1915). William Morris (1834–1896) created the fonts used for the title (Morris Troy) and subtitle (p22 Morris Golden). A key figure in the Arts and Crafts Movement and a contemporary of MacDonald (Morris purchased MacDonald's Hammersmith home and renamed it Kelmscott House), Morris's fantasy writings also influenced C. S. Lewis and J. R. R. Tolkien.

TABLE OF CONTENTS

Acknowledgements	1
Tribute to Stephen Prickett *Elisabeth Jay*	2
Introduction *Daniel Gabelman and Amanda B. Vernon*	5

PART I: MACDONALD AND CULTURE

George MacDonald and the Cambridge Apostles: **Literature, Theology, the Arts, and Social Reform** **in Victorian Britain** *Stephen Prickett*	17
George MacDonald: Unorthodox Anglican *Elisabeth Jay*	27
"A Guiding Radiance:" **George MacDonald's Science, Religion and Fantasy** **as a New Dialectic** *Franziska E. Kohlt*	43
Rethinking the Dark Side: **MacDonald's Subversive Challenges to "Enlightened"** **Theories of Social Darwinism** *Kerry Dearborn*	67

PART II: MACDONALD AND LITERATURE

Servants to Literature: **Scott, Maurice, and Their Medievalist Influence on MacDonald** *Kirstin Jeffrey Johnson*	97

Being and Truthfulness: 127
MacDonald's Vitalistic Theology of Personal Meaning
Gavin Budge

Uncommon Interpretation: 161
Reading Dante in Charles Kingsley
and George MacDonald's Fairytales
Amanda B. Vernon

PART III: MACDONALD AND THEOLOGY

***Phantastes* as Theological Critique of**   191
E. T. A. Hoffmann's *The Golden Pot*
Charles Beaucham

Another Serving of Orts: 217
Issues Theological, Literary, and Poetic in the Thought of
George MacDonald, F. D. Maurice, and Thomas Erskine
Trevor Hart

Children in the Midst: 239
A Deadly Playdate with MacDonald and Derrida
Daniel Gabelman

List of Contributors   267

The George MacDonald Society   271

Index   273

More George MacDonald Scholarship

ACKNOWLEDGEMENTS

With gratitude to Kirstin Jeffrey Johnson and Mike Partridge for their ceaseless efforts on behalf of the George MacDonald Society: first, for organizing the 2016 Cambridge Conference out of which this volume originated; second, for overseeing the initial stages of the editing process; and third, for their continued support throughout the project. Many thanks also to Robert Trexler for all he does to facilitate George MacDonald research generally and this volume particularly. Daniel would like to thank his family (Josie, Connie, and Beatrice) for allowing him to spend weekends and evenings wrangling footnotes and wrestling unruly apostrophes. Amanda would like to thank John and Linda (in-house cheerleaders) and Johannes (amanuensis extraordinaire). And finally, to our contributors for their patience and geniality through the many years it took to bring this work to fruition.

TRIBUTE TO STEPHEN PRICKETT

The origins of this book lie in a meeting of the George MacDonald Society held at Trinity Hall, Cambridge in the summer of 2016. This elegant but intimately-scaled ancient college, with its sunlit quadrangles and flourishing herbaceous borders, was the perfect venue for fostering conversation. But then, the Society's President, Stephen Prickett (1939–2020) was well aware of the magic that this environment might work for the MacDonald devotees who had travelled from near and far, having been an undergraduate there himself. It was characteristic of Stephen to want others to share the enjoyment he had himself experienced, be it of a place, a performance, a building, or a book. It was this capacity for infectious enthusiasm that made Stephen an excellent choice of president for the George MacDonald Society: wherever he lived and taught—Sussex, Canberra, Glasgow, North Carolina, Texas, and latterly, Kent and Italy—Stephen made converts to the authors, books, and disciplinary interests he espoused and eagerly urged friends, colleagues, and former students to attend the conferences in which he was involved.

In George MacDonald, Stephen found an author who drew together several of his academic preoccupations: the multidisciplinary study of literature, theology, Biblical studies, and the long nineteenth century. When Stephen first published *Victorian Fantasy* in 1979, both fantasy as a nineteenth-century genre and MacDonald as a leading Victorian practitioner could fairly be described as recherché academic interests. But, once his appetite for intellectual discovery and reflection had been whetted, Stephen was not one to be held back by thoughts of being seen as in the swim of whatever theory or subject area was temporarily in the ascendant. Perhaps that is the mark of the true literary explorer: to recognize a hitherto disregarded feature along the way and stop to ponder its unique features and its origins. When the second revised and enlarged edition of *Victorian Fantasy* appeared in 2005 Stephen was able to tie the genre, and more particularly MacDonald, into a German Romantic lineage which had formed a major area of his reading and research in the intervening quarter of a century. *European Romanticism: A Reader* (2010), a polyglot enterprise for which Stephen was General Editor, again speaks to his ability to convene scholars from different fields and countries to realize an idea which in book form became greater than the sum of its parts. The award of the Jean-Pierre Barricelli Prize that year for the best book in romanticism studies recognized the extent of this achievement.

It will not surprise any of those who met Stephen that in his final year he was working enthusiastically on his posthumously published book, *Secret Selves:*

A History of Our Inner Space (2021), anxious as always to share with others the fruits of his immense reading and scholarship.

Elisabeth Jay, September 2023

INTRODUCTION
UNSAYING THE COMMONPLACE

Daniel Gabelman and Amanda B. Vernon

That huge slug, The Commonplace.
It is the wearifulest dragon to fight in the whole miscreation.

Marquis of Lossie

One of MacDonald's lifelong foes was "the commonplace." In his writings, lectures, and sermons, he constantly battled commonplace opinions about science, race, theology, gender, literature, education, children, the Bible, money, class and many more (as will be seen in this volume). Unsurprisingly, his method of critiquing conventional views was also not the "commonplace" approach: he adopted an indirect way of undermining stereotypical thinking by exalting aspects of transcendental reality. To understand this oblique method, we first need to explore what MacDonald means by "the commonplace," because he does not mean the commonplace definition (neither the dictionary's "common or ordinary things" nor Oscar Wilde's aesthetic snobbery[1]), and his idiosyncratic usage is highly charged with symbolic resonances aimed to unsettle his readers' complacencies and redirect them toward higher things.

So, what exactly does MacDonald mean by "the commonplace"? If this word is one of his strongest insults, what precisely is he criticizing? He is not an elitist snob spurning common things to exalt the exclusive or the merely ornate—quite the opposite. "I love the common with all my heart," says the narrator, John Smith, in *Adela Cathcart*, "but I hate the common-place."[2] John Smith loves Christmas, feasts, and fairytales, but when he finds his "niece" Adela suffering from an unaccountable malaise he worries about "something of the commonplace in [her] expression" which makes her face look "too thick for the inward light to shine through."[3] In particular, he is shocked by "her worldliness," namely

---

[1] *Oxford English Dictionary*, s.v. "commonplace (adj.), sense 1," September 2023, https://doi.org/10.1093/OED/7231229364. "One of the chief causes that can be assigned for the curiously commonplace character of most of the literature of our age is undoubtedly the decay of Lying as an art, a science, and a social pleasure." Oscar Wilde, "The Decay of Lying," in *The Complete Writings of Oscar Wilde*, vol. 7, Intentions (New York: The Nottingham Society, 1909), 8.
[2] George MacDonald, *Adela Cathcart* (Whitehorn, CA: Johannesen, 2004), 312.
[3] MacDonald, *Adela Cathcart*, 313.

the way she speaks casually with "current worldly phrases of selfish contentment, or selfish care," and the book chronicles his efforts to pierce through this veil of the commonplace through stories, music, and fellowship.[4]

In addition to worldliness and selfishness, MacDonald also associates the commonplace with a willingness to settle for less than the divine, an over-reliance on conventional views, and a lack of imagination. So, in *Sir Gibbie* the narrator partially excuses a group of schoolgirls and their teacher for their poor assessment of the lowly shepherd and poet Donal Grant saying, "to the vulgar all things are vulgar, because only the vulgar can enter." Here "vulgar" does not mean either crude or lower class—the girls are ironically in something like a finishing school—but seems a synonym for MacDonald's "commonplace." Their vision of reality and interpretation of all things is necessarily filtered through the bourgeois "vulgarity" into which they have been inculcated, but they are still at fault:

> Wherein then is the commonplace man to be blamed? For as he is, so must he think! In this, that he consents to be commonplace, willing to live after his own idea of himself, and not after God's idea of him—the real idea, which, every now and then stirring in him, makes him uneasy with silent rebuke.[5]

The commonplace might be everywhere, but this does not excuse individuals from the responsibility to escape it and to aspire toward the transcendent ideal. And part of the reason why commonplace individuals do not listen to the "silent rebukes" of their elitism or see through their prejudices with the "inward light" is because they lack imagination as Mr. Walton in *The Seaboard Parish* claims: "because our minds are so commonplace, have so little of the divine imagination in them, therefore we do not recognize the spiritual meaning and worth, we do not perceive the beautiful will of God, in the things required of us, though they are full of it."[6] The problem is not with too much imagination (as a commonplace argument runs), but with too little. Or rather the problem is with an underdeveloped, cramped imagination, as MacDonald claims in his seminal essay "The Imagination: Its Functions and Its Culture," for if the imagination "be not occupied with the beautiful, she will be occupied with the pleasant; that which goes not out to worship, will remain at home to be sensual."[7] For MacDonald, the suppressed, commonplace imagination—in an eerie premonition of Freud—lowers itself to the "sensual," so he exhorts: "seek not that your sons and daughters should not see visions, should not dream dreams; seek that they should see true

---

[4] MacDonald, *Adela Cathcart*, 313.
[5] George MacDonald, *Sir Gibbie* (Whitehorn, CA: Johannesen, 2000), 337.
[6] George MacDonald, *The Seaboard Parish* (Whitehorn, CA: Johannesen, 1995), 77.
[7] George MacDonald, "The Imagination: Its Functions and Its Culture," in *A Dish of Orts* (Whitehorn, CA: Johannesen, 1996), 30.

visions, that they should dream noble dreams. Such out-going of the imagination is one with aspiration, and will do more to elevate above what is low and vile than all possible inculcations of morality."[8] The commonplace approach to improving people's lives and behavior is to denigrate beauty and desire, and replace these with more severe morality and religious doctrine. MacDonald inverts this: incite love of highest beauty, undermine the dullness of the commonplace, and you will elicit personal transformation at all levels and restore the delight bursting out of common things and common duties.

So, for instance, in one of MacDonald's longest and most symbolic discussions of the commonplace Alexander Graham (the schoolmaster from *Malcolm* who in *The Marquis of Lossie* is now living in London after losing his school in Scotland on a charge of heresy) is on his way to a London chapel on a wet, windy, dreary day when he starts thinking about "his dragon," which he describes as

> that huge slug, *The Commonplace*. It is the wearifulest dragon to fight in the whole miscreation. Wound it as you may, the jelly-mass of the monster closes, and the dull one is himself again—feeding all the time so cunningly that scarce one of the victims whom he has swallowed suspects that he is but pabulum slowly digesting in the belly of the monster.[9]

Graham imagines himself a knight "spurring to meet [his] dragon" in his "headquarters," and here MacDonald wryly comments, "What can be fuller of the wearisome, depressing, beauty-blasting commonplace than a dissenting chapel in London, on the night of the weekly prayer-meeting, and that night a drizzly one?" He further describes the pulpit as "gaping, empty, unsightly, the place is the very skull of the monster himself," but for this very reason it is

> the fittest place of all wherein to encounter the great slug, and deal him one of those death blows which every sunrise, every repentance, every childbirth, every true love deals him. Every hour he receives the blow that kills, but he takes long to die, for every hour he is right carefully fed and cherished by a whole army of purveyors, including every trade and profession, but officered chiefly by divines and men of science.[10]

The dragon now has an army. This army of the commonplace is associated with worldly business ("every trade and profession"), but it is ironically led by two types that should be mortal foes of the commonplace—religion and science. Religion and science were both dear to MacDonald, which is perhaps why they receive the highest blame, because they too often enabled "the destroying spirit,

---

[8] MacDonald, "The Imagination," 30.
[9] George MacDonald, *The Marquis of Lossie* (Whitehorn, CA: Johannesen, 2004), 110.
[10] MacDonald, *The Marquis of Lossie*, 111.

who works in the commonplace, [which] is ever covering the deep and clouding the high."[11]

Graham sits through the prayer service battling through boring music ("one of the monster's favourite hymns") and boring prayers ("then first the monster found tongue") before being asked to speak a word of exhortation, which he hears "as the Red-cross Knight when he heard Orgoglio in the wood staggered to meet him." Graham has some of the commonplace's "benumbing tendrils around his heart" as he rises, but "his business was nevertheless to fight him." And fight the monster he does. Seeing a charwoman "brooding over ways and means, calculating pence and shillings," Graham suddenly sees "the mere humanity of the woman" which breaks the "trance" of the commonplace, and he exhorts the audience to "seek the best first" and trust God for their "meat and drink and clothes."[12] Graham warms to his task, "and while he spoke, lo! The dragon-slug had vanished; the ugly chapel was no longer the den of the hideous monster; it was but the dusky bottom of a glory shaft adown which gazed the stars of the coming resurrection."[13] The great dragon is defeated in its den with nothing more than an appeal to divine love and an exhortation to seek the highest, the best, and the most beautiful, and then to leave worldly concerns to God. Graham thus speaks the commonplace monster out of existence without even directly acknowledging its presence.

Speaking things away indirectly (or *un*saying) was MacDonald's preferred mode of critique. He eschewed direct debate and frontal criticism not out of timidity or lack of passionate conviction, but out of an even deeper faith in the potency of beauty, goodness, and truth. He fervently believed that individuals must plant and nurture these transcendentals deep in their souls, not learn superficial criticisms or arguments by rote. Like Alexander Graham, "he rarely contradicted anything" but instead "would call up the opposing truth, set it face to face with the error, and leave the two to fight it out. [...] In a word, he would oppose error only by teaching truth."[14] In his first published essay, "Browning's 'Christmas Eve,'" MacDonald says the same thing in his own voice:

> Surely if a man would help his fellow-men, he can do so far more effectually by exhibiting truth than exposing error, by unveiling beauty than by a critical dissection of deformity. From the very nature of the things it must be so. Let the true and good destroy their opposites. It is only by the good and beautiful that the evil and ugly are known.[15]

---

[11] Geoge MacDonald, *The Miracles of Our Lord* (Whitehorn, CA: Johannesen, 2000), 245–6.
[12] MacDonald, *The Marquis of Lossie*, 113.
[13] MacDonald, *The Marquis of Lossie*, 114.
[14] George MacDonald, *Malcolm* (Whitehorn, CA: Johannesen, 2004), 32.
[15] George MacDonald, "Browning's 'Christmas Eve,'" in *A Dish of Orts*, 196–7.

Later in the essay, he explicitly rejects the rationalistic approach to convincing others, particularly as it relates to the highest things like faith, claiming that "the reality of Christ's nature is not to be proved by argument. He must be beheld. The manifestation of Him must 'gravitate inwards' on the soul."[16] This is why, despite holding many views that were diametrically opposed to his Victorian contemporaries, he rarely dissects or confronts them head on, and why in his works he can in W. H. Auden's words "create an atmosphere of goodness about which there is nothing phony or moralistic."[17]

MacDonald seems to have learned this unsaying method from his primary mentors—mystics. In his sermon "The New Name," MacDonald defines mysticism as "a certain mode of embodying truth" which seeks "the highest mode of conveying the deepest truth" through "[prosecuting] thought about truth by dealing with the symbols themselves."[18] Truth, he says, is not "an utterance, not even a *right* form of words," but instead "is a condition of heart, soul, mind and strength towards God and towards our fellow."[19] As such, fretting over doctrinal verbal precision or the consistency of logical arguments is relatively pointless, because it is "the person that speaks," and this personal manifestation of truth unsays more commonplace rationalistic approaches and concerns.[20]

MacDonald's approach to critique could thus be described as apophatic, for as Michael Sells reminds us, the etymology of *apophasis* is "un-saying or speaking away."[21] Yet, even though *apophasis* is associated with the "via negativa" and "negative theology," it is only ever partially or temporally negative because "all discourse on the transcendent contains both saying and unsaying."[22] MacDonald's version of apophatic unsaying might even be called a *via positiva*, because as we have seen he rarely negatively deconstructed a view he opposed but rather positively elevated something more grand and inspiring to do this work behind the scenes.

Unlike "commonplace," which appears repeatedly throughout MacDonald's oeuvre, "unsaying" was not used by MacDonald in the sense we are articulating here. Nevertheless, it seems a neat shorthand for his indirect method of critique, and he did use "unspoken" in the titles of his most condensed and influential

---

[16] MacDonald, "Browning's 'Christmas Eve,'" 206.
[17] W. H. Auden, "Afterword," in George MacDonald, *The Golden Key* (New York: Farrar, Straus & Giroux, 1967), 86.
[18] George MacDonald, "The New Name," in *Unspoken Sermons* (Whitehorn, CA: Johannesen, 2004), 67.
[19] MacDonald, "The New Name," 69.
[20] MacDonald, "The New Name," 69.
[21] Michael A. Sells, *Mystical Languages of Unsaying* (Chicago: Chicago University Press, 1994), 2.
[22] Sells, *Mystical Language of Unsaying*, 3.

theological works, *Unspoken Sermons*. For MacDonald to have repeated this title three times (his only reused title—and he wanted to use it for *Hope of the Gospel* as well[23]) suggests that he meant far more by "unspoken" than most reviewers and commentators have thought.[24] Our title is thus chosen to reflect MacDonald's distinctive, beneficent mode of battling the prejudices, injustices, and errors of his time not by lowering himself to fisticuffs with commonplaces but by elevating others to celestial dances. Similarly, the Arthur Hughes cover image (probably showing MacDonald with his daughter Mary Josephine) seems to depict MacDonald, like Alexander Graham, defeating "his dragon," "that huge slug, *The Commonplace*" without directly focusing on it. His innocent daughter lightly rests her slipper on the dragon's snout, serenely unconcerned by any threat while her arms are around her father—she is his attendant spirit, the reminder of the true vision of childlike joy. MacDonald meanwhile is a modern St. George who seems to have slain the dragon offhandedly not with a sword but with his writing. He kills it indirectly while busily imagining the starry sky behind him and contemplating the radiant light emanating from his writing desk.

—

The chapters in this book explore and delineate the varied ways in which MacDonald sought to slay the dragon of the commonplace through his writing. It is worth noting, however, that many of the chapters were developed with a different focus in mind as they were nearly all given as papers at the 2016 conference of the George MacDonald Society, "George MacDonald and the Cambridge Apostles," held at Trinity Hall, University of Cambridge. The papers at this conference explored the links between the work of MacDonald and various members of the Cambridge Apostles, many of whom were connected to MacDonald in some way. Several of the chapters are revised versions of these papers, which explains the frequency with which figures such as F. D. Maurice and Charles Kingsley (both Cambridge Apostles) are discussed.[25] A fairly extensive period elapsed between the conference and the first stages of compiling this book and therefore some of the material presented at the conference had already been published elsewhere. The decision was therefore made to widen the scope of this book in terms of theme in order to include subjects not necessarily connected with the Cambridge Apostles. As we compiled this volume, we noticed that each

---

[23] Rolland Hein, George MacDonald: Victorian Mythmaker (Nashville, TN: StarSong Publishing, 1993), 380.

[24] See Daniel Gabelman's chapter for further discussion of MacDonald's use of "unspoken."

[25] With the exception of a few changes to make the piece more appropriate for an audience of readers rather than listeners, Stephen Prickett's keynote (the first chapter of this volume) remains the same.

of the chapters examined how MacDonald, in some form or another, attempts to "unsay the commonplace."

The first four chapters are broadly concerned with "MacDonald and Culture." These chapters highlight MacDonald's critique of Victorian cultural convention and include discussions of MacDonald's relationships with key political and social reformers, Victorian Anglicanism, contemporary scientific discourse, and issues of gender and race. The three chapters on "MacDonald and Literature," highlight the fundamentally intertextual nature of MacDonald's writing and, in so doing, reveal the ways in which his work as a literary scholar and novelist offered him unique modes of unsaying the commonplace. The final section, "MacDonald and Theology," presents a set of chapters that, in offering varied—and even divergent—readings of MacDonald, enact a productive conversation on subjects ranging from MacDonald's engagement with Platonic philosophy, to his theory of language, to his understanding of atonement and incarnation. Contributors have referenced the editions of MacDonald's works that align with their individual preferences and research methodologies. As a result, readers will encounter citations from various editions across the chapters, reflecting the diverse approaches and perspectives of our contributing authors. To make publication details easier to find, full citations of editions are given in the footnote in which the edition is initially cited in each chapter even if full citation information for that edition has already been given in a previous chapter.

The first chapter, Stephen Prickett on MacDonald and the Cambridge Apostles, draws attention to the personal relationships that existed between MacDonald and various members of the group (especially Charles Kingsley and F. D. Maurice), as well as the interests they shared in art, theology, and social reform. Highlighting the ways in which Kingsley and Maurice's Christian Socialism offered a controversial challenge to Victorian convention, Prickett offers a window into the broader cultural context in which MacDonald undertook his work as a lecturer and writer in the cause of educational reform. Prickett's focus on the relationship between theology, art, and social reform reflects the claims MacDonald made about the necessity of the divine imagination to battle the worldly business and conventional thought that characterizes the commonplace.

Like Prickett, Elisabeth Jay highlights the relationship between MacDonald and the theologically- and socially-controversial F. D. Maurice. Her chapter explores the apparent conflict between MacDonald's "trajectory of increasing unorthodoxy" and his turn to Anglican worship (at Maurice's Church) in the 1860s and 1870s. Delving into the heated ecclesiastical debates of nineteenth-century Britain, and attending to accounts of the reception of MacDonald's *Annals of a Quiet Neighbourhood* trilogy, Jay offers a reading of the "Anglican trilogy" as MacDonald's intervention into contemporary debates about Anglican disestablishment. In so doing, Jay reveals MacDonald's critique of what he regarded as commonplace religion: forms of religious belief and practice that encourage schism and dull the divine imagination.

Franziska E. Kohlt's chapter considers MacDonald's fantasy works within their historical scientific context. She argues that, contrary to the prevailing narrative in MacDonald studies, attending to the role of science in MacDonald's life and fiction reveals his extensive participation in the scientific discourse of his day. Offering an examination of how MacDonald's mode of synthesizing religion and science was impacted by his studies at King's College Aberdeen, Kohlt goes on demonstrate how MacDonald's use of dream narrative, and his portrayal of the dream in *Phantastes*, functions as an alternative discursive sphere in which to resolve the scientific and philosophical questions with which he was preoccupied. MacDonald thus unsays the "destroying spirit" of commonplace scientific discourse and offers an imaginative alternative that transcends conventional modes of thought.

Kerry Dearborn's chapter reads MacDonald in light of questions of race, gender, class, and ability. She argues that MacDonald's theological convictions, which were shaped by his interpretation of the Bible and his Celtic worldview, offered him a framework for critiquing the conventional binary mode of thinking, which associated light with the good and darkness with the bad. Dearborn suggests that MacDonald's theological influences gave him both an ethical framework and imaginative resources to write stories critiquing commonplace prejudice. The chapter culminates in a reading of "Photogen and Nycteris," that draws attention to the ways in which the story might have offered a challenge to conventional Victorian understandings of race and gender.

Kirstin Jeffrey Johnson examines MacDonald's fiction in light of popular Victorian medievalism. She traces the roots of MacDonald's uncommon method as a literary scholar and draws attention to the extent and significance of his work on both Medieval texts and the literature that engages with them. Through her close readings of *Phantastes* and *The Seaboard Parish*, Jeffrey Johnson makes the case that MacDonald's scholarly work shaped his understanding of knighthood as a form of servanthood that, characterized by the inward light of imagination, is able to discern the beauty of common things and common duties. In doing so, she demonstrates how MacDonald's engagement with Arthurian tradition and contemporary popular medievalism offers a challenge to commonplace Victorian accounts of knighthood.

A critique of the commonplace in terms of a lack of individual authenticity is one aspect of the "vitalistic theology of personal meaning" that Gavin Budge delineates in his reading of MacDonald. Examining the typological resonances of MacDonald's fiction, Budge links the notion of "authentic" theology with MacDonald's emphasis on the centrality of the Incarnation. Tracing the influence of both Scottish Common Sense philosophy and Brunonian medical theory in MacDonald's thought, Budge's readings of narrative in *Adela Cathcart* and *At the Back of the North Wind*, highlight the relationships between mental, spiritual, and physical health and growth in MacDonald's work.

Amanda B. Vernon's chapter examines the uncommon links between Dante's *Divine Comedy* and the fairytales of Charles Kingsley and MacDonald. Her close readings of Kingsley's *The Water Babies* and MacDonald's *The Princess and Curdie* and "The Lost Princess: A Double Story," demonstrate the extent to which both writers appealed to Dante as a source of cultural authority and imaginative inspiration in order to articulate their ideas about the relationship between interpretation and revelation. Vernon argues that while Kingsley champions a mode of scientific enquiry that emphasizes revelation through moral and natural laws, MacDonald suggests an interpretive approach to nature and literature characterized by affect and creativity. MacDonald's reading of Dante unsays the Florentine poet's commonplace notion of punitive justice and offers an alternative notion of reparative justice in which the individual progresses to a higher stage of spiritual development via the imagination.

As is nearly always the case with MacDonald, literature and theology are intertwined. Building on the chapters from the previous section, the intertextuality of MacDonald's work is further explored by Charles Beaucham in his reading of *Phantastes* as a theological critique of E. T. A. Hoffmann's *The Golden Pot*. Attending to the Platonic influence evident in both texts, Beaucham explores how each writer's depiction of the pursuit of beauty illustrates both their shared rejection of capitalist misenchantment and their diverging notions of how the "ideal" and "commonplace" worlds relate. Beaucham draws out the social implications of Hoffmann's Romantic Platonism and of MacDonald's incarnational theology, arguing that the latter offers a disruptive and redemptive solution to the desacralizing forces of capitalism.

Beaucham's discussion of the ideal and commonplace worlds complements Trevor Hart's discussion of immanence, transcendence, and atonement in MacDonald's theology. In his chapter, Hart places MacDonald into conversation with F. D. Maurice and Thomas Erskine, exploring their responses to the apparent tension between God's immanence and transcendence, and its relationship with Trinitarian theology. Hart attends to the commonalities between Maurice and MacDonald's theology, examining the emphasis both placed upon the possibility of the reality and immediacy of God to the receptive soul—a reality that is encountered, in the case of MacDonald's sacramentalism, in Nature and in poetry. From his reading of MacDonald's sacramentalism, Hart moves into a discussion of Erskine, Maurice, and MacDonald's similar understanding of the doctrine of the atonement—a decidedly un-commonplace understanding that Hart claims is a distinctive and important contribution to the development of that doctrine in Christian theology.

Daniel Gabelman's chapter enacts a game of hide-and-seek as he playfully attempts to tease out the cryptic clues behind which are hidden MacDonald's theory of language. Placing MacDonald into conversation with Derrida, Gabelman brings to light the similarities between the two thinkers and their attempts to deconstruct—or unsay—the divine sign. Gabelman's reading of MacDonald's *Unspoken Sermon* "The Child in the Midst," similarly unsays commonplace interpretations of MacDonald as innocent dove, revealing him instead to be an agent of patricide and regicide when it comes to the unchildlike God of the dull disciple.

The chapters in this volume thus trace the various ways in which MacDonald—informed by the divine light of imagination—critiqued Victorian convention and battled the dragon of the commonplace. This volume also attempts, in its own way, to unsay some of the commonplaces about MacDonald in existing scholarly work. Whether critiquing conventional thought about MacDonald's relationship to science, challenging the perception of him as an innocuous theological thinker, or highlighting his often-overlooked work as a literary scholar, our contributors have essayed in new critical directions. It is our hope that this volume will also encourage further un-commonplace explorations of MacDonald and his unspoken method.

Part I
MacDonald and Culture

GEORGE MACDONALD AND THE CAMBRIDGE APOSTLES:
LITERATURE, THEOLOGY, THE ARTS, AND SOCIAL REFORM IN VICTORIAN ENGLAND

Stephen Prickett

When I first read Benjamin Disraeli's 1844 novel *Coningsby*—sometimes described as the first political novel in English—I was intrigued by the mention of a Cambridge tutor who, after teaching hours, initiated his pupils into what seemed to be dark and arcane secret knowledge—something by implication between black magic and a terrorist cell. It was many years later that I realized that this was one of the earliest references to the Cambridge Conversatzione Society that quickly became known as "The Apostles"—so called, because the membership was limited to twelve at any one time. Much more of a surprise to me was the news that, so far from practicing dark political arts, one of the goals of this society founded in 1820 was to develop an understanding of Samuel Taylor Coleridge's social and religious thought.

Coleridge is known to most of us primarily as a poet—author of such well-known poems as "The Ancient Mariner" or "Frost at Midnight"—and today his later career as a political and social thinker is largely overlooked, yet in his lifetime this was the other way round: he was much better known for his controversial social and theological ideas—(and also, by some, as a struggling drug addict). Remarkably, the foundation of the Apostles pre-dates much of Coleridge's best-known work in this area. *Church and State*, for instance, probably his most detailed piece of political ideology, belongs to the late 1820s, and explored contentious debates surrounding the Catholic Reform Bill of his time. The book had an unexpected and significant influence on later social policy. What seems to have been the main influence on the 1820 gathering was Coleridge's two Lay Sermons, *The Statesman's Manual*—the first subtitled *The Bible the Best Guide to Political Skill and Foresight* and the second, *"Blessed are ye that sow beside all waters!": A Lay Sermon addressed to the Higher and Middle Classes on the existing Distresses and Discontents.*

Anyone who reads of the maneuvering and chicanery of contemporary politics of the day—quite unlike our own, of course—will be even more astonished that these two deeply idealistic writings should have had any practical influence on real life. Ironically, it was probably Disraeli himself, who was never the graduate of any university but became one of the most popular novelists of the 1840s, who seems to have made more use of Coleridge in his "one nation" Toryism than any aspiring Liberal politician. Indeed, if we are to judge by practical results, Disraeli was arguably the greatest and most influential Coleridgean of all time. It was Richard Cross, Disraeli's first Home Secretary, who began the slow process of slum clearance and welfare programs for those left behind by industrialization, and provided a continuing counter-weight to the *laissez-fare* individualism of the Gladstonian liberals. Disraeli did not invent the Apostles, but he was to give them a totally unexpected glamor. It was a glamor coupled with a quite undeserved suggestion of secret power that was then, of course, absurd, but with its later accretion of the status of a secret society, and the revelation of the Cambridge spy ring of former members of Trinity Hall in Cold War days, a curiously prophetic attribution.

Though George MacDonald, a graduate of Aberdeen University, and from a superficially very different tradition, was obviously never an Apostle, it is significant how close his interests were to this young and idealistic group. The first link is his debt to Coleridge. This may come as something of a surprise from a quick glance at MacDonald's literary essays. His essay "The Imagination: Its Functions and Its Culture," for instance, has glowing references to Bacon, Carlyle, Keats, Milton, Shakespeare, Shelley, Spenser, Tennyson, and Wordsworth—yet in this panorama of Romantic taste, Coleridge's name is strangely absent. But this is less a matter of ignoring him than of acknowledging an omnipresence. To anyone familiar with chapter XIII of Coleridge's *Biographia Literaria*, an examination of the *structure* of MacDonald's essay immediately reveals some very familiar themes. The whole discussion is centered on the idea of a primary and secondary imagination, and turns on a discussion of how far human imagination reflects the infinitely greater divine imagination. As William Raeper puts it, for MacDonald "Wordsworth was the seer," and "Coleridge was the sage"— combining philosophy, poetry, and theology, drawing on the ancient classical tradition stemming from Plato and Plotinus.[1] Here is what MacDonald has to say in *England's Antiphon*, his 1868 anthology of English religious poetry: "Coleridge had much to do with the opening of Wordsworth's eyes to such visions; as, indeed, more than any other man of our times, he has opened the eyes of the English people to see wonderful things."[2] This was certainly the case with Disraeli's fictional Cambridge tutor, who was almost certainly based on Julius Hare (1795–1855), himself a tutor of Apostles such as Frederick Denison

---

[1] William Raeper, *George MacDonald: Novelist and Victorian Visionary* (Tring: Lion Publishing, 1987), 110–11.
[2] George MacDonald, *England's Antiphon* (London: Macmillan & Co, 1868), 307.

Maurice (1805–1872) and John Sterling (1806–1844). Though Hare's family were wealthy Sussex landowners, and from the center of the Anglican establishment, with bishops on both sides of the family, he was born at Valdagno, near Vicenza, in Italy. He came to England with his parents in 1799, but in 1804/05 spent a winter with them at Weimar, Germany, where as a precocious ten-year old, he learned German and met Goethe and Schiller, which triggered a lifelong interest in German literature and culture. In 1818, he became a fellow of Trinity College, Cambridge. After further trips abroad—no light undertaking at this period—he became assistant tutor at Trinity, from 1822 to 1832. If this sounds like a junior position, akin perhaps to an "assistant lecturer" in today's terms, this was, in fact, a senior post with (as Disraeli suggests) considerable power to influence favored pupils. He was ordained in 1826, and in 1832 he resigned his post to take up the family living of Herstmonceux, in Sussex. In 1853 he became chaplain to Queen Victoria.

Hare's personal library was said to have contained over 14,000 books—many of which were in German. An anonymous memoir from 1871 records that

> You entered and found the whole house one huge library,—books overflowing in all corners, in hall on landing places, in bedrooms, and in dressing rooms [...] though it would be too much to say their owner had read them all, yet he had at least bought them all with a special purpose, knew where they were, and what to find in them, and often in the midst of a discussion, he would dart off to some remote corner, and return in a few minutes with the passage which was wanted as an authority or illustration. Each group of books (and a traceable classification persisted throughout the house) represented some stage in the formation of his mind,—the earlier scholarship, the subsequent studies in European literature and philosophy, the later in patristic and foreign theology.[3]

Though Hare translated a number of important German works, including most notably, Niebuhr's massive *History of Rome*, he is chiefly remembered for a book with the distinctly un-arresting title of *Guesses at Truth*, which he produced together with his two brothers, Augustus and Marcus in 1827. Modelled vaguely on the *Athenaeum*, the short-lived journal of the German Jena Romantics—who, incidentally, invented the term "Romantic" in this literary sense—the Hare brothers' book was a collection of literary, philosophic, and religious aphorisms

---

[3] See the anonymously written "Memoir of Julius Hare," in Julius and Augustus Hare, *Guesses at Truth* (London: Macmillan, 1871), xlv. The author of this unsigned memoir, incidentally, was another Cambridge man who deserves a footnote of his own. Edward Henry Palmer, a local boy from a humble background was a self-taught linguist who managed to learn Romany from the gypsies while still at the Perse School in Cambridge, and eventually became Professor of Arabic, Hindustani, and Persian at Cambridge University. In 1882 he was shot by Arab brigands in Egypt while returning from a secret service mission for the British government.

and fragments. Surprisingly, it sold well, with a second, and much-enlarged edition in 1838, and third in 1847, and was reprinted thereafter in 1867, 1871, and 1874. It was, for instance, one of a parcel of books ordered by Charlotte Brontë from her publishers in November 1849, along with a translation of Goethe's *Conversations with Eckermann and Soret*.

Hare's enthusiasm for German literature, at a time when the language was rarely taught in Britain, and even more rarely read, is one of two important links with MacDonald. Whereas a knowledge of French was an essential for any educated person of the day, knowledge of German scarcely figured. The story of James Mill, the utilitarian philosopher, and father of John Stuart Mill, flipping through a volume of Kant's *Critique of Pure Reason*, and remarking, "Ah, yes. I see what poor Kant may be at," may well be apocryphal, but it captures the prevailing mood of patronizing ignorance very well. It is certainly true that when, in 1821, Edward Bouverie Pusey, later to become Regius Professor of Divinity at the University of Oxford, wanted to find out about recent developments in German theology, he could find only two men in the entire University who knew any German at all.[4] Cambridge was only marginally better off. Apart from Hare himself, there was Herbert Marsh, Lady Margaret Professor of Divinity, and the translator of Michaelis' *Introduction to the New Testament*, who had also done something to introduce German scholarship. A quick further check suggests something like five or six articulate Germanists in the whole country: Coleridge, Hare, Herbert Marsh, De Quincy, and Carlyle—and, of course, MacDonald himself who, according to Greville, was charged by the elders of his Congregational church in Arundel with being "tainted with German theology."[5]

For MacDonald, as for many at this period, to be a Coleridgean was also immediately to be interested in all things German. The end of the Napoleonic Wars in 1815 also ended twenty-five years of intellectual isolation from Continental ideas of all kinds, from French and German Romantic theologians, poets, and critics, to Kantian philosophy, the Jena Romantics, and the writings of Goethe. In the next quarter-century the tide changed sharply, with a flood of translations, and growing interest in a Germany that was still little known or understood. The improbable nexus of Coleridge's social thinking and enthusiasm for the German and the Gothic was not merely to herald a new intellectual fashion, it coincided with a much broader social trend—culminating, of course, with Queen Victoria's marriage to her German cousin, Albert of Saxe Coburg Gotha. In the 1840s and 50s things German were the flavor of the decade. Gloomy

---

[4] David Newsome, *The Parting of Friends: A Study of the Wilberforces and Henry Manning* (London: John Murray, 1966), 78.
[5] In fact, it doesn't seem to have been German theology so much as German poetry that attracted him.

pine forests, mysterious gothic castles, sinister witches, dark caverns inhabited by goblins, kobolds, and other creatures of the night were all the rage. A literary tradition perhaps begun by Horace Walpole, re-enforced by Novalis, Jean-Paul, and Goethe, not to mention Coleridge himself, was to be taken up by both Percy and Mary Shelley, MacDonald, William Morris, and continued down to Tolkien and J. K. Rowling in the present day.

It is in this fertile, even febrile, intellectual context that we need to see the no less strange, even Gothic, idea of a secret society with limited membership lurking under the sporting and philistine surface of this ancient university. In its earliest days the Apostles were little more than members of a self-perpetuating debating society—Tennyson, another early member from 1827, and a near contemporary of Maurice and Sterling, was remembered as lying on the floor during meetings, and never contributing to the discussions. Certainly, there was nothing very strange about university societies catering to all tastes—Oxford had the notorious Bullingdon Club, Cambridge the rather more sporting Hawks Club—but a secret *debating society* sounds rather more like a contradiction in terms. Who wants to shine just before an audience of never more than eleven others in some obscure undergraduate's room? Certainly not Disraeli, for instance!

The narrow, almost stifling, atmosphere of Hare's world is illustrated by his very close relationship with two of his students: Frederick Denison Maurice and John Sterling, both very early members of the Apostles. Hare was to write a *Memoir* of John Sterling after his untimely death in 1844, and the same year married Maurice's sister, Esther. However, literary matters were also important. During his short life Sterling also wrote a novel in 1833, almost unbelievably *also* called *Coningsby*, ten years before Disraeli's novel of the same name! He also produced a number of fantasy stories, "The Onyx Ring," "Land and Sea," "A Chronicle of England," and "The Palace of Morgana"—none of which achieved popularity anywhere nearly comparable with MacDonald's, but again, suggest the very closeness of interests between the Scottish writer and his English counterparts.

Frederick Denison Maurice represented another side of MacDonald's interests. Though he also wrote fiction—including a novel entitled *Eustace Conway*, which had at least the distinction of being praised by Coleridge himself—what he is mostly famous for is his theology. Raised as a Unitarian, his time at Trinity Hall, Cambridge was cut short by his refusal to accept a Cambridge degree awarded then, as now, in the name of the Trinity. In the late 1820s he moved steadily toward and eventually stepped into a firm Trinitarian position, and in 1835 he was ordained as an Anglican priest. *The Kingdom of Christ*, first published in 1838, was to establish him as one of the leading religious thinkers of his day, combining a Broad Church openness with what might be called High Church ecclesiology. This was quite enough to earn him the suspicion of conservative evangelicals and Anglo-Catholics alike. The Church, for Maurice, was by definition, a universal spiritual society. If it were not spiritual, it could not be universal; if it were not universal, it could not be spiritual. Unlike, say, Newman's conversion to Catholicism, where he was confronted from the outside by the historical certainty of the Roman Catholic Church, Maurice insisted that "conversion" was more a matter of discovering that one was *already* a member of the Church—in the same way one discovered oneself a member of a family. Though this attracted criticism which dogged him throughout his life, and even contributed to his (temporary) dismissal from a professorship at Queen's College, London in 1853, unlike many nineteenth-century theological tomes—not to mention his own fiction—*The Kingdom of Christ* has shown unexpected staying power. The last time I came across a copy, it was being read by an IT specialist in America who, with no hint of an antiquarian interest, recommended it to me as a "really good read!" It is a mark of Maurice's own spiritual qualities that, according to the twentieth-century Anglican theologian Alec Vidler, on one occasion a group of Victorian notables indulged in a game of who they wanted to be with them at their deathbed. Each wrote a name on a piece of paper. When they compared notes, they discovered that all of them had written the name of Maurice.

Though MacDonald had clearly read *The Kingdom of Christ* sometime before, he did not actually meet Maurice until 1858, when they became firm friends until Maurice's death in 1872. They not merely shared common views on Coleridge and German literature, but both had experience of persecution, having endured the humiliation of being expelled from their respective posts—MacDonald at Arundel; Maurice from Queens College, London. Both, moreover, saw the very closest connections between theology and literature—even, perhaps, that theology was a literary form. Both would have agreed with Julius Hare's aphorism in *Guesses at Truth* that "Poetry is philosophy, and philosophy is poetry."[6]

Another Cambridge man, Charles Kingsley, though not an Apostle, was also a Coleridgean and a friend of both Maurice and MacDonald. Like Hare and Maurice, he became an Anglican clergyman and theologian, as well as eventually becoming (to the surprise of many) Regius Professor of History. Like MacDonald, but unlike most of the Apostles, Kingsley was also at home in the scientific debates of the time—especially the debates over Darwinism after 1859. What really links him to MacDonald, however, is his role in the creation of the relatively new literary genre of fantasy. He was a friend of both Lewis Carroll

---

[6] Julius Hare, *Guesses at Truth* (London: Macmillan, 1871), xxii.

and MacDonald, and the manuscripts of the *Alice* books, *The Water Babies*, and *Phantastes* were circulated between them for appreciation and comment—the former especially by the Kingsley and MacDonald children. This is a literary development of major importance, and Kingsley and MacDonald were among the very first not merely to produce major works in the genre, but also to write critical essays about what they were trying to do.[7]

That, however, is not my main theme in this chapter. There is another strand to the complex relationships between MacDonald and this group of Cambridge Coleridgeans that has received much less attention—their social values. Not for nothing did I call attention to Disraeli's somewhat unusual use of Coleridge at the beginning of this chapter. It was he, of course, who first proclaimed the idea of "One Nation" Toryism that has received considerable debate—and, indeed, misattribution—in recent political debates, but the idea behind that somewhat revolutionary ideal, which first appears in Disraeli's novel, *Sybil: Or the Two Nations* (1845), can be traced straight back to Coleridge, even though he does not use those exact words in *Church and State*. That Disraeli, the convert Anglican Protestant Jew, should invoke the ideals of the monastic system in pre-reformation England (in contrast with what he damningly names the "Venetian Oligarchy" of the rich, as against the poor) in his own time tells us much about what Carlyle was to call "the condition of England question" of the first half of the nineteenth century. Current debates about social inequality in England country pale into insignificance compared with the controversies of that period—especially when Darwinism was drawn into the debate by writers like Herbert Spencer to demonstrate that social inequality (and even perhaps slavery) was a biological norm rather than a social perversion.

In contrast, what was to become known as "Christian Socialism," though it was founded and so named by the London barrister J. M. Ludlow in 1850, and included Kingsley, was for much of its early existence driven by former Apostles, especially, of course, by F. D. Maurice. The title was deliberately provocative. "Socialism" was a word for the most extreme anarchist beliefs in the 1840s. It was meant to shock, and for many of the middle classes it certainly did. It would be like "communist" in America of the 1950s, or "Taliban" today. The most potent form of socialism in the 1840s was probably in the writings of the French anarchist Pierre-Joseph Proudhon, who coined the inflammatory slogan "property is theft" in his book *What is Property?* (1840). Though he was to be soon overtaken by other extremists—most famously by Karl Marx—there was alongside this contemporary attack on capitalist materialism a much older strand of Christian equalitarianism reaching back as far as St. Ambrose, Basil of Caesarea, and best-

---

[7] See Stephen Prickett, *Victorian Fantasy* (Waco, TX: Baylor University Press, 2005).

known of all, St Francis of Assisi. Though Ludlow, who had been educated partly in Paris, was well aware of the French socialist movements of the period, the prime driving force of his new vision of society was, of course, these teachings and tradition of the New Testament. Despite Kingsley's famous—or notorious—declaration that he was "a Church of England clergyman and [...] a Chartist,"[8] which had for many much the same revolutionary frisson, this "socialism" was more akin to the model of the later Fabian Society, whose ideal was peaceful, non-violent, change, taking a long view of social development. In addition to Kingsley, Ludlow, and Maurice, the new Victorian Christian Socialists included such well-known contemporary figures as John Ruskin, Thomas Hughes (author of *Tom Brown's Schooldays*), many of the Pre-Raphaelite Brotherhood, such as Dante Gabriel Rossetti, and the indefatigable Frederick James Furnivall—another graduate of Trinity Hall, Cambridge who not merely helped to found the Oxford English Dictionary, but a whole raft of literary societies, including the Browning and the Shelley Societies. In particular, they pinned their hopes on an expansion of education—especially higher education. They were not, of course, the first to try to expand the university intake. Pioneered by the short-lived Warrington Academy (1756–82), the direct ancestor of today's Harris-Manchester College in Oxford, a series of new higher education institutions were planned. Jeremy Bentham's foundation of University College, London, followed in 1826, and then King's College (1829), and Durham University (1832), both Anglican foundations. Less well-known, but still significant was John Keble's failed attempt to democratize Oxford itself in the 1830s.[9]

What brought all these figures together in the 1850s, however, were the very practical ideals of the London Working Men's College, founded by Ludlow in 1854, with the aim of spreading university level academic study to a class who (like Hardy's *Jude the Obscure*) had previously had little or no opportunity of higher education. Naturally, MacDonald was in the audience to hear the opening lecture by Maurice, the first Principal of the College. Other working men's colleges in provincial cities quickly followed, in many cases, joining with the earlier, more secular, mechanics institutes to become embryonic provincial universities—as in the case of Manchester University. Anyone familiar with Oxbridge teaching of the period who reads these early lectures at the Working Men's College cannot fail to be impressed at their difficulty—especially when one remembers that these were evening lectures, delivered to men who had almost certainly already worked a ten-hour day. According to your viewpoint, these were either a tribute to the intelligence of these early socialist pioneers, or a monument to a gap in the

---

[8] Charles E. Raven, *Christian Socialism 1848–1854* (London: Routledge, 1968), 139.
[9] See Stephen Prickett, *Modernity and the Reinvention of Tradition* (Cambridge: Cambridge University Press, 2009), 156–68.

middle-class understanding of the needs of working men. Despite the warnings of John Stuart Mill, women of course were still largely ignored—or relegated to the new foundation of Queen's College.

What is very noticeable also is the range of material offered right from the start. Not merely were mechanics, engineering, and the necessary accompanying mathematics, on the curriculum, but with a rounded view of education, lectures on art criticism, history, literature, and theology were not merely represented, but actually delivered by many of the best-known public intellectuals of the day. Those associated with the college also included older radicals such as Thomas Cooper, William Lovett, and Charles Southwell (it is a pity how few lecture-notes we seem to have from the working men themselves).

In a sense, therefore, Disraeli may have been more right than he could have known. Coleridge's social ideas may not have been explosive in a modern journalistic sense—perhaps more like a slow-burning fuse—but, arguably, they were one of the few lasting political ideas to emerge, since Burke, in the last two hundred years. They are, moreover, relevant. The idea of "one-nation" Toryism—the belief that too great a gap between rich and poor is not merely immoral, but bad for the nation and in effect, therefore, bad politics—is central to current debates. Tony Blair declared at the beginning of this century that Christian Socialism had been the greatest single influence on his political beliefs (and, incidentally sent a whole phalanx of journalists scurrying off to the internet to find what Christian Socialism actually was). The idea of a Christian socio-political stance is not one that has disappeared from political life—indeed, it seems to have astonishing staying power.

"Some thoughts are acorns," wrote Julius Hare in the first edition of *Guesses at Truth*, "would that any in this book were."[10] He would no doubt have been gratified to see how, in the course of his century, the Coleridgean Christian social and political tradition was never to move far from its literary roots, and nevertheless to influence an increasing range of practical policies.

---

[10] Julius and Augustus Hare, *Guesses at Truth*, vol. 2 (London: J. Duncan for J. Taylor, 1827), 79.

GEORGE MACDONALD:

UNORTHODOX ANGLICAN

Elisabeth Jay

The case of George MacDonald (1824–1905), by turns Scottish Presbyterian, Congregationalist, Anglican, and theocratic individualist, suggests something of the fluidity of religious allegiance often observable in intellectual circles in mid-Victorian Britain where religion was frequently both a matter of intense personal inquiry and bound up in a public world of political engagement and social hierarchies.

Today George MacDonald is remembered as an unorthodox figure, celebrated for a distinctively individual Christian vision, frequently incorporated in fiction lying somewhere outside the canonical Great Tradition. Raised in a Congregationalist church and amid mixed family religious influences, by 1845, when he graduated from the University of Aberdeen, he had repudiated the rigid Scottish Calvinist doctrine of election. Migrating to London, he undertook a Congregational ministerial training, but finding himself unable to subscribe to "the extreme points either of Calvinism or Arminianism,"[1] he moved with his growing family to Manchester where he preached to his acquaintance in rented rooms on Sunday evenings. Given this trajectory of increasing unorthodoxy why did MacDonald, once back in London, turn, between the late 1860s and early 1870s, to Anglican worship? And why did he embark upon writing a trilogy devoted to a Church of England parson and his family?

This turn to the Established Church and its concerns appears all the more curious as the 1860s and 1870s might well be said to be a high-point of religious unorthodoxy in England. Roughly speaking, in the early years of the nineteenth century doubt had tended to be regarded as a sin bound to lead to further wickedness, while by the end of the century it would prove permissible to voice disbelief openly as long as it was done within the bounds of decency.[2] In the century's middle decades deviation from traditional Anglican doctrine could still carry penalties—such as the loss of a job, or the severing of ties with friends and family—but was nevertheless increasingly common in intellectual circles.

---

[1] George MacDonald, *An Expression of Character: The Letters of George MacDonald*, ed. Glenn Edward Sadler (Grand Rapids, MI: Eerdmans, 1994), 34.

[2] See Joss Marsh, *Word Crimes: Blasphemy, Culture, and Literature in Nineteenth-Century England* (Chicago: Chicago University Press, 1998).

Inevitably in a country where Anglicanism was hard-wired into the constitution as the Established Church, unorthodoxy involved a chain of associations involving class, nationality, and education, as well as religious belief. Take, for instance, the opinion of the Anglican clergyman, Charles Kingsley, on the subject of the poet Robert Browning, a poet of almost willfully erudite obscurity, whose Dissenting father had afforded him the best education money could buy, even employing the royal music tutor for his son:

> [Browning] was born and bred a Dissenter, a man of the common people, of the trois état, and [...] nothing will take the smell of tallow and brown sugar out of him. He cannot help being coarse and vulgar [...] if he had been born either a gentleman (of course I mean a churchman, for *all gentlemen owe that name to Church influence over themselves or their parents*), or a hard-working man, in contact with iron fact, he might have been a fine poet.[3]

With Kingsley's prejudices in mind, it is worth considering two apparently contradictory images, the one suggesting that MacDonald was very definitely excluded from the establishment, the other that he was very much included within it.

MacDonald's son, Greville, provides the first image with a recollection from his schoolboy days at King's College School, London:

> One morning, in class, suddenly rang forth the command, "Stand up the boys whose fathers are clergymen!" Three responded, myself not of them. Then I was called up to the desk. "Isn't your father a clergyman." "No, Sir." "Didn't he write *Annals of a Quiet Neighbourhood?*" "Yes, Sir." "But it's written by a clergyman!" "No, Sir; *but my father was once a dissenting minister.*" The Rev. B. Lobster [so nicknamed by Greville] turned scarlet with anger and screamed at me [...]. All the masters at that school were in Holy Orders.[4]

The school was the junior branch of King's College, London, established as an Anglican foundation in response to that avowedly dissenting institution, University College, London.[5] The quality of the staff (Gabriel Rossetti, father to Dante and Christina, taught Italian there, and the celebrated water-colorist John Sell Cotman was the art master), and the school's progressive curriculum made it a popular choice with middle-class parents. Reflecting in later life upon the period when he had become a pupil there, probably in 1869, Greville MacDonald

---

[3] Quoted in V. D. Cunningham, *Everywhere Spoken Against: Dissent in the Victorian Novel* (Oxford: Clarendon Press, 1975), 206–7.

[4] Greville MacDonald, *George MacDonald and His Wife* (London: George Allen & Unwin, 1924), 364–5.

[5] University College was backed by Christian denominations other than Church of England, as well as Jews and Unitarians. Prior to its existence the only university options in England were Oxford or Cambridge, which required Anglican membership for graduation.

assumed that his father had become an Anglican by virtue of the fact that he had taken to attending St. Peter's Chapel, Vere Street, although he also continued to preach in dissenting chapels. Whether Frederick Denison Maurice, who had been the incumbent of St. Peter's since 1860, had to vouch for the MacDonalds, father and son, being Anglicans is unclear. Perhaps George MacDonald had been able to use his position as an evening lecturer at King's College to secure his son's entry.

Attending Maurice's church in Vere Street was no guarantee of Anglican orthodoxy. Born into a Unitarian family, Maurice was twenty-six by the time that he was baptized into the avowedly Trinitarian Church of England in 1831. Even though his first controversial work, *The Kingdom of Christ; or, Hints to a Quaker, Respecting the Principles, Constitution and Ordinances of the Catholic Church* (1838) endorsed "the sacraments of baptism and the eucharist, to which must be added the creeds, the liturgy, the episcopate, and the scriptures—in fact, all the marks of catholicity as exemplified in the Church of England," as the signs of "a spiritual and universal Kingdom,"[6] he remained, theologically speaking, something of a square peg in a round hole. The Anglican apostate, Leslie Stephen, who resented what he saw as the dishonesty or cowardice of fellow clergymen who held onto their livelihoods while sharing many of the doubts which had led him to the eventual renunciation of his Anglican orders, vented a little of his bitterness when he came to pen Maurice's entry in the *Dictionary of National Biography*: there he noted that Maurice managed to sustain his Anglicanism although "opposed to the tenets of all the chief parties in the church."[7]

While modern scholarship would see Maurice as fitting within the capacious "Broad Church" wing of Anglicanism,[8] in 1860 Maurice's appointment to the Vere Street church had been mired in controversy. Twenty clergy, and *The Record*, the most virulent of the Anglican Evangelical papers, protested against his installation to the Bishop of London, Archibald Campbell Tait (himself a convert from Scottish Presbyterianism). However, among the 332 clergy and 487 lay signatories to a counter-protest in Maurice's favor were William Ewart Gladstone, then Chancellor of the Exchequer, Alfred Tennyson, poet laureate, and Bishop Connop Thirlwall. In the face of such Establishment support it seems

---

[6] Bernard M. G. Reardon, "Maurice, (John) Frederick Denison (1805–1872)," in *Oxford Dictionary of National Biography* (Sept. 23, 2004), www.oxforddnb.com/index/101018384/Frederick-Maurice.

[7] Leslie Stephen, "Maurice, Frederick Denison (1805–1872)," *Dictionary of National Biography, 1885–1900*, vol. 37 (London: Smith, Elder & Co., 1894), 97–105.

[8] The membership of this wing of the Victorian Anglican church remains difficult to define in that it included liberal anti-dogmatists; staunch defenders of the Established Church as both a bastion of religious freedom and a guarantor against dissenting excess, along with those prepared to extend a hand of friendship to both dissenters and doubters.

reasonable to question what "unorthodoxy," or "non-conformity" conveyed to the mid-Victorian mind. "Orthodoxy" is, of course, a similarly slippery term since it can imply anything from conformity to traditional doctrines to the acceptance of what in practice seems to be the majority consensual position at any particular point in time. The first definition is particularly difficult to apply at a period when the origin of the Anglican tradition was itself a matter of dispute, and the second, when applied to religion, might be said to take more account of numerical than spiritual force. Yet, since Anglicanism was born out of the imperative for unity rather than imposed uniformity, it seems not unreasonable to tend to the second definition. Even if the several parties embraced under the umbrella of the Church of England often found it difficult to agree between themselves, they were readier in recognizing threats to, or enemies of, their consensus, all the more so because the consensus was so fragile.

A handsomely-bound album of images mounted on stiff gilt-edged board, entitled *Celebrities of the Nineteenth Century: Politics, Literature, Science, and Art* was published in 1876; each plate was accompanied by a brief biographical account of those featured. The Royal coat of arms on the album's cover presumably suggested an imprimatur for inclusion within the establishment of those portrayed between its covers.[9] The pictures themselves, however, tell a strange story. The plate entitled "Authors and Novelists," like the others within the album, is neither painting nor photograph, but photomontage. The historian Lord Macaulay, second from the left on the front row, had been dead since 1859, his next-door neighbor on the far left, William Makepeace Thackeray had died in 1863. Dickens (far right, front row) had died in 1870, and Bulwer Lytton (center of the front row) is clearly sitting to another camera entirely. (Photo on page 33)

This illustration has been employed to point out the significant figure MacDonald cut in his own age.[10] Read differently it is a strange assemblage. Some obvious absentees were admittedly covered by a second plate, featuring Charles Lamb, John Stuart Mill, Charles Darwin, Herbert Spencer, Charles Kingsley, and John Ruskin, though omitting George Eliot, still very much alive in the mid-1870s. Those present include two aristocrats: the ennobled Macaulay, and Bulwer Lytton, born scion of a privileged family; and at least three authors notable for the unorthodox nature of their private lives: Lytton, Wilkie Collins (top row, third from the left) and Charles Dickens. What then does George MacDonald in a "half-Lytton" pose (top row, far left) share with the others pictured? Like Thomas Carlyle (second from right, front row) he was an émigré Scot, and could certainly

---

[9] *English Celebrities of the Nineteenth Century: Politics, Literature, Science and Art, Part I* (London: Hughes & Edmonds, 1876).
[10] Richard Reis, *George MacDonald's Fiction: A Twentieth-Century View* (Eureka, CA: Sunrise Book Publishers, 1989), 17–18.

have fallen under that broad descriptor "unorthodox" with Carlyle and the historian Froude (standing next to MacDonald); and, on a more frivolous note, looking across the board, George's beard cannot be seen as quite the extravagant protest against Victorian convention that his older Scottish relatives and indeed his son Greville certainly perceived it to be.[11]

Whoever made this selection did not conceive of MacDonald as out of place among this company. Moreover, arranging these men against a background suggestive of the library shelves of a gentlemen's club implied inclusion within a homosocial establishment world, where entry hung upon election by a membership who trusted any newcomer would share their values and extend their range of useful contacts. Despite the fact that several of the men pictured here had had bad fallings-out (Bulwer Lytton with Thackeray, and, more notoriously, Thackeray with Dickens over remarks made at their club, the Garrick), this carefully-constructed illusion of camaraderie obliterates considerable differences of class origin, and beliefs—or lack of them—to suggest an establishment group of gentlemen who would have found themselves at ease in each others' company.

The remainder of this article will explore what it was in the circumstances of the mid-Victorian period that allowed MacDonald to be seen, apparently contradictorily, as belonging either to an unorthodox, dissenting minority or to the mainstream establishment. MacDonald's own assumptions and beliefs at this period will be drawn largely from his so-called Anglican trilogy whose opening salvo, *Annals of a Quiet Neighbourhood* (1867) provoked Greville MacDonald's teacher to scarlet-faced screaming. If such an approach seems to smack of the biographical fallacy it should be remembered that MacDonald unabashedly directed sermonettes within his novels at his readers: "I wrote my sermon just as if I were preaching it to my unseen readers as I spoke it to my present parishioners," declares the first-person clerical narrator of *Annals of a Quiet Neighbourhood*.[12]

Contemporary reviews of *Annals* demonstrate none of the "Rev. B. Lobster's" apoplectic anger at MacDonald for posing, in his role as narrator, as an Anglican parson. Instead, though generally approving of MacDonald's poetic sensibility and of his idealist sentiments, they noted the constraints under which he had placed himself in composing this novel for Dr. Guthrie's *Sunday Magazine*: "In this book he is rather like a man who has given up natural breathing and gasps under the constraint of stays or a tight neckcloth," wrote the *Examiner*'s reviewer.[13] Reviews in the secular periodicals tended to agree that the ordinary

---

[11] Greville MacDonald, *George MacDonald and His Wife*, 76, 242.
[12] George MacDonald, *Annals of a Quiet Neighbourhood*, 3 vols. (London: Hurst and Blackett), 3:318.
[13] "Annals of a Quiet Neighbourhood," *Examiner* (Oct. 27, 1866): 678–9.

novel reader would be likely to find any novel tolerated by a religious periodical hopelessly insipid. Yet by the standards of the 1860s and 1870s the Scottish Free Church minister Thomas Guthrie (1803–73), editor of the *Sunday Magazine,* and his friend Norman MacLeod, Church of Scotland minister and editor of *Good Words,* both counted as liberals, and their attempts to leaven the diet of their lower middle-class, Evangelically-disposed readership by introducing fiction as appropriate fare, was a fraught proposition.[14] MacLeod had already had to renege on a contract to publish Anthony Trollope's *Rachel Ray* (1863), partly because the eagle-eyed *Record* newspaper, a strong opponent of fiction, as soon as it saw the novel advertised in the religious press, launched a six article attack on Trollope as a sensational novelist in whose "trashy tales the most ungodly sentiments are uttered and left to work their evil effects upon the young mind."[15]

MacDonald, however, trod carefully, prompting the *Saturday Review* to mock the pious clerical narrator of *Annals* as resembling:

> the ideal clergyman imagined by enthusiasts outside the pale of holy orders, rather than the actual vicars with whom we are accustomed to come into contact in country-houses, on the seat of justice, or at missionary or clerical meetings. By [MacDonald's clergyman] preferment is a thing unthought of; for him there is no extra savour in the crackling of the tithe-pig. He is at peace with all mankind, and can even shake hands with a Dissenter unmoved.[16]

Since the clergyman of the tale, a Mr. Walton, named after the gentle, eirenically-disposed biographer of those Anglican divines, Donne, Herbert and Hooker, is so idealized, it is at first glance difficult to see why Greville MacDonald's teacher should have been so exercised by the novelist father's appropriation of an Anglican cleric as his first-person narrator. The clue lies in Greville's innocent assertion that his father was not an Anglican clergyman but was "once a dissenting minister." Had Greville's father been a lay Nonconformist, matters might not have been so

---

[14] Evangelicals, whether Anglican or dissenting, had been taught in the early years of the nineteenth century to see the reading of fiction as a dissipation of imaginative sympathy best devoted to practical effect in the real world. More liberal views of the good to be done by harnessing the forces of fiction for religious profit influenced Evangelicals, dissenting and Anglican, at different rates over the middle decades of the century. A detailed account of the relative degrees and rate of liberalization in the Evangelical press, together with an account of the opprobrium *Good Words* attracted as a leader in the religious press' move to publishing fiction can be found in Elisabeth Jay, *The Religion of the Heart: Anglican Evangelicalism and the Nineteenth-Century Novel* (Oxford: Clarendon Press, 1979), 196–202.

[15] *Record* (Apr. 13, 1863), quoted in M. Sadleir, *Trollope: A Commentary* (London: Farrar, Constable & Co., 1945), 245; and N. John Hall, *Trollope: A Biography* (Oxford: Oxford University Press, 1991), 251–6.

[16] "Annals of a Quiet Neighbourhood," *Saturday Review of Politics, Literature, Science and Art* (Oct. 20, 1866): 495–6.

Top Row: George MacDonald, James A. Froude, Wilkie Collins, Anthony Trollope
Bottom Row: William Makepeace Thackeray, Thomas Babington Macaulay,
Edward Bulwer-Lytton, Thomas Carlyle, Charles Dickens

bad, but as a row over the publication of *Essays and Reviews* (1860), a collection of essays by one layman and six Anglican clerics, had recently revealed, different standards were expected from the clergy and the laity. Two of the Anglican clerical contributors to this book, which examined the state of Biblical scholarship in the light of German Higher Criticism and recent scientific discoveries, were charged with heresy and, although this verdict was overturned, the conclusion that Anglican clergy were to be held to tighter degrees of conformity was inescapable.

In the febrile state of ecclesiastical affairs which this controversy brought about it was unsurprising that a man in Holy Orders, teaching in an Anglican foundation, should be suspicious of the damage to orthodox belief that a dissenting cleric, masquerading as a parson of the established church, might wreak. The Oxford Movement, if it had done nothing else, had sensitized mid-Victorians to the notion that the Anglican ministerial commission, confirmed in a ceremony regarded by some Anglicans as in itself a sacrament, ordained priests into the universal Catholic church, descended directly from the apostles. Viewed from this perspective, dissenting clergy were just that—men who had chosen to dissociate themselves from the universal Catholic church and were free, within the bounds of their particular sect's chosen set of beliefs, to preach what they would, doctrinally-speaking. Therefore, for a man further to choose to liberate himself from even the bonds of his dissenting connection's beliefs, would to such an Anglican mind have suggested that he had had become what was known as a "freethinker," quite probably skeptical of all religious dogma.[17]

Viewing George MacDonald's spirituality retrospectively through the approving lens of a G. K. Chesterton[18] or a C. S. Lewis,[19] such a judgment may seem outrageous, but it was not that unreasonable a hypothesis in mid-nineteenth-century England when denominational affiliation was experiencing one of its more volatile periods. There had been many high-profile secessions from Anglicanism to Roman Catholicism, and to nonconformity and rationalism. Furthermore, MacDonald's Scottish background would have required some explanation. The Scottish university system in which he had been educated was considered by some as a honey-trap for the sons of English Dissenters because it did not require undergraduates to subscribe to a religious confession, either at the start of the degree as in Oxford, or upon graduation as in Cambridge. Moreover, when MacDonald sought ministerial training, it had not been in the Church of Scotland, whose kirks were bound by common adherence to the Westminster Confession, but in English Congregationalism, a sect renowned for its individual congregations retaining complete autonomy. A Congregational minister could of course easily find himself at odds with his congregation over matters which were not doctrinal. The Arundel deacons who visited MacDonald had at first hoped to "hint" to him that his ministrations were no longer wanted by mentioning that his ever-growing family would require their flock to pay for more expensive accommodation. Dumbfounded by his resolve to live on less, they were forced to raise doctrinal objections to his teaching: namely that it was "tainted with German Theology," and espoused heretical views on the afterlife.[20] MacDonald's subsequent trajectory, which had included not only the setting up of a non-denominational meeting room for Sunday evening worship in Manchester, but a winter spent in Algiers (1856) consorting with those notable Unitarian feminists, Barbara Bodichon and Bessie Rayner Parkes (who shortly thereafter became a Roman Catholic) would hardly have been reassuring to those who saw the

---

[17] The ostracism experienced by seceders such as James Anthony Froude or Francis William Newman, brother of the more famous John Henry, suggests that all but the most liberal "Broad Church" Anglicans were suspicious of, or openly hostile to, those who chose to renounce their Anglican affiliation.

[18] G. K. Chesterton, Introduction to *George MacDonald and His Wife*, by Greville MacDonald, (London: George Allen & Unwin, 1924), 9–15.

[19] C. S. Lewis, *Surprised by Joy: The Shape of My Early Life* (London: Collins, Fontana, 1964), 144–6, 171; Lewis also published a collection of MacDonald's spiritual sayings under the title, *George MacDonald: An Anthology* (London: Geoffrey Bles, 1946).

[20] Greville MacDonald, *George MacDonald and His Wife*, 178–9.

Church of England as a safeguard against many types of challenge to established ways.[21]

Given these divagations, MacDonald's subsequent decision to attend Maurice's Anglican chapel requires framing in a broader context. Émigré nineteenth-century Scots often found it hard to know where to worship in England. If they had continued in the Church of Scotland after the Great Disruption of 1843, and were thus to some extent accepting of the principle that patrons had a degree of control over conferment to livings they regarded as their property, the Presbyterian nature of the worship they were accustomed to would have made some Anglican practices seem almost Roman Catholic. If, on the other hand, émigré Scots had recently joined the exodus from the Church of Scotland into the Free Church, they were frequently dismayed to find themselves being treated by Anglicans as on a par with other English Dissenters—that is as doctrinally suspect and socially inferior. In the larger English cities, the Scots diaspora tended to socialize and worship together, choosing a sympathetic Anglican church when a Presbyterian equivalent was unavailable.

It seems plausible that it was through such a network of London-based Scots who found Maurice's ministry sympathetic that MacDonald first met the up-and-coming novelist and reviewer, Margaret Oliphant, who, according to Greville MacDonald, gave his father a literary leg-up at this period, approving as she did of his endeavors in the field of realist fiction.[22] Furthermore, as an expatriate Scot, Oliphant would also have understood MacDonald's wandering ecclesiastical allegiance. Her family had opted for the Free Church of Scotland in the wake of the Great Disruption of 1843, and in the late 1840s she had been a youthful housekeeper for an older brother who completed his ministerial training at the Presbyterian College in London. This wayward brother's subsequent dismissal from his Northumbrian parish led her to describe the Presbyterian service as "a strait ceremony undoubted[ly] from the time of the Puritans,"[23] and to the publication in 1862 of a sympathetic biography of that fellow Scot Edward Irving's estrangement from the Presbyterian church.[24] By the late 1850s

---

[21] No stranger herself to the reactions which might greet the decision to leave the security of the Established church, George Eliot neatly skewered this mindset in describing her character, Mrs. Bulstrode, "The unreformed provincial mind distrusted London; and while true religion was everywhere saving, honest Mrs. Bulstrode was convinced that to be saved in the Church was more respectable. She so much wished to ignore towards others that her husband had ever been a London Dissenter, that she liked to keep it out of sight even in talking to him." *Middlemarch: A Study of Provincial Life*, 3 vols. (Edinburgh and London: William Blackwood and Sons, 1871–72), 3:124.

[22] Greville MacDonald, *George MacDonald and His Wife*, 300, 358.

[23] *The Autobiography of Margaret Oliphant: The Complete Text*, ed. Elisabeth Jay (Oxford: Oxford University Press, 1990), 31.

[24] Again, it was a network of Scottish relations that had put Oliphant in touch with Irving's

when Oliphant met MacDonald she had become friendly with one of F. D. Maurice's sisters, Mrs. Powell, who had married into the very family from whom MacDonald was to take his bride, and Maurice knew her well enough to write to her on the occasion of her ten-year-old daughter's sudden death.[25] Over the years Oliphant became a regular Anglican communicant, though, like MacDonald, her theological views remained unorthodox.[26]

MacDonald's track record in the matter of religious allegiance was enough to have raised the eyebrow of many Anglican clergy at most times during the nineteenth century, but the immediate context of Anglican-Nonconformist relations during the 1860s and 1870s helps more fully in understanding "the Rev. B. Lobster's" outburst. Encouraged first by the suppression of ten Irish bishoprics in 1833, then by the Great Scottish Disruption of 1843, English Dissenters felt that the reforming spirit that was prompting the examination of so many of Britain's great national institutions would surely reach the Established Church, after it had finished with the universities and the army. The *Nonconformist* newspaper under its militant editor Edward Miall had been thundering forth the message "the Dissidence of Dissent and the Protestantism of the Protestant religion" since the 1840s, and Miall's regular tours, whipping up support for his campaigns in favor of disestablishment of the state church, had reached their apogee by the early 1870s.

The 1867 Reform Bill had left many Dissenters feeling entitled to a greater influence in parliament, and they were consequently immensely aggrieved when they did not prevail in the 1870 Education Act in freeing all state-financed elementary education from religious input and thus from Church influence. Encouraged by Prime Minister Gladstone's disestablishment of the Anglican Church in Ireland, Miall, by then a Member of Parliament, introduced three motions, between 1871 and 1873, for disestablishing the Church of England on the mainland. Each of these motions failed, but Anglicans were rattled enough to join ranks against the threat from Dissent in a way they had not done for almost a century.[27]

---

sister-in-law in the late 1840s.
[25] *The Autobiography of Margaret Oliphant*, 96, 11.
[26] See Elisabeth Jay, "A Scottish Widow's Speculations," in *Mrs. Oliphant: 'A Fiction to Herself': A Literary Life* (Oxford: Clarendon Press, 1995), 139–191. Oliphant's major religious biographies—of Edward Irving, Laurence Oliphant, and the Comte de Montalembert—were notably devoted to exploring men whose passionately-held convictions led them to beleaguered "outsider" positions. Her own speculations were mainly concerned with the afterlife where she was attracted by the conditional immortality theory, which held that the gift of immortality might be limited to believers.
[27] See for instance this slew of pamphlets by the militantly Evangelical Anglican, J. C. Ryle, later Bishop of Liverpool, who was eager to unite all churchmen in the cause of fighting disestablishment: *Church and Dissent: Or, Why Do I Prefer Church to Chapel?* (1870);

So, the "Rev. B. Lobster" was perhaps entitled to feel he was harboring in his class the son of a man who in speaking, albeit fictionally, as an Anglican cleric was a wolf in sheep's clothing. Even supposing that MacDonald, desperately writing to support his ever-growing family, was commercially inspired by the current vogue for clerical stories, such as Anthony Trollope's *The Warden* (1855) and *Barchester Towers* (1857); or George Eliot's *Scenes of Clerical Life* (1858); his friend Margaret Oliphant's *The Rector* (1861), *Salem Chapel* (1863), and *The Perpetual Curate* (1863), he could not have been unaware that by publishing in a Dissenting magazine, he was presenting an Anglican clergyman's life to a readership many of whom would have been politicized by the disestablishment lobby. The remainder of this article will therefore consider MacDonald's Anglican trilogy as an intervention in a contemporary debate.

Briefly summarized these three novels, *Annals of a Quiet Neighbourhood* (1867), *The Seaboard Parish* (1869) and *The Vicar's Daughter* (1871–72), look in turn at Christianity as practiced first in a country parish; second in a remote Cornish mining and fishing district, and third in the heart of London. The continuity, such as it is, lies in reappearing characters: Mr. Walton, an Anglican clergyman is the central figure in the first two novels, while one of his daughters carries the third. That MacDonald had intended the novels as a survey of Anglican parochial life in very different, rural, seaside, and urban surroundings is clear from a letter written some twenty years later in which he expressed his regret that *The Vicar's Daughter* had somehow survived to achieve a life independent of its companion pieces.[28] It is unsurprising that only the third survived. Its inner London setting, travelling across the artistic and literary worlds to the homes of wealthy merchants and the slum dwellings of the city's overcrowded alleyways off the Tottenham Court Road, is clearly based upon MacDonald's own social experiences at this period, and to that extent would have enjoyed some topical interest.[29] The two earlier novels, by contrast, seem to be set in another world entirely—a leisurely world of coach travel rather than railways, of clear-cut social hierarchies and semi-feudal deference to the established authorities—all combining to make Anglicanism seem an outdated system suitable for less progressive times.

This sense of being in a world wholly divorced from the realities of 1860s parochial life is enhanced in *The Annals of a Quiet Neighbourhood* by a sensational

---

Church Reform Papers (1870); *Yes or No! Is the Union of Church and State Worth Preserving?* (1871); *What Good Will It Do? A Question About the Disestablishment of the Church of England, Examined and Answered* (1872); *Church and State* (1877); *Churchmen and Dissenters* (1880); *Principles for Churchmen* (1884); *Disestablishment Papers* (1885); *I Am a Churchman and Why* (1886); *Thoughts on the Prayer Book and on Church and Dissent* (1887).

[28] Sadler, *An Expression of Character*, 366.
[29] Greville MacDonald, *George MacDonald and His Wife*, 300–13.

Gothic romance concerning the appropriately named Oldcastle family at the local big house, who, for two generations at least, have been immersed in events which totally undermine the notion of this as a "quiet neighbourhood." The plot involves daughters terrorized into forced marriages, Hindostanee servants kidnapping babies, and murky events taking place in the underground cellars and passages of the vast and gloomy Oldcastle Hall. Setting aside these elements, clearly designed to appeal to sensationally-inclined readers, the novel should really have been entitled "The Education of an Anglican Clergyman by a Dissenting Author."

From the opening chapter, the young narrator, who has just been presented to his first living, doubts his own worthiness: could he really be accused of being in it for the "loaves and fishes" of an easy income, as Dissenting propaganda of the 1860s and 1870s period so notably expressed it? From the first this clergyman, Mr. Walton, makes it clear that he holds ordination into the priesthood in no high esteem: although the clergy bear greater responsibility to set an example, they are *au fond* as other men, and will eventually be swallowed up, their role effaced, in the greater brotherhood of all mankind. Walton's role is to act as servant of his people and practical caretaker of a church-building which he should ensure is comfortable enough for his congregation to be able to concentrate upon the sermon. This clergyman is suspicious of a liturgy which might make him into "a mere praying-machine,"[30] and focuses upon preaching, supplemented by parish-visiting, as his central duties. There is no mention of the sacraments other than in an aside about the way that the communion offering should best be administered.[31] Rather, as means of grace, this priest introduces evening lectures, and decides that the best way of creating a sense of community is to hold a party on Christmas Eve, believing, as MacDonald's spokesman puts it, that "a few country dances" with reading of "Wordsworth's ballads" in between "would not only do them good, but help them to see what is in the Bible, and therefore to love it more. For I never could believe that a man who did not find God in other places as well as in the Bible ever found Him there at all."[32] Walton's eventual marriage provides occasion for MacDonald to expatiate at length upon the role of the clergy-wife, before concluding, "but there cannot be many clergymen's wives amongst my readers; and I may have occupied more space than reasonable with this 'large discourse.'"[33]

Walton's marriage to the wealthy Oldcastle heiress and subsequent move to her family mansion contributes to the impression this novel gives of

---

[30] MacDonald, *Annals of a Quiet Neighbourhood*, 1:107.
[31] MacDonald, *Annals of a Quiet Neighbourhood*, 3:243–4.
[32] MacDonald, *Annals of a Quiet Neighbourhood*, 1:305–6.
[33] MacDonald, *Annals of a Quiet Neighbourhood*, 3:247.

Anglican clergy operating as completely free agents, untrammeled by a bishop's oversight, or their churchwardens' watchful eyes. Walton is in effect, as "the Rev. B. Lobster" perceived with appalled clarity, a Dissenting preacher in Anglican clothing. Indeed, equipped with his wife's inheritance, Walton fulfills a Dissenting program for educational equality, sending the local carpenter's son to Oxford, and appointing him as his curate.

The second novel, *The Seaboard Parish*, by taking us to Mr. Walton's locum duty in a ritualist church in Cornwall, transports Anglicanism into a Dissenting heartland. Once again the opening chapters start by establishing Walton as the sternest type of Dissenting critic of the Established church. "I would never have any vessel used in the eucharist but wooden platters and wooden cups. […] I would send all the church-plate to fight the devil with his own weapons in our overcrowded cities," he somewhat improbably declares.[34] MacDonald's Anglicanism turns out to be largely a matter of aesthetics. In old Anglican churches, declares Walton, "we […] can worship the God of Abraham, of Isaac, and of Jacob—the God of Sidney, of Hooker, of Herbert," yet he hastens to add that old Puritan conventicles are capable of arousing the same awe in him,[35] and his admiration of the Anglican poets is balanced by an earlier paean to that Dissenting hero, John Milton.[36] Walton feels that the Anglican liturgy leaves insufficient space for spontaneous prayer and preaching, castigates his fellow clergy for clinging to God's word as fossilized in the Bible and Prayer-Book and for "look[ing] down upon the prophesying—that is, the preaching of the word."[37] Although some of Walton's teaching is encoded in little homilies to the parishioners he visits, the informal space of Sunday evening family gatherings is as much to his taste as a space for preaching.

In the third and final novel the narrative is handed over to one of the Vicar's daughters.[38] While this could be construed as part of the novel's response to the increasing urgency of the contemporary debate about women's education, women's rights, and women's religious role, it may also have been an attempt to distance MacDonald from the bitter party politics of Miall's disestablishment campaign. The novel's title, *The Vicar's Daughter*, indicates that we have moved on a generation, and the only episode featuring Mr. Walton, involving

---

[34] George MacDonald, *The Seaboard Parish*, 3 vols. (London: Tinsley Brothers, 1868), 1:65–6.
[35] MacDonald, *The Seaboard Parish*, 1:212.
[36] MacDonald, *The Seaboard Parish*, 1:48–50.
[37] MacDonald, *The Seaboard Parish*, 1:223–4.
[38] Using Walton's daughter as a narrator was not entirely successful: a vitriolic article in the *Saturday Review* claimed that by taking the voice "of a feeble woman" MacDonald had achieved "the last word in the abandonment of masculinity." "The Vicar's Daughter," *Saturday Review of Politics, Literature, Science and Art*, 34.876 (Aug. 10, 1872), 196–7.

a confrontation with a gipsy encampment believed to have kidnapped a baby, belongs more properly to the world of early nineteenth-century romances than to the 1870s.

The third novel instead represents the *modus vivendi* of the Anglican parson, with his proprietorial certainty that all to be found within the parish boundaries are his parishioners, as, at best, irrelevant in modern London. In the city's suburbs the old hierarchies seem to count for little and it is more urgent to form bonds with like-minded individuals across the many small villages that make up London, than to establish networks within immediate neighborhoods where the inhabitants are inclined to change swiftly with any success or failure in the commercial world. And as for the city's slums, a London cleric tells Mr. Walton, no new model has as yet been invented for Anglican clergy to practice their vocation there: parish visiting is intrusive, he claims, when imposed upon the poor; and the work of spiritual counseling has long been bedeviled by confusing it with charitable handouts.[39]

MacDonald's solution to these problems comes in the shape of a saintly young woman who chooses to spend her life among the dwellers of the crowded tenement buildings and brings even wife-beating laborers to the Christian life through a combination of piano recitals, trips to the National Gallery, and Sunday evening readings from the Apocrypha. Named Marion Clare, presumably with reference to the Virgin Mary and the Poor Clares, she prefers remaining wedded to the poor to becoming the wife of a worthy Anglican clergyman. She declares that "though still a communicant of the Church of England" she regards the differences between dissenting chapels and churches "with absolute indifference: to one hungering for bread, it is of little consequence in what sort of platter it is handed him."[40] Furthermore, MacDonald has her claim that she was herself brought back to regular worship by an earnest dissenting preacher. The novelist then seeks to even the sectarian score a little by telling the reader in a footnote that he derived the idea of the preacher's religious affiliation being unimportant from F. D. Maurice's interpretation of the text "by their fruits ye shall know them."[41]

Marion Clare, a nun without habit or religious order, is effectively MacDonald's proxy, preaching, like him, the brotherhood of man to be brought about by a religious education, consisting of the Bible, English poetry, imaginative preaching, nature rambles, country dancing, and visits to the National Gallery.

---

[39] George MacDonald, *The Vicar's Daughter: An Autobiographical Story*, vol. 1 (London: Tinsley Brothers, 1872), 211–13.

[40] MacDonald, *The Vicar's Daughter*, 2:63.

[41] MacDonald, *The Vicar's Daughter*, 2:63–6.

Effectively her mission is MacDonald's: "I want to lead some poor stray sheep home—not home to the church [...]. I never think of what they call the church. I only care to lead them home to the bosom of God, where alone man is true man."[42]

Drawn for a time to Anglicanism by a combination of its aesthetic, the society of his fellow Scots exiles, and above all his admiration for Maurice, while disestablishment still seemed on the cards, MacDonald was happy to embrace both Anglican clergy and Dissenting ministers who seemed in sympathy with his program. Indeed Maurice, who claimed in 1869 that he had been filling his sermons with his dominant interest of the time, "the Unity of the Church" and the possibility of bringing men to a sense of shame for their "sectarian enmity," wrote to MacDonald in the hope that he would agree to contribute hymns to a joint book on the subject.[43] Yet, as MacDonald's son shrewdly observed, his father had probably only become an Anglican "as allowing a greater freedom in faith than any other Christian organization," and at base believed in "a theocratic individualism."[44]

By 1876, when MacDonald wrote his next novel involving Anglicanism, Maurice was dead (d.1872), and the possibility of disestablishment, and thus the immediate prospect of Anglican reform, had disappeared for a generation. *Thomas Wingfold, Curate* (1876) contains a far more hard-hitting attack on a Church of England clergyman. The novel begins with a cynical non-believer confronting the curate with the accusation, true in this particular case, that, like most of his kind, he has assumed ministerial orders simply as a consequence of family expectation. But that, as they say, is another story.

---

[42] MacDonald, *The Vicar's Daughter*, 2:66–7.
[43] Greville MacDonald, *George MacDonald and His Wife*, 399.
[44] Greville MacDonald, *George MacDonald and His Wife*, 401.

"A GUIDING RADIANCE:"
GEORGE MACDONALD'S SCIENCE AND FANTASY AS A NEW DIALECTIC[1]

Franziska E. Kohlt

George MacDonald's *Phantastes* (1858), opens in a seemingly mundane, even cliché fashion. The protagonist, Anodos, enters his deceased father's study on the night of his twenty-first birthday to discover the "land or moneys" the estate might hold for him, secretly longing to uncover his family's mysterious history, and thus his own identity.[2] The way in which MacDonald describes the thought process of his protagonist is, however, comparably peculiar: "Perhaps, like a geologist, I was about to turn up to the light some of the buried strata of the human world, with its fossil remains charred by passion and petrified by tears."[3] A geologist of emotion, Anodos anticipates transcending the material world into a dimension of past human thought turned natural-historical specimen. The description of the scene indeed evokes a physical descent. Darkness clings to the walls "bat-like" as he approaches the "long-neglected" room's inner sanctum, a secretary, with "reverence" as if it were a grave, and with a "curiosity" as if a scientist on a geoarchaeological expedition.

What he finds is a psychological reward, or rather, the promise of it. Instead of money or land, a phantom appears to him and diagnoses Anodos with an imbalanced mind that prevents him from finding what he seeks. What has caused it, is a "philosophy" that believes nothing it cannot touch, and is convinced only by "mere repetition."[4] Anxious and restless, the mind of the young science graduate lacked, as MacDonald puts it elsewhere, one of the two "twain wings" necessary to lift the scientific mind to discovery of truth: the fantastic imagination.[5] With the clashing philosophies of seeking in the *material* the fulfilment of an *immaterial* desire, this opening heralds a journey into the psychological fabric of

---

[1] James Clerk Maxwell, "Dreamland," in *The Scientific Letters and Papers of James Clerk Maxwell*, ed. P. M. Harman, 3 vols. (Cambridge: Cambridge University Press, 2009), 1:443.
[2] George MacDonald, *Phantastes: A Faerie Romance for Men and Women* (London: Chatto & Windus, 1894), 3.
[3] MacDonald, *Phantastes*, 4.
[4] MacDonald, *Phantastes*, 5.
[5] George MacDonald, "The Imagination: Its Functions and Its Culture," in *Orts: Chiefly Papers on the Imagination and Shakspere* (London: Sampson Low, 1882), 6.

the dreamer. On this journey he must negotiate the unbalancing influence of the specific kind of scientific education he received upon his psyche, to mitigate any effects of the actions sprung from a mind thus shaped.

Through the psycho-geological metaphor, MacDonald blurs the boundaries between individual, psyche, and environment, and he grounds his dream-novel in a potent framework of scientific analogy in which scientific thinking is made visible and scientific discovery may arise via the imagination: narrative techniques, seemingly literary, but borrowed, perhaps counter-intuitively, from Victorian science writing.

All this challenges past reception of MacDonald's engagement with science and establishes it as an integral part of his life, philosophy, and writing, which scholarship has traditionally neglected or even dismissed. According to Broome, MacDonald "rejected science altogether," or as Manlove asserts even more emphatically he "turned away" from all pursuits of science "*absolutely,*" allowing it, "*no place* in the discovery of *worthwhile* knowledge."[6] It also raises questions as to the writing out of MacDonald's biography his scientific preoccupations, and his odd position within the canon of Victorian literature. While such scientific metaphors and analogies as those found in *Phantastes* were a common trait of Victorian fantastic literature, they have remained almost entirely unremarked upon in studies of it, in the same way in which MacDonald himself is oddly absent from Victorian studies—a coincidence, as this chapter will explore, representative of the larger, underexplored intersection of fantasy and science for which MacDonald serves as a striking example.

In more than half a century of fantasy scholarship in which MacDonald has periodically resurfaced, he has remained somewhat of a paradox, in ways that closer attention to his engagement with science can help to reconcile. Scholarship has typically characterized the Scotsman as a primarily fervently Christian writer, whom religious interpretations have, however, paradoxically found "impenetrable."[7] Impenetrability has, at times, led to neglect, so much so, that MacDonald is not only noted as an "unjustly neglected author," but the image has, as William Raeper states, "almost become a cliché."[8] On the other hand,

---

[6] F. Hal Broome, "The Scientific Basis of MacDonald's Dream-Frame," in *The Gold Thread: Essays on George MacDonald*, ed. William Raeper (Edinburgh: Edinburgh University Press, 1991), 88 (italics added); Colin Manlove, *Modern Fantasy: Five Studies* (Cambridge: Cambridge University Press, 1975), 58 (italics added).

[7] John Pennington, "A 'Wolff' in Sheep's Clothing," in *George MacDonald: Literary Heritage and Heirs*, ed. Roderick McGillis (Wayne, PA: Zossima Press, 2008), 241; Colin Manlove, *Christian Fantasy: From 1200 to the Present* (Notre Dame: University of Notre Dame Press, 1992), 166.

[8] William Raeper, *George MacDonald: Novelist and Victorian Visionary* (Tring: Lion Publishing, 1987), 11.

while nearly every protagonist in his over thirty novels is a scientist or medic by training, like MacDonald himself, many critics and biographers reiterate almost compulsively that he "rejected science."[9] But it was MacDonald's portrayal of science, that attracted much of the early interest in his novels—the "exceptional interest," for instance, of such admirers as H. G. Wells. He described the "realistic wonderlands of Dr MacDonald" as "neat in the extreme," which suggests there may be more to MacDonald's fantasy than has met the eye of more recent fantasy critics that bridges the gap between interest and neglect, and diffuses paradox.[10] This chapter will probe, therefore, whether MacDonald's texts have to some degree remained cryptic because of the exclusion of the science-historical dimension, which have severed his texts from the complexities of the historical context that shaped them, in which science and religion were everything but mutually exclusive.

The phenomenon of the pre-emptive exclusion of science from fantasy can be observed more widely, as can historiographies that construct science and religion as conflicting endeavors—both of which have affected the critical conceptualization of MacDonald. Definitions of fantasy, such as for instance most recently by Edward James and Farah Mendlesohn juxtapose literary fantasy with its sister genre science fiction, stating fantasy was "the construction of the impossible whereas science fiction may be about the unlikely, but it is grounded in the scientifically possible."[11] Such definitions, however, risk labelling science fiction authors as the ones who engage with and solve real-life crises, casting aside fantasists as escapists, pre-emptively limiting the remit of texts classed as fantasy, or preventing such texts that do engage with science from being considered fantasy, despite evidence to the contrary.

Writers like MacDonald were situated firmly between the two poles defined by James and Mendlesohn—who saw fantastic writing as able to construct the *seemingly* impossible by scientific and narrative means. He represents a genre which emerged from engaging with prominent scientific developments of the Victorian age in the second half of the nineteenth century, from which such a bifurcation observed by James and Mendlesohn only eventually emerges, and never consistently manifests. Yet, in the corresponding scholarly field of literature and science studies, as Martin Willis highlights, subjects from

---

[9] Broome, "MacDonald's Dream-Frame," 88; see also Rolland Hein, "Doors In: The Fairy Tale World of George MacDonald," YouTube, February 20, 2019, recorded lecture, 52.24 to 53.20, https://youtu.be/bgtcHsB6kjY?feature=shared&t=3144.

[10] H.G. Wells, quoted in Greville MacDonald, *Reminiscences of a Specialist* (London: Allen & Unwin, 1932), 323.

[11] Edward James and Farah Mendlesohn, *Introduction to The Cambridge Companion to Fantasy Literature*, ed. Edward James and Farah Mendlesohn (Cambridge: Cambridge University Press, 2012), 1.

"Renaissance drama, the Victorian novel, the modernist poem, sensation fiction and the Gothic, [and] the Victorian stage," have been "widely explored"—yet not fantasy or science fiction.[12] While the latter is slowly being addressed, this is mostly through single author studies, which, as Mendlesohn observes, often lack comparativism. The more general fantasy studies that have also turned to MacDonald concerned themselves for much of the twentieth century with extrapolating, by psychoanalytic means, the "universal" concerns its imagery encapsulated, rather than the more immediate historical contexts, such the scientific developments of the Victorian age. This has resulted in such distortions of the supposed remit of the texts studied, as MacDonald's case, and its purely theological framing, exemplifies.

This chapter will reframe these fantasy works within the history of science, its impact on epistemologies and society, and the ways in which fantasists engaged with science. It will do so to demonstrate how attention to scientific contexts can aid in re-evaluating and demystifying author biographies and give new and historicist depth not only to their writing, but also to the critical consensus that fantasy is profoundly psychological.[13] Psychology, a field in which both MacDonald, and his contemporary fantasists, such as Lewis Carroll or Charles Kingsley, were well-read, will serve as an example. An emerging science, psychology was an "open" and "multidisciplinary" discourse, in which authors of the fantastic participated especially through fiction situated in dreams, and thus the realm of the psyche, rather than escaping from it. This is particularly true of the use of scientific narrative forms, which, increasingly de-prioritized by the professionalization of the sciences, continued to play a significant role in them. Analogies and metaphors, such as those of MacDonald's *Phantastes*, reveal an alternative discursive space at the intersection of the sciences and literature that can offer insights into changing practices and perceptions of scientific writing, and what constituted it.

George MacDonald and Nineteenth-Century Science

Considering MacDonald's scientific education, it becomes clear that, rather than rejecting his education, it fundamentally shaped his outlook on everything in life. George MacDonald studied for an A. M. (Artium Magister) at King's College Aberdeen from 1840–1845, which covered Natural Philosophy, Natural History,

---

[12] Martin Willis, *Mesmerists, Monsters and Machines: Science Fiction and the Cultures of Science in the Nineteenth Century* (Kent, OH: Kent State University Press, 2006), 2.

[13] Cf. Colin Manlove, *The Fantasy Literature of England* (London: Macmillan, 1999), 1; Rosemary Jackson, *Fantasy: The Literature of Subversion*, 3rd ed. (London: Routledge, 1981), 4; Bruno Bettelheim, *The Uses of Enchantment*, 3rd ed. (London: Penguin, 1991), 3.

Moral Philosophy, and Mathematics.[14] MacDonald was a contemporary, for a time, of Alexander Bain, the psychologist and future founder of *Mind*. Other notable Victorian Aberdonians included James Clerk Maxwell.[15] While Aberdeen had been a beacon of the Scottish Enlightenment in the eighteenth century, consulting student notes of lectures the young MacDonald attended makes clear that by the 1840s, there was lingering resentment against its associated Common-Sense tradition.[16] Instead of the typical focus on rationalism and materialism, the lectures MacDonald attended presented the study of science as a means of self-improvement that functioned alongside Christian moral teachings, more akin to Natural Theology. A question in a Natural Philosophy examination which MacDonald passed reads:

> What advantage is to be derived from the study of Natural Philosophy as a system of mental training? And is any danger to be apprehended to religion from the study of Physical Science?

The model answer, at first, praises the philosophical purpose of science and promotes facts and reason:

> The study of Natural Philosophy forms an admirable system of mental culture, as it habituates the mind to a rigorous investigation of the causes of the phenomena of nature. It likewise forms a disposition to search after truth, and to take nothing for granted, as hypothetical reasonings are null and void in Natural Philosophy, but all conclusions must be drawn from facts previously established.

Yet it goes on to highlight the apparent danger that "superficial knowledge of Natural Philosophy may sometimes be accompanied by a spirit of infidelity." The primary aim of scientific study was to "elevate and invigorate the mind" and its chief purpose was to lay "open to our view the wisdom, power, and magnificence displayed in the works of God."[17] MacDonald was thus not exposed to an

---

[14] Aberdeen had two colleges, Marischal College and King's College, which were joined into the University of Aberdeen in 1860. Until then, each university had their own chair in each subject, and while students were enrolled at either of the two colleges, they were able to borrow from a common library, and attended each other's lectures; they shared a Debating and Literary Society, and MacDonald was a member of both.

[15] James Clerk Maxwell was professor of Natural Philosophy from 1856 until the merging of the two Aberdeen colleges in 1860, when he accepted their chair in the same field, teaching alongside Bain and MacDonald, who taught English Language and Literature there respectively.

[16] These notes were taken by students or student assistants to be kept in the archives of the university, often lectures delivered by the same lecturers were identical every year. One set of notes of lectures MacDonald would have attended is written by Alexander Bain, cf. MS M 172, Alexander Bain, "William Knight's Lecture Notes Natural Philosophy 1938–9," Sir Duncan Rice Library Special Collections, University of Aberdeen.

[17] MS K 211 [MS 3340] "Questions on Natural Philosophy," Sir Duncan Rice Library Special Collections, University of Aberdeen, 189–90.

institutional antagonism to science on religious grounds at his alma mater, nor its opposite, but rather a perhaps idealistic synthesis of the two: an idea that pervades all of MacDonald's writing.

The view of science as an integrated philosophy was complemented by Aberdeen's focus on applied science.[18] The Aberdeen Colleges had begun catering to the fabric and agriculture industries of Aberdeenshire, and while their students had commonly sought vacation employment in these industries, as indeed did Bain, an increasing number started building their careers in their administration, diverging from more traditional career paths in medicine, the church and law.[19] Agriculture and population health were by far the most prominent applications of science at Aberdeen, but the practical focus also pervaded other subjects. Moral Philosophy dedicated several lectures in "psychology" to diagnosing and curing the mind, and Geology, which was taught over the course of half a year—an unusually long timespan for a single topic in the curriculum—focused largely on mining.[20] Practical knowledge of both subjects features prominently in MacDonald's fiction. In the *Princess and the Goblin* (1872), Curdie, a miner boy alters the course of the tale with his knowledge of underground structures, and *Lilith* (1895) is founded upon an elaborate analogy of gemstone purity that is alluded to in less complex form in nearly every MacDonald novel.[21]

One of the few details of MacDonald's scientific biography that has been commonly acknowledged by modern MacDonald critics is that he was particularly interested in the study of chemistry. While there has, so far, only been speculation as to why this subject in particular may have attracted his interest, unpublished correspondence with his tutor William Gregory confirms, provides insight, and, in fact, reshapes fundamentally the focus of past biographies and their view on science in MacDonald's life and writing. A descendant of a dynasty of Scottish

---

[18] Keith Hannabus notes that, for instance, the University of Oxford, which features as a counterpoint, a contrast to Scottish university education, for instance in MacDonald's *Lilith*, only began including the modern Natural Sciences (which had been taught much earlier at Scottish Universities) into its degrees in the 1860s; "Mathematics in Victorian Oxford," in *Mathematics in Victorian Britain*, Raymond Flood, Adrian Rice and Robin Wilson, eds. (Oxford: Oxford University Press, 2011), 37.

[19] Colin A. McLaren, *Aberdeen Students, 1600–1860* (Aberdeen: University of Aberdeen, 2005), 99, 108.

[20] Cf. MS M 186, James Beattie, "Dr Beattie's Lectures in the Philosophy of the Mind and Logick," Sir Duncan Rice Library Special Collections, University of Aberdeen.

[21] MacDonald's characters are often named after precious and gem stones, such as Diamond and Ruby in *At the Back of the North Wind* (1868); The purity of their souls is analogous to the purity of the crystals; the quack doctor Count von Funkelstein is exposed through his name as a disingenuous in *David Elginbrod* (1863)—Funkelstein, in German, meaning a mere "sparkly stone," a contrast especially when juxtaposed with the pure diamond.

academics and scientists,[22] Gregory taught Organic Chemistry and translated Justus von Liebig's works on chemistry in agriculture and life sciences into English, among them *Analysis of Organic Bodies* (1839) and *Organic Chemistry in its Applications to Physiology and Pathology* (1842). He left Aberdeen for Edinburgh in 1845, where, as he writes to MacDonald, he had set up laboratories and "*practical* instruction" on the same model as Liebig's in Germany, where he also employed "first-rate" German assistants.[23] Gregory expanded on Liebig's work on the improvement of farming but also population health, especially the issue of malnourishment which preoccupied the impoverished MacDonald, who for much of his later life participated in efforts to improve the living conditions of the poor.

These letters, moreover, clarify the reasons for MacDonald not pursuing further study or a career in science. This was not because he "abandoned" or "rejected" it, or because he was not "qualified" for it, as William Raeper has argued.[24] In fact, the opposite emerges in all points. Gregory, firstly, expressed no concerns about MacDonald's academic capabilities: he writes that "although *at the present* you are not qualified for the duties" of an academic assistant, "you may probably become so *in no long period*."[25] Although MacDonald's original letter is lost, Gregory clearly responds to his former student's worries about the cost of studying abroad, listing in great detail the fees for his laboratories over more than one page. While the whereabouts of MacDonald's response are also unknown, the thoughts of his protagonist in *Castle Warlock* (1881) appear to give insight into what it might have said. Cosmo passes his science degree with identical results as MacDonald, and agonizes over his future:

> The one profession he had a leaning to was that of chemistry, at the time receiving much attention in view of agricultural and manufacturing prospects [...]. But for the realisation of the possible hope [...] a large sum must be spent before his knowledge would be of money-value, and fit for offer in the scientific market. For that he must go to Germany to Liebig, or to Edinburgh to Gregory.[26]

Many of MacDonald's contemporaries vouched for the historical accuracy of his fiction. Former fellow student William Duguid Geddes, later principal

---

[22] Cf. Agnes Grainger Stewart, *The Academic Gregories* (Edinburgh: Oliphant Anderson & Ferrier, 1901).
[23] MS MacDonald 1/1/1, William Gregory to George MacDonald, 14 Apr 1845, King's College London Archives, n.p. (italics added).
[24] Cf. Manlove, *Modern Fantasy*, 58; Raeper, *George MacDonald: Novelist and Victorian Visionary*, 55; Broome, "MacDonald's Dream-Frame," 87.
[25] MS MacDonald 1/1/1, n.p. (italics added).
[26] George MacDonald, *Castle Warlock: A Homely Romance* (London: Kegan Paul, 1890), 169–70 (italics added).

of Aberdeen University, referred to them as the "Classic Epic of Student Life in Aberdeen," and reconsidered in this setting the autobiographical content of MacDonald's fiction grates against modern critical consensus.[27]

Cosmo's thoughts, however, do seem to confirm the opinion of Greville MacDonald's views on his father's abandoned scientific career. Greville asserted that, then, a "strong desire took hold of" his father to train as a doctor, a common career for "more affluent" graduates of his degree, but it was "the want of money" which "stood in the way."[28] He repeats this when recalling that regret about this missed opportunity was still felt when he began to study medicine at King's College London in 1870. Greville recalls his career choice "made [his father] very happy [...] seeing that he himself would have *been* a doctor if [his father] could have afforded it," confirming that no ideological grounds prevented MacDonald senior's scientific career, but his poverty.[29]

Instead of giving up on the path of science he had wished to pursue, George MacDonald found a different way of doing so, and considering the third major component of his time at Aberdeen underlines how becoming a writer and teacher of literature was precisely that alternative path of pursuing his scientific interest. MacDonald interrupted his study in his third year due to a lack of finance, and worked in cataloguing a private library in which he encountered the works of Goethe and Novalis, who expressed their scientific thought through literature,[30] and became the most significant influences on MacDonald's writing and philosophy. Only shortly after graduating MacDonald published a translation of Novalis' *Hymnen an die Nacht*. He also translated poetry by Schiller, Goethe, Heine, and others. His first novel is littered with lengthy quotations from Novalis, especially *Heinrich von Ofterdingen* and *Fragmente*, and references to Hegel; Goethe's *Faust* and *Farbenlehre* ("Theory of Colors") continued to shape the intellectual basis of his magnum opus *Lilith*. MacDonald did not pursue literature in spite of science, but as an alternative way of participating in it, outside a professional career.

In accordance with his training, MacDonald understood science as an integrated philosophy, and something that had to be applied for the improvement of society. This is fundamental to understanding its function within the author's philosophy, which has been mistaken for a comprehensive rejection of science. A

---

[27] Greville MacDonald, *George MacDonald and his Wife* (London: George Allen & Unwin, 1924), 57.
[28] McLaren, Aberdeen Students, 134; Greville MacDonald, *George MacDonald and his Wife*, 68.
[29] Greville MacDonald, *Reminiscences of a Specialist*, 36 (italics added).
[30] See Dalia Nassar, "'Idealism is nothing but genuine empiricism:' Novalis, Goethe, and the Ideal of Romantic Science," *Goethe Yearbook* 18 (2011): 67–95.

lecture on Wordsworth's poetry delivered by MacDonald decades after graduating from Aberdeen, whose dramatic imagery has almost uniformly been used to cement this point, in fact proves the opposite. MacDonald refers to Wordsworth's often-evoked lines on the "meddling intellect" that "misshapes beauteous forms of things; / We murder to dissect," in which "scientists" are seemingly castigated a "fingering slave / One that would peep and botanize / Upon his mother's grave," recklessly irreverent of nature, and scientific materialism a threat to beauty, art and nature as revelations of God.[31] MacDonald parallels this passage, stating that finding "the first primrose of the year," was as beautiful "as if you had found a child;" but "Science, in the person of the botanist," regardless, "pulls it to pieces to see its construction:" it "kills what it touches."[32] But while the science, and the poetry of nature were two fundamentally different things to MacDonald, they were neither rejected, nor considered mutually exclusive, but are merely flawed on their own: "The poet may be man of science, and the man of science may be a poet; but poetry includes science, and the man who will advance science most, is the man who, other qualifications being equal, has most of the poetic faculty in him."[33] But it was not merely a case that poetry, in its reverence of nature closer to religion, and therefore the more important of the two, improved the scientist, but also vice versa. William Paley's *Natural Theology* (1802) on its own, for instance, is shown to be as limited as any materialist: "[Paley] taught us to believe there is a God from the mechanism of the world. But […] what does it prove? A mechanical God, and nothing more."[34]

MacDonald believed Wordsworth's poetry provided a "teaching" in what was missing from scientific study, emphasizing the value of poetry in its power to visualize processes of the imagination, the faculty, which MacDonald believed to be strongest in the poet, that could bring "two levels of experience […] together as a coherent whole."[35]

MacDonald's applied and integrated understanding of science and literary portrayals of scientific matters is mirrored in his protagonists' views. In *Castle Warlock*, Cosmo's reading in the library of a similar "great house" as the one in which MacDonald had worked, enlightens his search for knowledge during his Aberdeen science degree:

> And already he saw a glimmer here and there in regions of mathematics from which had *never* fallen a ray into the corner of an eye of those grinding

---

[31] William Wordsworth, "The Tables Turned," *Lyrical Ballads and Other Poems* (Ware: Wordsworth Editions, 2003), 83; Rylance, *Victorian Psychology*, 152.
[32] MacDonald, "Wordsworth's Poetry," 257–8.
[33] MacDonald, "Wordsworth's Poetry," 256–7.
[34] MacDonald, "Wordsworth's Poetry," 246.
[35] MacDonald, "The Imagination," 8.

men. That was because he read books of poetry and philosophy of which *they* had never heard.³⁶

Near-identical scenes are described in MacDonald's final novel *Lilith*, and *The Portent*, which fill in the details of what MacDonald may have read in those years. *Lilith*'s Vane notes the "fine library" in which he read contained "Ptolemy, Dante, the two Bacons, and Boyle [who] were even more to me than Darwin or Maxwell;" earlier drafts also include Herbert Spencer and T. H. Huxley.³⁷ *The Portent*'s Duncan finds there also a "whole nest of German classics [...]—I found in these volumes a mine of wealth unexhaustive."³⁸ The wording is notable, when considering the flawed search of Anodos for wealth in his father's secretary, as opposed to what it is he finds. It was in these multidisciplinary libraries that *Lilith*'s Vane also states he

> was constantly seeing, and on the outlook to see, strange analogies, not only between the facts of different sciences of the same order, or between physical and metaphysical facts, but between physical hypotheses and suggestions glimmering out of the metaphysical dreams into which I was in the habit of falling.³⁹

Rather than having "turned away from his early studies in physics and chemistry *absolutely*, allowing science *no place* in the discovery of worthwhile knowledge," as Colin Manlove has claimed, "two levels of experience" are brought "together as a coherent whole:" a synthesis that happens through the dream.⁴⁰

Although the dream has been almost universally acknowledged as the main narrative element of MacDonald's fantasies, the content of its frame, and in what relationship the mind of the dreamer stands to it, has remained unexplored. By having treated MacDonald's realist and fantastic novels largely separately, scholarship has, so far, never viewed in conjunction this main fantastic narrative element and its vital realist basis. Acknowledging MacDonald's personal engagement with the science of his time, as outlined above, aims to illuminate how MacDonald's portrayal of the dream is rooted deeply in the scientific and philosophical conundrums which the author was so engrossed in, and which he navigates and negotiates, in a process made manifest, via the mind of the dreamer in his novels. It is an alternative discursive sphere in which to resolve them. As Frederic Jameson notes, irrespective of genre classification, and "no matter how escapist their surfaces," literary works "embody" the "realities that shaped

---

³⁶ MacDonald, *Castle Warlock*, 164 (italics added).
³⁷ George MacDonald, *Lilith* (London: Chatto & Windus, 1895), 1; George MacDonald, *Lilith B*, MS 46187 B, (London, British Library), 1.
³⁸ George MacDonald, *The Portent: A Story* (London: Smith & Elder, 1864), 80.
³⁹ MacDonald, *Lilith*, 1.
⁴⁰ MacDonald, "The Imagination," 8; Manlove, *Modern Fantasy*, 58.

them," the referential framework exists always as the "unconscious" of a literary text.[41] MacDonald's fantastic dreams, as the following section will show, give "conscious" and "unconscious" insight into how the Victorian fantastic engaged with science, and revealed its potential social impact, and how dreaming, and its literary imitation, held diagnostic and curative potential.

"Chemical Analogies" and "Experimental Physics of the Mind" in MacDonald's Fiction

Returning to the analogy of descent, and Anodos transcending the material world on a psycho-geological journey to cure his unbalanced materialist mindset, it is striking that this is a trope which is, like the library scene, replayed with minor variations throughout MacDonald's fiction, thus underlining the continuing influence of his formative years. The analogy performs a scientific function, mirroring a technique that gained currency in the Victorian psychological discourse in the second half of the nineteenth century. Most famously formulated by James Sully, and quoted by Freud in his *Interpretation of Dreams* (1899), this image conveyed Sully's belief that dreams revealed the "stratified," "hidden" layers of the of the "palimpsest" of the mind and the "organic substrate of our conscious personality."[42] Crucially, Sully utilized the natural, geological metaphor to express that the "subconscious," was the revelation of a "*nobler*" impulse," a better choice not made in life, the dream as a *childish*, *regressive* activity revealing its *purer*, natural character.[43] This stood in contrast to the dominating narrative of the second half of the nineteenth century, represented by the likes of Henry Holland or Arthur Ladbroke Wigan, who understood the unconscious as a threat. Wigan formulated this in his theory of "double consciousness," in which each "cerebrum" was "capable of a distinct and separate volition," one *rational*, and in the "*healthy* brain," dominant; the other inhabited by the "*passions*," the creative mind, which, if it took over, rendered the mind "*morbid*;" making dreams, as Frances Power Cobbe, stated a sign of "the reasonable soul run mad."[44]

---

[41] Adam Roberts, Frederic Jameson (London: Routledge, 2000), 76, 83; Frederic Jameson, *The Political Unconscious: Narrative as a Socially Symbolic Act* (Ithaca, NY: Cornell University Press, 1982), 110.

[42] Sully, "Dream as Revelation," 359, 358. In a footnote in the fourth chapter of his *Interpretation of Dreams* (1899), Freud cites a lengthy passage from Sully's "The Dream as Revelation."

[43] Sully, "Dream as Revelation," 364 (italics added).

[44] Frances Power Cobbe, "Dreams as Illustrations of Unconscious Cerebration," *Macmillan's Magazine* (Apr. 1871): 523; Arthur Ladbroke Wigan, *A New View of Insanity: The Duality of Mind: Proved By The Structure, Functions, And Diseases of The Brain And By The Phenomena Of Mental Derangement, And Shown To Be Essential To Moral Responsibility* (London: Longman, 1844), 26, 30.

Arthur Hughes, "Anodos Awakens"

The unconscious mind, as Holland had himself noted, had not emerged as a field of study before the second half of the century—the phrase "unconscious thought" would have rather appeared an oxymoron—but it became a dominating discourse which MacDonald interrogates in *Phantastes*.[45] Anodos begins his journey on the opposite end of the spectrum to which MacDonald and Sully stood on the issue of the nature of the unconscious, which is evident right from the beginning of the dream vision into which Anodos drifts after the appearance of the specter of the White Lady. He awakes, or so it seems, to find his habitual surroundings transformed, in a way similar to *A Midsummer Night's Dream* or *The Divine Comedy*: into a forest scene. "A stream of clear water was running over the carpet […] which *I had myself designed* to imitate a field of grass and daisies" and "seemed to wave in a tiny breeze that followed the water's flow;" "the branches

---

[45] Henry Holland, Chapter on Mental Physiology (London: Longman, 1852), 109, 79; Anon, "Works on Mental Philosophy, Mesmerism, Electro-Biology &c.," North British Review (1854): 180.

and leaves *designed upon the curtains* of my bed were slightly in motion."[46] Anodos' gaze seeks the man-made, only to find that all he made *into* material, is in fact natural: his dream transports him into the creative unconscious, the source of his creation, his "poieos"—showing the unconscious mind, the unfettered imagination, as an image of God the *creator*, and his creation which *is* nature, much in accordance with what Sully would write half a century later. Reversing the creative process, Anodos finds himself at the source of thought, where natural imagery functions analogically to the psyche. From a "green marble basin," flows a "stream of cool water:" the "stream of consciousness" (an image William James is usually credited to have popularized).

MacDonald enacts the conflict between his own belief (that it is the immaterial that guides the material) and Anodos' opposing view in a crucial scene of *Phantastes*. Evoking the tale of Pygmalion quickening the statue he carves, MacDonald stages the sequence of how different philosophies are translated into actions, and how philosophies may thus improve or worsen self and society. Anodos follows the stream to a cave, in which he falls into "delicious reverie" in which "lovely forms, and colors, and sounds," a kaleidoscopic "assembly of forms and spiritual sensations," "seemed to use my brain as a common hall"—Anodos has for the first time let go of the material, become passive, and given his mind over to unconscious thought.[47] Referring to the cave as an "antenatal tomb," a quote from Shelley, a place "where butterflies dream of the life to come," this is an awakening of the soul, for which butterflies are a symbol: the Greek "psyche" stands for both "soul" and "butterfly"—a popular metaphor employed also by Lewis Carroll or Charles Kingsley to refer to the liberation of the soul in dream, as a naturally intended evolution of mental function.[48]

The evocation of kaleidoscopic imagery further enhances the psychological imagery. MacDonald had studied the works of David Brewster, a collaborator of his tutor Gregory credited with the invention of the kaleidoscope, and references to his kaleidoscope and multiplying glass feature throughout *Phantastes*. The kaleidoscope was a popular "philosophical toy," almost in itself an embodied

---

[46] George MacDonald, *Phantastes*, 14 (italics added).
[47] George MacDonald, *Phantastes*, 81.
[48] In discarded drafts of *Lilith* MacDonald compares the curative power of dreaming to "turning worms into psyches," or turning "bookworms" into psyches, the worm being a reference to the devil, as I will discuss below; the butterfly image is associated with the goddess Psyche, whose Roman name, Anima, is likewise found in psychological terminology; Percy Bysshe Shelley, "The Sensitive Plant," in *The Sensitive Plant*, ed. Edmund Gosse (London: Heinemann, 1820), 79; with this image MacDonald also seems to draw on Dante's lines: "Do you not understand that we are worms / Each born to form the angelic butterfly / That flies defenseless to the Final Judge," quoted and discussed in Daniel Gabelman, *George MacDonald: Divine Carelessness and Fairytale Levity* (Waco, TX: Baylor University Press, 2013), 194.

metaphor. Brewster explained it was designed for "creating and exhibiting beautiful forms" from reality by fragmentation, "multiplication," and recombination, and by "arrangement of the images" into a new order according to "the principle of symmetry:" an image of reality "beyond description splendid and beautiful."[49] The unconscious vision, the first dream of profound sleep, reveals the substrata of thought, that rearranges, like Brewster's instrument, the fragments of waking thought of the material world into a meaningful picture.

This vision, of liberated thought reordering his mind, produces unexperienced insight, and Anodos leaps into action. Inspired by a kind of thought that arises from reading fairy-stories, he creates out of alabaster the image of the White Lady—the symbol of the perfect union of the material quickened by the "poeios." MacDonald had studied the curative and intellectually enhancing effect of rendering the scientific mind passive and giving it over to the unconscious in his psychology lectures at Aberdeen in which dreams were described as "useful fables" in which "a man of prudence might make discoveries concerning his health," as the vision of the diagnostic specter. Considered to be "giving variety to our thoughts and forcing the mind to exert itself into new directions," it was those "who are most addicted to intense thinking" that were "most apt to dream," and MacDonald had full confidence in the intellectual products of this process.[50]

However, the dream models not only what is good, but, since it reveals the mental structure of its dreamer, it also illuminates his flaws. Thus, the perfect union falls victim to Anodos' still materially focused mind. As in the opening scene, he wishes to possess the ideal, and as he tries to grasp her with this objective, she escapes—and his vision becomes understandable to him, once again—as Wigan or Holland conceptualized unconscious thought—a "delusion of my brain."[51] Neither the first nor the second descent were sufficient as a cure, despite their ever-greater revelations.

The relevance of this scene becomes clear in juxtaposition with its uncanny re-enactment. The plot of *Phantastes* is made up of recurring patterns, mirroring mental descents and ascents, accompanied by striking oscillations between darkness and light. In the twin-scene of the light-immersed encounter in the meadow, Anodos diverts his wanderings, away from the stream that embodied unconscious thought, towards a spired gothic building, in which the search for insight is re-enacted, but this time in the absence of that light, that kind of unconscious thought that had just been revealed to him. After disobeying a warning not to enter the "church of darkness," and yet entering the second dark

---

[49] David Brewster, *A Treatise on Optics* (London: Longman, 1853), 443–5.
[50] Beattie, *Philosophy of the Mind*, n.p.
[51] MacDonald, *Phantastes*, 129.

space—this time a man-made structure—he yields, despite a second warning, to a still more "irresistible desire" to penetrate into it even further and open a cupboard in it.[52] He disregards even a third warning and enters, unleashing a shadow that attaches itself to his heels: a creature, as an ogre woman observes, "you call [...] by a different name in your world."[53] The chapter's epigraph ("part of the part which was at first a whole") a quote from Goethe's *Faust* (1790), links the Shadow to Mephistopheles, who only enters into Faust's "high vaulted, narrow Gothic study" after being invited "thrice."[54] As the Shadow likewise requires three rejections of what the unconscious advises, it becomes clear that the Shadow is Anodos' devil.

Although the devil is a fundamentally theological image, it provides crucial insight into how MacDonald's religion is intimately linked with his philosophy of science, of nature, and of the mind. Faust, like Anodos, and many other MacDonald protagonists, is a scientist, who, in the pivotal "Studierzimmer" scene MacDonald evokes—an equivalent to his library scenes—despairs over the struggle of his "two souls" and his inability to find what "what binds the world and guides its course"—a struggle Mephistopheles tantalizingly promises to resolve.[55] MacDonald considered the devil, as he clarified in the "Poet-Physician," "the Shadow of thy own self"—a Mephistophelean embodiment of worldly desires, and "self-centredness:" a two-dimensional, "lower," representation of the self, the latter being an image of God.[56] This is precisely the flawed mindset Anodos initially betrays in his interaction with the specter, and which *Lilith*'s Vane shows when he resists leaving the waking world for his dream vision, exclaiming, "let me *first* go home [...] and come again after *I* have *found* or *made, invented*, or at least *discovered* something," when he fears he may not return from it.[57] Their self-centered approach to scientific study for its own sake, and discovery only for possessing its outcomes out of vanity, are motifs diametrically opposed to the application of scientific study for the improvement of self and society, which MacDonald saw as its purpose.

The vision makes graspable how this mindset is fundamentally against nature (thus implicitly dismissing such views as Wigan's as inherently wrong), as knowledge ("scientia") is implicit in nature, and therefore unpossessable, and only translatable into mental and societal structures which must mirror it. Attempts at

---

[52] MacDonald, *Phantastes*, 129.
[53] MacDonald, *Phantastes*, 108.
[54] Johann Wolfgang von Goethe, *Faust: Der Tragödie Erster Teil* (Husum: Hamburger Lesehefte, 2004), 44.
[55] Goethe, *Faust*, 15.
[56] George MacDonald, *St. George and St Michael* (London: Kegan Paul, 1876), 129.
[57] MacDonald, *Lilith*, 30.

possessing scientific knowledge were thus, fundamentally, an act of unbalancing, and MacDonald echoes theories of analogous structures of nature and society, such as Spencer's of man as the "social atom."[58] As Beattie suggested, the dream could reveal much about a man's health, and the nature-based analogy of dreams shows how both protagonists' rationalist-materialist teaching has had an adverse effect on their minds. Trapped in a misconception of the relationship of science to nature, their mind is in*sane*, as the type of scientist Wordsworth proclaimed, "murders to dissect."[59]

The way in which this fictionalized, and yet scientifically founded analogy performs a counterpoint to such theories as Wigan's and Holland's illuminates the kindred nature of the medical term "diagnosis" and "fantasy" which both come to bear in the framework of dreaming. Through diagnosis (to "see / to know through"), and "fantasy," from "phantasai" ("to make visible"), the dream acts as a psychological diagnostic device "making visible" the immaterial influences that shape the mind of the dreamer—in this case, the effect of a certain school of scientific teaching, rather than science in general—and how these, in turn, affect his actions and the world around him.

After having experienced the two ways of thinking in juxtaposition, Anodos longs for a resolution of the tension between them. As he was now able to *feel* that the rivulet's course is "surely the path to Fairy Land," Anodos enters a boat, and lets himself drift down the stream, once more letting his unconscious take over. He thus arrives at the fairy castle, where a dialectic resolution of this tension takes place.[60] This resolution relies heavily on its referential framework of Edmund Spenser's *Faerie Queene* (1590) and its House of Alma, an allegory of the "soul in perfect command of the body," which illuminates the ways in which MacDonald uses the castle as—another recurring—spatial metaphor for the ideal workings of the mind; it is also the source of the novel's name.[61]

In *The Faerie Queene*, two knights had ascended, under the guidance of the white lady Alma, to the chambers of the "higher faculties of the sensitive

---

[58] Herbert Spencer, *Social Statics: or, The Conditions Essential to Happiness Specified, and the First of them Developed* (London: Chapman, 1851), 17.

[59] As Alice Jenkins elaborates, this was a subject of great public concern: university study that was too "mathematical" was feared to fostered "overactive habits of analysis" and a sense of mathematics as "the only logic," which could lead to "permanent mental damage," "Mathematics and Mental Health in Early Nineteenth-Century England," *Journal BSHM Bulletin: Journal of the British Society for the History of Mathematics* 25, vol. 2 (2010): 94.

[60] MacDonald, *Phantastes*, 47, 49.

[61] Roderick McGillis, "*Phantastes* and *Lilith*: Femininity and Freedom," in *The Gold Thread: Essays on George MacDonald*, ed. William Raeper (Edinburgh: Edinburgh University Press, 1991), 35; John Docherty, "Anodos and Kathodos in Alice's Adventures in Wonderland," *The Carrollian: The Lewis Carroll Journal*, 9 (2002): 46.

soul," embodied in the allegories "Memoree" and "Phantastes," embodiments also of the two systems of thought MacDonald showed at work in the mind, who, only in synthesis, facilitate good "Judgement."[62] "Phantastes," who is "of years yet fresh," and knows "all artes, all science, all Philosophy" inhabits a room filled with "sondry colours" of reflections, "visions" and "dreames:" he corresponds to the kaleidoscopic vision of the "antenatal tomb," which Anodos strives to regain.[63] Memoree, an "old man" of "infinite remembrance," "recorded" all "things foregone," catalogued them in his "library," a "chamber" full of "old records," "some made in books" of two kinds: factual or fairy histories.[64]

Like Spenser's knights, Anodos reads the two distinct types of books in the library based on the House of Alma, and MacDonald layers contemporary science into Spenser's literary allegory. When, reading a fairy-tale, Anodos turns into Cosmo—a model for later characters by this name—who in accordance with it, have brought their mind into "order," MacDonald models the psychology of his novel's anticipated educational impact upon the readers' minds:

> While I read it, I was Cosmo, and his history was mine. Yet, all the time, I seemed to have a kind of *double consciousness*, and the story a double meaning. Sometimes it seemed only to represent a simple story of *ordinary life*, perhaps almost of *universal life*; wherein *two souls*, loving each other and longing to come nearer, do, after all, but behold each other as in a glass darkly.[65]

The analogy explicitly aligns Faust's two souls with the waking, rational thought, and fantastic imagination of dreams of "double consciousness" theories.

But having considered MacDonald's biography, a third type of books in the fairy library, towards which less critical attention has been turned, moves into sharper focus. These "other books" sought after the source "whence the spiritual vision sprang," and hoped to

> *combine two propositions, both apparently true* [...], and to find the point in which their invisibly converging lines would *unite in one*, revealing *a truth higher than either* [...] whence each derived its life and power.[66]

Presenting the two types of thought as thesis and antithesis, MacDonald illuminates the place he envisages for dream-consciousness in its practical application with regard to digesting, and advancing scientific thought in their synthesis—a pattern of thought that also aligns with the German Romantic and philosophical influences of MacDonald's, notably of Hegel and Schelling's

---

[62] Docherty, "Anodos and Kathodos," 46.
[63] Edmund Spenser, *The Faerie Queene*, Longman Annotated English Poets, 2nd ed. (Harlow: Pearson Longman, 2007), II.9.50–1, 53
[64] Spenser, *Faerie Queene*, II.9. 55–7.
[65] MacDonald, *Phantastes*, 148 (italics added).
[66] MacDonald, *Phantastes*, 137–8 (italics added).

naturphilosophie. This synthesis was not only ideal, but a change in the fabric of the mind, staged in the final descent into the geological strata of the mind, which thus also reveals the physiological, electro-chemical basis of its workings—enacted, in turn, in the subsequent scene.

The tone of this third descent conveys finality: after his most recent failure not to touch the White Lady, Anodos is drawn to a "waste windy hill," where "great stones like tombstones stood all about" him.[67] He descends down a "natural staircase" within the "deep chasm" of a grave-like "excavated well," recognizing, "at once that this was my path."[68] The analogy of geology and psychology is evident, and John Docherty underlines how the tortuous descent into this underworld reveals "malfunctioning parts of [the] soul which have created regions of hell [is] closely comparable to those of the traditional subterranean hell."[69] Anodos reflects that "ever as I went, darker grew my thoughts:" the actual topographical descent in his dream is equivalent to getting to the bottom of his conundrum; consequently, "whenever a choice was necessary" he "always chose the path which seemed to lead downwards."[70] The torturing memories of what is now apparent to him as moral failures chase him in the shape of "queer goblin creatures" of "all varieties of fantastic ugliness, both in form and feature." With "harsh grating laughter full of evil humour" they mockingly sing the "song with which I had brought the light into the eyes of the White Lady."[71] When he attempts "to run, but they all [rush] on [him]," leaving him unable to move or escape, Anodos gives in, and "no longer call[s] her" to himself "*my* White Lady." At the lowest point of his journey, he faces and re-evaluates memory fragments, to experience catharsis, and "the *galvanic torrent* of this *battery* of malevolence *stung* to life within me a *spark of nobleness*, and I said aloud, "Well, if he is a better man, let him have her.""[72]

This turning point is expressed, strikingly, in terms of geological chemistry and galvanism, which function analogously on a psychological level. The "noble" change in character crystalizes as a chemical process, in which the subconscious strata are analogous to the subconscious. Once the deeply-rooted problem is thus solved in the unconscious mind—a process as observable scientifically, as the analogous process in geological chemistry, the crystalized insight can ascend, be transported, to the waking mind.

---

[67] MacDonald, *Phantastes*, 187.
[68] MacDonald, *Phantastes*, 188.
[69] Docherty, "Anodos and Kathodos," 45.
[70] MacDonald, *Phantastes*, 188.
[71] MacDonald, *Phantastes*, 191.
[72] MacDonald, *Phantastes*, 190.

MacDonald's complex layered system of analogies thus comes full circle in this scene through the overarching framework of the mythological katabasis: his hero's journey into the underworld in which allegorical embodiments of sin are encountered, and upon which Anodos' journey is modelled. The name Anodos itself is linked to this framework: it derives from ancient Greek, "a way up," or "a way back," and foreshadows the outcome of his kathodos, his "way down."[73] The "anodos" denotes the return of the hero, having experienced catharsis, a spiritual "cleansing, purifying" from "the contagion of sin" or "disobedience to divine will," a figurative rebirth.[74] This framework had in MacDonald's time famously already been appropriated for scientific purposes in Victorian electro-biology—to which the galvanic shock marks the turning point, as Soto also points out, a swing in the "dynamic" of "the two-world nature of life and energy."[75] To a "man trained in electro-chemistry," Soto tentatively suggests, "the *anodos* and *kathodos* would have had primarily scientific connotations," and Broome, who describes the dreams in MacDonald's fiction as "scientific portals," likewise suspects he possessed "significant knowledge on biochemical processes"—yet both Broome and Soto stop short of drawing any conclusions from the connection of mythological to scientific concepts.[76]

Such an interpretation is, however, fruitful, as the entanglement of fantastic and scientific languages was something MacDonald was aware of, and actively utilized for making meaning through combining both in the scientifically based fantastic spaces constructed in his novel. MacDonald had indeed learned in his lectures on electricity that "cathode" and "anode" had been coined in 1834 by Michael Faraday, who had derived the water-based metaphor of the "electrical current" from the "terrestrial globe," and consequently settled on "directional" terms for visualizing electricity that "signify way up and way down."[77] Metaphors were abundant in Victorian science writing. Alexander Bain expressed the dynamic nervous system through metaphors of railways and telegraph wires. Likewise, Alice

---

[73] Nick Page, ed., Introduction to *Phantastes: A Faerie Romance for Men and Women*, George MacDonald (London: Paternoster, 2008), 44; Fernando Soto, "Chthonic Aspects of Phantastes: From the Rising of the Goddess to the Anodos of Anodos," *North Wind: A Journal of George MacDonald Studies* 19 (2000): 20.

[74] Joseph Campbell, *The Hero with a Thousand Faces*, 3rd ed. (Novato: New World Library, 2008), 1. There can be little doubt about MacDonald's awareness of the linguistic and mythological implications of the name he chose for his protagonist. As a student at Aberdeen he was examined on the translation Xenophon's anabasis, obtained a distinction in his degree, and he continued to study Ancient Greek at Highbury. Variations of this terminology recur throughout his fiction: *Lilith*'s temporary working title was "Anacosm," and its protagonist's ancestor, evoking Anodos' knightly name, is called "Sir Upward."

[75] Soto, "Chthonic Aspects," 20, 44.

[76] Soto, "Chthonic Aspects," 44; Broome, "MacDonald's Dream-Frame," 87, 88.

[77] Alice Jenkins, Space and the "March of Mind" (Oxford: Oxford University Press, 2007), 126; MS M 172 Bain, "Lecture 119," Lectures in Natural Philosophy, n.p.

Jenkins notes that Faraday "did not attempt to expunge metaphor," but rather allowed "for the possibility of interpretation of their referents as either concrete or conceptual."[78] And it is through this metaphoric freedom that MacDonald here proposes (through the means of imaginative literature) a scientifically based theory of dream-consciousness.

"More than a Figment of Scientific Fancy:"
Science, Literature, and Fantasy

Through the use of such linguistic imagery, common to scientific discourse, but with a parallel life in mythology and fantastic narrative, MacDonald participates not only in fantasy writing, but also in the ongoing discussion of the place of the imagination in science at a time in which it is popularly seen to lean ever more toward empirical methods, professionalization, and institutionalization. The discussions around the concept of the imagination and the unconscious, and thus also dream, were a crucible of Victorian intellectual discourse, and one at which the limits of science and the limits of human knowledge were negotiated. MacDonald's fantasies thus constitute an innovative literary endeavor but also a serious, scientifically informed participation in this discussion, pushing its boundaries. MacDonald thus took a place alongside many of the most prominent names in Victorian science—among them many, who, like him, brought philosophies shaped by their particularly Scottish education to bear in this debate, in which narrative and metaphor played a crucial role.

Among those prominent names we re-encounter Faraday, who, while he had judged reason "the noblest," had called imagination "the most enticing" means of pursuing science.[79] Men like Faraday, who became icons of a public-facing science, were well-versed in the potential of imaginative language, and metaphors were evoked to *embody*, to make graspable and enact the limits of perception, and to overcome the limits posed on scientific debate by specialist language. Faraday's fellow Royal Institution-based science popularizer, John Tyndall thus drew on the potential of narrative devices to "make visible," and thus graspable, invisible parts of science—as MacDonald had done for psychology. The scientific principles underlying sound, Tyndall had thus articulated as follows: as the "bodily eye [...] cannot see the condensations and rarefactions of the waves of sound," "we constructed them in thought." The imagination, and imaginative narrative were thus crucial to the pursuit of science—in ways that MacDonald had discovered for himself through his studies at Aberdeen. Tyndall, like MacDonald, saw

---

[78] Jenkins, *March of Mind*, 128, 131.
[79] Alice Jenkins, *Michael Faraday's Mental Exercises: An Artisan Essay Circle in Regency London* (Liverpool: Liverpool University Press, 2008).

scientifically based metaphorical and analogous narrative, as a continuation of experiment and observation, crucial to the formation of scientific hypothesis, and thus the formation of new insights, as an integral part of the pursuit of science. He asserted that if imagination was guided by scientific "syllogism and mechanical laws," it carried "our experience into a new region," and back into "the world of sense," and "always lands on the solid shores of fact," an act of "creation" that could produce "something more than a mere figment of the scientific fancy," but discover scientific fact beyond the limits of the empirically possible.[80] This was the very journey that MacDonald's fantasies elevated to a literary form.

Finally, one of the most absolute claims on the power of fantastic narrative elements in science came from MacDonald's fellow Aberdonian, James Clerk Maxwell. Like MacDonald, Maxwell believed that imagination (which was being pushed out of science by forces arguing for reason, observation, and experimentation as the only valid methods of pursuing science—as embodied by Anodos at the beginning of *Phantastes*) was of vital importance to science. Giving space to imagination, to which narrative, metaphor and analogy were handmaidens, prevented the "limiting [of] the range and free play of thought [by] both positivist phenomenalism and *a priori* systems of mathematics threaten to preordain further scientific knowledge"—addressing precisely the mathematically focused mind MacDonald criticized in Anodos and throughout his non-fiction.[81]

Victorian literary dreams acted as a mirror to such scientific debates as an alternative discursive space for their subjects, and while *Phantastes* is a mid-Victorian text, investigation of similar contemporary and later texts by MacDonald, Carroll, Kingsley, and ultimately the generation of inheritors of their narrative tradition, such as H. G. Wells, show that such scientific narrative forms remained current, while their place within scientific writing shifts.

Gillian Beer has foregrounded the importance of literature and literary forms in Victorian scientific discourse, and the continuing significance of the imagination and fantastic forms. These, in turn, indicate a space for the importance of fantasy within the Victorian scientific context. When Maxwell formulated his own contribution to the psychology of the unconscious, he chose to do so through the fantastic means of a poetic dream in which the functions of the fantastic crystallize. As analogy was crucial to him as the imaginative extension to science, so poetry was, vice versa, the means for "establishing epistemological

---

[80] Tyndall, *Imagination*, 10.
[81] James Clerk Maxwell, "Are there real analogies in nature?" in *The Life of James Clerk Maxwell with a Selection from his Correspondence and Occasional Writings and a Sketch of his Contributions to Science*, ed. Lewis Campbell and William Garnett (London: Macmillan, 1882), 235–6.

foundations of scientific discovery."[82] In Maxwell's poem, the first-person narrator steps back, and by means of a "hydrodynamic" analogy of the mind, similar to that of MacDonald's caves, examines "the peculiar personal forces that compose its subconscious ground."[83] Were the "bubbles floating upwards through the current of the mind" merely "lawless force," or did they trace back the "stream of conscious action" to its source arising from "where the self in secret lies," between "rocks and eddies hidden in the depths below?" The dreamer "rise[s] afresh" and sees their duty "lie before [them] straight and plain:" he has gained (as J. R. R. Tolkien suggested was the ultimate aim of fantasy) "clearer thought."[84] His vision expresses his scientific stance on dreaming: at once the revelation of the true self, which rises in the shape of synthetic and cathartic insight into the mind, the dream also fulfils a character-shaping function. Thus, Maxwell refines Beattie's notion of the healthful dream into a potentially crucial contributor to physiological, as well as mental health, in addition to its intellectual applications.

Maxwell's aims, means, and outcomes align precisely with MacDonald's fantastic fiction, his use of scientifically informed metaphor and analogy, on the same scientific basis, and thus anticipating the same effects as in the outcome of Anodos' vision. Rising from his dream, Anodos has, accordingly, acquired a new way of thinking through this kind of self-reflection, which has formed new habits of thought in his mind. He draws on it "unconsciously almost, looking" for the "ideals that guided him in Fairy Land" whenever in doubt about how to run the newly acquired estate: feeling "somewhat instructed [...] by the adventures that had befallen me in Fairy Land," he "translates the experience" into "common life."[85] The novel ends with a voice echoing from Fairy Land, mirroring the same triple invitation of his Shadow, "A great good is coming—is coming—is coming to thee, Anodos" to confirm the physio-psychological change is completed.[86]

MacDonald's portrayal, in turn, aligns with the forms of "escape" that focus upon its "returns" described in fantasy criticism, giving them a science-historical, rather than speculative basis. Bruno Bettelheim had noted that the "enchantment" of fantasy responded, as Jackson also notes, to the "difficult inner problems" caused since the 1800s by the "destabilising psychological effects of inhabiting a materialistic culture."[87] Bettelheim asserts if "we hope to live life [...] in true consciousness of existence, then our greatest need is [...] to find meaning

---

[82] Daniel Brown, *The Poetry of Victorian Scientists: Style, Science and Nonsense* (Cambridge: Cambridge University Press, 2015), 56.
[83] Brown, *Poetry of Victorian Scientists*, 75.
[84] Maxwell, *Scientific Letters and Papers*, 443.
[85] MacDonald, *Phantastes*, 271.
[86] MacDonald, *Phantastes*, 272.
[87] Jackson, *Fantasy*, 4; Bettelheim, *Uses of Enchantment*, 3.

in existence," and "intelligent understanding" of which can only be gained from transcending the "narrow confines of *self*-centred existence"—as that embodied in Anodos' Shadow.[88] The ultimate aim of fantastic literature in this process was to "develop one's inner resources" so "emotions, imagination, and intellect mutually support and enrich one another."[89] Thus, fantasy is not only "founded in reality" and "sublimates it," but is in fact "grounded in the scientifically possible," when, on the basis of existing scientific theory, it creates an experience akin to imagination: escaping the realm of the scientifically possible but, as Tyndall and Maxwell prescribe, adhering to its rules to return improved—to improve.[90]

A reconsideration of McDonald in the context of his engagements with science sheds light not only on his biography, but enhances the scope for interpretations of his works, and their intellectual depth—especially when integrated, via his use of metaphor and analogy common to scientific discourse, into a wider intellectual debate. Opportunities for comparison, commonalities, and true innovation of MacDonald's literary texts thus arise that would not become evident when considering MacDonald along more traditional lines, as a writer of realistic, children's, fantastic, or theological fiction exclusively. MacDonald's works then emerge as even more complex engagements with (and scientifically grounded) avenues through which to navigate the anxieties arising from the impact of scientific theory, and its societal applications in education and industry, and upon Victorian epistemologies and society more widely, through fiction.

The history of science can thus illuminate the purpose of MacDonald and his fellow fantasists' work, opening new ways of looking at their impact, audiences, and influences. This also holds potential for reconceptualizing fantastic literature, and literary writing in general, through their contribution to the public understandings of science. Such approaches assert the importance of what is customarily considered non-scientific narrative as participators in scientific discourse, and, in turn, highlight the crucial role of cultural and literary forms in shaping this discourse. This remains vital, especially in the context of scholarship in science communication, and its historical forms, a history which such re-examinations of literary works, traditionally excluded from this context, can enrich—an essential endeavor, perhaps, in the current age of crisis, in which storytelling once more, emerges as a foremost agent of meaning-making.

---

[88] Bettelheim, *Uses of Enchantment*, 3.
[89] Jackson, *Fantasy*, 3; Bettelheim, *Uses of Enchantment*, 4.
[90] Bettelheim, *Uses of Enchantment*, 5, 8.

RETHINKING THE DARK SIDE:
MACDONALD'S SUBVERSIVE CHALLENGES TO "ENLIGHTENED" THEORIES OF SOCIAL DARWINISM[1]

Kerry Dearborn

I will open my mouth in a parable; I will utter dark sayings from of old [...]. glorious deeds of the Lord and his might and the wonders that he has done.[2]

George MacDonald's context was heavily shaped by the Enlightenment. His was an era when many bowed to reason as the supreme good. Rationality, scientific discovery, and empirical methodology were associated with light, and darkness was aligned with ignorance, evil, and ominous mystery. "Dark Ages" was a phrase applied to periods of history considered less rational and educationally oriented, and more captive to mythological beliefs than scientific ones. Dark skin was associated with mental and moral inferiority. Dark imaginings were associated with artists, people of color, and women, and dark curses were attributed to the disabled.[3]

Discriminatory anthropological theories grew virulently in the nineteenth century. Such theories had already grown in the soil of prejudice for centuries, but during MacDonald's lifetime they were given the strengthening fertilizer of pseudo-scientific rationalism and methodology. Prejudicial theories were useful to a ravenous empire seeking to swallow up other nations and extend its reach and control to the far ends of the world—particularly since people in desirable lands were primarily dark-skinned. To be able to discredit dark-skinned people through so-called scientific, empirical methodologies, was to create powerful rationales for conquering their lands and bringing Western forms of civilization, education, and even salvation to "dark savages." Thus, Alfred Russel Wallace presented his ideas to the Anthropological Society in 1864, stating that "more mentally and morally advanced and socially cohesive races would overtake,

---

[1] This chapter is a revised and expanded version of an article of the same title published in *North Wind: A Journal of George MacDonald Studies*, 38 (2019): 1–24.
[2] Ps. 78: 2, 4. All subsequent biblical quotations are from the NRSV translation.
[3] See for example, "Dark Ages," in *The Oxford Companion to British History*, ed. Robert Crowcroft and John Cannon (Oxford: Oxford University Press, 2018), 63; Michael E. Ruane, "A brief history of the enduring phony science that perpetuates white supremacy," *The Washington Post* (Apr. 30, 2019).

conquer, and ultimately exterminate the less advanced, just as in the animal and plant world, more fit varieties eliminated inferior varieties."[4]

It was during this period that, according to social scientists Jackson and Weidman, "All the resources of the new evolutionary science were now brought to bear as organizing concepts, models, and metaphors on the pre-evolutionary goal of explaining and justifying the inferiority of Asian, African, and American Indian peoples."[5] Such theories were also effective in justifying the use of British resources for only certain members of the population and denying them to others. If science could document the idea that people of color, immigrants, women, and those who are disabled are less human, less rational, and less able to be educated, why bother with allocating money for educating and training them?

George MacDonald employed his own theological insight and imaginative gifts to resist such discrimination and dehumanization of women, people of color, and those with disabilities throughout his works. Much has been written of MacDonald's advocacy for women, even the fact that he taught at a women's college, and that often his heroines, and even a Christ figure in his books, were female.[6] In this chapter I would also like to focus on MacDonald's radical challenges to the theories of his day, which ascribed full humanity and normalcy to white aristocratic British males and tended to view other people as outside the norm, or as part of those considered less fit for society and for life.

Based on his biblically informed, Celtic worldview, MacDonald offered a number of paradigm shifts in his work that challenged and disrupted commonplace Victorian thinking. First, he challenged the binary thinking that attributed what is good to the light, and what is bad to the darkness. Second, he challenged the negatively weighted associations of darkness and depravity with women, people of color, those who are poor, disabled, struggling with addiction, and/or with violations of the law. He also critiqued the implications drawn from such negative associations, which justified eugenics, prejudiced allocation of resources, and limited access to education. Third, he sought to bring out old and new treasure from the kingdom of God, the teaching of Jesus, and the values of

---

[4] Quoted in John P. Jackson and Nadine M. Weidman, "Race and Evolution, 1859–1900," *Race, Racism and Science: Social Impact and Interaction* (New Brunswick, NJ: Rutgers University Press, 2006), 68.

[5] Jackson and Weidman, "Race and Evolution, 1859–1900," 63.

[6] See for example the great-great-great grandmother in *The Princess and the Goblin* and *The Princess and Curdie* as explained in Kerry Dearborn, *Baptized Imagination: The Theology of George MacDonald* (Farnham: Ashgate Publishing, 2006), 114–17. Kirstin Jeffrey Johnson argues that "maybe Great-great-grandmother is, in a sense, 'a Wise Imagination,' which MacDonald calls the 'presence of the Spirit of God.'" "George MacDonald: A Life of Relationships," The Rabbit Room (Nov. 22, 2021) https://www.rabbitroom.com/post/george-macdonald-a-life-of-relationships.

the Celts to portray his belief that values of the kingdom of God are the inverse of those of the kingdoms of this world.[7] The ideas which shaped his views of the dignity of all people, which caused him to challenge the dehumanizing views of his era, and from which he created alternate narratives will be highlighted in the concluding section.

I. Challenging Binary Judgments about Light and Darkness

First, MacDonald challenged the tendency to disparage aspects of our world that are linked with darkness. Certainly, he wrote about the problems of moral darkness where a person would resist the light of God's truth and love. He did not romanticize the notion of moral darkness or try to claim that it was superior to the light. Thus, in one of MacDonald's English novels, the young curate Thomas Wingfold's mentor, Polworth, "looked so anxiously for the news of light in [Wingfold's] darkness."[8] He yearned for wisdom and insight to penetrate Wingfold's doubts and lack of faith. Of the handsome, well-educated, finely evolved, but morally weak and atheistic George Bascombe, MacDonald wrote that in Bascombe's view, he "had come out of the darkness and would return to the darkness."[9] MacDonald acknowledged associations of chaos and a return to non-being with darkness as well. Through Mr. Polworth, MacDonald expressed his firm conviction to the dying Leopold, that God "will not forget you, for that would be ceasing to be God. If God were to forget for one moment, the universe would grow black—vanish—rush out again from the realm of law and order into chaos and night."[10] MacDonald did not idealize darkness, for he recognized the goal of becoming a people who walk in the light of God's loving presence, associating his beloved Lord with the "Father of Lights." But he also saw redemptive purposes and value to darkness, and he was unwilling to associate God's redemptive purposes with the light alone.

Throughout his work MacDonald challenged a number of negative views of darkness that have been fairly pervasive throughout history. He affirmed biblical descriptions such as: "The people who walked in darkness have seen a great light,"

---

[7] "Every scribe who has been trained for the kingdom of heaven is like the master of a household who brings out of his treasure what is new and what is old" (Matt. 13:51–52). MacDonald evokes this idea in his poem, "To Aurelio Saffi:" "To God and man be simply true; / Do as thou hast been wont to do; / Bring out thy treasures, old and new," *Poetical Works, vol. 1* (London: Chatto & Windus, 1893), 442. Examples of inverse values include, "the last will be first, and the first will be last" (Matt. 20:16); "the greatest among you will be your servant" (Matt. 23:11); and "Blessed are the meek, for they will inherit the earth" (Matt. 5:5).

[8] George MacDonald, *Thomas Wingfold, Curate* (London: Kegan Paul, Trench & Co,. Paternoster Square, 1887), 147.

[9] MacDonald, *Thomas Wingfold, Curate*, 32.

[10] MacDonald, *Thomas Wingfold, Curate*, 438.

and "If the light within you is darkness how great is that darkness."[11] He was, however, willing to challenge views that categorically identified darkness as bad and then extended and exploited those views to justify dehumanizing approaches to others who were correlated with darkness. As Willie Jennings has carefully described in *The Christian Imagination*, colonializing endeavors took advantage of some biblical and archetypal categories related to darkness and light to build a foundation upon which greed, territorial growth, and ethnocentrism would appear noble and good.[12] If one could develop a framework in which anything linked with darkness would be associated with depravity and destructiveness, and anything related to light would be associated with goodness and illumination, it could serve well the purposes of those who were lighter skinned and had the power of determining who and what fit into each category. As Brian Bantum elucidates, "The story of race is the story of painting guilt upon the dark bodies of the world."[13]

Before describing MacDonald's debunking of typical correlations of various types of people with the light or the darkness, this chapter will explore his challenges to the framework itself: the binary thinking that affirmed light as good and darkness or night as bad. Because he was grounded in the biblical creation narrative, he considered both night and day, darkness and light, as part of God's very good creation. The darkness of moral depravity was not to be equated with God's good creation of night and the gifts that can arise from times, seasons, and creatures connected in any way with darkness. In fact, the day as described in the creation story of Genesis begins with the evening, "the evening and the morning were the first day. [...] the second day."[14] Biblically, the day begins when the light is fading and the darkness appears. Humans were created to embrace the reality of evening darkness in their day before ever awakening to the morning light. That means that the first job each day is to quit our activity and go to sleep. As Eugene Peterson writes:

> The Hebrew evening/morning sequence conditions us to the rhythms of grace. We go to sleep, and God begins his work. As we sleep, he develops his covenant. We wake and are called out to participate in God's creative action. We respond in faith, in work. But always grace is previous. Grace is primary. We wake into a world we did not make, into a salvation we did not earn.[15]

---

[11] Isa. 9:2; Matt. 6:23.
[12] Willie James Jennings, *The Christian Imagination: Theology and the Origins of Race* (New Haven, CT: Yale University Press, 2010).
[13] Brian Bantum, *The Death of Race, Building a New Christianity in a Racial World* (Philadelphia: Fortress Press, 2016), 62.
[14] Gen. 1:5, 8.
[15] Eugene Peterson, *Working the Angles* (Grand Rapids, MI: Eerdmans, 1987), 48.

In much of MacDonald's writing, his immature characters approach life with a sense of self-sufficiency and self-centeredness. As they mature, they learn that freedom, fullness of life, and meaning flow from living out of grace and participating in God's ways instead.

Moreover, MacDonald's works also model something very like Peterson's "rhythms of grace," with night often depicted positively as a time of rest, repentance, and transformation. In *Lilith*, Vane's first encounter with his "mentor," Mr. Raven, happens "in the evening of a gloomy day in August."[16] The process of transformation for Vane begins in the evening and moves into a dream-like experience. Over the course of the novel MacDonald surfaces commonplace concerns about darkness. There are numerous and fairly stereotypical suspicions raised about Mr. Raven, who is misperceived as "probably the devil himself" by an ancient woman of the village, and who appears initially as a "shadow."[17] Can anything good come from such a dark shadowy creature, the reader wonders? We soon learn that he is a sexton at a certain "graveyard—cemetery, more properly."[18] Once Vane has crossed over into the other world, his "mentor" has become an "ancient raven," "purply black" but "here and there softened with gray."[19] Vane correlates the experience of this other world with a kind of sleep in which its images and realities are like a dream, which to try to describe becomes elusive as when awakening from a dream.[20] Early in their conversation, Vane tries to assert evolutionary and categorical valuations, "Am I wrong in presuming that a man is superior to a bird?" Raven's response is quintessential MacDonald, "We do not waste our intellects in generalizing, but take man or bird as we find him." The Raven "saw through accident into entity."[21] In his way, MacDonald challenges essentializing ways of judging creatures according to the inherent, biological characteristics of their "group."

The challenge for Vane in entering this dream-like world is to discover himself a relative "nobody," to face the reality of death, and to rise by grace to the challenge of finding himself at home, interconnected with all who originate from the one great heart.[22] Yet, Vane is continually concerned with acting to "justify

---

[16] George MacDonald, *Lilith* (London: Lion Paperback, 1982), 6. Raven says his business as a sexton is to "have the air full of worms," that is taking worms from the dark ground and flinging them into the air to become butterflies. He says, "If only the rest of the clergy understood it [that to be their business] as well." Vane is worried lest creatures forget their origins, whereas Raven says, "it is well, surely, if it be to rise higher and grow larger," 20.

[17] MacDonald, *Lilith*, 9.

[18] MacDonald, *Lilith*, 20.

[19] MacDonald, *Lilith*, 11.

[20] MacDonald, *Lilith*, 13.

[21] MacDonald, *Lilith*, 14.

[22] MacDonald, *Lilith*, 15.

his existence" to earn his food and his rest. Raven takes him through a "sacred gloom" to the cemetery by the church ruins on Vane's actual property—a place where people still come to pray, but which Vane prefers to make a wilderness.[23] He learns that people still come to pray to join their hearts with the "one heart," the "one great Thinker" to send aloft prayers that become exquisite prayer-flowers, or soaring pigeons. All live things find their origin initially in this one great Source.[24] "All live things were thoughts to begin with, and are fit therefore to be used by those that think," he writes. This is the central basis from which all creatures are worthy and to be valued, that they were thoughts, dreams of the one heart and great Thinker.

Mr. Raven has led Vane into a secondary world to meet Raven's wife in the midst of the "burial-ground of the universe."[25] Light and dark are used in interconnected and mutually enhancing ways throughout this section. While dressed all in white:

> The life of her face and her whole person was gathered and concentrated in her eyes, where it became light. It might have been coming death that made her face luminous, but the eyes had life in them for a nation—large, and dark with a darkness ever deepening as I gazed. A whole night-heaven lay condensed in each pupil; all the stars were in its blackness, and flashed; while round it for a horizon lay coiled an iris of the eternal twilight. What any eye *is*, God only knows: her eyes must have been coming direct out of his own! The still face might be a primeval perfection; the live eyes were a continuous creation.[26]

Here we see darkness linked with the darkness from which creation emerged, with the very eyes of God, with primeval perfection, and with a "night-heaven" in whose blackness all the stars dwelt.[27] This is darkness linked with death, and also with beauty, glory, and new creation.

Raven's wife's initial questions and comments draw out the parallels with the Hebrew concept of day, and express MacDonald's work to denote the promises latent in welcoming aspects of the darkness. She asks, "Will he sleep?" Raven responds, "I fear not [...] he is neither weary nor heavy laden."[28] Here is an allusion to Jesus' invitation to all who are weary and heavy laden to come to him.[29] Somehow a willingness to sleep connects for MacDonald with awareness of need and coming with that need to Jesus. Vane's response to this is, "surely a

---

[23] MacDonald, *Lilith*, 23, 24.
[24] MacDonald, *Lilith*, 25–6.
[25] MacDonald, *Lilith*, 27.
[26] MacDonald, *Lilith*, 28.
[27] MacDonald, *Lilith*, 28.
[28] MacDonald, *Lilith*, 28.
[29] Matt. 11:28.

man must do a day's work first! [...] Let me first go home [...] and come again after I have found or made, invented, or at least discovered something!" Raven's wife responds by speaking to her husband, "He has not yet learned that the day begins with sleep! [...] Tell him he must rest before he can do anything."[30]

Even after being given the great eucharistic feast pointing to death and new life, bread and wine, and though he is tired and ready to sleep, when Vane realizes that sleep is somehow linked with dying and relinquishment of control, he plots his escape. Raven urges him, "Do not be a coward, Mr. Vane. Turn your back on fear, and your face to whatever may come. Give yourself up to the night, and you will rest indeed. Harm will not come to you, but a good you cannot foreknow."[31] Allowing fear rather than faith to guide his response he rushes out of the cold sleep/death chamber and into a context where his self-assertiveness and autonomy can find expression. Throughout the book, MacDonald reveals that Vane's rejection of darkness and dying has grave consequences for him and for others. He will remain both vane (as vacillating as a weather vane) and vain (self-absorbed) as long as he is unwilling to wrestle with truths that emerge in the darkness and new life that flows from death. Throughout the novel, both Raven (or Adam) and Eve, repeatedly urge Vane to sleep before he acts. Vane resists again and again, desperate to launch into his heroic activities, to be the savior, the victor, the center. But Raven knows that wise action must come from another source than oneself. It must come from the great heart, the great Thinker. One must sleep, even die to one's own self-centeredness and temptation to make oneself God.

Vane desperately needs to come to terms with his own limitations, and to see that he is not the source, the center, the hero. Raven explains, "They cannot empty an egg but they turn into the shell, and lie down!"[32] Vane needs to sleep first, to admit his own dependency before he can emerge into the life for which he had been created, and awaken to the reality of which he is only a small part. He has to learn that he will cause a lot more harm than good when he insists on doing things his way, according to the rhythm of self-centered action rather than the rhythm of grace. This requires embracing the darkness, acknowledging his own limitations, and trusting in something greater than himself.

For MacDonald, throughout his books, night and darkness offer liminal space in which his characters (and hopefully his readers) can experience and accept their weaknesses, their need for others, and ultimately their need for God. The fact that MacDonald would include this emphasis even in his short

---

[30] MacDonald, *Lilith*, 29.
[31] MacDonald, *Lilith*, 36.
[32] MacDonald, *Lilith*, 29.

stories, reveals what an important perspective it was for him. For example, in his short story, "The Shadows," MacDonald portrays darkness and shadows as encouraging times of reflection, repentance, and transformation, out of which a transformed life could emerge. The Shadows seem to reveal the importance of something like Peterson's "rhythms of grace" in the way they always go to church before going to work. The shadows are "gentle and respectful."[33] The question is raised, "Can that be true that loves the night?" and the response of the Shadow is, "The darkness is the nurse of light."[34] We see this theme developed more fully in *Phantastes*, as described below.[35] Furthermore, MacDonald reveals that until one comes to terms with one's limitations, it remains possible to live in the illusion of inflated self-importance and to inflict great damage on others.

These challenges are evident in Anodos in *Phantastes*, an aristocratic young white male who comes of age at the beginning of the book. Though he is given many guides—mostly female sources of wisdom, and though he repeatedly hurts the ones he loves because he trusts no wisdom outside of his own, he remains largely a dangerous and clueless presence wherever he goes. MacDonald offers a complex view of darkness in this book. Anodos allows darkness and his shadow to play a damaging role in his life; however, darkness and nighttime are also the places of his deepest reckoning and preparation for transformation. It requires a lengthy process before Anodos is ready for nighttime and darkness to bear its full fruit in him.

Negatively, he acquires a shadow by entering into the church of darkness, a shadow that influences him to demystify the world and the others in it, to see them from merely an empirical, analytic mind-set. Rather than questioning and resisting the shadow, he becomes completely identified with it, and eventually allows it to imprison him in "a dreary square tower."[36] "One miserable square hole in the roof was the only visible suggestion of a window."[37] During Anodos' imprisonment, it was only during the nighttime that he felt free, with moonlight descending through the high window "down the wall, as I might have watched, adown the sky, the long, swift approach of a helping angel."[38] The days were "hateful," "dreary," and "wretched."[39] Whereas he had struggled in the fairy palace, because "My soul was not still enough for songs. Only in the silence and darkness of the soul's night, do those stars of the inward firmament sink to

---

[33] MacDonald, "The Shadows," in *The Light Princess and Other Tales* (Edinburgh: Canongate, 1961), 92.
[34] MacDonald, "The Shadows," 97.
[35] George MacDonald, *Phantastes: A Faerie Romance* (London: Lion Paperback, 1986).
[36] MacDonald, *Phantastes*, 160.
[37] MacDonald, *Phantastes*, 160.
[38] MacDonald, *Phantastes*, 162.
[39] MacDonald, *Phantastes*, 162.

its lower surface from the singing realms beyond and shine upon the conscious spirit."⁴⁰ In this space he learns to welcome silence and darkness, which take him into his "soul's night."⁴¹ Thus, his awareness expands to see the people whom he loves and his own past more clearly. Moonlit nights become the time of nurturing new wisdom and life in him, a womb in which he can grow to accept his limitations, his humanity, and his need for others.

Ultimately, he learns to acknowledge that he is not self-sufficient, but rather weary and heavy-laden from all his efforts at self-generated grand deeds. In the fairy palace he had sought to create a song to "unveil his Isis," his "marble beauty upon her black pedestal," so that he could grasp and hold her, in violation of the command, "Touch not!"⁴² In this time of solitude and imprisonment, he finally becomes free enough to hear a song from another source than his grasping desire. He becomes capable of receiving the gift of forgiveness from the one he has most damaged, the girl whose musical globe he has shattered, whose greatest treasure he has violated. Unlike Anodos who sang the maiden free from imprisonment in marble in order to grasp and hold her, this maiden sings him free in order to liberate him from his shadow, from the prison tower, from his grasping form of love, and from the illusions of his own grandeur and nobility. Anodos describes this liberation: "A great weight was lifted from my thoughts. I knelt before her, and thanked her [...]."⁴³ And he describes the new vision it gives him, "She went like a radiance through the dark wood, which was henceforth bright to me, from simply knowing that such a creature was in it."⁴⁴ Furthermore, "Then first I knew the delight of being lowly; of saying to myself, 'I am what I am, nothing more.' 'I have failed,' I said; "I have lost myself—would it had been my shadow." I looked round: the shadow was nowhere to be seen. Ere long, I learned that it was not myself, but only my shadow, that I had lost. I learned that it is better, a thousand-fold, for a proud man to fall and be humbled, than to hold up his head in his pride and fancied innocence."⁴⁵ Even so, Anodos realizes that he will need to experience the death, burial, and rebirth of the self again and again.

Numerous MacDonald stories demonstrate the critical need to move beyond the devaluation of darkness and exultation of only the light. It is during the nighttime that Diamond encounters the North Wind in *At the Back of the North Wind*, grows in his active compassion for others, and is empowered to face the ultimate trials of sickness and death. It is the nighttime in which he develops

---

⁴⁰ MacDonald, *Phantastes*, 111.
⁴¹ MacDonald, *Phantastes*, 111.
⁴² MacDonald, *Phantastes*, 111, 109, 107.
⁴³ MacDonald, *Phantastes*, 163.
⁴⁴ MacDonald, *Phantastes*, 165.
⁴⁵ MacDonald, *Phantastes*, 166.

connections with others who are poor and suffering, and becomes available to assist even the aristocratic who have fallen in status. Nighttime for MacDonald is often when "strength of soul"[46] is fostered in his characters.

MacDonald saw the potential of night being a nurturing space. Thus, in *Thomas Wingfold, Curate* he writes, "the night on her nest was brooding upon the egg of tomorrow."[47] For MacDonald, maturity was equated with being at "home with twilight" and understanding that "the night, silent with thought" is able to hold the pangs of one's heart "also in its bosom."[48] Places described as dark spaces, such as Polwarth's dark parlor smelling of last year's roses, could be places of profound relational and spiritual encounter and wisdom.[49] It is in this place with Polwarth that Wingfold faces the reality of "how ignorant I am," and where he learns to become a true curate for his parishioners.[50] For those who were suffering and afraid, like Helen Lingard, the "covering wings of the darkness had protection in them."[51] And for MacDonald, "deepest midnights" are part of life's welcome rhythms.[52] Rachel, who was discriminated against because of her physical disability, thanked God for giving her the "health and riches of the night to strengthen me for the pain and poverties of the day."[53]

MacDonald perceived a sacredness and beauty to night and even the darker shades. He wrote that, "the brown feathers of twilight were beautiful as the wings of the silver dove sprung heavenwards [...]."[54] Night is a time when one can give one's gifts and minister in anonymity.[55] Similar themes are evident in *Sir Gibbie*. Nighttime was when Gibbie went into action whether leading his drunken father home or cleaning a farm kitchen. MacDonald wrote of Robert and Janet's cottage, "Night is as sacred as the day in that dear house."[56]

My favorite story of MacDonald's in which he overcomes the binary view of darkness as bad and light as good is "Photogen and Nycteris."[57] Roger Lancelyn Green refers to this story as "one perfect short tale" reflecting MacDonald's

---

[46] Ps. 138:3
[47] MacDonald, *Thomas Wingfold, Curate*, 136.
[48] MacDonald, *Thomas Wingfold, Curate*, 160.
[49] MacDonald, *Thomas Wingfold, Curate*, 67.
[50] MacDonald, *Thomas Wingfold, Curate*, 75.
[51] MacDonald, *Thomas Wingfold, Curate*, 109.
[52] MacDonald, *Thomas Wingfold, Curate*, 417.
[53] MacDonald, *Thomas Wingfold, Curate*, 206.
[54] MacDonald, *Thomas Wingfold, Curate*, 217.
[55] MacDonald, *Thomas Wingfold, Curate*, 302.
[56] George MacDonald, *Sir Gibbie* (Eureka, CA: Sunrise Books, 1988), 274.
[57] George MacDonald, "The Day Boy and the Night Girl" in T*he Light Princess and Other Tales* (Edinburgh: Canongate, 1961), 13–63. This story was originally published with the title "The History of Photogen and Nycteris."

"highest peak" of writing.[58] Since much in that story correlates with my second main point, in which I will continue to describe how MacDonald challenges negative views of night and darkness, I will also explore how through this story he challenges negatively-weighted correlations of darkness to women, people of color, those who are disabled, poor, and uneducated.

II. Challenging the Correlation of Darkness and Depravity with Those Who are Considered "Other"

MacDonald challenged derogatory associations of darkness and depravity with women, people of color, the poor, strangers, and those struggling with disabilities, addiction, and violations of the law. And he challenged the implications drawn from such negative associations, which justified eugenics, lack of economic, social, healthcare, and educational resources, and unequal access to education. I aim to show how in "Photogen and Nycteris" MacDonald begins with those constructed and commonly accepted correlations and then proceeds to deconstruct many of them.

To see how remarkably subversive MacDonald was, it is worth exploring more fully the nature and extent of these negative associations in his context. Jennings writes "Christianity in the Western world lives and moves within a diseased social imagination."[59] As he argues, this diseased social imagination did not just arise from the Enlightenment, but it did receive substantial fertilizer there.[60] Prior to the Enlightenment, "Christian theological imagination was woven into processes of colonial dominance."[61] Part of western Christianity's ethos was to assert its superiority and priority wherever colonial efforts extended: "It claimed to be the host, the owner of the spaces it entered, and demanded native peoples enter its cultural logics, its ways of being in the world, and its conceptualities."[62]

A strong component of colonial conceptualities was the correlation of moral darkness with certain types of human beings, especially those defined as having dark skin, but it also included those seen as deficient according to western standards in any way. The convenience of these attributions is that they could be altered for various people groups over time for utilitarian purposes. During certain eras, people in Japan were described as being "white" according to the

---

[58] Roger Lancelyn Green, Introduction to *The Light Princess and Other Tales*, by George MacDonald (Edinburgh: Canongate, 1961), 10.
[59] Jennings, *The Christian Imagination*, 6.
[60] Jennings, *The Christian Imagination*, 7.
[61] Jennings, *The Christian Imagination*, 8.
[62] Jennings, *The Christian Imagination*, 8.

colonial logic, since they were seen as civilized and reasonable like the colonizers. East Indians were described as "black" and "therefore very difficult to improve and turn into good Christians."[63] At other times, the Japanese were described as "Niggers and their customs barbarous."[64] This was also true for the Chinese and for indigenous peoples in the Americas. When they cooperated with the colonial powers, they were considered light-skinned. When they refused to cede their land to the colonizers and co-operate with them, they were categorized as dark savages.

White rulers and power brokers ascribed to themselves the role of supreme judge of other human beings. They developed scales of value correlating their own whiteness with the top of the scale, along with superior intelligence and morality. Those in power then linked whiteness with their determination of people's capacity to be fully converted to Christian faith and to minister to others. The Jesuit Valignano (1539–1606) identified Africans with Jewish and Muslim converts (Christian Moors) in this way:

> They are a very untalented race...incapable of grasping our holy religion or practicing it; because of their naturally low intelligence they cannot rise above the level of the senses...; they lack any culture and are given to savage ways and vices, and as a consequence they live like brute beasts.... In fine, they are a race born to serve, with no natural aptitude for governing.... like a sterile reprobate land which gives no hope of yielding fruit for a long time to come.[65]

As Jennings documents through a letter written by Zurara, the royal chronicler of Prince Henry of Portugal, Zurara invokes in his writing "a scale of existence, with white at one end and black at the other end and all others placed in between."[66] Only those at or near the top were considered full human beings. Those below the highest attribution of whiteness were considered less and less human as the scale descended. Ultimately, "whiteness emerges not simply as a marker of the European but as the rarely spoken but always understood organizing conceptual frame. And blackness appears as the fundamental tool of that organizing conceptuality. Black bodies are the ever-visible counterweight of an unusually *invisible* white identity."[67] Yet MacDonald was willing to defy such attributions of value based on skin color and claims of normativity. He offered a helpful contrast to these pervasive theories, so deeply rooted in racial prejudice and in the self-aggrandizement of those who claimed the power to attribute normalcy to themselves.

---

[63] Jennings, *The Christian Imagination*, 32.
[64] Jennings, *The Christian Imagination*, 32.
[65] Jennings, *The Christian Imagination*, 34.
[66] Jennings, *The Christian Imagination*, 23.
[67] Jennings, *The Christian Imagination*, 25.

To see a window into MacDonald's response we now turn to the more specific contexts in which "The History of Photogen and Nycteris" was written. This short story was published in 1882 but began as a series in *Harper's Young People* in 1879. It came out shortly after the British Prime Minister, Benjamin Disraeli, had proclaimed Queen Victoria as the Empress of India in 1877. Furthermore, MacDonald published it after his 1872 tour to the United States, which included Boston, New York, Chicago, Philadelphia, Washington DC, and Detroit. At that time racial segregation was common in these cities.[68] The MacDonalds were largely based in Boston, where they met Harriet Beecher Stowe and were exposed to circumstances from which the "separate but equal doctrine" had already emerged. This "doctrine" would become known as "Jim Crow" laws, which formalized practices already in place and which prevented contact between white and black peoples in all public facilities.[69] Boston, the only city in Massachusetts to segregate blacks and whites in school, had been segregating children according to skin color since 1798.

The one school in which Negro children were allowed was greatly inferior to schools for those deemed white: "The school for the black children was [sic] rooms that were too small, paint much defaced, and with manifest evidence of shameful negligence and abuse. The yards were about 15 feet square and only accessible through a 'dark, damp cellar.'"[70] Segregation was often justified theologically according to a theory of creation. According to an 1846 report on Boston public schools, "The real reason, according to the report, was 'one of races, not of colors, merely.' Having been established by the 'All-wise Creator,' the difference between

---

[68] For a helpful window on the racism against dark-skinned people in the Philadelphia that MacDonald would have witnessed, see *The Annals of the American Academy of Political and Social Science* (Jan. 1979): "Opportunities for upward mobility created by an expanding economy—which provided the boot-straps for the Irish and German immigrants—were so limited for blacks that they were virtually nonexistent," Wade Clark Roof, "Race and Residence: The Shifting Basis of American Race Relations," 65; "The ecological 'rules' that explain important elements of the white immigrant experience do not explain, for most of Philadelphia's history, what happened to blacks. Where blacks were concerned the rules were inoperative, suspending as it were by the force of racism. Racism, particularly its manifestation in discriminatory hiring and housing practices, is the final dimension in the explanatory framework," Theodore Hershberg, Alan N. Burstein, Eugene P. Ericksen, Stephanie Greenberg and William L. Yancey, "A Tale of Three Cities: Blacks and Immigrants in Philadelphia: 1850–1880, 1930 and 1970," 57.

[69] Jim Crow laws emerged in the 1870s and 1880s in the former Confederate states but were also practiced in the north. See Leonard W. Levy and Douglas L. Jones, ed., *Jim Crow in Boston: The Origin of the Separate but Equal Doctrine* (New York: Da Capo Press, 1974).

[70] xxiv, Reports of the Annual Visiting Committees of the Public Schools of the City of Boston, Documents of the City of Boston for the Year 1846 (Boston, 1846), 206, 227.

whites and blacks existed in 'the physical, mental and moral natures of the two races. No legislation, no social customs, can efface this distinction.'"[71]

Though school segregation in Boston was outlawed in 1855, Judge Lemuel Shaw's opinion on the Massachusetts Supreme Court in 1849 became the leading precedent for Jim Crow laws, which would be established nationally by the US Supreme Court in 1896. Shaw's opinion was "that Negroes are not denied equal protection of the law when provided with separate facilities that are substantially the same as those for white."[72] MacDonald's "Photogen and Nycteris" seems to depict and deconstructs the notion of "separate but equal" and the theological rationales on which it was based. The story begins by describing Watho,[73] who is something of a scientist, conducting an empirical study of the effects of light and darkness on two different individuals. Watho is described as having white skin and as someone with a wolf in her mind and the desire to know everything: "She was not naturally cruel, but the wolf had made her cruel."[74] MacDonald raises questions about her early on by calling her a witch, who cared "for nothing in itself—only for knowing it."[75] Her way of knowing is to separate, to divide, and to study not according to relations between things but for mastery over those things.

One of Watho's guests (or, perhaps more accurately, research subjects) is Lady Aurora, whose "skin was fair, not white like Watho's," according to MacDonald.[76] This would raise questions for readers for whom it was commonplace to correlate "whiteness" with purity, intelligence, and higher levels of evolution, rather than that which was evil. Lady Aurora has golden hair, and heavenly blue eyes, and is housed in bright spacious apartments with southern exposure and plentiful sunlight. She is also given abundant resources of "musical instruments, books, pictures, curiosities" and Watho's own charming company.[77] Her food consists of venison and feathered game and her drink of pale sunny sparkling wine. Here we see a woman of privilege who is exceptionally well resourced in a refreshing and liberating space.

Vesper, on the other hand, though beautiful, is a widow and without the status of being a lady like Aurora. Additionally, she has a disability, having lost her sight after her husband's death. She is referred to as "the dark lady," with dark

---

[71] Reports of the Annual Visiting Committees 1846, 10, 11, 12, 13.
[72] Reports of the Annual Visiting Committees 1846, 7–8.
[73] It is fascinating to discover that "watho" is a Kikuyu word meaning "law, rule," which may have come to MacDonald via British incursions into Kenya at the time.
[74] MacDonald, "The Day Boy and the Night Girl," 241.
[75] MacDonald, "The Day Boy and the Night Girl," 241.
[76] MacDonald, "The Day Boy and the Night Girl," 241.
[77] MacDonald, "The Day Boy and the Night Girl," 241.

skin ("her skin had a look of darkened silver"), black hair and black eyes with long black lashes.[78] And she is given lodging in a tomb-like space carved out of rock that MacDonald describes as constructed after the tomb of an Egyptian King, and with a sarcophagus at the center of one of the chambers. Because she is blind, she doesn't know she's lodged in a tomb, but is given rich carpets, silk lined couches, dark wine, pomegranates, marshy birds and purple grapes. Everything associated with her is "dark." She is attended by wailful violins and sad tales. Both women are expecting the births of their first child.

In MacDonald's context, Aurora would be among those considered more highly evolved who should continue to bear children. And for those who ascribed to theories of natural selection and/or eugenics, Vesper would be viewed by some as unfit to live or to propagate. In fact, Francis Galton, a cousin of Darwin's, published an article six years before this story came out in which he made such a claim. If the "non-gifted class" "continued to procreate children, inferior in moral, intellectual and physical qualities, it is easy to believe the time may come when such persons would be considered as enemies to the State, and to have forfeited all claims to kindness."[79]

Even so in MacDonald's story Vesper, "the dark lady," dies after giving birth "in the dead of night" to a baby girl, whom Watho names "Nycteris." She also has dark skin and dark hair, but mysteriously has blue eyes. And she is raised in a way that reflects depravations and discrimination often inflicted on those considered less worthy. She is never allowed to see the daylight but is kept in the tombs where her mother had been lodged and kept to a schedule where she is allowed to be awake only during the nighttime. The only education she is granted is by word of mouth.[80] Watho intends that she will not have enough light to read and denies her access to books and to any light except that of a dull lamp. However, like many enslaved people who were denied access to education, Nycteris is very eager to learn and coaxes Falca, her caregiver, to teach her to read. And she loves the one thing she is trained to do and that is to play her musical instrument. Her curiosity, intelligence, and hunger for more space, more room, and more light ultimately guide her out of her tomb and into her first experiences of nature and nighttime outside.

The fair Lady Aurora gives birth to a splendid baby boy as the sun is rising but is falsely told that he died immediately after birth, which prompts her departure. The boy is named "Photogen" and is prevented from ever seeing

---

[78] MacDonald, "The Day Boy and the Night Girl," 244, 243.
[79] Francis Galton, "Hereditary Improvement," *Fraser's Magazine* (1873): 129.
[80] MacDonald, "The Day Boy and the Night Girl," 247.

any darkness.⁸¹ Watho never allows him to "see anything black" or even "dull colours."⁸² She tries to keep even the shadows from falling on him. She desires to so acclimate him to the sunlight that he can bear more than "any dark-skinned African."⁸³ This itself is a fascinating move for MacDonald to make in this story. The aristocracy was meant to be so white their superficial veins would be evident through their white skin—thus the term "blue-blooded." Sun-darkened skin was associated with the lower classes, and the peasants who had to work out in the fields. African flesh was considered "damaged flesh" and at the bottom of the scale, while while white flesh was thought to be "unharmed flesh" at the highest end of the spectrum.⁸⁴ Here is a privileged young, tanned man who is more like a twenty-first century traveler than a nineteenth-century aristocrat. Photogen's "hair was of the red gold, but his eyes grew darker as he grew, until they were as black as Vesper's."⁸⁵ MacDonald is already deconstructing the idea of racial purity and revealing something of the fluidity of identities even within these rigidly fixed states. In contrast to Nycteris, Photogen is given every resource necessary for a vibrant education and for growth. He is given wide open spaces to explore, multitudes of animals to hunt, the best training he could receive, and "pony after pony, larger and larger as he grew, every one less manageable than that which had preceded it, and [they would] advance him from pony to horse, and from horse to horse, until he was equal to anything in that kind which the country produced."⁸⁶ He is carefully protected from any darkness at all, so he grows up not knowing what fear is: "For the boy had been so steeped in the sun, from childhood so saturated with his influence, that he looked upon every danger from a sovereign height of courage."⁸⁷ When Watho commanded him never to be out when the rim of the sun should touch the horizon, "Photogen listened respectfully, but, knowing neither the taste of fear nor the temptation of the night, her words were but sounds to him."⁸⁸

The way in which MacDonald constructs the story connects with much of social Darwinian thought in his era and the adoption of "survival of the fittest" ideas from biology to sociology. Further description of the context will clarify the remarkable nature of MacDonald's own approach. The English sociologist, Herbert Spencer, who is credited with developing the phrase "survival of the

---

[81] The word "Photogen" was first recorded in 1855, combining the word photo (meaning "light") with gen (meaning "that which produces").
[82] MacDonald, "The Day Boy and the Night Girl," 244.
[83] MacDonald, "The Day Boy and the Night Girl," 244.
[84] Jennings, *The Christian Imagination*, 24.
[85] MacDonald, "The Day Boy and the Night Girl," 244.
[86] MacDonald, "The Day Boy and the Night Girl," 246.
[87] MacDonald, "The Day Boy and the Night Girl," 247.
[88] MacDonald, "The Day Boy and the Night Girl," 247.

fittest," was prominent in the efforts to adapt biological evolutionary ideas to sociological theories. In 1842, he argued that the government should not be responsible for education, building roads or administering charity.[89] People should be responsible to pull themselves up by their own bootstraps, with no allowance for systemic injustice as a factor. In fact, if people were unable to provide for themselves and to compete, they should be deemed unfit and unworthy to survive.

Writing in 1851, Spencer argued that as with biological organisms, society also should "excret[e] its unhealthy, imbecile, slow, vacillating, faithless members."[90] And he attributed such social dynamics to providence. The suffering of the weak might seem unkind for the moment, but it was all for the greater good: "The poverty of the incapable, the distresses that come upon the imprudent, the starvation of the idle, and those shoulderings aside of the weak by the strong, which leave so many 'in shallows and in miseries,' are the decrees of a larger, far-seeing benevolence."[91] People were encouraged to take up their different stations in life and to attend to their own division of labor.

The assertion was that "members of all the races lower than the Caucasian had minds that were rigid and unadaptable, automatic or reflex in character, impulsive and uncontrolled."[92] In fact, the so-called lower races had smaller and less evolved brains than those of the so-called higher races who had inherited a "larger brain mass."[93] "And the higher the race, according to Spencer, the greater the contrast between men and women in physical appearance and social role."[94] Such correlations of status with assigned gender roles and appearance were a convenient way to intensify binary gender polarities, largely to the advantage of the males and the disadvantage of females.

Though the "savage" and the Caucasian child were equated at times, Caucasian men were the only ones who were seen as full adults. Women, the lower classes, and criminals were also childlike or savage, in certain ways. All were subordinate in different realms of life, all lacked the ability to look after or control themselves, and all represented lower positions on the unilinear scale. Victorian philosophers, scientists, and social thinkers equated and spoke in similar terms about women, children, peasants, laborers, criminals, madmen, Irishmen, and

---

[89] Herbert Spencer, "The Proper Sphere of Government," in *Race, Racism and Science: Social Impact and Interaction*, (New Brunswick, NJ: Rutgers University Press 2006), 76.
[90] Spencer, "The Proper Sphere of Government," 78.
[91] Spencer, "The Proper Sphere of Government," 78.
[92] Spencer, "The Proper Sphere of Government," 81.
[93] Spencer, "The Proper Sphere of Government," 81.
[94] Spencer, "The Proper Sphere of Government," 82.

savages. And there were warnings about the dangers of educating such primitive lower orders of humanity, especially "Negroes and women."[95]

In MacDonald's story, Watho seems to be of a similar mindset, giving all the educational and training resources to the Caucasian male in this story. Photogen epitomizes white male privilege. He is led to believe that he is the master of all he sees. In contrast, MacDonald depicts Nycteris as very much falling into the restrictive life allotted to women and people of color: confined, domesticated, "protected," and virtually entombed. Nycteris, like the women of her day, was expected to remain within the private sphere, and not to concern herself with other matters. Women were seen as more emotional and less rational, and prone to mental and physical illness.[96] Thus the ideal woman was considered passive, weak, dependent, and in a state of perpetual childhood. As Barbara MacHaffie writes in *Her Story*, "In many nineteenth-century novels, the qualities of willfulness and independence belong to the world of white men, while white women, children, and black people are celebrated for their submission and the moral power that comes from this."[97]

MacDonald's story initially reflects these presuppositions and then moves to deconstruct such binary categories and demeaning ideas about people of color and women. Nycteris has a very inquisitive mind and a rich imagination. She eventually finds her way out of the tomb and is utterly enthralled by all that she sees and experiences. MacDonald writes, "It was a resurrection—nay, a birth itself, to Nycteris."[98] She had known darkness, and a form of death (such as MacDonald's Vane had resisted), and now was able to emerge from them very much alive: "She saw with the eyes made for seeing, and saw indeed what many men are too wise to see."[99] The wind of the night was like "spiritual wine" to her "filling her whole being with an intoxication of purest joy. [...] Possessed by the power of the gorgeous night, she seemed at one and the same moment annihilated and glorified."[100] "Losing one's life" could be a means by which to gain a much richer and more profound life. Nycteris now understands that her caregivers have actually been her "gaolers" [sic] to keep her in ignorance. "Life was a mighty bliss, and they had scraped hers to the bare bone."[101] And now similar to many women and people of color, she realizes she "must hide her knowledge."[102]

---

[95] Spencer, "The Proper Sphere of Government," 83.
[96] Barbara MacHaffie, *Her Story* (Philadelphia: Fortress Press, 1983), 160.
[97] MacHaffie, *Her Story*, 162.
[98] MacDonald, "The Day Boy and the Night Girl," 253.
[99] MacDonald, "The Day Boy and the Night Girl," 253.
[100] MacDonald, "The Day Boy and the Night Girl," 253.
[101] MacDonald, "The Day Boy and the Night Girl," 254.
[102] MacDonald, "The Day Boy and the Night Girl," 254.

Ultimately, Photogen defies Watho's prohibition and seeks to hunt an animal that he has learned prefers to stay out past the sunset. Darkness is an overpowering liminal experience for him, in which "fear inexplicable laid hold of the youth; [...] the very fear itself terrified him" such that his "horror seemed to blossom into very madness." He has to confront an entirely new self-perception, "He was no longer the man he had known, or rather thought himself."[103] He falls into self-loathing and thinking it is the "night itself! the darkness alive" that is after him, "He gave a sob," fled, and "fell senseless on the grass."[104]

In a similar way, Old Testament scholar, Walter Brueggemann reflects on the humbling and clarifying capacity of the night, in terms of its impact on King Nebuchadnezzar from the book of Daniel, "In the night, by contrast, the king is vulnerable, even defenseless. Voices other than his own get a chance to speak. It turns out in such times of vulnerability, that the world is not ordered as well or as regally as he had imagined. The other voices, of God, of spirit, of the night, of darkness, penetrate the empire's Strategic Defense Initiatives."[105] It is difficult to hold the illusion of control and mastery when faced with one's human vulnerability in darkness.

Even as MacDonald challenges the stereotype of white male invulnerability, he also challenges the stereotype of women as the weak, ignorant, and the emotional ones. He conveys the truth that all people must confront their limitations and weakness at some point in their lives. He reveals through Photogen that fixing the odds in favor of white males, only makes it all the more difficult when disruption hits and their privilege can no longer keep at bay the challenges others have had to face their entire lives. Photogen's response could be seen as a nineteenth-century depiction of what today is referred to as "white fragility."[106]

When Nycteris encounters Photogen in this collapsed state, she feels immediate compassion for him and identification with him: "Her heart—like every heart, if only its fallen sides were cleared away—was an inexhaustible fountain of love: she loved everything she saw."[107] She thinks he is a girl like her, having never seen a boy, and seeks to comfort this one of whom she says, "How sensitive you must be!" Photogen classifies and objectifies her as a "creature of the darkness," who loves the night, and thus he fears her.[108] MacDonald humorously

---

[103] MacDonald, "The Day Boy and the Night Girl," 260.
[104] MacDonald, "The Day Boy and the Night Girl," 261.
[105] Walter Brueggemann, *Finally Comes the Poet* (Minneapolis, MN: Fortress Press, 1989), 127.
[106] See Robin DiAngelo, *White Fragility: Why It's So Hard for White People to Talk About Racism* (Boston: Beacon Press, 2018).
[107] MacDonald, "The Day Boy and the Night Girl," 264.
[108] MacDonald, "The Day Boy and the Night Girl," 265.

reverses common gender stereotypes related to courage, emotionalism, and rationality. When Nycteris tries to strengthen his courage, saying, "You must be a brave girl [...]" he erupts in fury, "If you were a man, I should kill you." Whereas she has approached him with a sense of courage and solidarity, he quickly acts in fear and pride to distinguish himself from this other, this one he judges as inferior to him. Nycteris' response reflects MacDonald's humor and conviction, "No, of course! You can't be a girl: girls are not afraid—without reason. I understand now: it is because you are not a girl that you are so frightened."[109] Forgetting danger to herself, she pledges to take care of him throughout the night. And MacDonald describes them as "two Pharaohs in one pyramid" resting in "the heart of the great-cone shadow of the earth."[110] For MacDonald, both are regal, both are empowered, and both are created to be God's image bearers, whether here, or in a non-European-like domain, or in darkness. As soon as the sun has risen, and when it is Nycteris' great time of fear and testing, Photogen rushes off, utterly insensitive to her own human frailty and fear. She is now confronted for the first time with what for her is excruciating sunlight, because she has put aside her own safety and norms to care for him. MacDonald notes Photogen's indifference, "'What is the matter with you, girl?' said Photogen, with the arrogance of all male creatures until they have been taught by the other kind."[111]

After much suffering they both learn that they must find strength together against their true enemy the white witch, Watho, who has become more and more wolf-like each day. They both must learn to value that which is other for each of them, day and night, male and female, light and dark. Evil is not in the darkness, or in the other. Evil resides in those who will use knowledge for power over the other, to divide and conquer, to objectify and control. In this story, as in *Lilith*, the controlling and destructive power is someone who is very white, not dark-skinned.[112] MacDonald in fact emphasized Watho's extremely white skin, which finds echoes in his later writing when he describes Lilith's paleness as "not a pallor, but a pure whiteness."[113] Not only has MacDonald deconstructed the binary correlations of white with all that is good and dark with all that is bad,

---

[109] MacDonald, "The Day Boy and the Night Girl," 267.
[110] MacDonald, "The Day Boy and the Night Girl," 269.
[111] MacDonald, "The Day Boy and the Night Girl," 271.
[112] Cf. Michelle Alexander, *The New Jim Crow* (New York: The New Press, 2010); Bryan Stevenson, *Just Mercy* (London: One World, 2015).
[113] MacDonald, *Lilith*, 109. According to Hannah Lauren Murray, "It is in the nineteenth century that Whiteness becomes formalized as a racial identity through the convergence of race science, settler colonialism, slavery, and imperialism—all of which cement racial hierarchies." Murray, "Critical Whiteness Studies and Teaching Nineteenth-Century American Literature," *English: Journal of the English Association* 70, no. 271 (Winter 2021): 333–9.

he has also challenged the idealization of the purification of the white race, and "pure whiteness" as the pinnacle of human evolution.

MacDonald's fiction exposes and challenges deeply embedded social biases that have severe social and personal consequences. MacDonald may have felt the pain of the eugenics movement personally and directed at his own cultural origins. In 1868, a German biologist, Ernst Haeckel, had published his own adaptation of Darwin's thought in a book entitled, History of Creation. He "divided human beings into ten races, of which the Caucasian was the highest and the primitives were doomed to extinction."[114] One result of these racial theories were efforts to determine, measure, and define that which separates the races—Watho-type efforts. One scientist, Broca, "developed over forty measurements, including various kinds of calipers, pelvimeters, craniostats, and torsiometers, to make the increasingly precise cranial and body measurements that his science demanded. [...] 25 million Europeans were measured throughout the late nineteenth century."[115] The principle means of dividing European populations became the cephalic index, which had been developed in 1844. Among Europeans, three major delineations were developed, the Teutonic, the Alpine and the Mediterranean. Aryan, or Nordic was envisioned as the superior race, and the Aryans were divided into the superior Saxon and the inferior Celt: "The Celtic type was represented by the Irish, who were commonly portrayed as monkeys in newspapers and popular journals."[116] MacDonald very clearly saw himself as a Celt and would have experienced the challenge of living as a Scot in the midst of the English class system.

This was not only personal for MacDonald, but also theological. MacDonald worked diligently to challenge the prevailing social hierarchies established by those who exploited scientific strategies to advance their own power and strength. His belief was that the true origin of all people was the one great heart, the one Great Thinker—the very love and creating power of God. Thus, it is the very people thought to be least of all that MacDonald raised up as his heroes and heroines throughout his books. It is the poor, mute, Gibbie, son of an alcoholic, that is shown to be the most Christ-like of all, and who rises to the highest position of any character in that novel—a position of power he uses with great love. It is Sambo, the black African sailor in *Sir Gibbie*, who is one of the most compassionate people of the narrative, who loves Gibbie like a mother would and who reappears in Gibbie's memory throughout the book as his hero.

---

[114] Jackson and Weidman, "Race and Evolution, 1859–1900," 87.
[115] Jackson and Weidman, "Race and Evolution, 1859–1900," 72.
[116] Jackson and Weidman, "Race and Evolution, 1859–1900," 75.

It is particularly striking that MacDonald places an entire chapter of *Sir Gibbie* under the heading of "Sambo." In this chapter, Sambo is introduced after MacDonald has argued with cynical readers about whether portraying a noble character is realistic, particularly referring to the character of Gibbie. "But whatever the demand of the age, I insist that that which *ought* to be presented to its beholding, is the common good uncommonly developed, and that not because of its rarity, but because it is truer to humanity."[117] MacDonald emphasizes Gibbie's "ever active love of his kind" and the way in which "The human face was the one attraction to him in the universe." So, it seems subversive that, at a time when black people were seen as sub-human, MacDonald would emphasis how very drawn Gibbie was to Sambo's face and being. Thus, "in a few days a strong mutual affection had sprung up between them. To Gibbie Sambo speedily became absolutely loving and tender, and Gibbie made him full return of devotion."[118] In Sambo, MacDonald is also describing "the common good uncommonly developed." In ways that evokes the character of Christ, Sambo is described as "long-suffering," one who "bore even with those who treated him with far worse than the ordinary superciliousness of white to black; and when the rudest of city boys mocked him, only showed his teeth by way of smile."[119] When a tumbler is thrown at him, striking Gibbie on the head, Sambo overturns the tables, and then carries Gibbie gently to his bed. Sambo is murdered by a group of men and his last words are, "*O Lord Jesus!*" Throughout the remainder of the book, Gibbie is given strength when reflecting on Sambo's heroic and loving nature.

MacDonald's challenge to the commonplace social hierarchies and their correlations with light and dark, is also evident in the *Princess* books. Curdie, in *The Princess and Goblin* and *The Princess and Curdie* is a poor miner who works in dark places yet has greater vision and insight than those who are well-placed and more privileged. He helps to save the rural kingdom from the goblins, and the city kingdom from the crooked nobility. Curdie is one who has learned to find treasure in the darkness, and who is able to see the self-revelation of the Great-Grandmother in the deepest caverns. It is there, in the midst of deepest darkness, that she reveals herself: "All he knew of the whole creation, seemed gathered in one centre of harmony and loveliness in the person of the ancient lady who stood before him in the very summer of beauty and strength."[120] Though some judge her as decrepit, devious, and power-hungry—more like a witch—MacDonald reveals her to be a Christ-figure in these books.

---

[117] MacDonald, *Sir Gibbie*, 45.
[118] MacDonald, *Sir Gibbie*, 45.
[119] MacDonald, *Sir Gibbie*, 46.
[120] George MacDonald, *The Princess and Curdie* (Philadelphia: J.B. Lippincott, 1914), 69.

Similarly, in *Thomas Wingfold* Joseph Polwarth and his niece Rachel are deemed unfit to live by the handsome and aristocratic Bascombe because of their disabilities. MacDonald, however, portrays them as sources of spiritual wisdom, love, and beauty. They guide Wingfold through his journey from ignorance and doubt to faith and trusting obedience. And the Polwarths also guide Leopold, a man convicted of murder and struggling with addiction, from fleeing to facing and confessing his own deed, dying with the gift of dignity. Polwarth and his niece are called "temples of the Holy Ghost."[121] In one more stroke against the illusion of white supremacy, MacDonald depicts Leopold as the dark-skinned son of an East Indian Hindu woman and an English father. Even this dark man, addicted to a drug he had been given in India, and who, under the influence of that drug, had murdered his beloved is conveyed as a gentle soul "of a lovely nature."[122] Wingfold says of Leopold, "I never saw a lovelier disposition."[123]

The very people who were seen as threats to British civilization and progress, MacDonald reveals as those who can offer the source of greatest compassion, wisdom, and insight. Those who judged them as unfit and as "others" to be feared were actually only exposing something of their own inner realities. Helen Lingard's aunt exposes her own shallowness and warped nature when she expresses the cultural attitudes of the day: "People that are crooked in body are always crooked in mind too."[124] MacDonald offers the alternative that Polwarth (who also has Jewish ancestry) has "a soul [...] as grand and beautiful and patient as his body is insignificant and troubled, [...] the wisest and best man I have ever known."[125]

In another reversal, MacDonald depicts so-called "progress" actually leading to devolution, as with the hardheaded and weak-soled goblins in *The Princess and the Goblin*, who thought their creations underground were superior to anything in nature. Certain types of "development" could mean losing one's joy, laughter, wisdom, and love of the other, like the Giants who though they developed from Little Ones, were greedy, selfish, and gluttonous in *Lilith*. The more admirable Little Ones remain very wary of such growth and development rather than enamored by it. And rather than creating a society that was more loving, caring, and inclusive of strangers, children, and those who are poor and needy, such "progress" could actually result in hardened hearts as in Gwyntystorm (*The Princess and Curdie*) and Bulika (*Lilith*) where like-mindedness meant selfish closed- heartedness.

---

[121] MacDonald, *Thomas Wingfold, Curate*, 207.
[122] MacDonald, *Thomas Wingfold, Curate*, 460.
[123] MacDonald, *Thomas Wingfold, Curate*, 285.
[124] MacDonald, *Thomas Wingfold, Curate*, 438.
[125] MacDonald, *Thomas Wingfold, Curate*, 286.

For example, Vane questions a woman whom he has helped after first entering Bulika, "Is there no place in the city for the taking in of strangers?" Her response reflects something akin to certain types of responses in our own contexts, "How is purity to be preserved except by keeping low people at a proper distance? Dignity is such a delicate thing."[126] This woman expresses nationalist pride declaring, "we are more ancient and noble than any other nation—Therefore [...] we always turn strangers out before night."[127] Though she is terrified of the Princess (a devious force who seeks absolute control of the city, of children, of water, etc.) and her white leopard, she seems to relish the thought that "She it is who keeps us safe and free and rich." Personal security and affluence are more highly valued than compassion, connection, and the common good. Similarly, Vane is told that there is no room in Bulika for children or the poor. "When one goes poor," explains the woman, "we forget him. That is how we keep rich. We mean to be rich always."[128] In these ways, MacDonald conveys the devolution that flows from the commonplace priorities of wealth, individualism, nationalism, and homogeneity. This is in contrast to the Christ-like characters he creates (Gibbie, Sambo, Curdie, Polwarth), who welcome strangers and stand in solidarity with those considered outsiders, poor, weak, and disabled.

III. Treasures from the Kingdom of God: Jesus' Teaching and Celtic Wisdom

Third, it is important to explore the influences in George MacDonald's life and context that fostered such radically different perspectives than those of many of his contemporaries. MacDonald was significantly influenced by his Celtic Christian context, and by the life and teaching of Jesus.[129] And he sought to bring out "old and new treasure" from the teaching of Jesus and from Celtic Christian influences demonstrating the values of the kingdom of God to be the inverse of those of the kingdoms of this world.

As MacDonald's son Greville attested, his Celtic background significantly influenced George MacDonald's life and much of what he wrote: "George MacDonald inherited all the characteristic virtues; [...] a social law built upon Faith rather than Competition, may in large measure explain his rooted fidelity to God and man."[130] Greville also believed that his father's "devotion to the soil,

---

[126] MacDonald, *Lilith*, 121.
[127] MacDonald, *Lilith*, 121.
[128] MacDonald, *Lilith*, 120.
[129] See Dearborn, *Baptized Imagination*, 14–24.
[130] Greville MacDonald, *George MacDonald and His Wife* (London: George Allen and Unwin, 1932), 39. See also, "Letter to his Father" (5 April 1853), in *An Expression of Character: The Letters of George MacDonald*, ed. Glenn Sadler (Grand Rapids, MI: Eerdmans, 1994), 57.

his love of liberty, his intolerance of injustice, his eloquence and love of learning," derived from Celtic tradition.[131] Thus, as noted above, MacDonald challenged and exposed systems of injustice throughout his writing, including those based on biases against the poor, women, people of color, and those with disabilities. This was quite extraordinary in his context, especially since he not only exposed systems of injustice but often made people from these very marginalized groups his heroes.[132] Unlike many of his contemporaries MacDonald did not associate them with inferiority and moral darkness, but often portrayed them as sources of wisdom and light.

MacDonald's concern for justice combined with the Celtic Christian view of the sacramental nature of all creation resulted in his depiction of all creatures with dignity. Thus, he conveyed a sense of the sacredness of all people and a rejection of rigid social hierarchies based on gender, wealth, ability, or insider status. The dignity and worth of the stranger (whatever their skin color) was a key tenet of Celtic Christian thought.[133] So, a stranger and outsider like Sambo in *Sir Gibbie* is depicted as someone who nurtures and offers refuge for the orphaned Gibbie. On the other hand, Gwyntystorm's resistance and cruelty to strangers in *The Princess and Curdie* reflect hard-heartedness and portend the eventual collapse of the city.

A hospitable and honoring posture to the other was central to Celtic Christianity most importantly because of the strong emphasis on God as a Triune Communion of Persons, who exist eternally in loving relationship and who extend love to welcome others into that Communion. As those created in the image of the Triune God, people are meant to reflect and participate in God's loving and hospitable nature. Even so, embracing the wonder of a God, who exists in mutual, self-giving relationships, fostered community life that was based on mutuality and unity with diversity.[134] The diversity evident in gender, race, ethnicity, and ability was not perceived as a problem, but rather as an enhancement. Celtic

---

[131] Greville MacDonald, *George MacDonald and His Wife*, 39.
[132] Of Victorian dominant ideology Rosemary Jackson writes, "The shadow on the edges of bourgeois culture is variously identified, as black, mad, primitive, criminal, socially deprived, deviant, crippled, or [...] female." *Fantasy, the Literature of Subversion* (London: Methuen, 1981), 121. It is interesting that MacDonald honors individuals from each of these social groupings in his writing (e.g. Sambo, who is black, *Sir Gibbie*; the mad laird who is mad and primitive, *Malcolm*; James Blatherwick, who is a criminal of sorts, *Salted with Fire*; Aggie in *Castle Warlock*; Polwarth and Rachel in *Thomas Wingfold, Curate*).
[133] Granted that Celtic clans were notoriously in conflict with one another, but these were tribal disputes not based in racial discrimination.
[134] Kerry Dearborn, "Recovering a Trinitarian and Sacramental Ecclesiology," in *Evangelical Ecclesiology*, ed. John G. Stackhouse (Ada, MI: Baker Academic, 2003), 51.

Runes of hospitality to strangers flowed from the belief that in each person the sacramental presence of Christ waited to be discovered.[135]

The Triune nature of God and the belief that humans are created in the image of a Triune God of love and creativity also freed Celtic Christians and MacDonald to move beyond either/or binaries that identified part of God's creation as bad or inferior (e.g. night, darkness, women) and other parts of God's creation as good or superior (e.g. day, light, males). MacDonald learned to value the third way, the creative alternative rather than to be locked into binary modes of thought. Thus, rather than submit to the idea that women were inferior and less inclined toward math and higher education, he taught women at a women's college and his protagonists often tutored women.[136]

In addition to an affinity for Celtic thought, MacDonald was convinced that Jesus' life and teaching were the fount of wisdom and truth, "soul of everything on earth."[137] Thus, it is no surprise that he challenged prevailing beliefs and presented the alternatives in ways that correlated with Jesus' own life of welcoming those who are poor, blind, mute, treated as unclean, outsiders, or criminals. Jesus' inclusion of women in his ministry,[138] and the invitation to sit at his feet and learn as disciples,[139] were also sources for MacDonald's empowerment of women through his life and stories. Jesus' priorities were evident in his inaugural sermon, in which he quotes Isaiah to describe his own ministry and purpose:

> The Spirit of the Lord is upon me,
> because he has anointed me
> to bring good news to the poor.
> He has sent me to proclaim release to the captives
> and recovery of sight to the blind,
> to set free those who are oppressed,
> to proclaim the year of the Lord's favor.[140]

Jesus' compassion was extended to all. Jesus' illustration of this truth from Isaiah, in which he highlighted outsiders (non-Israelites) as those whom God blessed, provoked the wrath of his listeners. He violated many protocols of his day in the ways he extended healing, hospitality, touch, and affirmation to those deemed less worthy, including children.

Even so, MacDonald's writing reflects Jesus' priorities in those whom MacDonald honored and lifted up. He urged people throughout his books to

---

[135] John Miriam Jones, *With an Eagle's Eye* (Notre Dame, IN: Ave Maria Press, 1998), 29.
[136] See for example, Hugh Sutherland who tutors Margaret in *David Elginbrod*.
[137] George MacDonald, *A Book of Strife in the Form of The Diary of an Old Soul* (London: Hughes, 1880), "February 6," 31.
[138] Luke 8:2
[139] Luke 10:38–42
[140] Luke 4:18–19

move beyond a cerebral faith and to heed Jesus' call for those who believed in him to follow in his ways. Thomas Wingfold's growth in faith required not conceptual awareness of doctrine, but rather increased Christlikeness of being. Wingfold in his evolving faith would become more like Jesus, as he reached out to the marginalized of his day, to care for people who were socially disdained, uneducated, dark-skinned, struggling with disabilities, the law, or addictions. He too would become a person of mercy, rather than of eugenically motivated scorn or fear. In Christlikeness, he would link his reputation with those most questionable to his parishioners, joining in solidarity with them, learning from them, and growing with them.

MacDonald conveys Jesus' teaching that "the last will be the first,"[141] whether Gibbie, a homeless and mute street urchin, whom most thought was mentally challenged, or Curdie, a child laborer in the mines who enters the sophisticated city of Gwyntystorm, ultimately to become its king. Similarly, MacDonald portrayed Jesus' teaching that "the least among all of you is the greatest,"[142] whether Nycteris entombed and restricted, or the great-grandmother in the "Curdie" books, looking old and withered at the spinning wheel. MacDonald depicted cities that shut their doors to strangers and children as cities that were shutting out life, for the Author of life told the children, "Come unto me," and said, "I was a stranger and you welcomed me."[143] A sure sign of a city or culture's decadence for MacDonald was its hard-heartedness toward those in need. In God's kingdom the least will be the greatest of all, and to welcome the least of these is to welcome the king himself.

For a British commonwealth that was increasingly fearful of paupers and lower classes and believed such people to be more inclined to criminal lifestyles,[144] MacDonald offered different visions to challenge their moral imaginations in ways that reflected the kingdom of God rather than the kingdoms of this world. Thus, for example, Anodos' maturation process leads him to become a servant rather than a knight in shining armor. Vane reflects moral and spiritual development when he realizes his need for diverse others, the idea that it is the "development of the differences which make a large and lofty unity possible, and which alone can make millions into a church."[145]

---

[141] Matt. 20:16
[142] Luke 9:48
[143] Matt. 25:35
[144] Richard Johnson, "Educational Policy and Social Control in Early Victorian England," *Past and Present* 49 (Nov. 1970): 104, 110; See also, "Life for Children in Victorian Britain," Birmingham City Council, https://www.birmingham.gov.uk/info/50139/explore_and_discover/1609/life_for_children_in_victorian_britain/2.
[145] MacDonald, *Lilith*, 102.

There is a reason why MacDonald's novels and writing were so popular in his own time, why at one point "his reputation in England rivaled that of his contemporary Charles Dickens," and that his works are read internationally today.[146] Many people then and now hunger for truth that challenges their fears and offers a vision of the Kingdom of God where love is stronger than fear, our common humanity is a deeper bond than our ethnicity, ability, or gender, and where death, though painful and grievous, is a doorway into newness of life. The invitation is to join with MacDonald in praise:

> Nothing is alien in thy world immense—
> No look of sky or earth or man or beast;
> In the great hand of God I stand, and thence
> Look out on life, his endless, holy feast.[147]

MacDonald's radical challenges to the prejudices of his day have enduring relevance. He found ways to reach deeply rooted biases that derive from warped imaginations and fearful hearts. He offered stories that can reshape and heal our moral imagination, deepen trust in the One Great Heart, and help us to face our fears of darkness and death, freeing us see our solidarity with and need for all people.

---

[146] Michael R. Phillips, *George MacDonald: Scotland's Beloved Storyteller* (Minneapolis, MN: Bethany House, 1987), 275.

[147] MacDonald, *A Book of Strife in the Form of The Diary of an Old Soul*, "July 31," 155.

Part II
MacDonald and Literature

SERVANTS TO LITERATURE:
SCOTT, MAURICE, & THEIR MEDIEVALIST INFLUENCE ON MACDONALD[1]

KIRSTIN JEFFREY JOHNSON

A true knowledge of the present, in literature, as in everything else, could only be founded upon a knowledge of what had gone before.

The Seaboard Parish

No man could sing as he has sung, had not others sung before him. Deep answereth unto deep, face to face, praise to praise. To the sound of the trumpet the harp returns its own vibrating response—alike, but how different!

England's Antiphon

To become a better reader of George MacDonald's works, it is helpful to understand that two of his primary mentors—and closest friends—were two of the founders and first lecturers of a new academic discipline called "English Literature."[2] The myriad ways in which Alexander John Scott and Frederic Denison Maurice influenced, sharpened, encouraged, and engaged with MacDonald are possibly beyond measure and certainly worthy of far more scholarship.[3] So too are the

---

[1] As this chapter is based on my 2016 Cambridge keynote, some of the material has since appeared elsewhere, in particular: "Servants of All: Arthurian Peregrinations in George MacDonald," *The Inklings and King Arthur*, ed. Sørina Higgins (Berkeley, CA: Apocryphile Press, 2017), 421–34; "How Shall We Then Read? George MacDonald and the Beginnings of a Discipline Called English Literature," in *The Undiscovered C. S. Lewis: Essays in Memory of Christopher W. Mitchell*, ed. Bruce R. Johnson (Hampden, CT: Winged Lion, 2021) 88–111.

[2] MacDonald dedicated a book to each—*Robert Falconer* to Scott, and *Miracles of Our Lord* to Maurice—and wrote a poem for each. In addition, Greville MacDonald names Scott, Maurice, John Ruskin, and Greville Matheson as his father's four closest friends. Greville MacDonald, *George MacDonald and His Wife* (London: George Allen & Unwin, 1924), 192.

[3] Scott and Maurice were highly successful campaigners, founders, and teachers of institutionalized secondary and post-secondary education in England for persons regardless of class, gender, or religious affiliation: these were all privileges contested in Parliamentary debate throughout the century. It was not until 1871 that the "University Test Act" finally opened Cambridge and Oxford to all religious faiths. For more detailed discussion on Scott and Maurice, see Kirstin Jeffrey Johnson, "Rooted in All Its Story: More Is Meant Than Meets the Ear" (PhD thesis, University of St Andrews, 2010). For more specifically on their Christian Socialism, see J. Philip Newell, "A. J. Scott and his Circle" (PhD thesis,

decades they spent arguing for their English audiences to better value (and thus better read) England's own stories—a passion which culminated in their forging the discipline of "English Literature" for post-secondary education.[4] This chapter will delve into some of the early influences found by both Scott and Maurice in that shared vocation as purveyors of literature—specifically their participation in the Victorian Medieval revival. It will then consider how MacDonald responds to and engages with that movement-turned-trend within two particular texts, *Phantastes: A Fairie Romance for Men and Women* (1858) and *The Seaboard Parish* (1868). Storytelling is both playful *and* meaningful for MacDonald—as explained by one of his storytellers: "what distinguishes the true bard in such work is, that more is meant than meets the ear; and although I am no bard, I should scorn to write anything that only spoke to the ear, which signifies the surface understanding."[5] Thus, acquaintance with Scott and Maurice's conviction for the need to better know the stories of one's inheritance will simultaneously facilitate the hearing of "more than meets the ear" in the works of their student, George MacDonald.[6]

University of Edinburgh, 1981). For Scott's theological practice alongside that of Thomas Erskine, see Margaret McKerron, "Theological Learning as Formation in Holy Love: The Lives and Works of Thomas Erskine of Linlathen & Alexander John Scott" (PhD thesis, University of St Andrews, 2023).

[4] The term "English Literature" has shifted in its meaning since those first classes, as will become evident in this chapter. Initially the courses focused very specifically upon literature by (perceived) English nationals—rather than British let alone English-language writers. MacDonald's public literature lectures included three non-English nationals (the Scottish Robert Burns and Sir Walter Scott, and the Italian Dante), and his writing references English language writers of multiple nationalities—as well as a pantheon of writers from non-English-speaking countries. For a detailed list of MacDonald's lectures, see Ricke, Chu, Smalley, Dwyer, and Hoelscher, "George MacDonald: A Timeline of Lectures and Performance 1855–1891," *North Wind: A Journal of George MacDonald Studies* 37 (2018): 107–179. When Maurice later wrote a testimonial for MacDonald to teach in Edinburgh he recognized MacDonald as a Scot who could also teach Scottish literature: "He appears to me to have as keen a delight in the literature of his own country and of other countries as any man I have ever met with; to study books as only a man does who really appreciates the authors of them; and to have a peculiar facility for communicating his thoughts to others, and for awakening in them an interest like his own. [...] He would be a great acquisition to any university—to none, I should imagine, more than to that with which he has already the strongest patriotic sympathies." Greville MacDonald, *George MacDonald and His Wife*, 357.

[5] George MacDonald, *Adela Cathcart* (Whitehorn, CA: Johannesen, 2000), 57. For more on MacDonald's playfulness see Daniel Gabelman, *George MacDonald: Divine Carelessness and Fairytale Levity* (Waco, TX: Baylor University Press, 2013).

[6] Although introduced by Scott, MacDonald and Maurice had an independent relationship. From 1860–69 Maurice was the MacDonald family's priest, and in 1864 he became godfather and namesake to MacDonald's fourth son. In 1869 Maurice wrote that he would "deem it a great honour" if MacDonald would collaborate with him on a book combining his prayers and meditations with MacDonald's hymns, with the intent of promoting and encouraging "the Unity of the Church." Maurice's ill health impeded the project, however,

The Mentors

The man MacDonald acknowledged to be his greatest mentor (alongside his own father) was Alexander John Scott—"Sandy" amongst his friends, and "A. J. Scott" to the public.[7] He was born in 1805 in the ship-building port of Greenock, Scotland. A minister's son and graduate of Glasgow University, Scott was mentored by the renowned divine Thomas Chalmers, who sought to fight community disintegration and the loss of identity and of education incurred by the rapid urbanization of the Industrial Revolution. Scott and his wife Ann later moved to London when he was invited to assist pastoring a church there, and before long he was pastoring his own, not far from the dockyards of London. Scottish connections quickly introduced the couple to a culturally and theologically diverse group of people, and they frequently hosted large gatherings that included regulars such as Francis Newman, the Wedgewoods, Erasmus Darwin, Charles Kingsley, W.M. Thackeray, John Ruskin, Archdeacon Julius Hare, William and Elizabeth Gaskell, and Karl Gützlaff. Scott's active encouragement of artists meant that actress Fanny Kemble, painter Frederic Shields, and musician Frédéric Chopin were also amongst the guests.[8]

But this was only one side of London—and one side of Scott. Despite his experiences of industrialized Glasgow and Leith, Scott was overwhelmed by the amplification of England's capital (just then becoming the largest city in the world). In London he observed an even greater evisceration of community and roots and stories of identity—thousands of rural people pouring into urban unfamiliarity—and he was discovering that not only were most of these new residents suffering from a lack of supportive and hereditary community, but also that few had ever had any education. More shocking than England's rates of illiteracy—and for Scott even more concerning—was how many were

---

and he died in 1872—six years after Scott. See Greville MacDonald, *George MacDonald and His Wife*, 399.

[7] MacDonald addressed Scott in letters as "My Master," and wrote to Scott's daughter: "I looked up to your father more than to any man except my own father." William Raeper, *George MacDonald: Novelist and Victorian Visionary* (Tring: Lion Publishing, 1987), 228. Upon Scott's death MacDonald wrote to Scott's wife Ann, "He who has left us was the best and greatest of our time. [...] All my prosperity in literary life besides has come chiefly through him and you." Greville MacDonald, *George MacDonald and His Wife*, 359. Elsewhere MacDonald said simply that Scott was "the greatest man I have ever known." John Hunter, "A Lecture Given Before the London Society for the Study of Religion," *The Expositor* 21 (London: Hodder and Stoughton, 1921), 391.

[8] Shields painted a striking portrait of Scott (his father's cousin) in 1865, when his health was already in decline, and that was likely the model for his later image of St Paul in the "Chapel of the Ascension." The chapel (bombed in the Blitz) was funded by another Scott friend, Amelia Russell Gurney. She and her husband had helped finance some of MacDonald's early London literature lectures.

"unstoried." Nineteenth-century urban labor demands left little time to read (if one could) or tell children folk stories or family stories or Bible stories or national stories. England's literacy rates were significantly behind Scotland's (where parish schools were part of every community, even in the remote Highlands).[9] Whilst a lucky few children might find a charity proffering education (such as the Ragged Schools), certainly there was no opportunity for continued education—the only universities in England were the denominationally- and class-exclusive Oxford and Cambridge. Struck by an even greater lack of education and identity than he had found in the new factory communities of urban Scotland and convinced that self-understanding is a matter of great theological import, Scott began giving evening lectures in the dockyards to interested workers. He lectured on topics that he thought affected the daily lives of these men: on recent science and technological advances, on philosophical concepts, on general church history, on English church history, and on English Literature.[10]

Scott's audiences increased exponentially, and soon his friends convinced him to diversify that audience, because he was teaching material that was new to most of them as well—whether or not they were Oxbridge graduates—and he was integrating concepts and material in novel ways to which they also wanted access. Both in boys' private schools and at Oxford and Cambridge (limited at that time to males), the only literature that was taught was Classical—in Greek and in Latin. It was assumed that an educated man would study modern and vernacular works independently. It is difficult to believe, but Scott had to argue vigorously in his lectures that his audience should consider Chaucer, Shakespeare, and Milton not only important to read but also worthy of formal teaching. But so he did—and some listeners were convinced. As a Scottish ex-pat, Scott marveled to learn that many of his "literary peers" had read more German and Italian texts than they had specifically English texts. He pushed against their general antipathy toward "regional writing," and sought to engage interest in texts he was dusting off in the British Library, such as *Beowulf* and the works of Bede. He admonished his audiences for considering classical and foreign literature better than their own, noting for example the growing interest in the *Niebelungen*, whilst

---

[9] In 1855—the earliest available records—Scotland's literacy rate was 89% for men and 77% for women, compared with 70% and 59% for England and Wales. In the majority of the Lowland counties, outside of the industrializing areas, male literacy was over 90%. This staggering difference between neighboring nations is largely due to the fact that while public education had been available in Scotland since the mid-sixteenth century, England did not have free primary education until the establishment of the National Board of Education in 1899—three and a half centuries later. Secondary education was not publicly available in England until 1902. Robert Anderson, *Education and Opportunity in Victorian Scotland: Schools and Universities* (Oxford: Clarendon Press, 1983), 1.

[10] For specific lecture and course lists, as well as detailed descriptions, see Johnson, "Rooted in All Its Story."

scarcely anyone had yet read *Beowulf*.[11] He repeatedly spoke of King Alfred's efforts to unify and fortify his kingdom by having the history, the stories, of his people translated out of Latin into the vernacular, and of Aelfric's endeavors to familiarize the people with the "history of their own country."[12] Scott's material and perspective were novel, and audiences climbed into the thousands, and not only in London: "Philosophical Societies" across Britain started inviting him to lecture. Soon such teaching became his full-time occupation.

The "Interweaving of England's Literature and History" was one of Scott's most popular series—the other was on the mutual relations and essential harmony of religion, philosophy, and science. Regardless of topic, Scott repeatedly lectured against *schism*: he was adamant that both seeking and exploring all variety of relationships would lead one into deeper and fuller theological truths—the Trinity itself being relationship most fully realized. Because of this, Scott considered the literature of one's own heritage to be a particularly powerful medium of relating (and revealing) these truths. In observing the changes and developments from Homer through to Goethe, Scott identified a continuum of common threads, common signs, and common truths. Such commonalities demanded attention, and attention could precipitate change. To follow these threads from Chaucer and early England, through Wycliffe, Shakespeare, and beyond, was to trace "a history of the mind of England."[13] Scott hoped to equip his audience to recognize "the mind of England" in the specific stories that had shaped their own cultural identity. He believed that out of such truer self-knowledge would be born a greater facility in relating with God, neighbors, and nations. And that in such self-knowledge would also be forged a hospitable maturity towards diversity. Understanding the complex roots of their own stories could help English readers shift attitudes from imperialistic individualism towards compassionate communion, towards a greater openness and reception to the stories of others.

One of the English audience members riveted by A. J. Scott's arguments and practice was F. D. Maurice. In a sense, Scott was manifesting the culmination

---

[11] "The prevalent English tone is that of disdain for their own ancient literature; they like to disparage the remote past of their own country—to cut themselves off from all association with the times before the Reformation. I will not stay to ask whether this is the spirit of the Reformation." A. J. Scott, *Notes of Four Lectures on the Literature and Philosophy of the Middle Ages* (Edinburgh: T. Constable, 1857), 14. The situation was exacerbated by limited access to texts—most people did not own many books, and public lending libraries (another project Scott would assist) had not yet come into existence.

[12] Scott, *Middle Ages*, 20.

[13] A. J. Scott, *Two Discourses* (London: Darling, 1848), 227. MacDonald's *England's Antiphon* echoes these arguments, explaining some of the culture, beliefs, relationships of each poet, to better facilitate the poetry's reception: "No man could sing as he has sung, had not others sung before him. Deep answereth unto deep." *England's Antiphon* (London: Macmillan, 1868), 3.

of what Maurice had been working towards since his undergraduate days at Cambridge. Born the same year as Scott, and also a minister's son, Maurice grew up mostly in Glouchestershire. But whilst Scott's father was Presbyterian, Maurice's was Unitarian—thus, when Maurice declared himself to be trinitarian, it was a declaration born of careful, thoughtful intentionality.[14] From a young age Maurice advocated respectful discussion of differing perspectives, the seeking out of not just new knowledge but also wisdom and integrity, and the practical application of consequent understanding. When he arrived at Cambridge, he was invited to join a new select intellectual discussion group called "The Cambridge Apostles." According to Cambridge Apostle scholars such as Peter Allen and Richard Deacon, Maurice influenced not only the Apostles of his own peer group but shaped a distinctive foundational ethos that came to be known as "the Spirit of the Apostles." Both authors write about Maurice's influence on establishing principles that were key to the long-term success of the Society, and which permeated other groups of later years either founded by or well-populated by Cambridge Apostles—such as the Stirling Club, the Philosophy Club, even the leadership of the Working Men's Colleges (at which Scott, Maurice, and MacDonald would all teach). Cambridge Apostle and philosopher Henry Sidgwick described this "Spirit of the Apostles" as: "the spirit of the pursuit of truth with absolute devotion and unreserve by a group of intimate friends, who were perfectly frank with each other."[15] Changes in opinion were allowed within the Society, and questioning encouraged, so long as truly in pursuit of truth—there was no place for swaggering devil's advocacy. The distinctive insistence on respecting alternative voices marked an identity proudly defined by unity in diversity. Maurice and his peers believed that progress (better and truer understanding) could only come through this manner of respectful attention to multiple perspectives and ideas. They were passionately against inculcation of any sort, particularly religious, but this did not mean they were against religious feeling—quite the opposite: most of them were very sincere about their faith. But, importantly, not all of them were Christians, and those who were came from (and went towards) different perspectives on various doctrines. With youthful idealism they held that what one believed, how one worked, and even how one

---

[14] There occasionally arises a question of MacDonald's own trinitarianism, which can be readily challenged in numerous ways—and would be bemusing given how central that doctrine was for these two mentors. In discussion of the Incarnation Greville writes that Maurice and his father agreed on all key doctrinal points (400). Another son, Ronald, writes: "he always stipulated for liberty to maintain the doctrine of the Trinity; by which orthodoxy I do not think he ever gained a Sunday's rest." Ronald MacDonald, *From a Northern Window: A Personal Reminiscence of George MacDonald by His Son* (Eureka, CA: Sunrise Books, 1989), 35.

[15] Arthur and Eleanor Sidgwick, *Henry Sidgwick: A Memoir* (London: Macmillan, 1906), 34.

played, should all hold together, each aspect informing the other. It was a cohesive worldview that informed not only how one thought, spoke, and argued, but also how one lived. For Maurice these aspirations became a rule of life that would shape his career—and were later reflected in the novels of his future student, colleague, and parishioner, George MacDonald.

Such vision as the young Maurice and his colleagues held necessarily demanded that they participate in reform. One of the key areas in which they saw the need for reform was that of education: that it should be available for all peoples, regardless of class, religion, or gender. They believed that one of the most effective ways of facilitating such change was through the medium of literature—it is striking that these students believed their own university sorely lacked in literary education. So, they addressed this in their Apostle gatherings, where they gave particular attention to British Romantic Literature, but were uniquely versed in German literature as well—not only holding discussions, but setting essays for mutual examination.[16] In their post-university careers, many who remained passionate about the reforming power of literature shifted their teaching and writing energies towards the then particularly uncommon field of pre-Reformation English Literature. In consequence, amongst this circle of friends emerged some of England's most significant medievalists.

Given all of this, it is no surprise that when Maurice began attending Scott's public lectures, he discovered a kindred spirit and fellow reformer. This immigrant Scot, through experience and theology and culture-shock, had come to very similar conclusions—and appeared not only determined to do his best at re-storying his new country with its literature and history, but was convinced that doing so would both facilitate reform and provide a platform for richer theological understanding.[17] The men were soon working together, drawing each

---

[16] Samuel Taylor Coleridge was a primary source of inspiration, with whom various members had met. Working knowledge of German language and literature was still uncommon at this point in Britain: the select company included Coleridge, Scott, Thomas Erskine, Thomas Carlyle, John Sterling, Connop Thirlwell, and Julius Hare. See Newell, "Scott and his Circle," 197.

[17] When the new University College London opened as an alternative to the exclusive Oxford and Cambridge, its largely Scottish council determined that the literature of England should be one of the courses. Although not entirely sure how it should be taught, they knew that the course should be neither a vehicle for other material or purposes nor a mere introduction to worthy leisure material. Initially there was little success in their choices of instructors. The hiring of Maurice began a new trajectory, and the council was delighted when his successor Scott was appointed Chair English Language and Literature in 1848—thus earning the distinction of being the first to commit himself to a career of teaching "English Literature." Although Cambridge did not offer English Literature until 1878, it became a standard course for each of the new "inclusive" universities and educational institutions in England. For more on this and the attitudes, methodologies, and pedagogies of these two pre-Arnold literary critics and teachers, see Franklin E. Court,

into the other's projects and circles. Perhaps best known for their membership and leadership of what came to be called "Christian Socialism,"[18] more pertinent to this chapter is that out of their united passions and their mutual commitment to praxis was born the very discipline of "English Literature," with Scott and Maurice as England's first English Literature professors, and MacDonald as their enthusiastic heir.[19]

As their heir MacDonald is adamant that to consider the "womb of the time" into which an author is born—the pulses of the culture, the characters of the author's parents, the company the author kept—is to better understand that author's works. This is the critical approach MacDonald learned from these teachers: that a text does not stand independent of authorial lived experience. These men did not eschew "close readings," or even the validity of the reader finding within a text that which the author was unaware; rather, they were interested in a piece of writing both as a piece of communication as well as—to borrow Tolkien's term—of sub-creation. For them this was a theological matter: to know something about the author, and about how a piece of work came about, is to understand that piece of work even better. For me, applying these critical mandates of the pioneer teachers of the study of English Literature has shifted and shaped my subsequent readings of MacDonald's work generally, and *Phantastes*

Institutionalizing English Literature: the Culture and Politics of Literary Study, 1750–1900 (Stanford: Stanford University Press, 1992), and D. J. Palmer, *The Rise of English Studies* (Oxford: Oxford University Press, 1965).

[18] Nineteenth-century "Christian Socialism" was a reform movement that sought to apply the social principles of Christianity to modern industrial life—working through cross-class relationships—and thus improve life especially for lower classes and impoverished peoples. The term was first used by Maurice himself, although John Malcolm Ludlow is often considered the founder, and Scott sometimes the inspiring mentor.

[19] MacDonald was, like his two mentors who pioneered the field, an English Literature professor: a teacher and a literary critic. For myself, one of the most startling reconsiderations upon assessing primary data in this field of research was the misleading image of MacDonald as preacher-author. MacDonald indeed began his vocational life employed as a minister in Arundel—but he was only in that position for 28 months, whilst in his twenties. For ten years he was a professor of English literature; for forty years a lecturer on British Literature (and Dante). Failure to recognize this forty-year vocation of MacDonald will impede not only literary critique, but also reading of his theology. When in 1859 MacDonald became Scott's successor as professor of English Literature at Bedford Ladies College, London, his testimonials were written by Scott and Maurice. I am delighted to note that in the period since this chapter was given as a paper, several scholars have delivered new work on MacDonald's literary criticism and teaching. See, for example, Amanda B. Vernon, "Reading with the Trinity: Theology and Literary Form in George MacDonald" (PhD thesis, Lancaster University, 2021); Daniel Gabelman, "Surprised by Percival: Arthurian Transtextuality and the Reader in George MacDonald's *Phantastes*," *Journal of the International Arthurian Society* 9, no. 1 (2021): 118–142; Joe Ricke and Ashley Chu, "Remembrance and Response: George MacDonald and the Blank Page," *North Wind: A Journal of George MacDonald Studies* 38 (2019): 105–124.

and *The Seaboard Parish* particularly. This is why a chapter that intends a close reading of aspects of both MacDonald's debut novel and a work written a decade later, begins with Scott and Maurice. And why the chapter will now focus even more closely on a particular area of Scott and Maurice's literary study: Victorian Medieval Revivalism.

Medieval Revivalism

Medieval Revivalism began gradually in Victorian England. During the eighteenth century, medieval matters had been largely the preserve of antiquarians, and the Arthurian legend remained a minority interest primarily of social historians.[20] When in 1817 Poet Laureate Robert Southey wrote an introduction to the new edition of Malory's *Morte D'Arthur* (previously out of print since 1634) the text was little-known.[21] As mentioned, there had existed little interest in what was regarded as "regional literature." By the end of the century, however, references to Malory were ubiquitous from political cartoons through to mundane advertising. Although today this Arthurian revival is commonly attributed to iconic names such as Alfred Lord Tennyson (Southey's successor and a fellow Cambridge Apostle with Maurice) and F. J. Furnivall (a student of Maurice), and to William Morris and the Pre-Raphaelites, in reality these famed writers and artists were but few amongst many, and their enduring work emerged from a burgeoning company of fellow enthusiasts.[22] Scott and Maurice had each generated early enthusiasm amongst peers and students with their impassioned arguments that England was insufficiently familiar with her own stories. Scott, a gifted medievalist and linguist, was named one of the best Medieval scholars of the age by the likes of Southey, Carlyle, and Ruskin. These scholars boasted of Scott's practice of spending hours translating forgotten texts in the British Museum, and then regaling his students and public audiences with their contents. His

---

[20] Elizabeth Jenkins, *The Mystery of King Arthur* (New York: Coward, McCann & Geoghegan, 1975), 182–4.

[21] 1816 was the first run; Southey wrote the introduction for the second run in 1817. By 1853 it was still plausible that a well-educated Archdeacon's son (as seen in Yonge's popular novel The Heir of Redclyffe) was ignorant of Malory's *Morte d'Arthur*; but by the 1870s such ignorance would have been impossible; Jenkins, *The Mystery of King Arthur*, 211. William Morris' Arts & Crafts movement was largely inspired by the medievalism and social critiques of John Ruskin and Augustus Pugin. The aesthetic and social vision was first developed in the 1850s, and had cohered by the 1860s. MacDonald, like Morris, was a careful student of Ruskin's *Modern Painters*. And the legacy of both Scott and Maurice's influences upon Ruskin should not be ignored when noting Ruskin's influences upon the Pre-Raphaelite affiliates. An acquaintance between Ruskin and MacDonald in 1863 quickly turned to deep friendship and enabled for the latter an even greater familiarity with both the Pre-Raphaelite and Arts & Crafts circles.

[22] See Inga Bryden, *Reinventing Arthur: The Arthurian Legends in Victorian Culture* (London: Ashgate, 2005).

enthusiasm inspired them and helped establish a firm foundation for early Anglo-Saxon literature, particularly through his emphasis on language: "Great value was placed on tracing the histories and converging lines of development of words in order to construct a 'philosophy' of language that would reveal the specificity of a culture as it was expressed through comparative connections among the meaning of the language, its literature, and the [cultural] consciousness that gave rise to both."[23] Scott's incredibly popular lectures and classes were attended by various of Maurice's fellow Cambridge Apostles, as well as associates such as Carlyle, Ruskin, Francis Newman, the Gaskells, and Thackeray. Considering himself Scott's student, Maurice had also furthered interest in Medieval literature through his writings for journals such as the *Athenaeum* and *The Literary Chronicle*, and later through his own teaching, and in texts such as *Medieval Philosophy* (dedicated to Scott). It is hard to over-emphasize the role this pair of friends and colleagues played in the revival, through writing, teaching, and mentorship.

Interestingly, the more one looks at not just Maurice and Scott, but also their compatriot scholars involved in the rise of Victorian medievalism, the more evident it becomes that the *majority* of these scholars were simultaneously involved in social reform. Despite a diversity of social backgrounds, educational experiences, and theological, philosophical, and political perspectives, this social network of reformers and writers were not just keen on but had actually been inspired by England's early texts and myths—Arthurian legend in particular—just as Maurice and his fellow Apostles had anticipated back in their undergraduate days. Sharing more than ideologies (despite diversities), many of these medievalists worked and socialized together. Tennyson had met Maurice at university when he joined the Cambridge Apostles, and although less involved in the educational reform than many other early Mallory-enthusiasts, he did write a poem to celebrate Maurice's endeavors for female education.[24] Furnivall (after studying under Maurice) took up both social and educational causes, and responded to the call for better awareness of England's own literature by facilitating the publication of many medieval texts, beginning with Arthuriana. Apostle John Kemble—briefly a revolutionary in Spain, also editor of a political journal—was a keen advocate of Scott's lectures, and Scott a keen advocate of Kemble's work on Old English Literature. Social and philosophical reformers Ruskin and Carlyle had, like Tennyson, profound influence upon the younger

---

[23] Court uses the word "racial" here, rather than "cultural"—but I believe that the latter conveys Scott's intent, while the former may be misconstrued; Court, *Institutionalizing English Literature*, 97.

[24] Maurice founded Queen's College in 1848 for women and girls—the first institution in the world to award academic qualifications to women. Tennyson (godfather to one of Maurice's sons) wrote "The Princess" whilst living with Maurice one winter.

Pre-Raphaelites and their associates—men and women who produced a vast array of Arthurian-inspired paintings, writings, and literary reproductions.[25] A number of these joined Scott and Maurice in their social and education programs (some even identifying as "Christian Socialists"), and the Pre-Raphaelite associate William Morris earned his own reputation for his social reform initiatives.

Situated amid this collective enthusiasm for both literary and social reform was George MacDonald: Ruskin was an intimate friend; Maurice was his minister; Tennyson borrowed his books. When Furnivall founded a Shakespeare society, MacDonald was a vice-president. Members of the Pre-Raphaelite circle were guests of MacDonald both in England and in Italy and his children were occasionally models for them; as a magazine editor, he produced some of their work; letters indicate that he also counselled and gave pastoral care to some.[26] One Pre-Raphaelite associate, Arthur Hughes, became MacDonald's primary illustrator. Most importantly, Scott and Maurice—those scholars who argued so vociferously for a rediscovery of England's literary past—became MacDonald's mentors, educationally and spiritually. Maurice was MacDonald's minister at St. Peter's Vere Street, when MacDonald officially joined the Church of England in 1866. But even before then, he counselled, taught, and even helped tend MacDonald when he was ill. Maurice's reading of Ruskin to a convalescing MacDonald in Bude in 1865 directly influenced the Arthurian novel that echoes that family sojourn to Cornwall: *The Seaboard Parish*. MacDonald first attended Scott's lectures in the mid-1840s, and soon thereafter was seeking the discipleship of both Scott and his wife Ann, with whom he even lived whilst invalided in Manchester. Scott invested deeply in MacDonald's literary training, recruited him for reform efforts, and encouraged his writing and teaching. Both Scott and Maurice were active champions and facilitators of MacDonald's literary career. And their willingness to draw him into their larger circles, both vocationally and socially, brought him right into the midst of the Medieval Revivalists.

As the spheres of engagement of these medievalist writers, teachers, and artists widened and diverged over the decades, so advancements in technology and industry vastly increased the audiences. During the Industrial Revolution, England expanded and changed at a speed not experienced since the Renaissance, and unease with some of the negative consequences heightened the popular

---

[25] See "The Late Professor A. J. Scott," *The Scotsman* (Jan. 19, 1866) 23; The Carlyle Letters Online 20, 72–4; and John Ruskin, *The Winnington Letters: John Ruskin's Correspondence with Margaret Alexis Bell and the Children at Winnington Hall*, ed. V. A. Burd (London: Allen & Unwin, 1969), 109–10.

[26] See Beinecke Archives for further details. Morris, though unimpressed with the home-spun décor, even purchased Kelmscott House from MacDonald in 1875.

appeal of what appeared a simpler, cleaner, more heroic past.²⁷ Whilst early in the Medieval Revival the Arthurian legend primarily evoked a model of British Christian heroism, as the legends entered common vernacular the emphasis shifted to "'knight' heroes of contemporary society."²⁸ Despite the foci of the early medievalists, the general population became more interested in medieval literature and Arthurian legend as mythic inspiration than as history, or even literary text.²⁹ By the 1850s the popular concept of Arthurian England was that of an idealized realm, "where the borders of national, cultural, and mythological identities overlap."³⁰ Its allure was nation-wide: Arthurian images adorned the Queen's Robing Room at Parliament, the Oxford Students Union, and many village memorials to fallen soldiers.³¹ Gothic architecture pervaded public spaces in both the North and South; societies for social reform bore names such as "The Guild of St George"; and the Arts & Craft movement brought regal medieval design into middle-class homes. There was a notion that "Arthurian chivalry should inform modern behavior," which became "an important Victorian phenomenon"— yet, one that was fairly gender and class-specific.³² A popular text describing how to manifest chivalry in modern life, *The Broad Stone of Honour: Or, Rules for the Gentlemen of England*, defined chivalry as "only a name for that general spirit or state of mind which disposes men to heroic actions, and keeps them conversant with all that is beautiful and sublime in the intellectual and moral world."³³ Whilst superficially resonant, this emerging "spirit of the age" lacked the desire for personal growth and commitment to reformational praxis aspired to either by the "spirit" of the young Cambridge Apostles or the commitments of the later Christian Socialists.

MacDonald the Medievalist

As indicated, it was before this great popularization occurred that MacDonald began engaging with these early Medievalists. Since 1845 these people had been

---

²⁷ Jenkins, *The Mystery of King Arthur*, 182
²⁸ Bryden, *Reinventing Arthur*, 2–3.
²⁹ David Matthews, "Scholarship and Popular Culture in the Nineteenth Century," *A Companion to Arthurian Literature*, ed. Helen Fulton (Oxford: Wiley-Blackwell, 2009), 359.
³⁰ Bryden, *Reinventing Arthur*, 1. Edward Bulwer-Lytton's *King Arthur* (1849) was a key text in the appropriation of Arthur as part of emerging racial and ethnographical discourses of national identity. In contrast, Scott and Maurice were both convinced that better study of England's literature would reveal how much an engagement with—and borrowing from— other cultures had enriched England's own, and that that would help defend against the unhealthy nationalism they saw gaining ground in the Age of Empire.
³¹ George Landlow, *Ruskin* (Oxford: Oxford University Press, 1985), 72.
³² Matthews, 359.
³³ Matthews, 359; *Kenelm Henry Digby, The Broad Stone of Honour: Goefridus* (London: Wyman & Sons, 1877), 109.

his intellectual, social, and spiritual community. After seminary and a short spell as a minister, he joined Maurice and Scott in the newly developed profession of teaching English Literature. Privately, in colleges and public lectures, MacDonald taught medieval tales and the literature that engaged with them—from Sidney, Spenser, and Shakespeare, right up to contemporaries such as Tennyson—to classrooms of women, working class men, and dissenters. Strikingly, MacDonald was also amongst the earliest of these Victorian scholars to compose his own fiction based on Arthurian topics such as the Grail, Galahad, and Percival. His first such piece, the novel *Phantastes: A Faerie Romance for Men and Women*, was published in 1858, a year before the first of Tennyson's *Idylls*.[34] And although according to Tennyson critic David Staines the specific "revival of interest" in the Grail element of the legends only began in the early 1860s (probably instigated by Furnivall's 1861 reprint of the fifteenth-century epic *Seynt Graal*), MacDonald had begun work on that aspect as early as 1859.[35] His poem "The Sangreal: A Part of the Story Omitted in the Old Romances" was one of the first Victorian poems to focus specifically on the Holy Grail, published in June 1863 (six years before Tennyson focused on the subject).[36] Nor were such Arthurian references a passing phase for MacDonald: they figure throughout his corpus, frequently significant to the plot; even his essays and sermons draw upon Arthurian imagery.

Thus, MacDonald was not simply taking advantage of a promising trend: from *Phantastes* onwards this student of Maurice and Scott carefully manifested a mythopoeic approach to literature: engaging in new ways with old myths, crafting new stories, exploring old truths. The popularization of Arthurian legend had been lessening the interest in authenticity and accuracy, thereby increasing the propensity to use its images to promote agendas—particularly those connecting Arthurian legend to England's national identity and an elitist perception of English gallantry. Aware of this, MacDonald intentionally met his audience "where the borders of national, cultural, and mythological identities overlap."[37] Setting Lancelot and Guinevere aside, he relegated Arthur more to his

---

[34] William Morris' "Sir Galahad: A Christmas Mystery" was also published in 1858. The period widely recognized as prime artistic output on Arthurian and medieval themes—the 1850s to 80s—are MacDonald's prime writing years.

[35] David Staines, *Tennyson's Camelot* (Waterloo: Wilfrid Laurier University Press, 1982), 65.

[36] In a letter to Lady Byron on November 2, 1859, MacDonald discusses the Grail poem that he has completed. The later publication was accompanied by an engraving by Horatio Joseph Lucas; *Good Words* 4 (London: Strahan, 1863): 454–55. The next year, Robert Hawker published "The Quest of Sangraal," which was followed by Thomas Westwood's "The Quest of Sancgreall" in 1868. Although Tennyson mentioned the Grail in his idyll of "Sir Galahad," it is not the focus of the poem. His poem on the Grail was published in 1869.

[37] Bryden, *Reinventing Arthur*, 1.

role as Spenserian knight than as king.³⁸ Using his knowledge of the medieval Arthurian texts, and the engagements with them that follow, MacDonald the literature scholar (and student of Scott who insisted on attention to the threads of Anglo-Saxon language) reminds his readers—*re*-images for them—what the Old English word *knight* (*cniht*) technically means: "one who serves." MacDonald seeks to redefine the concept for his generation by showing how one can be an *authentically* English knight-hero. He initially does so implicitly in *Phantastes*, a fantasy novel about a young man eager to take on his role as family patriarch and filled with romantic notions of his gallantry. The tale is guided throughout by MacDonald's readings of authors for whom the chivalric vision was not make-believe, even if the settings in which they explored it might be. And the authors are not merely English, for as all Scott and Maurice's students learned, the most English of stories have roots in many cultures. But the writings MacDonald references uphold that Old English (Anglo-Saxon) vision of *cniht*, in contrast to populist "knight heroes of contemporary society."³⁹ A decade after *Phantastes*, however, MacDonald is more explicit about what knighthood actually is and the social reform it might—perhaps uncomfortably—evoke. In *The Seaboard Parish*, set on England's very real west coast, he spells it out in careful detail:

> No man could rise to the honour of knighthood without service. A nobleman's son even had to wait on his father, or to go into the family of another nobleman, and wait upon him as a page, standing behind his chair at dinner. This was an honour. No notion of degradation was in it. It was a necessary step to higher honour. And what was the next higher honour? To be set free from service? No. To serve in the harder service of the field; to be a squire to some noble knight; to tend his horse, to clean his armour, to see that every rivet was sound, every buckle true, every strap strong; to ride behind him, and carry his spear, and if more than one attacked him, to rush to his aid. This service was the more honourable because it was harder, and was the next step to higher honour yet. And what was this higher honour? That of knighthood. Wherein did this knighthood consist? The very word means simply *service*. And for what was the knight thus waited upon by his squire? That he might be free to do as he pleased? No, but that he might be free to be the servant of all. By being a squire first, the servant of one, he

---

³⁸ This would have pleased Furnivall. The year after MacDonald published "The Sangreal," Furnivall—whilst declaring his highest esteem for Tennyson—expressed his revulsion at the combination of Arthur's nobleness from early legend and the appearance of Guinevere in the later versions, stressing that in the early legends nothing is said of the sin of Arthur, nor of Guinevere with Lancelot; Staines, 66. For MacDonald, Spenser's *Faerie Queene*—full of Arthurian reference—is "the great poem of the period." He writes of "the profound religious truth contained in this poem," quoting as example a passage which declares the Redcross Knight's survival due to the care of his female companion, Una. MacDonald, *England's Antiphon*, 63.

³⁹ Bryden, *Reinventing Arthur*, 2–3.

learned to rise to the higher rank, that of servant of all.[40]

For MacDonald, an *English* "chivalry," including one's sense of identity and understanding of gallantry, must be that of an etymologically-faithful English *cniht*.

As MacDonald explored and modelled an etymologically true knight in *Phantastes* and *The Seaboard Parish*, he set aside the Holy Grail. In Malory the Grail first appears before Arthur and his knights during the Feast of Pentecost, and—as shown in MacDonald's poem "Sangreal"—it is because Galahad is a pursuant of holiness rather than of gallant deeds that he is successful in his Grail quest. Thus, the motif of *peregrinatio* is as important as the Grail itself. Adventures of the "solitary knight-errant" serve as progressive self-revelation, with epiphanic confrontations typically arising in consequence of the traveler's own sin, "as much from sin within as without."[41] Beginning in Malory (who followed Chrétien de Troyes and medieval ballads) this wandering motif continues in English chivalric tales from Spenser right up to Bunyan and beyond, all the time emphasizing the servanthood of the *cniht*. MacDonald participated in this tradition, frequently referencing the peregrinations of Sir Percival and Spenser's Redcross Knight— perhaps most explicitly in *Phantastes*. Percival's wandering journey is central to *Phantastes*, and is evoked again by his namesake in *The Seaboard Parish*. But just as both tales merge the medieval Percival with Spenser's Renaissance knight, both tales also detail the peregrinations of more than one adventurer. In *Phantastes*, the *peregrinatio* of the modern "gentleman" receiving education in the land of faerie is repeatedly contrasted to that of a "Repentant Knight" who more successfully emulates the noble acts of Sir Percival.[42] In *The Seaboard Parish*, a journey to the West Country and the actual English landscape of Tintagel (supposed location of Arthur's birth, and Merlin's cave) requires a Londoner named Percivale and his senior, Reverend Walton—contemporary versions of the newly-questing and the well-travelled knight—to negotiate their chivalric relationship not only with each other, but with the various "damsels-in-distress."

In these challenges to populist Victorian medievalism, MacDonald's literary commitment is evident: Arthurian history, literature, and myth all meet and intertwine—and invite. In both *Phantastes* and *The Seaboard Parish* he explicitly and implicitly alludes to an abundant number of external texts, from Biblical

---

[40] George MacDonald, *The Seaboard Parish* (Whitehorn, CA: Johannesen, 1995), 94. Reiterated almost verbatim in "True Christian Ministering" (1882).

[41] David L. Jeffrey, *A Dictionary of Biblical Tradition in English Literature* (Grand Rapids, MI: Eerdmans, 1992), 256. The specific term knygt erraunt, meaning wandering or roving knight, first appears in the 14th century Sir Gawain and the Green Knight.

[42] Or arguably at times Sir Galahad—the story he reads at the novel's beginning is of both. See Gabelman, "Surprised by Percival," 131–7.

and Classical, through to contemporary. Out of careful attention to the ongoing engagement of these tales emerge MacDonald's new tales: the mythopoeia of which Tolkien and Lewis named him a master.[43] These two Arthurian novels are densely infused with acknowledgements of dramas and poems, scripture and exposition, ballads and folklore, romances (from different British cultures as well as French) and Romanticism (English, Scottish, and German). *Phantastes* weighs more heavily with Jacobean and Elizabethan references, and *The Seaboard Parish* more heavily with the Metaphysical poets. While MacDonald's audience would recognize Dante, Chaucer, Shakespeare, Milton, and Bunyan, and perhaps even all the classical mythologies referenced, a vast number of his literary references would have been as novel to most readers in 1858 and 1868 as they are today. For MacDonald these are not only displays of synergistic intertextuality: they are introductions and invitations to other makers and engagers of myth. From his first novel he calls Arthuriana fans to delve deeper and discover the multiculturally and historically rich roots that gave rise to the popular culture—and to respond to what they find.

In both his realistic and fantastic writing, MacDonald's central characters are typically readers of myths and fairy tales. Rather than simply being caught up in a new trend, these characters are familiar with multiple engagements with Arthurian legend and consider this akin to spiritual nourishment—sometimes the familiarity even directly aids their survival. MacDonald's "educated" protagonists—male or female—read Sidney's *Arcadia* and Spenser's *Faerie Queene,* and have "read a good deal of the history of Prince Arthur."[44] It is as a result of such reading that his characters become "conscious of a desire after honour" as expressed by the protagonist of *Wilfrid Cumbermede*: "their spirit had wrought upon my spirit, and armour and war-horses and mighty swords were only the instruments with which faithful knights wrought honourable deeds."[45] Such tales give a hue of faerie to the commonplace world, all the more so for being the "genetic literary history" of the readers. MacDonald specifically encourages his readers to make connections between the swords and grails within his tales and those of myth. The hearts of his protagonists glow at such legends, their daydreams are fed by the visions; they retell them to their peers. The more mature characters "read rejoicingly" when they page through England's poets, engaging so deeply that they share a sort of "song-worship with [...] all who have thus at

---

[43] Lewis, *George MacDonald: An Anthology*, 17; J. R. R. Tolkien, "On Fairy Stories," *Tree and Leaf* (London: Harper Collins, 2001), 26.

[44] George MacDonald, *Wilfrid Cumbermede*, vol. 1 (London: Hurst and Blackett, 1872), 193.

[45] MacDonald, *Wilfrid Cumbermede*, 68. This is strikingly akin to Lewis' reflection on the effect of reading *Phantastes* upon his own young self; it is reminiscent too of Tolkien's careful representation of Faramir, with repeated emphasis on that character's preparation for "knighthood" through literary study.

any time shared in his feelings, even if he has passed centuries ago into the 'high countries' of song."⁴⁶ In doing so, MacDonald's characters recognize that these writings of the past equip them to better assess and engage with the present. As the narrator of *The Seaboard Parish* explains:

> A true knowledge of the present, in literature, as in everything else, could only be founded upon a knowledge of what had gone before; therefore, that any judgment, in regard to the literature of the present day, was of no value which was not guided and influenced by a real acquaintance with the best of what had gone before, being liable to be dazzled and misled by novelty of form and other qualities which, whatever might be the real worth of the substance, were, in themselves, purely ephemeral.⁴⁷

Thus, when a reader of MacDonald turns to *Phantastes* and discovers that in this tale the protagonist has no knowledge of what has gone before—is relatively unstoried, and even unaware of his actual genetic fairy heritage—it is clear that Anodos is an Englishman little aware of what it truly means to be a knight. He must endure a long peregrination of *aventures* before he wins his spurs. Unsurprisingly both of MacDonald's mentors were delighted by this first novel that made manifest so much of their own teaching. Newell writes that the book "won the keen appreciation of Scott" who wrote of its "purity and delicate beauty," and that Maurice arranged MacDonald's meeting with the publishers, who immediately accepted and paid for the manuscript.⁴⁸

PHANTASTIC PEREGRINATIONS

As *Phantastes* begins, the protagonist Anodos has just celebrated his twenty-first birthday.⁴⁹ A young "Victorian gentleman," he has reached the age of legal

---

⁴⁶ MacDonald, *England's Antiphon*, 2.
⁴⁷ MacDonald, *The Seaboard Parish*, 204.
⁴⁸ Newell, "Scott and his Circle," 368; Greville MacDonald, *George MacDonald and His Wife*, 19. MacDonald wrote to Ann Scott: "I hope Mr. Scott will like my fairy-tale. I don't see what right the Athenaeum has to call it an allegory and judge or misjudge it accordingly—as if nothing but an allegory could have two meanings!" Unfortunately, the publication of MacDonald's reference to the Athenaeum review singled it out for attention—leading to the common misconception that the review was representative. British publication scholar Mary Ann Gillies clarifies that in general the reviews of *Phantastes* "were actually quite positive" and that any negative response seemed to come from reviewers who "were nonplussed by MacDonald's fusion of fairy-tale form with religious or spiritual truths." Gillies records that a few years after the publication of *Phantastes* a literary journal declares that it "has proved a success even as regards its circulation, and a very decided success as concerns the influence it has exerted on minds of the highest order." Mary Ann Gillies, *The Professional Literary Agent in Britain, 1880–1920* (Toronto: Toronto University Press, 2007), 43, 186.
⁴⁹ His name in Greek has the potential of a curious double-entendre: it can be construed as indicating "without a way," even though the arguably more accurate translation is "progress upward." A careful reader of Plato, and of *The Republic* in particular, MacDonald

responsibility and must now take charge of his family's castle estate, be guardian of his sisters, and execute new duties. But though he is apparently of noble blood and has grand ideas of gallantry, Anodos is barely practiced (as the Repentant Knight later explains) in nobility of thought, let alone of deed. He has little more than a Victorian populist concept of chivalry: he knows the trends, but not the texts. Mere hours before Anodos assumes his role as lord of the manor he is accosted by a faerie ancestress who chides him for knowing so little of his genetic inheritance.[50] As she further chastises him for his general atheism regarding faerie, her star-gaze fills him with "an unknown longing" for a celestial sea. She tells him he will find it "in Fairy Land."[51] The next morning, Anodos awakens as his bedchamber transforms from a room with Arts & Craft décor into an actual sylvan bower, and he follows a path leading out of his room, in search of Fairy Land and the sea. His awakened interest in his inheritance of faerie is but the beginning of a long peregrination of self-revelation in which he will have to gradually set self aside, and learn to serve others. Although he is certainly *disposed* to heroic actions and believes himself conversant with the "beautiful and sublime"—thus, culturally a "Gentleman of England"—Anodos is quickly forced to accept that this does not make him a knight, English or otherwise.

It is Anodos' fairy blood that enables him to wander through these stories, and although Arthurian legends are dominant, they are not the only ones evident: Faerie is not confined by nationality. *Contes de fées* flow into *märchen* that flow into Celtic myth. Anodos discovers early on, from another person of similarly mixed genes, that those who have ancestry such as theirs needs must live by faerie borders and eat at least occasionally of its food, else they become ill. This woman infers that Anodos is less aware of the want than she, due to his "education and the activity of [his] mind," but it is dubious whether this is a compliment. Identifying her as of "the lower orders" (a mere cottager), Anodos is astonished at the woman's facility with language: "It seemed that intercourse with the fairies

---

would also know of Plato's use of the word anodos to indicate enlightenment. In his last fantastical novel, *Lilith* (1895), MacDonald hints that the protagonist Mr. Vane is a descendant of this Anodos—for Vane's ancestor is referred to as "Sir Upward" (reiterated eight times). Vane later recognizes a song, as will the reader of *Phantastes*: "Many a wrong, and its curing song; / [...] / Room to roam, but only one home." George MacDonald, *Lilith* (Whitehorn, CA: Johannesen, 2001), 325.

[50] In subtle contest to Spenser's hint of nationalism in *The Faerie Queene*, Anodos is shown to be the inverse of the Redcross Knight: while Spenser's knight is purportedly of English blood yet raised in Fairy Land, Anodos has fairy blood and yet has lived thus far only in England. It is in coming to know this foreign land of his ancestry—and the stories that inhabit it—that Anodos will be better enabled to venture well in his terram patrum.

[51] George MacDonald, *Phantastes: A Faerie Romance for Men and Women* (London: Smith, Elder & Co., 1858), 8.

was no bad education in itself."⁵² Anodos' surprise at the intellectual abilities of a woman of this class is representative of many of his contemporaries—and likely some of the first readers of *Phantastes* too. The concurrent Parliamentary arguments in London against education reform efforts were often based on the inability of both lower classes and women to sustain such intellectual strain.⁵³ Although Anodos is forced to acknowledge this cottager's abilities and accept her hospitality, he yet remains "disinclined to talk" with her and as a result misses the opportunity to learn important information. Nonetheless, it is under the auspices of her hospitality that he begins to supplement the education that he does have, taking up to read her "great old volume" that contains "many wondrous tales of Fairy Land, and olden times, and the Knights of King Arthur's table."⁵⁴ Thus, one of Anodos' first positive acts in Fairy Land is not a physical engagement in adventure, but rather a reading of adventure. He reads for hours, following the exploits of Sir Galahad and Sir Percival. Just as he is about to discover why Sir Percival appears in such a dishonored state beside the shining Sir Galahad—and how this relates to the wiles of the evil Alder-maid—he is interrupted and reads no more. The consequences of leaving the tale unfinished prove dire.

As the novel unfolds, it becomes evident that in not having conquered that trial of the Alder-maid alongside Sir Percival on the page, Anodos is ill-equipped to avoid her wiles in person. Nor does he heed the warnings of the knight he meets, whom he dubs "the repentant knight;" for despite the fact that this knight has rescued Anodos, his attitude of repentance over past chivalric failure does not match Anodos' image of a "knight hero." Given Anodos' inability to recognize this repentant attitude as a noble virtue, it should not surprise the reader that over time his attempts to prove himself a *knight errant* only sink him deeper into errancy. As he increasingly recognizes the selfish motivations behind even his seemingly good deeds, he starts to see the actions of the Repentant Knight in a new light. When finally sufficiently mature to feel honored to travel with the knight and learn from him, it is but a short passage. A shadow acquired through an encounter of willful disobedience impedes this and every one of Anodos' relationships. It besmirches good will, and causes him either to frequently distrust or dislike others:

> In a land like this, with so many illusions everywhere, I need [the Shadow] to disenchant the things around me. He does away with all appearances, and shows me things in their true colour and form. And I am not one to be

---

⁵² MacDonald, *Phantastes*, 17, 26.
⁵³ For further discussion on this topic, see Joan N. Burstyn, "Education and Sex: The Medical Case against Higher Education for Women in England, 1870–1900," *Proceedings of the American Philosophical Society* 117, no. 2 (1973): 79–89.
⁵⁴ MacDonald, *Phantastes*, 20.

fooled with the vanities of the common crowd. I will not see beauty where there is none. I will dare to behold things as they are. And if I live in a waste instead of a paradise, I will live knowing where I live.[55]

Self-satisfied with his own realism, Anodos becomes determined not to be taken in. He chooses cunning over companionship.

But when Anodos' self-oriented errors eventually lead to his abusing the trust of a young maid, the resultant self-loathing in this would-be knight can be healed only by the food, drink, and ritual washing proffered at the Fairy Palace. A greater maturity comes to him in this period of repose, during which day upon day of reading finally improves his fashion-fed knowledge of "Victorian chivalry" with the literary education he has lacked. Anodos becomes an itinerant traveler by paging through the books of a most astounding library—recognizing as he does so that this is also a form of peregrination, through which he is vicariously living many lives. The experiences are fortifying: in a narrative aside, he informs the reader that once back in England, "portions of what [he] read there have often come to [him] again, with an unexpected comforting."[56] However, Anodos still does not understand that the new life he has found within these books is but cerebral: that he must put it into practice or it will become null and void, or worse. This is evidenced when, attempting to free an imprisoned "White Lady," he himself is too free, assuming a champion's right to the damsel. His vision of chivalric glory, even for all the tales he has read, is still self-oriented: to conquer evil, earn the maiden, gain the glory. In consequence, the Lady flees and Anodos is banished from the Palace.

Anodos has much to learn in his relationships with women before he earns the title of a knight, rather than being a mere gallant. He must eschew his chauvinist attitude that a woman is either something to be rescued and claimed if beautiful and noble, bested if a temptress, or ignored if common. This progress takes him time, even though right from the beginning of his adventures he was both rescued and instructed by a matron cottager, her daughter, and a female tree.[57] After his banishment, when he is in the depths of despair, a character identified as the Wise Woman takes Anodos into her humble dwelling. By now he is sufficiently chivalric to give her the respect he did not have for his earlier lowly hostess. The experiences with this old woman guide him to reconsider his relationships back home in England—it is an emotionally difficult advancement in his peregrination of self-knowledge. Yet despite his learning Anodos still

---

[55] MacDonald, *Phantastes*, 104.
[56] MacDonald, *Phantastes*, 183.
[57] The Beech-maid who saves Anodos early in his journey, whilst yet remaining in arboreal confinement herself, gives him a leafy girdle of protection—one of a myriad of such references to Arthurian legend that occur in Phantastes.

endangers both himself and his hostess in an impetuous moment of willful disobedience, and the Wise Woman makes an immense sacrifice to save him. Her actions model the enormity of forgiveness—a lesson reinforced later by that young maid whose trust Anodos had abused near the novel's beginning. Precipitating the tale's end, it is this maid's forgiveness that sets Anodos free from both physical and emotional entrapment.

Thus, it is quite late in the tale that Anodos is finally able to recognize true knights when he sees them, though he remains for some time yet unable to assess accurately his own proximity to this state. Through the model of character in a pair of brothers, he finally understands that a knight does not rush headlong from one glorious rescue to another but must labor: that mental, emotional, and physical rigor are required to serve well. He also learns the importance of preparation for future endeavors, and of seeking advice: these knights have spent years readying themselves, requesting guidance from the old Wise Woman. Yet though he delights in the experience of being part of their team, Anodos still believes he can be a knight on his own. He becomes cavalier about the shadow that continues to haunt him, and numbers himself "amongst the glorious knights of old," even "an equal to Sir Galahad."[58] His self-delusion eventually results in solitary confinement, and it is from this that the absolving maiden frees him, her forgiveness all the more powerful for her honesty at the hurt that he had caused. Finally, Anodos recognizes that the truly valiant individual is not he who would be champion, but rather the lowly young female who has rescued him. He strips himself of his armor, declaring: "I might do for a squire; but I honoured knighthood too highly, to call myself any longer one of the noble brotherhood."[59] In this act of self-abasement, he finally loses his evil shadow.

No longer self-aggrandizing, Anodos' comprehension of what it means to be a knight is radically improved, but it is not until he willingly puts himself in service to one who intentionally seeks to be a servant that he really understands. In his first "adventure" as squire, Anodos discovers that the Repentant Knight makes no distinction between low- and high-born for his chivalric missions: he risks his life to rescue a mere peasant child. Although this knight has already "won" his damsel (over whom he does not rule, but rather with whom he confers) and has achieved the valiant shine of Galahad, he yet continues to face deep peril regardless of reward. Anodos marvels as his knight treats the petrified parents of the peasant child with the same dignity as he does his own lady, accepting their hospitality and sitting with them in their lowly cottage. The knight honestly enjoys their lowborn company, "talking most familiarly with the simple host"

---

[58] MacDonald, *Phantastes*, 272.
[59] MacDonald, *Phantastes*, 287.

and tending to the child "if possible even more gently than the mother."⁶⁰ This scene is a striking contrast to Anodos' own treatment of his peasant hostess earlier in the tale. Anodos now understands that the knight's countenance is noble not because he is high-born, but because "loving-kindness beamed from every line of his face."⁶¹ The knight builds upon this experience for Anodos in a later conversation with him, challenging the romantic notion of questing for fame and fortune:

> "All a man has to do, is to better what he can. And if he will settle it with himself, that even renown and success are in themselves of no great value, and be content to be defeated, if so be that the fault is not his; and so go to his work with a cool brain and a strong will, he will get it done; and fare none the worse in the end, that he was not burdened with provision and precaution."
>
> "But he will not always come off well," I ventured to say.
>
> "Perhaps not," rejoined the knight, "in the individual act; but the result of his lifetime will content him."⁶²

Anodos finally recognizes that *this* is noble service. This is true knighthood.

Once Anodos understands what being a true knight means, his time in Fairy Land is complete. Proving that he is finally able to put into deed a nobleness that is true, he commits a sacrificial act that he knows will cost his life, and fully dies to self. He is allowed to taste the "clear mountain-air of the land of Death" and to reflect on his journeying in Fairy Land, but, as soon as he vows a future of selfless service, he is abruptly returned alive to his childhood home.⁶³ While his sisters receive the returned Anodos with profound joy, they also observe that he is changed. He, too, is aware that he is now equipped with "a power of calm endurance to which [he] had hitherto been a stranger."⁶⁴ The reader is reminded that before the adventures in Fairy Land Anodos was about to take up a new mantle of responsibility, by his reflection: "I began the duties of my new position, somewhat instructed, I hoped, by the adventures that had befallen me in Fairy Land. Could I translate the experience of my travels there, into common life?

---

⁶⁰ MacDonald, *Phantastes*, 221. It is difficult to appreciate today just how shocking such an act would be not just to Anodos, but also to MacDonald's readers. Years later reviewers would balk at his even making mention in novels of such vulgarities as dirt floors in cottages; see Anonymous, "New Books: *Malcolm* by George MacDonald," *Wingfold* 42 (Spring, 2003): 25.

⁶¹ MacDonald, *Phantastes*, 294. The partnership of the Repentant Knight and his White Lady, in addition to her name, repeatedly recalls Spenser's *Faerie Queene* and the Percivalian knight who only succeeds through his partnership with Truth.

⁶² MacDonald, *Phantastes*, 296.

⁶³ MacDonald, *Phantastes*, 313.

⁶⁴ MacDonald, *Phantastes*, 318.

This was the question."⁶⁵ Anodos knows that he will continue to face trials and even failures. He must stay on guard, laboring in mental, emotional, and physical preparation, so that he "might be free, strong, unwearied, to shoot like an arrow to the rescue of *any and every* one who needed his ready aid."⁶⁶ He is now a true knight rather than an aspiring hero; knowing that at times he will be defeated, he yet will continue to serve. Anodos' memories of his faerie adventures—those read, observed, and partaken—will fortify him as he puts into practice the actions required of an English *cniht*.

A Modern Foray

Phantastes was well received by the reading public, unique as it was in its melding Arthurian legend into a fantastical novel. This tale of a man who, on his quest for knighthood, is rescued repeatedly by women, hosted and educated by peasants, and finally realizes his goal once he learns to serve others regardless of status or potential reward, has remained one of MacDonald's best-known tales. It is often credited for being at the beginning of a whole new genre of English literature. But despite its reception, as Victorian passion for Arthurian chivalry reached new heights mid-nineteenth century, MacDonald chose to change his tack. Ten years after the publication of Anodos' adventure in *Phantastes,* and now a popular author of realistic novels as well as fantasies, MacDonald wrote *The Seaboard Parish*. Significant advancements had been made in education reform, but MacDonald the Scottish suffragist, now a father of several teenage girls, was well aware of remaining cultural repressions. That he was ten years further into his career as an English Literature professor and lecturer is evidenced in the complex discourse of literary criticism that lies beneath the surface of *The Seaboard Parish,* and not least in his engagements with Ruskin's *Modern Painters*, Dante's *Commedia,* and the Greek myth of Psyche. Conversation of texts within texts remained a delight for MacDonald, and this composition is another rich dialogue of multiple literatures (and real history) on a number of inter-related themes. But the Arthurian overtones are the most explicit, and MacDonald's continued evangelism of an etymologically consistent concept of knighthood remains an important element of the textual conversation. However, this novel is not a stylistically ancient, episodic fantasy. Instead, *The Seaboard Parish* addresses the same themes in the "realistic" medium, rooted in an identifiably contemporary English time and place.

G. K. Chesterton writes that in MacDonald's non-fantasy, "the fairytale was the inside of the ordinary story and not the outside," yet in the *The Seaboard*

---
⁶⁵ MacDonald, *Phantastes*, 320.
⁶⁶ MacDonald, *The Seaboard Parish,* 83 (italics added).

Parish faery is both inside and out.[67] In response to the new stage of Arthurian hype, MacDonald has his characters become Victorian tourists (tourism itself was a swelling trend), occasioning their explorations of true knighthood whilst journeying in a region that claims Arthur's historic origins. That MacDonald has the Walton family travel to this specific location is all the more remarkable for the novel being written before the transformation of nineteenth-century Tintagel into a shrine of Victorian tourism.[68] Awareness of the anticipatory nature of this setting gives today's reader a context for just how contemporary MacDonald's novel is. Not only did he still have his finger on the pulse of popular culture, but his family conducted first-hand research for this novel. Just three years before *The Seaboard Parish* was published, the MacDonalds had travelled to Cornwall and Devon and visited the not-yet famous Tintagel.[69] In general it was a trip of recovery and convalescence as it is in the novel, only MacDonald was the convalescent, recovering from one of his bad bouts of tubercular hemorrhaging.[70] The location, adventures, and persons with which MacDonald engaged on that visit shaped the framework for *The Seaboard Parish*. During this time Maurice came down to visit and read to him from Ruskin's *Modern Painters*; his wife Louisa spent the time landscape painting; his family visited Tintagel.[71] The Pre-Raphaelitesque Arthurian painting MacDonald discusses within the novel, *Knight of the Sun* (by Arthur Hughes), actually exists and was then new to England's public: one rendition paired with a poem by MacDonald (1862) had sold at Christie's only months before *The Seaboard Parish* began appearing in installments in *The Sunday Magazine*.[72]

---

[67] G. K. Chesterton, Introduction to *George MacDonald and His Wife*, Greville MacDonald, George MacDonald and His Wife, 11.

[68] Amy Hale, "The Land Near the Dark Cornish Sea: The Development of Tintagel as a Celtic Pilgrimage Site," *Journal for the Academic Study of Magic* 2 (2004): 2.

[69] Tennyson had been here years before, guided by the poet-priest Robert Hawker whose "Quest of Sangraal" had been published a year after MacDonald's Sangreal poem. Charles Kingsley, author and reformer in the same circles as MacDonald, had also visited Hawker, and it is possible that some of MacDonald's inspiration for *The Seaboard Parish* comes from tales of this coastal vicar who helped with shipwrecks and shared poetry with his parishioners. Sabine Baring Gould, *The Vicar of Morwenstow*, R. S. Hawker (London: Henry S. King & Co., 1876), 69, 70.

[70] Greville MacDonald, *George MacDonald and His Wife*, 262.

[71] Five years later MacDonald's daughter Mary Josephine became engaged to a tall, handsome, bearded Pre-Raphaelite follower, strikingly similar to the character Charles Percivale. He was a nephew of Arthur Hughes, the real-life artist of the *Knight of the Sun*. Sadly she died of the family haunt of TB before she and E. R. (Ted) Hughes were married.

[72] Hughes worked on various versions of this painting throughout the decade. See Leonard Roberts, *Arthur Hughes: His Life and Works: a Catalogue Raisonné* (Woodbridge: Antique Collectors' Club, 1997).

This realistic Arthurian novel begins in considerable contrast to *Phantastes*. Rather than the speculations of a young pathless protagonist, the reader of *The Seaboard Parish* is presented with the ruminations of an aging minister upon the complexities of audience and story, and with his warning to older readers not to become complacent and thus stagnate. This narrator of *The Seaboard Parish* explains that *peregrinatio* is life-long; the adventure of living never ceases, it is an on-going pilgrimage in which none is too elderly to participate nor, indeed, to serve. Reverend Henry Walton is familiar to readers of *The Seaboard Parish* as the book is the second in a trilogy. In the first, *Annals of a Quiet Neighbourhood*, a much younger Walton discovered sacred vocation in his ecclesial occupation and also introduced his congregation to English literary heroes. Walton had also proved rather chivalric in dashing fashion: he triumphed over the vile machinations of a local evil matriarch, rescuing—and marrying—her daughter, a veritable damsel-in-distress once imprisoned in a real (former) castle. Now in *The Seaboard Parish* Walton is "settled into [being] a gray-haired, quite elderly, yet active man."[73] He is also a contemplative, and the novel is filled with his ruminations and sermons. While the story weaves in and out of these, it is a mistake to think that either tale or exposition stands alone; each exegetes the other, and both serve to explore an etymologically accurate understanding of English knighthood.

When a dramatic horse-riding accident in the first few pages renders Walton's vivacious daughter Constance a physical prisoner of paralysis, it is quickly evident that she refuses to be confined in spirit. This is set in contrast to her elder sister Winnie, who is physically fit but entrapped by spiritual malaise. Once so successful in rescuing his wife, Walton now struggles with impotence at the travails of these two daughters. When an invitation offers him an opportunity to take the entire family on a visit to the Devonshire and Cornish coast, "a vision of the sea [...] rush[es] in upon [him]" and soon the household is a cavalcade, invalid and all, travelling to the West Country.[74] While there they visit Tintagel, the birthplace of England's greatest crowned knight and of its greatest myth. They also find a wandering young Percivale, painting visions on the shore. This ever-present sea, the whole family learns, is a place of mystery and myth; of new beginnings (the reader is reminded that nothing lies between the Coast and "New-found-land," a land of promise towards which emigrants journey); and of death (drownings and storms are a constant theme, even for the emigrants). Ruminating upon this variously beautiful and foreboding entity, life-giving and life-claiming, Walton details the immaterial seas of which he is also aware: "one of the unseen world, that is, of death; one of the spirit—the devouring ocean of evil—and might I not have added yet another, encompassing and silencing all the

---

[73] MacDonald, *The Seaboard Parish*, 6.
[74] MacDonald, *The Seaboard Parish*, 111.

rest—that of truth!"[75] It is at the convergence of such physical and metaphysical shores that they meet the artist Percivale. He has transformed a jagged, rocky island into Dante's Purgatorial mountain, upon which Beatrice leads the poet ever higher. In his late twenties, Percivale (his first name, "Charles," is only used twice) is of noble and ancient English blood, though when teasingly asked if he is "a descendant of Sir Percivale of King Arthur's Round Table," he replies that he "cannot count quite so far back."[76] It is quickly established that Percivale is a fervent admirer of Dante's *Divine Comedy* and of Ruskin's *Modern Painters*, and he wrestles deeply with questions of life, death, and the divine: "the mere romantic [he] never had much taste for."[77] In his commitment to "the pursuit of truth with absolute devotion and unreserve," his respectful but "absolute candour" in discourse, his pursuit of education through literature, Percivale could have been a Cambridge reformer with young Maurice and his peers.

Both pastorally and personally, Walton is drawn to this exceedingly chivalrous young man who is fluent in Italian and a student of the Pre-Raphaelite school. He would willingly mentor Percivale on his pilgrimage. However, much to his chagrin, Percivale and Walton's spiritually struggling daughter Winnie are clearly romantically drawn to each other.[78] While Walton had no issue being a knight to his wife Ethelwyn in their own courtship, rescuing her in both body and soul, he does have an issue with Percivale being the gallant savior of his daughter. Percivale is still on his own spiritual journey: not yet a Christian, let alone a Galahad. In discussions over this dilemma (most pointedly after Percivale physically rescues Winnie from plunging over a cliff), Ethelwyn challenges Walton. Now in partnership with him, as his Spenserian Una, she reminds him that he himself was struggling in his faith-journey when they fell in love, and that still the two of them are progressing yet far from any final state of sanctification. Ethelwyn implies that Walton might be jealous in his desire that he be the knight who rescues his daughter. She suggests that perhaps Winnie and Percivale might be of assistance to each other if they journey together in their search for truth, each so driven in their "Holy Longing" for something more. Walton concedes but continues to struggle in allowing another to be his daughter's champion.

Walton and Percivale must resolve their tensions and physically work together once they are at Tintagel (Arthur's birthplace), for there they carry the chivalric invalid Constance up a dangerously steep path into the castle ruins,

---

[75] MacDonald, *The Seaboard Parish*, 208.
[76] MacDonald, *The Seaboard Parish*, 249.
[77] MacDonald, *The Seaboard Parish*, 327.
[78] Although Winnie is sometimes used as a nickname for variants of Guinevere, MacDonald is very clear that in this situation Winnie is an abbreviation of the name Ethelwyn: the daughter being named after her mother.

so that she might look out upon the shining seas. The image they create as they share their burden echoes that of a painting by Percivale, in which a dying knight is carried by his squires "on the edge of a steep descent."[79] This painting is based on an actual work of art, executed by MacDonald's friend Arthur Hughes, titled both *Knight of the Sun* and *Morte D'Arthur*. The subject is a devout knight whose dying wish is to see the setting sun, the inspiration of the insignia borne on his own personal heraldry.[80] Not till long after the event with Connie does Walton see Percivale's painting, which upon viewing he calls "a grand picture, full of feeling—a picture and a parable."[81] Percivale's gallant conduct throughout the Tintagel adventure goes a long way towards reconciling Walton to relinquish his grip as Winnie's prime protector. Walton's final release is made when Percivale risks his life in order to rescue some strangers in peril of drowning in the stormy sea.

These characters, Winnie and Percivale, struggle with doubt, but they *are* in pursuit of the truth. They are "reverent doubters" (a term MacDonald used for agnostics in whom he identified integrity), seeking to serve without spiritual assurance or eschatological hope.[82] They may not be as secure as Walton, or even Constance, in their sense of Truth or Home, but they quest onward nonetheless, and—as Walton eventually indicates—are perhaps even more to be admired for doing so, for in their quest they seek to serve without expecting reward. It is a chivalry for which MacDonald the author had much respect. In time the shared quest of Winnie and Percivale does eventually result in their release from what Walton sees as spiritual confinement, but that is in another book, and both reader and father have to relinquish assurance, and wait.

In keeping with the broader understanding of knighthood communicated in *Phantastes*, Walton also explicitly acknowledges some of the social reform issues being argued in England's Parliament even as *The Seaboard Parish* was published. He discusses particular forms of societal confinement to which the women in his lifetime are bound. Like MacDonald, Walton is a suffragist, and while he struggles with whether he would "like to see any woman [he] cared much for either in parliament or in an anatomical class-room," he clearly states that that is her decision to make—"not his or that of any man."[83] Consistent throughout the

---

[79] MacDonald, *The Seaboard Parish*, 614.
[80] Anonymous, "Review of 'Knight of the Sun,'" *Athenaeum* 20 (Sep. 1873): 374. On the frame, Hughes had inscribed half a stanza from MacDonald's poem "Better Things": "Better a death when work is done, / Than earth's most favoured birth." The remainder of the stanza, the last in the poem, is: "Better a child in God's great house / Than the king of all the earth."
[81] MacDonald, *The Seaboard Parish*, 615.
[82] MacDonald, *England's Antiphon*, 326.
[83] MacDonald, *The Seaboard Parish*, 291. Already part of the movement to provide post-

text are reminders to the reader that Una and Beatrice both have occasion to be rescuers and guides to the Redcross Knight and Dante (physically, emotionally, and spiritually), just as Ethelwyn—now Walton's helpmeet and partner—rescues him repeatedly from inner turmoil (jealousy, impatience, willfulness). Both Walton and Anodos learn that whilst sometimes they will be rescuers, they will also at times have to be rescued, and may even have to accept that, at times, the rescuing is not theirs to do. In both novels, the successful knights are those who become socially progressive, working as partners, being educated by, and even at times being dependent upon both women and persons of lower social status. For Walton, this list of partners also includes persons with different beliefs. In the words of Maurice's Spirit of the Apostles, "better and truer understanding [came] through respectful attention to multiple perspectives and ideas."[84]

Storied Reform, Regardless of Genre

The Seaboard Parish is a modern and "realistic" contrast to the fantastical peregrinations of *Phantastes*. The change in genre emphasizes MacDonald's endeavor to usurp an ever-growing romanticized notion of knighthood. MacDonald's message is for his modern audience, regardless of gender or class. *Phantastes* was written at the beginning of a fad, before it became a national obsession, and MacDonald engages in the new trend in a manner that calls his readers to a better knowledge of their own heritage. In doing so, the novel challenges readers to reconsider their definition of knighthood and their understanding of true English chivalry. A reader of *Phantastes* and *The Seaboard Parish* who expects the gallant knight (or gentleman) to save the damsel-in-distress and win the glory will be disappointed, perhaps even frustrated. The reader is asked instead to accept numerous concepts subversive to populist Victorian medievalism: that chivalry and valor is gender- and class-neutral, both for those who give and those who receive; that patience, preparation, and waiting are necessary acts of service; that not all good deeds are rewarded, or even succeed; that saving the girl does not equate to winning the girl, nor finding the grail indicate the adventure's end; and, that the true chivalric quest never does end. *Phantastes* shows this with the youthful protagonist Anodos; *The Seaboard Parish* (perhaps even more surprisingly) shows it with a late middle-aged pastor. The *Perigrinatio* of a *cniht* is life-long.

In these two novels, MacDonald responds to the renewed fascination with Arthurian myth in his contemporary culture. Fortified by his own privileged

---

secondary education for women, MacDonald's friendships with and support of such as Barbara Bodichon, Elizabeth Gaskell, Josephine Butler, Octavia Hill, Elizabeth Reid, and (physician!) Elizabeth Garrett indicates the breadth of his suffragism.

[84] Deacon, 6.

education from other medieval scholars, his creative engagements with these ancient stories remind his readers that behind this new trend lies their own rich literary past. The novels are themselves each a course in "English Literature." When MacDonald first began to write, the Arthurian revival was only beginning: Tintagel was not yet a tourist shrine, and Tennyson's first *Idylls* were not yet published. As taught by Maurice and Scott, MacDonald met the cultural hunger for identity and the need for reform with an invitation for readers to join with their own ancient tales of transformation. In doing so he invokes the mythic into their present. He critiques the misconstrued notion of modern English chivalry that manifests as a paternalistic *noblesse oblige*, or a shallow gallantry, and which perpetuates common tropes such as damsels-in-distress and gallivanting knights. He "stories" how an etymologically accurate understanding of the word demands a conscience of social reform, whether that involves issues of suffrage, class, education, or theological orientation.

Yet as a steward of such ancient tales, MacDonald is not hesitant to challenge familiar patterns: literature is for him a conversation. He defies the convention of the "solitary knight," incongruent as it is with the English definition of *cniht*: none of his adventurers succeed on their own. Nor does their service end with the completion of a quest: to be a *cnight* is a lifelong journey. Whether for young Anodos and the artist Percivale, or the elder Walton and well-travelled Repentant Knight, death to self is likewise a continuous battle. Anodos was once eager to be a knight who fights evil through deeds of valiance, yet the mentor he comes to admire is one who proves that the true quest is discerning whom to serve and how, and then doing so. For MacDonald every reader has the potential to be such a knight: an adventurer choosing how to venture.

BEING AND TRUTHFULNESS:
MACDONALD'S VITALISTIC THEOLOGY OF PERSONAL MEANING

GAVIN BUDGE

MACDONALD AND HIS SCOTTISH INTELLECTUAL CONTEXT

Despite the religious and philosophical themes with which most of his writing is preoccupied, George MacDonald avoided discursive argumentative prose in favor of the parabolic mode of his imaginative work, with even the explicitly religious writings collected in his *Unspoken Sermons* ultimately adducing the ethos of God's being, rather than employing a Paleyan deductive register. In this essay, I would like to suggest that MacDonald's marked avoidance of the rationalistic register of argument is not just personal idiosyncrasy, or a merely pragmatic strategy, but constitutes a fundamental feature of his religious and philosophical outlook. For MacDonald, I will claim, the act of communicating truth is an embodied and existential enterprise which transcends mere intellectual correctness. MacDonald's writing highlights questions about individual authenticity in such a way as to insist upon the indispensability of belief to everyday living.

In this, of course, MacDonald is far from being alone among writers of the mid- to late nineteenth century, as the popularity of the theme of Evangelical hypocrisy amongst Victorian novelists testifies. The little boy whom Mr. Brocklehurst in *Jane Eyre* is prepared to reward with two ginger-nuts for expressing his preference for learning a verse of a psalm over eating a single ginger-nut, exposes the fundamental insincerity of an Evangelical theology centered on the notion of heavenly reward.[1] A similar point can be made about the rather less well known tale by Charlotte M. Yonge, *The Six Cushions* (1867). In the conclusion of Yonge's tale, a young girl who has put her faith in an imaginary Evangelical story-book outcome for her own situation where "the widow's daughter in the little house, who never goes to parties, would be superior to all the grand young ladies,"[2] to the extent of neglecting the actual embroidery task with which their vicar has entrusted them all, is shown to have engaged in an elaborate, and spiritually perilous act of self-deception.

---

[1] Charlotte Brontë, *Jane Eyre*, ed. Margaret Smith (Oxford: Oxford University Press, 1993), 34.
[2] Charlotte M. Yonge, *The Six Cushions* (London: Mozley, 1867), 195.

MacDonald's Scottish education, I will argue, makes him particularly sensitive to questions of personal authenticity and their relationship to mental and spiritual health in a way which by the end of his career in the 1890s, as reflected in his fantastic narrative *Lilith*, aligns him with the themes of the Decadent movement. MacDonald's exposure to the Scottish tradition of Common Sense philosophy inaugurated by Aberdonian philosopher Thomas Reid would have familiarized him with a mode of critique which aimed to expose the philosophical "bad faith" of Pyrrhonist skepticism of the kind represented by David Hume (the principal target of Reid's philosophical reformulation of Berkeleyan idealism). For Reid and his followers (collectively known as the Common Sense school) the existential argument that it is impossible to live in accordance with the dictates of Humean skepticism is conclusive against any claim for its intellectual validity.[3] Really to act according to the conclusions of Humean skepticism would be to make any kind of knowledge or action in the world impossible,[4] given that Hume denies the possibility of proving the existence of a world external to the mind, and for the Common Sense school this demonstrates Hume's philosophical bad faith, since notwithstanding his skeptical philosophy he managed to function very successfully in the society of his day.[5]

Scottish universities, however, were also leading European centers of medical education at the time, and, as Colin Manlove has recently shown, MacDonald's scientific studies made a significant contribution to his visionary romances.[6] As this essay will suggest, the Scottish medical context, in which MacDonald's struggle with tuberculosis would have led him to take a personal interest, intersects with the Common Sense school's own existentialist emphasis on the essential requirement for a valid philosophical position to promote action-orientated healthy-mindedness (something reflected in the German translation of "common sense" as "gesunder Menschenverstand").[7] The search for a healthy attitude to life, which this essay will suggest forms a consistent thread in

---

[3] Thomas Reid, *Works*, 8th ed., ed. William Hamilton (Edinburgh: Maclachlan and Stewart, 1872), 109; See also James Beattie, *An Essay on the Nature and Immutability of Truth*, 6th ed. (Edinburgh: Creech, Dilly and Cadell, 1777), 127–8.
[4] Reid, *Works*, 196–97.
[5] Beattie, *Essay on Truth*, 345; See also Reid, *Works*, 488.
[6] Colin Manlove, "The Electromagnetic World of George MacDonald's Visionary Romances," *Journal of Scottish Thought* 12 (2020): 144.
[7] "Gesunder Menschenverstand" translates literally as "healthy human understanding." Reid comments that from the perspective of common sense, philosophical skepticism about the existence of a world external to the mind is naturally regarded as "a kind of metaphysical lunacy," Reid, *Works*, 127. Beattie argues that philosophical disputation is counterproductive since human beings are "destined for action rather than for knowledge, and governed more by instinct than by reason," Beattie, *Essay on Truth*, 355.

MacDonald's writing, thus has, in the Scottish context both philosophical and medical resonances.

The Common Sense school's existentialist rejection of the Humean conception of philosophy as a merely theoretical enterprise, with no implications for practical, everyday life,[8] is also closely linked in the Scottish context with arguments about Calvinist doctrine, in a way which, as I will show, has important implications for the religious themes of MacDonald's writing. The Common Sense school's emphasis on the embodied context in which philosophical thought necessarily takes place[9] ushers in a wider transition away from what comes to be perceived as the excessive abstraction and purely theoretical nature of the Calvinist account of Atonement and the justification of the elect toward a theology in which the embodiment of incarnation is central.[10] MacDonald's commitment to embodying a theological understanding of life in the imaginative form of his fiction testifies to his participation in this general theological shift toward an incarnational perspective.

MacDonald's Religious Parables as a Personal Form of Knowledge

Recent critical commentary on MacDonald has rejected the assumption that the interest in writing a kind of fiction with religious, or theological, significance, which led him to turn down the secure career of Congregationalist minister in favor of a precarious and peripatetic existence, necessarily implies that his fiction must be preachy and sanctimonious.[11] In this, of course, such commentary takes its cue from MacDonald himself, who emphasized that Jesus himself "had no design of constructing a system of truth in intellectual forms," but "spoke out of a region of realities which he knew could only be suggested—not represented—in the forms of intellect and speech."[12] MacDonald's emphasis here on the necessity of suggesting, rather than representing, religious reality, expresses a caution about

---

[8] David Hume, *A Treatise of Human Nature*, ed. L. A. Selby-Bigge and P. H. Nidditch (Oxford: Clarendon Press, 1978), 269–70.
[9] Beattie asks, in relation to the Berkeleyan philosophical claim that matter does not exist, "Where is the harm of my believing, that if I were to fall down yonder precipice, and break my neck, I should be no more a man of this world? My neck, Sir, may be an idea to you, but it is a reality to me, and an important one too," Beattie, *Essay on Truth*, 244.
[10] The importance of the transition from the theology of Atonement to the theology of Incarnation for an understanding of nineteenth-century intellectual history is examined at length in Boyd Hilton, *The Age of Atonement: The Influence of Evangelicalism on Social and Economic Thought, 1795–1865* (Oxford: Clarendon Press, 1988).
[11] See Roderick McGillis, "Childhood and Growth: George MacDonald and William Wordsworth," in *Romanticism and Children's Literature in Nineteenth-Century England*, ed. James Holt McGavran (Athens, GA: University of Georgia Press, 1991), 150–67.
[12] George MacDonald, "It Shall Not Be Forgiven," in *Unspoken Sermons* (London: Strahan, 1867), 66–7.

the attempt to embody religion in any linguistic form, which needs must require especial self-consciousness and stylistic subtlety when it comes to fiction.[13]

Aubrey Plourde, for example, has acknowledged the literary sophistication with which MacDonald handles his universalist theology, adoption of which was one of the factors behind his resignation as a Congregationalist minister. Plourde notes MacDonald's ability to sidestep "determinism, whereby the individual faith he valued so deeply is reduced to meaninglessness under the crushing weight of God's design," in favor of "a developmental paradigm that allowed for paradoxical impulses: the simultaneous confidence that all would be right in the end, combined with a focus on incremental and often invisible change."[14] For Plourde, MacDonald's suspension of the totalizing drive of universalism is a specifically literary achievement of theological ambiguity, of which she finds emblematic Princess Irene's following of the grandmother's thread in *The Princess and the Goblin*. Rather than conducting Irene infallibly back home "the thread of her faith leads her further away" so that "when the ordeal is resolved successfully, the grandmother is nowhere to be found."[15] As Plourde notes, "God's conspicuous absence" here makes Irene look less "like the ideal child believer and more like Hardy, Eliot, or Tennyson—that is, a figure of continual spiritual negotiation rather than confirmation."[16] In Plourde's reading, MacDonald's literariness opens up a space for the living indeterminacy of faith and doubt which would seem to be precluded by his universalist theological position. A kindred emphasis on indeterminacy underlies Daniel Gabelman's extended reading of MacDonald in terms of the notion of playfulness, on which I will comment later.[17]

Similarly, the account given by Lori Branch and Mark Knight of the postsecular approach to literary interpretation makes MacDonald's writing exemplary of the Bakhtinian dialogical quality they identify in "the best sort of theological thought" in that "throughout his fiction, the commitment to God's mysterious activity in and through creation endows all events with a divine purpose that eschews easy answers, registers the contribution of all creatures, and remains open to different interpretations."[18] The open-endedness which Branch

---

[13] I have argued for a similarly religiously motivated self-consciousness in the work of the Tractarian novelist Charlotte M. Yonge in my study *Charlotte M. Yonge: Religion, Feminism and Realism in the Victorian Novel* (Bern and New York: Peter Lang Publishing, 2007).

[14] Aubrey Plourde, "George MacDonald's Doors: Suspended Telos and the Child Believer," *Victorian Literature and Culture* 49, no. 2 (2021): 238.

[15] Plourde, "George MacDonald's Doors," 241.

[16] Plourde, "George MacDonald's Doors," 241.

[17] Daniel Gabelman, *George MacDonald: Divine Carelessness and Fairytale Levity* (Waco, TX: Baylor University Press, 2013).

[18] Lori Branch and Mark Knight, "Why the Postsecular Matters: Literary Studies and the Rise of the Novel," *Christianity and Literature* 67, no. 3 (2018): 502, 500.

and Knight identify in MacDonald's work, resistant to the fixed correspondences of allegory, underlies the contrast Amanda B. Vernon draws between Tractarian religious formalism and MacDonald's belief "that particular religious forms were temporary means by which a person related to God and which, with the passing of time, would almost inevitably be outgrown," a belief which underwrites a quasi-Symbolist faith in poetry as an immediate, if momentary, revelation of the divine.[19] Steven Sprott's Ruskinian approach to MacDonald also points in the direction of the aesthetics of the Symbolist movement, by drawing attention to the open-ended interaction between "the memory of Gothic architecture" and "MacDonald's depictions of God's creation," in which "it is not only that our perceptions of nature affect our architecture, but that our architecture in turn affects our perception of nature."[20] The way in which "the human mind alters what it perceives" makes even our perceptions of external nature essentially personal.[21]

In later nineteenth-century thinking, the very category of the "personal" carries a theological charge, invoking the theological "personhood" or "personality" of Jesus himself[22] in a way that anticipates existentialism (a theological movement before it became a secular philosophy).[23] The "personal knowledge"[24] of which MacDonald and his fictional characters are in quest is thus fundamentally an incarnational, or embodied, meaning. In a nineteenth-century intellectual context, to refer to the body as an intellectual paradigm is to invoke a strong tradition of vitalist thought, which informs not only Romantic thinking about the symbol, but also most nineteenth-century medicine (insofar, at least, as it is

---

[19] Amanda B. Vernon, "A Form of (Spiritual) Knowing: Word-Music and the Verticality of Prayer in George MacDonald," *Victorian Review: An Interdisciplinary Journal of Victorian Studies* 47, no. 2 (2021): 283, 286.
[20] Steven Sprott, "The Architectural Psyche in the Works of George MacDonald and John Ruskin," *North Wind: A Journal of George MacDonald Studies* 39 (2020): 24.
[21] Sprott, "The Architectural Psyche," 24.
[22] Cf. Hilton, *The Age of Atonement*, 285.
[23] Although the theological existentialism of Kierkegaard was not widely available in English before the twentieth century, M. G. Piety notes that MacDonald could have encountered it in German during the 1870s, commenting that "MacDonald's thought is remarkably similar to Kierkegaard's." M. G. Piety, "Kierkegaard's Early Reception in Germany," Piety on Kierkegaard, June 22, 2022, https://www.pietyonkierkegaard.com/2022/06/22/kierkegaards-early-reception-in-germany/. An even more likely influence is the proto-existentialist German religious thinker, and contemporary of Kant, J. G. Hamann, whose rejection of systematic philosophizing in favor of more literary modes of writing is likely to have appealed to MacDonald. Hamann, as Walter Lowrie notes, was "the only author by whom S. K. [Kierkegaard] was profoundly influenced," Walter Lowrie, *Kierkegaard*, 2 vols. (New York: Harper & Brothers, 1962), 1:164.
[24] Michael Polanyi, *Personal Knowledge: Towards Post-Critical Philosophy* (London: Routledge and Kegan Paul, 1962), vii–viii.

part of the period's general culture).[25] In this context, the consumptive illness which MacDonald shared with his character Diamond in *At the Back of the North Wind*, and which necessitated his residence in Italy for the last two decades of his life,[26] becomes connected to his literary production in a way which links it to the thematics of the Decadent movement.[27]

The way in which MacDonald's theological emphasis on the personal entails a focus on embodiment can be seen in Danielle E. Price's reading of "The Light Princess" in terms of disability. Citing the work of Patrick McDonagh, Price notes that "that women with cognitive impairments or mental illness were represented not only as having "a threatening sexuality which was either controlled or absent in 'normal' women," but also "as sexual innocents," a tendency which, as she observes, pushes to the limit "the seeming contradiction—woman as whore or virgin—which runs through much mid-century Victorian literature and art."[28] The "curse" of disability[29] positions the princess outside the norms of her society, meaning that the prince who seeks her hand can only relate to her on a personal and embodied level, by taking her swimming (it may be relevant that swimming was something commonly done naked by men in the Victorian period, though MacDonald's narrative does not emphasize this). In chapter four of this volume on the critique of social Darwinism implied by MacDonald's challenge to "the negatively weighted associations of darkness and depravity with women, people of color, those who are poor, disabled, struggling with addiction, and/or with violations of the law,"[30] Dearborn suggests political implications to this linkage of embodiment and a theology of the personal in MacDonald's work.

---

[25] I have explored this relationship at length in Gavin Budge, *Romanticism, Medicine and the Natural Supernatural: Transcendent Vision and Bodily Spectres, 1789–1852* (Basingstoke: Palgrave, 2013).

[26] Rolland Hein, *George MacDonald: Victorian Mythmaker* (Whitethorn, CA: Johannesen, 1999), 439.

[27] Cf. the emphasis on the unhealthiness of decadent literature in Arthur Symons, "The Decadent Movement in Literature," in *Aesthetes and Decadents of the 1890s*, ed. Karl Beckson (Chicago: Academy Publishers Chicago, 1993), 135–6. I discuss the relationship between literary Decadence and medical ideas in *Romanticism, Medicine and the Natural Supernatural*, 199.

[28] Danielle E. Price, "'This Effect Defective Comes by Cause': Disability and George MacDonald's *The Light Princess*," *The Lion and the Unicorn: A Critical Journal of Children's Literature* 43, no. 1 (2019): 3.

[29] Price, "Disability and *The Light Princess*," 6.

[30] Kerry Dearborn, "Rethinking the Dark Side," Chapter Four.

Personal Authenticity and the Existential Focus of Scottish Common Sense Philosophy

In her 2006 monograph, *Baptized Imagination: The Theology of George MacDonald*, Dearborn emphasizes the important role played by personal authenticity in MacDonald's conception of theology:

> For MacDonald, the business of the theologian is first to *be* true, that one may be able to speak the truth. A central conviction was that one's vision of the truth becomes clearer as one becomes increasingly true in one's own being. The character of the theologian and the character of theology are thus interdependent. [...] Much of his own credibility theologically is based on his own *trueness* as a person, and the reality of his life, which, like his theology, was not based on refractions of the truth, but focused primarily on the source of Truth.[31]

Dearborn describes the conviction that the ability to communicate religious truth is fundamentally ontological in its demands for a personal truth of character as characteristic of MacDonald. Although Dearborn situates MacDonald's thinking primarily in a German context (albeit one mediated by Coleridge), I would argue that the ontological emphasis which leads to the primacy of incarnation in his theology is just as much a product of his Scottish university education, dominated as it was by the Common Sense school of Reid and Stewart.[32] The essentially Scottish nature of MacDonald's interests is suggested by comparison with the Calvinist religious satire of the slightly earlier Scottish writer James Hogg's *Confessions of a Justified Sinner*, which could be seen as an exercise in taking to its logical conclusion the opposite theological pole, of an insistence on the all-sufficiency of Atonement (for the elect) which does not require an authentic personal commitment. The conviction of Hogg's Robert Wringhim that he is one of the elect leads him to become the prey of a plausible character who is well able to spout theological justifications of the crimes Wringhim is led to commit (and whom the narrative hints is the Devil himself), with the eventual disintegration of his personal identity through moments late on in the narrative when Wringham, as the first-person narrator, wakes to discover he has apparently committed crimes of which he is completely unaware.[33]

Where Dearborn's emphasis on the influence of Coleridge on MacDonald is very valuable, however, is the way it brings out Coleridge's role in formulating the

---

[31] Kerry Dearborn, *Baptized Imagination: The Theology of George MacDonald* (Aldershot: Ashgate, 2006), 22.

[32] For Reid's protest against philosophical neglect of the ontological dimension of human experience, see Reid, *Works*, 109.

[33] James Hogg, *The Private Memoirs and Confessions of a Justified Sinner* (Ware: Wordsworth Classics, 2003), 119–26.

principle of "polarity" as way of negotiating the relationship between the personal and the divine,[34] something which offers to resolve a fundamental aporia in the Scottish philosophical heritage, divided as it is between Thomas Reid and his successors, and the skepticism of David Hume. The nature of this aporia, and its relationship to the category of the personal, is suggested by the early nineteenth-century Scottish philosopher Thomas Brown's conversational remark, in response to a comment that Reid and Hume "differed more in words than in opinion," observing that "Reid bawled out, We must believe an outward world; but added in a whisper, We can give no reason for our belief. Hume cries out, We can give no reason for such a notion; and whispers, I own we cannot get rid of it."[35] Brown later elaborated an influential philosophical account of the nature of causality in response to the impasse between the philosophical outlooks of Reid and Hume which his remark identifies.[36]

Reid's critique of Hume, in which he was followed by members of the Common Sense school, such as James Beattie and James Oswald, addressing a more popular audience, hinged on the question of the philosopher's personal relationship to their own philosophy. Reid argued that the impossibility of a philosopher such as Hume actually acting on the radically skeptical conclusions of their own philosophy, about the lack of evidence of existence of an external world, showed that there was something fundamentally flawed about the nature of the philosophical posture they had chosen to adopt.[37] For Hume, on the other hand, the impossibility of putting the conclusions of philosophy into practice authorized a radical skepticism about the sufficiency of human reason itself.[38] MacDonald would have been made familiar with Common Sense philosophy and its critique of Hume through his Scottish university education, and recognizably echoes its language in *At the Back of the North Wind*, whose narrator comments that Diamond "was a true child in this, that he was given to metaphysics."[39]

Common Sense philosophy rejects philosophical "system" in favor of a focus on the individual's existential response to perception.[40] Both Reid and

[34] Dearborn, *Baptized Imagination*, 30.
[35] Galen Strawson, "What's So Good About Reid?," *London Review of Books* 12, no. 4 (Feb. 1990): 6.
[36] Thomas Brown, *Inquiry into the Relation of Cause and Effect*, 3rd ed. (Edinburgh: Constable, 1818).
[37] Reid, *Works*, 444–6.
[38] Hume famously claimed, for example, that "reason is, and ought only to be the slave of the passions." Hume, *A Treatise of Human Nature*, 415.
[39] George MacDonald, *At the Back of the North Wind* (London: Strahan, 1871), 83. Beattie denounces metaphysics as "puerile," i.e. childish. Beattie, *Essay on Truth*, 408.
[40] For representative denunciations of the influence of "system" in philosophy, see Reid, *Works*, 474–5; Beattie, *Essay on Truth*, 307–8. Reid contrasts the philosophical "debate about the existence of a material world" with "the belief of a material world" which, he notes, is

Hume, however, have a problem with the category of the personal. In Reid's case, this is because his Berkeleyan account of perception as an intuitive response to divinely-instituted signs does not allow any interval between the individual mind and the mind of God himself.[41] Hume's associationist account of knowledge, on the other hand, threatens to dissolve the individual mind into the universe. Dearborn's emphasis on Coleridge's "stereoscopic" view of language, as holding in tension the transcendence of the divine with the immanence of "relationships, community and culture,"[42] suggests a way of holding these two philosophical perspectives in tension, without seeking to resolve their competing claims, an intellectual strategy that allows epistemological space for the category of the personal to be articulated.

The Category of the Personal in MacDonald's Fiction

The fundamental importance in MacDonald's thinking of the personal (as inflected by theological overtones of Jesus' incarnational "personality") is reflected in a particularly striking image in his late work *Lilith*. The passage is well summarized by Dearborn:

> Vane sees a dimly lit hall filled with dancers "gorgeously dressed and gracefully robed," many with beautiful, flowing locks of hair, but none of whom has a human face. Instead, they have only skull fronts, with lidless living eyes, and are unable to speak or to smile. Thus Vane inquires: "Had they used their faces, not for communication, not to utter thought and feeling, not to share existence with their neighbors, but to appear what they wished to appear, and conceal what they were? and, having made their faces masks, were they therefore deprived of those masks, and condemned to go without faces until they repented?"[43]

Dearborn links this image of the face as a dead skull front to T. S. Eliot's emphasis in "The Love Song of J. Alfred Prufrock" on the intolerable burden of having to "prepare a face to meet the faces that you meet,"[44] in a way which testifies to the existentialist resonance of MacDonald's fantasy. The refusal of personal authenticity represented by the conventionality of polite "society" which was satirized around the same time by Oscar Wilde in *The Importance of Being Earnest*, is graphically imaged by MacDonald as the reduction of the living face to the dead skull. MacDonald's emphasis on the expression of individual

---

"older, and of more authority, than any principles of philosophy." Reid, *Works*, 127.
[41] Reid, following Berkeley, describes "the visible appearance of objects" as "a kind of language used by nature, to inform us of their distance, magnitude and figure," with perception being comparable to a direct revelation from God. Reid, *Works*, 134–5.
[42] Dearborn, *Baptized Imagination*, 32.
[43] Dearborn, *Baptized Imagination*, 121.
[44] Dearborn, *Baptized Imagination*, 146, fn.193

personality as so fundamental to the divine endowment of human beings with faces that the suppression of personality means they might as well not have faces at all witnesses to the vitalist roots of his insistence on the personal. MacDonald's image is interestingly referenced in the title of *Till We Have Faces*, the late retelling of the Cupid and Psyche myth by C. S. Lewis, another twentieth-century writer who was significantly influenced by MacDonald's work.

MacDonald's emphasis on the fundamental importance of the personal to any meaningful engagement with social problems appears in an episode of his well-known children's book *At the Back of the North Wind*, which centers on a groom and his wife's ailing young boy Diamond, whose extreme naïvety doubles in the narrative as exceptional spiritual insight. Diamond is a kind of Wordsworthian child,[45] whose ambiguous status between visionary religious seer and unworldly fool is conveyed by MacDonald's comment that because Diamond's face is "so quiet and sweet" his father's fellow stablemen regard him as not "all there, meaning that he was half an idiot, whereas he was a great deal more there than they had the sense to see."[46]

Diamond's visionary tendencies have been rendered particularly acute through a bout of near-fatal illness, figured in the narrative as an extended visit to a supernatural country without a sun but lit by "a certain still rayless light,"[47] to which he has been taken by the supernatural character North Wind, who, at a literal level, is the draught which blows through a chink in the hay-loft where he sleeps and which is responsible for the consumption of which he dies at the end of the book. In the mews where the family end up living after his father loses his regular job as a coachman, Diamond is woken by an argument he hears though the wall, between a "drunken cabman" and his wife, which ends with "a cry from the woman, and then a scream from the baby."[48] Diamond goes to investigate, guided by "the voice of the crying baby," to find a scene which could be a melodramatic tableau:

> There, leaning back in a chair, with his arms hanging down by his sides, and his legs stretched out before him and supported on his heels, sat the drunken cabman. His wife lay in her clothes upon the bed, sobbing, and the baby was wailing in the cradle. It was very miserable altogether.[49]

Diamond's personal and practical engagement with the misery which surrounds the cabman by attending to the baby is presented by MacDonald as a providential

---

[45] Cf. Robert A. Davis, "Brilliance of a Fire: Innocence, Experience and the Theory of Childhood," *Journal of Philosophy of Education* 45, no. 2 (2011): 390–1.
[46] MacDonald, *At the Back of the North Wind*, 166.
[47] MacDonald, *At the Back of the North Wind*, 115. This phrase echoes Rev. 22:5.
[48] MacDonald, *At the Back of the North Wind*, 177.
[49] MacDonald, *At the Back of the North Wind*, 178.

intervention which makes him "one of God's messengers."⁵⁰ The narrator contrasts Diamond's response with the stereotypical Evangelical approach of merely lecturing the cabman and his wife about their behavior, and leaving religious tracts ("ill-bred though well-meant shabby little books"), an approach which would have been ineffectual because it doesn't engage with the couple's personal circumstances.⁵¹ Diamond's active intervention by dandling the baby is shown as allowing space for the cabman to become conscious of a divine intuition within himself (reflecting MacDonald's incarnational theology), namely "that great Love [which] speaks in the most wretched and dirty hearts," which he experiences as the "misery" of remorse.⁵² The cabman overhears Diamond prattling to the baby about the "thirsty devil creeps into a man's inside when he takes a drink," and how that "devil is always crying out for more drink, and that makes the man thirsty, and so he drinks more and more, till he kills himself with it." This message about alcoholism, as MacDonald presents it, is more effective than all the temperance tracts in the world because Diamond is wholly unconscious of giving it (Diamond prattles to the baby because "he thought the cabman was asleep").⁵³ The cabman is all the more struck by what Diamond says because he doesn't recognize him, and half thinks he is an angel, although his wife in their subsequent dialogue puts him straight. Nevertheless, he starts trying to avoid "the public-house" and "is never quite so bad after that," although MacDonald realistically notes that "it was some time before he really began to reform," something MacDonald blames on the fact that "a certain rich brewer had built [... a public-house] like a trap to catch souls and bodies in, at almost every corner he had to pass on his way home."⁵⁴

MacDonald's insistence on the personal dimension as essential to any kind of religious action or significance can be traced back to Coleridge's criticism of Evangelical doctrines of plenary inspiration as emptying the Bible of any of its authors' personal meaning, reducing it, in Coleridge's words, to "a colossal Memnon's head, a hollow passage for a Voice, a Voice that mocks the voices of many men, and speaks in their names, and yet is but one voice and the same—'and no man uttered it, and never in a human heart was it conceived.'"⁵⁵ For Coleridge, the removal of the biblical text from the embodied context of its human authors'

---

⁵⁰ MacDonald, *At the Back of the North Wind*, 179.
⁵¹ MacDonald, *At the Back of the North Wind*, 179.
⁵² MacDonald, *At the Back of the North Wind*, 180.
⁵³ MacDonald, *At the Back of the North Wind*, 182, 181.
⁵⁴ MacDonald, *At the Back of the North Wind*, 184.
⁵⁵ S. T. Coleridge, *Shorter Works and Fragments*, 2 vols., H. J. Jackson and J. R. de J. Jackson, eds. (London and Princeton: Routledge and Princeton University Press, 1995), 1134. I discuss this passage at greater length in *Romanticism, Medicine and the Natural Supernatural*, 82.

life fundamentally denatures it, turning it into a blasphemous parody of itself due to its being conceived of as divorced from individual personality.[56]

MacDonald makes a similar point about the essential embodiedness, and hence personality, of any religious response to the world when he emphasizes the "altogether human" duty of "the imagination of man [...] the duty, namely, which springs from his immediate relation to the Father, that of following and finding out the divine imagination in whose image it was made."[57] The echo here of Coleridge's well-known definition in the *Biographia Literaria* of the human imagination as a "secondary" repetition of "the infinite I AM"[58] suggests the fundamentally incarnational nature of the imagination in finding ways to embody divine immateriality within the finitude of nature.

The Incarnational Focus and Refusal of Theological Totalization in MacDonald's Fiction

Timothy Larsen has recently drawn attention to the way MacDonald's writing participates in the "new spiritual sensibility" represented by the "generational" shift in the mid nineteenth century from the "Age of Atonement" to the "Age of Incarnation."[59] Larsen's argument draws on Boyd Hilton's pioneering 1988 study *The Age of Atonement: the Influence of Evangelicalism on Social and Economic Thought, 1795–1865*, which explores the shift away, in the mid-nineteenth century, from the kind of abstract and transactional perspective represented by substitutionary theological accounts of the Atonement (in which Christ's death on the cross pays humanity's "debt" to God incurred by sin) in favor of a new emphasis on the fundamentally personal nature of an authentic relationship with God.

Larsen notes that this mid-nineteenth-century incarnational theology is accompanied by a new emphasis on the celebration of a family Christmas, a practice which at the time the extensive MacDonald family were regarded as unusual for prioritizing.[60] For Larsen, this incarnational theology explains why the celebration of Christmas is so key to MacDonald's novel *Adela Cathcart*, whose

---

[56] The consistency of Coleridge's interest in the embodied nature of religious meaning can be seen in his jokey reference in the *Biographia Literaria* to the "most censurable application" he made as a young man of the phrase from Isaiah "the noise of my bowels shall sound as an harp," Coleridge, *Biographia Literaria*, 1:184.

[57] George MacDonald, "The Imagination: Its Functions and Its Culture," in *Orts: Chiefly Papers on the Imagination and Shakspere* (London: Sampson Low, Marston, Searle & Rivington, 1882), 10.

[58] Coleridge, *Biographia Literaria*, 1:304.

[59] Timothy Larsen, *George MacDonald in the Age of Miracles* (Downers Grove, IL: IVP Academic, 2018), 18.

[60] Larsen, *George MacDonald in the Age of Miracles*, 22.

structure, in the manner of Boccaccio's *Decameron*, revolves around a revival of the "Christmas-time [...] season for story-telling"[61] by the genial elderly bachelor (somewhat anonymously named John Smith),[62] who is the novel's narrator, and, as the novel's opening makes clear, a great enthusiast for Christmas celebrations, giving the typological justification that "it is the Christmas feast that justifies all feasts, as the bread and wine of the communion are the essence of all bread and wine, of all strength and rejoicing."[63]

As Charles Beaucham comments, from the incarnational perspective, which MacDonald shares with F. D. Maurice, the material world is not a pale shadow of "the transcendental realm of ideal forms," as it would be in a conventional Platonic view, but holds the potential to be a "revelatory embodiment" of the supernatural.[64] Widely held nineteenth-century ideas deriving from Brunonian medicine complement this incarnational view of the supernatural by supplying a disconcertingly literal explanation for why Christmas feasting finds a naturally appropriate accompaniment in story-telling, and particularly in tales of the supernatural. Although these medical ideas circulated generally in nineteenth-century culture,[65] MacDonald can reasonably be assumed to have been particularly aware of them, given his early interest in studying electro-biology[66] and their relevance to the consumption from which he and his family suffered.[67]

Brunonian medicine, which, as systematized by the famous doctor Erasmus Darwin, was an important influence on Coleridge, had a monistic conception of the relationship between body and mind in which disease itself could be understood as consequence of disordered associations between ideas (themselves regarded as ultimately constituted by material bodily states).[68] Seeing ghosts and visions, in this Brunonian view, represented an important symptom of such a disordered state of association (which naturally, of course, accompanied the delirium of fever).[69] A less extreme visionary state, however, could also be induced by indigestion, in which the stomach's laboring to assimilate food diverted

---

[61] George MacDonald, *Adela Cathcart*, 3 vols. (London: Hurst and Blackett, 1864), 1:119.
[62] The narrator comments that he does "not want to be distinguished from other people" and so does not feel his name to be "a hardship." MacDonald, *Adela Cathcart*, 1:10.
[63] MacDonald, *Adela Cathcart*, 1:12.
[64] Charles Beaucham, "*Phantastes* as Theological Critique of Hoffmann's The Golden Pot," *North Wind: A Journal of George MacDonald Studies* 38 (2019): 102, 104.
[65] I have explored the presence of ideas derived from Brunonian medicine in a wide variety of nineteenth-century cultural contexts in my study *Romanticism, Medicine and the Natural Supernatural*.
[66] Manlove, "The Electromagnetic World of George MacDonald's Visionary Romances," 144.
[67] Budge, *Romanticism, Medicine and the Natural Supernatural*, 59–60.
[68] Budge, *Romanticism, Medicine and the Natural Supernatural*, 51–5.
[69] Budge, *Romanticism, Medicine and the Natural Supernatural*, 16–17.

bodily vitality which would ordinarily be monopolized by the brain in its usual operation of quantitatively weighing the distinction between the stronger ideas excited by external perceptions and the weaker ideas excited by association.[70] Without its usual resources of vitality to draw on, the brain, for Darwin, found it hard to distinguish between externally induced ideas and the internal ideas of association. The wide cultural currency of this medical explanation of ghost-seeing is indicated by its use by Dickens at the beginning of "A Christmas Carol," where Scrooge dismisses his vision of Marley's face in the doorknocker as down to "an undigested bit of beef."[71]

From the Brunonian medical perspective, Christmas feasting provides the perfect context for tales of the supernatural (and other narratives) to make a vivid impression, given that the brain's energies will in any case be diverted from their immediate sensory context by the process of digestion. Although Erasmus Darwin himself was a materialist (and very probably an atheist), his Brunonian monism did not necessarily have to be interpreted materialistically, as the example of Coleridge shows.[72] The materialization of the spiritual implied by Brunonianism could equally well be interpreted as a spiritualization of the material, a fundamental ambiguity which is central to the Romantic discourse of the imagination.[73]

The new liminality of the relationship between the spiritual and the material in the nineteenth century, and its relationship to narrative, can be illustrated by the project of publishing lives of the saints pursued by John Henry Newman and other Tractarians in the 1840s,[74] where traditional Protestant objections to the legendary and non-factual status of many such lives become irrelevant in the face of a typological conception of truth. The events recounted in the saint's life may not actually have happened, but typologically they stand for an eternal religious truth of which the saint has become the local embodiment through an accumulative process of association.[75] In the context of nineteenth-century ideas about digestion I have been discussing, it may be relevant that, in a monastic context, such saints' lives were often read at meals. Certainly, regarded

---

[70] Budge, *Romanticism, Medicine and the Natural Supernatural*, 86–8, 103–6.
[71] Charles Dickens, "A Christmas Carol," in *Christmas Books*, vol. 1, ed. Michael Slater (Harmondsworth: Penguin, 1971), 59.
[72] Budge, *Romanticism, Medicine and the Natural Supernatural*, 86–7.
[73] Budge, *Romanticism, Medicine and the Natural Supernatural*, 97–101.
[74] Elizabeth MacFarlane, "John Henry Newman's *Lives of the English Saints*," in *Making and Remaking Saints in Nineteenth-Century Britain*, ed. Gareth Atkins (Manchester: Manchester University Press, 2016), 245–61.
[75] J. A. Froude, "Introduction to the Life of St. Neot," in *The Mind of The Oxford Movement*, ed. Owen Chadwick (London: Adam and Charles Black, 1960), 173.

as a typological narrative, the saint's life provides an easy way for its audience to assimilate Christian doctrine.

The Tractarians' relaxed acceptance of the legendary nature of saints' lives parallels the "light touch," which Gabelman identifies as characterizing MacDonald's understanding of the genre of the fairy tale, in which the author is unable "to control meanings because 'there is layer upon layer of ascending significance.'"[76] Gabelman convincingly characterizes MacDonald's playful conception of fairy tales as, from the point of view of its attitude toward authorial intentionality, post-structuralist *avant la lettre*.[77] He draws a contrast between the way in which MacDonald's fairy tales, "by signaling the inadequacy of their own representations [...] simultaneously point toward and attempt to keep open their connection to vital energies beyond themselves," with the attempt of other Victorians such as George Cruikshank to write fairy tales which would, like the children's stories of Maria Edgeworth, Sarah Trimmer, and Anna Barbauld, "teach moral lessons that grounded children in reality."[78] As Gabelman shows, other Victorians such as Dickens and Ruskin were aware that such attempts to exert authorial control over the signification of fairy tales result in the lifelessness of allegory.[79] In contrast, within what I would describe as MacDonald's typological approach (an approach to interpretation which has a very long history in Biblical hermeneutics), the ultimate significance of a narrative is regarded as providentially determined in a way which transcends the intention of an individual author, without giving up on the possibility of an ascertainable meaning altogether.[80]

In suggesting that the refusal of a totalizing approach to meaning which Gabelman identifies as underlying MacDonald's resort to the fairy tale form aligns his work with a typological mode of writing,[81] I have in mind the prominent role a typological conception of poetic meaning plays in the thinking of John Keble, not only a leading light of the Tractarian revolt against the institutionalized Protestantism of the early nineteenth-century Church of England, but also one of the most prominent poets of the mid-nineteenth century. In his lengthy Tract 89, *On the Mysticism attributed to the Early Fathers of the Church*, Keble argues that the divine inspiration of the Bible renders any "metaphor and similitude"

---

[76] Gabelman, *Divine Carelessness and Fairytale Levity*, 97. Gabelman is quoting from MacDonald's *A Dish of Orts*.
[77] I present a similar characterization of the narrative technique of the Victorian novelist Charlotte M. Yonge in my *Yonge*, 19. As Gabelman argues in *Divine Carelessness and Fairytale Levity*, this theologically motivated "postmodern" playfulness reflects a wider theological understanding of the universe as providentially ordered, 49.
[78] Gabelman, *Divine Carelessness and Fairytale Levity*, 97, 86.
[79] Gabelman, *Divine Carelessness and Fairytale Levity*, 85–6.
[80] Budge, *Yonge*, 65–7.
[81] Gabelman, *Divine Carelessness and Fairytale Levity*, 97.

employed in it potentially a gateway into the mind of God himself, removing it from "the number of ordinary figures of speech and resources of language," so that it "partakes thenceforth of the nature of a Type."[82] As Keble emphasizes, "the Author of Scripture is the Author of Nature," so that, regarded from a religious point of view, any figural expression appearing in the Bible may be considered to have a potentially privileged access to the very nature of reality itself.[83]

The connection between MacDonald's opposition to totalizing forms of theology, which presume to speak for God himself, and his privileging of the localized mode of signification of the divine represented by typology, is revealed in his collection of *Unspoken Sermons*. MacDonald insists on the necessarily "partial" nature of all divine revelation implicit in communication from "the infinite God" to a finite creature, noting that "a more partial revelation might be truer than that would be which constituted a fuller revelation to one in a higher condition; for the former might reveal much to him, the latter might reveal nothing."[84] Divine revelation is necessarily incomplete in a way that must condescend to the limited capacity of mortals to take it in, because anything more adequate runs the risk of overwhelming the human mind and so of actually communicating nothing. MacDonald applies this hermeneutic position to the words of Jesus himself, who, he notes, "had no design of constructing a system of truth in intellectual forms," being concerned solely with "the truth of the moment in its relation to him," since "he spoke out of a region of realities which he knew could only be suggested—not represented—in the forms of intellect and speech."[85] The divine reality which Jesus, as the incarnate Son of God, inhabited, can only be conveyed through the incomplete and fragmentary suggestions of typology, rather than anything more systematic.

Typology and Incarnation in MacDonald's Fiction:
The Therapeutic Function of Narrative

MacDonald's narrative deployment of a typological mode of signification is intimately connected to the incarnational emphasis of his theology, in that incarnation implies that the divine has scandalously been incorporated within creaturely limitation, rendering that very limitation somehow numinous and infinite. In *Adela Cathcart*, the insistent physicality of the clergyman with whom the narrator, on his way to spend Christmas with his friend Colonel Cathcart, shares a railway carriage, represents this kind of incarnational paradox. The

---

[82] John Keble, *On the Mysticism Attributed to the Early Fathers of the Church* in *Aesthetics and Religion in Nineteenth-Century Britain*, 6 vols., ed. Gavin Budge (Bristol: Thoemmes, 2003), 3:170.
[83] Keble, *Tract 89*, 169.
[84] George MacDonald, "The Consuming Fire," in *Unspoken Sermons*, 35.
[85] MacDonald, "It Shall Not Be Forgiven," 66–7.

narrator finds that this clergyman's face does not "fit into the clerical mould which I had all ready in my own mind for it," as it is "at all events, the face of a man, in spite of waistcoat and depilation."[86] This unstereotypically manly figure turns out to be the new curate in the small town where Colonel Cathcart lives. He gives a Christmas Day sermon which is inserted wholesale into the narrative, and is strikingly typological in its rhetoric (it was later expanded and rewritten in MacDonald's first collection of *Unspoken Sermons*).[87] In this sermon the curate urges members of the congregation, using highly rhetorical epistrophic repetition, to "become a child" in their celebration of "this blessed birth-time."[88]

As MacDonald comments in another of his *Unspoken Sermons*, what, in the context of religious faith, becoming a "child" means is not limiting your belief to the explicit textual meaning of Scripture, but believing in the truth of God's "Being."[89] This view of the nature of a truly religious belief can be regarded as an existential rationale for adopting a typological perspective, as, for MacDonald, the child's belief is always exceeding the strict limits of Scripture through "some outburst of unusual feeling, some scintillation of a lively hope, some wide-reaching imagination that draws into the circle of religious theory the world of nature, and the yet wider world of humanity."[90] The typological impulse is a way out of what MacDonald elsewhere in the *Unspoken Sermons* calls "the dungeon of self," in which man's "consciousness" is isolated from the interpersonal "spiritual region" to which "God, his friends, his neighbors, his brothers all" belong.[91]

As MacDonald's emphasis on the legitimate role of imagination in religious belief suggests, his attitude here is akin to Wordsworth's complaint in *The Prelude* that the "modern system" of education leaves the child imprisoned "within the pinfold of his own conceit," a harmful effect Wordsworth contrasts with that of traditional fairy tales from which the child at least reaps "one previous gain, that he forgets himself."[92] Wordsworth's description of such a child as characterized by "unnatural growth"[93] suggests the fundamental unhealthiness of this self-regarding mental state.[94] The malaise Wordsworth identifies is paralleled in MacDonald's *Adela Cathcart* by the listless condition in which the narrator finds

---

[86] MacDonald, *Adela Cathcart*, 1:4.
[87] George MacDonald, "The Child in the Midst," in *Unspoken Sermons*, 1–26.
[88] MacDonald, *Adela Cathcart*, 1:40.
[89] George MacDonald, "The Higher Faith," in *Unspoken Sermons*, 50–1, 59.
[90] MacDonald, "The Higher Faith," 50.
[91] George MacDonald, "Love Thy Neighbour," in *Unspoken Sermons*, 214–15.
[92] William Wordsworth, *The Prelude* (1850 version), Book Fifth, ll. 295, 336, 346, in *The Prelude 1799, 1805, 1850*, eds., Jonathan Wordsworth, M. H. Abrams, and Stephen Gill (New York and London: Norton, 1979), 171.
[93] Wordsworth, *The Prelude* (1850 version), Book Fifth, l. 328, 171.
[94] I explore Wordsworth's preoccupation with healthy and diseased states of mind at length in *Romanticism, Medicine and the Natural Supernatural*, 67–69.

Colonel Cathcart's daughter, the eponymous Adela, who confides to him that her "overpowering sense of blackness and misery" leads her to "wake wretched every morning" and be "crowded with wretched, if not wicked, thoughts, all day."[95] MacDonald's novel enacts Adela's cure from this dangerous condition of moral wretchedness through the recuperative power of narrative itself. Adela's cure through the power of narrative reflects not only the monistic Brunonian conception of both physical and mental disease as the product of disordered associations but also the incarnational theological perspective suggested by the curate's exhortation in his sermon, slightly earlier in the same chapter (as a remedy for the inevitable corruptions of age and experience) to "take the child Jesus to your bosoms, into your very souls, and let him grow there till he is one with your every thought, and purpose, and hope."[96]

The curate, unusually middle-aged for this early stage in a clerical career, turns out to be the older brother of a new doctor trying to build up a practice in the area, whom Colonel Cathcart is advised to consult over the established Dr. Wade about the treatment of his daughter Adela for her mysterious longstanding illness.[97] Having been invited to dinner on a Saturday night, and observed Adela at home, the doctor, Henry Armstrong, discusses her with Colonel Cathcart before church on Sunday, remarking "I have seen such a case before. There are a good many of them amongst girls of her age. It is as if, without any disease, life were gradually withdrawing itself,—ebbing back as it were to its source. Whether this has a physical or psychological cause, it is impossible to tell."[98] He adds that "the best thing that can be done for her is, to interest her in something, if possible,—no matter what it is."[99]

As the doctor's reference to "girls of her age" suggests, Adela's decline, in the context of the Brunonian paradigm that dominated medical thinking in the mid-nineteenth century, is linked to the onset of menstruation, regarded as an intensely demanding physical process which drains the body of its stores of vitality and so potentially the cause of a morbid condition of understimulation (sthenia) unless counteracted by outside stimulus.[100] Interesting her in something would supply such a stimulus, a suggestion that is eagerly taken up by the narrator who suggests the plan of "telling her stories" as a way of encouraging "the tide of life

---

[95] MacDonald, *Adela Cathcart*, 1:53–54.
[96] MacDonald, *Adela Cathcart*, 1:42–43.
[97] MacDonald, *Adela Cathcart*, 1:63–65.
[98] MacDonald, *Adela Cathcart*, 1:107.
[99] MacDonald, *Adela Cathcart*, 1:107.
[100] The influence of Brunonian medicine on nineteenth-century literature is discussed extensively in *Romanticism, Medicine and the Natural Supernatural*, see especially 56.

[...] to flow again."[101] In a private conversation with the narrator after church, the doctor is more explicit about his diagnosis:

> I feel I may say to you what I could not well say to the colonel—I suspect the cause of her illness is rather a spiritual one. She has evidently a strong mental constitution, and this strong frame, so to speak, has been fed upon slops, and an atrophy is the consequence. My hope in your plan is, partly, that it may furnish a better mental table for her for the time, and set her foraging in new directions for the future. [...] I watched everything about her; and interpreted it by what I know about women. I believe that many of them go into a consumption just from discontent,—the righteous discontent of a soul which is meant to sit at the Father's table, and so cannot content itself with the husks which the swine eat. The theological nourishment which is offered them is generally no better than husks. They cannot live upon it, and so die and go home to their Father. And without good spiritual food to keep the spiritual senses healthy and true, they cannot see the things about them as they really are. They cannot find interest in them, because they cannot find their *own* place amongst them.[102]

Adela's active mind (her "strong mental constitution") has been starved by lack of education, and this, in the Brunonian model at which this description hints, has led to an understimulated condition, or "atrophy," in which her vital processes start to undermine her bodily health, threatening to send her into "a consumption."[103] The remedy of story-telling sessions which the narrator has proposed is regarded by the doctor as a suitable treatment, because, in Brunonian terms, it offers a mild stimulus which will gradually counteract the self-reinforcing downward spiral which Adela's health, both mental and physical, has taken.[104] In the narrator's later account of Adela's condition to her father, the parallel between physical and mental digestion which underpins this diagnosis is spelt out explicitly:

> Adela is in a kind of moral atrophy, for she cannot digest the food provided for her, so as to get any good of it. Suppose a patient, in a corresponding physical condition, should show a relish for anything proposed to him, would you not take it for a sign that that was just the thing to do him good? And we may accept the interest Adela shows in any kind of mental pabulum provided for her, as an analogous sign. It corresponds to relish, and is a ground for expecting some benefit to follow,—in a word, some nourishment of the spiritual life. Relish may be called the digestion of the palate; interest, the digestion of the inner ears; both significant of further digestion to follow. The food thus relished may not be the best food; and yet it may be the best for the patient, because she feels no repugnance to it, and

---

[101] MacDonald, *Adela Cathcart*, 1:108.
[102] MacDonald, *Adela Cathcart*, 1:112–13.
[103] Budge, *Romanticism, Medicine and the Natural Supernatural*, 59–60.
[104] Cf. Budge, *Romanticism, Medicine and the Natural Supernatural*, 127.

can digest and assimilate, as well as swallow it.[105]

As I have argued elsewhere, the paradigm of digestion invoked by the narrator here, conceived as a process occurring both at a physical and a mental level, occupies a key role in Brunonian medical thinking, which doesn't separate mental and bodily processes.[106] At a theological level, this Brunonian monism can be regarded as literalizing the doctrine of incarnation: Christian teaching is "inwardly digested" (as Cranmer's collect puts it),[107] and manifests itself in the believer's life. Although the stories Adela is to be told are not themselves religious teaching, they can pique sufficient interest to raise her out of the boredom and indifference which prevent her assimilating the health-giving elements of daily life (which correspond on a mental level to the indigestion which prevents the body from benefiting from its food), acting as the kind of easily digestible pap, or "pabulum," which a doctor might prescribe for a patient who has suffered from a debilitating illness. Far from MacDonald's characterization of Adela's illness as "a manifestation of a spiritual problem" being "eccentric and dubious," as Larsen claims,[108] it is very much within the mainstream of nineteenth-century medical thinking, which was also prepared to assign a central role in the healing process to the imagination.[109]

Adela's "moral atrophy," as the narrator's words suggest, can be regarded as a kind of indigestion, in that it prevents her assimilating any "nourishment of the spiritual life." In Adela's case, general listlessness and low spirits suggest that her problem is caused by the understimulation which Brunonian medicine identified as responsible for many of the health problems of respectable nineteenth-century women.[110] The other pole of Brunonian medicine's radically simplified diagnostic continuum, however, was overstimulation ("sthenia"),[111] a diagnosis which can also be seen to inform MacDonald's incarnational theology through his narrative portrayal of religious hypocrisy.

MacDonald, of course, shares the theme of nineteenth-century Evangelicals' "hypocrisy" with other mid-Victorian novelists such as Dickens and Charlotte Brontë,[112] but in his case it is more explicitly linked to a person-centered

---

[105] MacDonald, *Adela Cathcart*, 1:236–37.
[106] Budge, *Romanticism, Medicine and the Natural Supernatural*, 84–6.
[107] "Collect for the Second Sunday in Advent, Book of Common Prayer," The Church of England, https://www.churchofengland.org/prayer-and-worship/worship-texts-and-resources/book-common-prayer/collects-epistles-and-gospels-2.
[108] Larsen, *George MacDonald in the Age of Miracles*, 106.
[109] Budge, *Romanticism, Medicine and the Natural Supernatural*, 62.
[110] Budge, *Romanticism, Medicine and the Natural Supernatural*, 126–7.
[111] Budge, *Romanticism, Medicine and the Natural Supernatural*, 31–2.
[112] Cf. the blackmailing Evangelical minister Mr. Chadband in Dickens' *Bleak House*, and the daughters of Mr. Brocklehurst, who arrive "splendidly attired in velvet, silk and furs"

theological emphasis on incarnation. Regarded in terms of Brunonian medicine, the religious ostentation of which Evangelicals were often regarded as guilty[113] can also be regarded as a kind of moral indigestion, in that it reflects a failure fully to incorporate religion within the practice of everyday life. It is, in other words, a failure in the incarnation of religious belief. The ambiguity with which the same underlying cause, a failure of assimilation (in this case of religious doctrine), can present either as a state of overstimulation (e.g. Evangelical bibliolatry) or of understimulation (such as Adela's religious indifference), and also alternate between the two states, is fundamental to the approach taken to diagnosis in Brunonian medicine.[114]

MacDonald's Vitalist Conception of Religious Truth and Satire of Bourgeois Individualism

From the Brunonian perspective, which I am suggesting underlies MacDonald's portrayal of religious belief, the feverish religious over-emphasis which led nineteenth-century Evangelicals to be accused of hypocrisy testifies to their failure to embody in their personal lives the religious teaching to which they are theoretically committed. In MacDonald's early bildungsroman *David Elginbrod*, for example, the novel's hero Hugh is taken on as tutor to the family of a well-to-do London grocer, who asks him to attend Sunday morning service at his Congregationalist chapel. MacDonald gives a vivid description of the sermon, in a way which reflects his own personal rejection of the role of a Congregationalist minister:

> It was in truth a strange, grotesque, and somewhat awful medley—not unlike a dance of Death, in which the painter has given here a lovely face, and there a beautiful arm or an exquisite foot, to the wild-prancing and exultant skeletons. But the parts of the sermon corresponding to the beautiful face or arm or foot, were but the fragments of Scripture, shining like gold amidst the worthless ore of the man's own production—worthless, save as gravel or chaff or husks have worth, in a world where dilution, and not always concentration, is necessary for healthfulness.[115]

In language which reveals MacDonald's Brunonian vitalist conception of religious truth, the only living parts of the sermon's "dance of Death" are the "fragments of Scripture" surrounded by the inorganic roughage of the minister's

---

immediately after he has inveighed against the naturally curly hair of one of the girls at Lowood School, Brontë, *Jane Eyre*, 67.
[113] John Foster, "On Some of the Causes by Which Evangelical Religion Has Been Rendered Less Acceptable to Persons of Cultivated Taste," in *Essays, in a Series of Letters to a Friend* (London: Longman, 1805), 125.
[114] Budge, *Romanticism, Medicine and the Natural Supernatural*, 56.
[115] George MacDonald, *David Elginbrod* (London: Hurst and Blackett, 1863), 3:100.

theological discourse, which Hugh's sympathetically portrayed pious landlady devoutly absorbs.[116] The sermon requires exceptionally tough mental digestion to be of any spiritual benefit. Hugh later goes back for Sunday lunch to the grocer's house in a newly-built crescent, where the dining-room is "full of what is called handsome furniture, in a high state of polish,"[117] a detail which is reminiscent of Wilkie Collins' emphasis on the "aching newness" of the furniture belonging to a somewhat similar *nouveau riche* family in his early sensation novel *Basil*.[118] The lack of wear on the furniture reflects not only the family's *parvenu* status, but also, more fundamentally, their conventionality and consequent lack of lived personal authenticity. As in Collins' novel, the newness of the furniture hints at an inability fully to assimilate the family's rapidly changed social status, which explains its members' pretentiousness and snobbery.

MacDonald's portrayal of the goblins in *The Princess and the Goblin* can be seen as a satire on the kind of Evangelical attitudes he depicts in the realist mode of his early bildungsroman. When Curdie, the book's youthful hero who can drive away the goblin hordes by extemporizing poetry,[119] is finally captured by the goblins, he overhears the goblin queen musing out loud:

> But [...] he is so troublesome. For poor creatures as they are, there is something about those sun-people that is *very* troublesome. I cannot imagine how it is that with such superior strength and skill and understanding as ours, we permit them to exist at all. Why do we not destroy them entirely, and use their cattle and grazing lands at our pleasure? Of course we don't want to live in their horrid country! It is far too glaring for our quieter and more refined tastes. But we might use it as a sort of outhouse, you know.[120]

MacDonald's parody of the language of gentility, in the queen's reference to the "quieter and more refined tastes" which prevent the goblins from inhabiting the world above ground, implicitly identifies the goblins with the *petit bourgeois* attitudes of the newly wealthy commercial middle class who feature in *David Elginbrod*. Early on in *The Princess and the Goblin*, MacDonald describes the goblins' recourse to living underground as a response to social restrictions that are reminiscent of those that had been imposed in Britain on religious Dissenters from the seventeenth to the early nineteenth centuries: "the king had laid what

---

[116] I have discussed the implications of the kind of digestive metaphor underlying this passage, and its connection with vitalism, at length in *Romanticism, Medicine and the Natural Supernatural*, 84–94.

[117] MacDonald, *David Elginbrod*, 3:106.

[118] I discuss this passage in *Romanticism, Medicine and the Natural Supernatural*, 191–2.

[119] George MacDonald, *The Princess and the Goblin* (New York: Routledge, 1871), 48–9, 56, 66.

[120] MacDonald, *The Princess and the Goblin*, 192–3.

they thought too severe taxes upon them, or had begun to treat them with more severity, in some way or other, and impose stricter laws."[121]

MacDonald's fairy tale can thus be seen to share a vein of social satire with H. G. Wells' *The Time Machine*, where the division between the decadent but graceful Eloi, who live above ground, and the vigorous but brutal Morlocks, who live underground (and, like MacDonald's goblins, as Curdie discovers when he overhears the queen of the goblins discussing what he would be like to eat,[122] dine on the other group's flesh), is an exaggerated version of late-nineteenth-century class relations between industrial workers and the rentier capitalists who benefit from their labor.[123] MacDonald's sympathies, however, lie closer to Matthew Arnold's aestheticist advocacy of Culture's "sweetness and light" as a way of maintaining social cohesion in the face of bourgeois Philistinism's emphasis on "doing as one likes,"[124] than to the early Wells' more starkly polarized vision of irreconcilable class conflict. In MacDonald's fable, the industrial working class are identifiable as the "household animals" kept by the goblins, whose underground life has led to "the various parts of their bodies assuming, in an apparently arbitrary and self-willed manner, the most abnormal developments."[125] The goblins' bourgeois individualism has here encouraged a disproportionate over-development of some capacities over others, which renders the animals "grotesque," a term which recalls Ruskin's account of aesthetic and social degeneration in *The Stones of Venice*.[126] The overground society to which Curdie and Princes Irene belong is, by contrast, organized along feudal lines, reflecting the Ruskinian characterization of medieval social organization as a truly human form of society in comparison to industrialism.[127]

In the sequel MacDonald wrote to his fairy tale, *The Princess and Curdie*, this satire on industrialist individualism is further developed in the portrayal of the city of Gwyntystorm which Curdie visits:

> The fortifications had been long neglected, for the whole country was now under one king, and all men said there was no more need for weapons or walls. No man pretended to love his neighbour, but everyone said he knew that peace and quiet behaviour was the best thing for himself, and that, he

---

[121] MacDonald, *The Princess and the Goblin*, 4.
[122] MacDonald, *The Princess and the Goblin*, 191.
[123] Michael R. Page, *The Literary Imagination from Erasmus Darwin to H. G. Wells: Science, Evolution, and Ecology* (Farnham: Ashgate, 2012), 165.
[124] Matthew Arnold, *Culture and Anarchy*, vol. 5, *Complete Prose Works*, 11 vols., ed. R. H. Super (Ann Arbor, MI: The University of Michigan Press, 1965), 117–23.
[125] MacDonald, *The Princess and the Goblin*, 133.
[126] John Ruskin, *Works*, 39 vols., E. T. Cook and Alexander Wedderburn, eds. (London: Allen, 1903–12), 9:157–8.
[127] Ruskin, *Works*, 10: 185–94.

said, was quite as useful, and great deal more reasonable. [...] Commerce and self-interest, they said, had got the better of violence, and the troubles of the past were whelmed in the riches that flowed in at their open gates. Indeed, there was one sect of philosophers in it which taught that it would be better to forget all the past history of the city, were it not that its former imperfections taught its present inhabitants how superior they and their times were, and enabled them to glory over their ancestors. [...] Indeed, the general theme of discourse when they met was how much wiser they were than their fathers.[128]

MacDonald's satire here is directed against the kind of political economy which Boyd Hilton has shown was bound up with a theological emphasis on the doctrine of Atonement,[129] and which purported to derive all social cohesion from rational self-interest. MacDonald's allusion to the "sect of philosophers" whose "general theme [...] was how much wiser they were than their fathers" recalls Coleridge's withering references to the complacency of those who glorify the present by referring to "this *enlightened* age."[130]

PERSONAL AUTHENTICITY AND RELIGIOUS BELIEF IN MACDONALD

In *Adela Cathcart*, the conflict between an inauthentic kind of theology centered on the doctrine of Atonement, and an authentic theology centered on incarnation is dramatized by the personal narrative recounted to the narrator by the curate, Mr. Armstrong, which is comparable in length and prominence to many of the other stories told in the novel. The curate explains that he has embarked late upon his clerical career due to a personal crisis of belief in which he abandoned holy orders in order to pay off a debt to a Jewish moneylender incurred through extravagant behavior whilst an undergraduate at Oxford.[131] Before coming to this decision, he is haunted by a feeling of the spiritual unreality of his clerical occupation:

> What I suffered most from was the fact that I must seem to the poor of my parish unsympathetic and unkind. [...] Add to this a feeling of hypocrisy, in the knowledge that I, the dispenser of sacred things to the people, was myself the slave of a money-lending Jew, and you will easily see how my life could not be to me the reality which it must be, for any true and healthy action, to every man. In a word, I felt that I was a humbug. As to my preaching, that could not have had much reality in it of any kind, for I had no experience

---

[128] George MacDonald, *The Princess and Curdie* (London: Chatto & Windus, 1883), 102–3.
[129] Hilton, *Age of Atonement*.
[130] S. T. Coleridge, *On the Constitution of the Church and State*, ed. John Colmer (Princeton: Princeton University Press, 1976), 14.
[131] MacDonald, *Adela Cathcart*, 2:15–17 His narrative drops a discreet hint that he maintained a mistress at Oxford, though MacDonald, in line with Victorian propriety, refrains from spelling this out.

yet of the relation of Christian Faith to Christian Action.[132]

MacDonald's repeated use of the word "reality" here hints at the existential dimension of the crisis experienced by the clergyman,[133] which is further emphasized by the question he puts to the narrator:

> As far as regards the *profession*, is it a manly kind of work, to put on a white gown once a week, and read out of a book; and then put on a black gown, and read out of a paper you bought or wrote,— all about certain old time-honoured legends which have some influence in keeping the common people on their good behaviour, by promising them happiness after they are dead, if they are respectable, and everlasting torture if they are blackguards? Is it manly?[134]

The curate's doubt as to the "manliness" of being a clergyman articulates his unease over the existential inauthenticity of the conventional Establishment religion he is expected to purvey. This suspicion of the unmanliness of "talking *goody* to old wives and sentimental young ladies," is reinforced by his awareness of Lizzie, "the daughter of a lieutenant in the army [...] living with her mother and elder sister, on a very scanty income, in the village where I had the good fortune to be the unhappy curate."[135] The curate wonders why "while she was most attentive and devout during the reading of the service, her face assumed, during the sermon, a far-off look of abstraction that indicated no reception of what I said, further than an influence of soporific quality," which he feels as a "reproof [...which] made me doubt whether there was anything genuine in me at all."[136] Lizzie's boredom during the curate's sermons reflects their lack of any lived personal authenticity.

Meeting Lizzie by chance one day, the curate strikes up a conversation about her behavior in church:

> "You don't seem to like going to church, Miss Lizzie?"
> Her face flushed.
> "Who dares to say so? I am very regular in my attendance."
> "Not a doubt of it. But you don't enjoy being there?"
> "I do."
> "Confess now. You don't like my sermons."
> "Do you like them yourself, Mr. Armstrong?"
> Here was a floorer! Did I like them myself? I really couldn't honestly say that

---

[132] MacDonald, *Adela Cathcart*, 2:18–19. MacDonald's narrative here obviously participates in the casual antisemitism which was common in nineteenth-century British culture.
[133] I discuss Carlyle's comparable sense of the unreality of modern life in *Romanticism, Medicine and the Natural Supernatural*, 14–15.
[134] MacDonald, *Adela Cathcart*, 2:20–1.
[135] MacDonald, *Adela Cathcart*, 2:21, 24.
[136] MacDonald, *Adela Cathcart*, 2:25–6.

> I did. [...] She stood looking at me out of clear grey eyes.
> "Now you have begun this conversation, Mr. Armstrong, I will go on with it," she said, at length. "It was not of my seeking. I do not think you believe what you say in the pulpit."
>
> Not believe what I said! Did I believe what I said? Or did I only believe that it was to be believed? The tables were turned with a vengeance. Here was the lay lamb, attacked and about to be worried by the wolf clerical, turning and driving the said wolf to bay. I stood and felt like a convicted criminal before the grey eyes of my judge.[137]

The curate's inauthenticity and lack of spiritual seriousness, his unthinking reliance on the authority of a belief that he has done nothing personally to earn, is exposed by this existential reversal of roles. He is so disconcerted that he falls on his knees "and made speechless love to her,"[138] an act he describes as "the simplest and truest thing I ever did in my life."

> How was I to help it? There stood the visible truth before me, looking out of the woman's grey eyes. What was I to do? I thank God I have never seen the truth plain before me, let it look ever so ghostly, without rushing at it. All my advances have been by a sudden act,—to me like an inspiration:—an act done in terror, almost, lest I should stop and think about it, and fail to do it. And here was no ghost, but a woman-angel, whose *Thou art the man* was spoken out of profundities of sweetness and truth. Could I turn my back upon her? Could I parley with her?—with the Truth? No. I fell on my knees, weeping like a child; for all my misery, all my sense of bondage and untruth, broke from me in those tears.[139]

As is shown by the reference, in the well-known Biblical quotation "Thou art the man," to the prophet Nathan's prompting (through a parable about the killing of a poor man's pet lamb by a rich man who had "exceeding many flocks and herds"),[140] of King David's self-condemnation for arranging the death of Uriah the Hittite in battle so that he could take Uriah's widow Bathsheba as his wife, Lizzie's intuition of an absence of heartfelt sincerity in his preaching constitutes for the curate a moment of revelation of his fundamental lack of spiritual authenticity,[141] his failure to make personal religious belief vital by incarnating it in the practice of his own life. This ability to embody the hidden promptings of the curate's own conscience renders Lizzie the ideal "woman-angel" of Victorian

---

[137] MacDonald, *Adela Cathcart*, 2:28–30.
[138] MacDonald, *Adela Cathcart*, 2:31.
[139] MacDonald, *Adela Cathcart*, 2:31–2.
[140] 2 Sam. 12:7, 2. This and all subsequent biblical quotations are taken from the KJV.
[141] Lionel Trilling has discussed the transition from the eighteenth-century ideal of "sincerity" to the modern ideal of existential "authenticity" during the nineteenth century in *Sincerity and Authenticity* (Cambridge, MA: Harvard University Press, 1972).

gender ideology,[142] and so makes her the woman he is bound to marry, as indeed he eventually does. "Having disclosed my whole bondage and grief," the curate asks Lizzie what he should do, and receives the answer that he must pay his debts before he undertakes to do anything more as a clergyman.[143] He then proceeds to take a position as an accountant in his worldly and commonplace dissenting cousin's business,[144] living as cheaply as possible in "a lodging-house in Hatton Garden" in consequence of his resolution "to regard the money I earned as the ransom-money of the church, paid by her for the redemption of an erring servant from the power of Mammon."[145]

In his modest lodgings, he eventually gets over "the disgust I felt at the coarseness of the men I met," recognizing that the "bond [...] between these men and me [...] was a tolerably broad and visible one,—nothing less than our human nature recognized as such."[146] He comes to the realization that "*the* work of the church" is to lead everyone to the "secret chamber, to which God has access from behind by a hidden door; while they know nothing of this chamber; and the other door, toward their own consciousness, is hidden by darkness and wrong, and ruin of all kinds," with the goal of encouraging them to tear "the door open, and, lo! there is the Father, at the heart of us, at the heart of all things."[147] This theology of religiously-inspired social solidarity is expressed in imagery reminiscent of William Holman Hunt's famous 1854 religious painting *The Light of the World*. For the curate, the work of the preacher becomes that of leading hearers to a recognition of the Incarnation already at work in themselves. He describes this insight as "a new life [... awaking] in me from that hour, feeble and dim, but yet life; and often as it has stopped growing, that has always been my own fault," which renders "existence [...] an awful grandeur and delight."[148] This vitalistic language, in which renewed personal consciousness of a spiritual dimension to existence is figured as a growing "life," invokes the important Victorian discourse of "character."[149]

After this religious awakening, the curate accidentally encounters Lizzie in an omnibus, and it turns out she has followed him to London and, abandoning

---

[142] Mary Poovey, *Uneven Developments: The Ideological Work of Gender in Mid-Victorian England* (Chicago: University of Chicago Press, 1988), 11.
[143] MacDonald, *Adela Cathcart*, 2:37–8.
[144] The curate describes him as "a good-hearted man [... who] never did anything plainly wicked, and consequently never repented of anything. He thought no harm of being petty and unfair," MacDonald, *Adela Cathcart*, 2:63.
[145] MacDonald, *Adela Cathcart*, 2:44.
[146] MacDonald, *Adela Cathcart*, 2:53.
[147] MacDonald, *Adela Cathcart*, 2:59–60.
[148] MacDonald, *Adela Cathcart*, 2:58–9.
[149] Budge, *Romanticism, Medicine and the Natural Supernatural*, 85–7.

her genteel social position, taken up "a good situation with a dressmaker in Bond street."[150] Every quarter from then on, she contributes "all she could spare of her salary for the Jew to gorge upon" and so "shortened my purgatory by a whole year."[151] The curate then goes "at once to a certain bishop, told him the whole story [...] and begged him to reinstate me in my office."[152]

As indicated by the reference to the Roman Catholic doctrine of purgatory, the narrative literalizes a movement away from a theology based on Atonement, in the form of the curate's debt to the Jew (which remains unrepayable while he fails to take personal responsibility for it),[153] toward one based on incarnation, as represented by the curate's developing awareness of "the Father, at the heart of us, at the heart of all things."[154] A similar sympathy for the doctrine of purgatory, also prompted by a vitalist emphasis on the ongoing and developing process of incarnation of religious belief in the Christian believer, can be found in Kingsley,[155] despite what was in some respects his thorough-going Protestantism.[156]

THE DEFAMILIARIZATION OF THEOLOGY IN MACDONALD'S NARRATIVE

This (re)narrativization of theological concepts is something *Adela Cathcart* shares with *At the Back of the North Wind*. After Diamond returns from his lengthy stay at the back of the North Wind (which is at the level of the realist narrative a lengthy and near fatal bout of fever), we are told the sinking of a ship brought about by North Wind during Diamond's journey with her (in which she acts as a personification of divine providence has led to the bankruptcy of his father's employer, due to him having "speculated a great more than was right," and the consequent sale of his "house, carriage, horses, furniture, and everything."[157] Whilst Diamond is convalescing with his aunt and being nursed by his mother, Diamond picks up on his mother's anxieties, asking why she is worried about their ability to "eat" when there is a "piece of gingerbread in the basket."[158] When she responds that Diamond has "no more sense than a sparrow that picks what it wants, and never thinks of the winter and the frost and, the snow," Diamond comments that "the birds get through the winter," and naively expresses his faith

---

[150] MacDonald, *Adela Cathcart*, 2:65–66.
[151] MacDonald, *Adela Cathcart*, 2:67.
[152] MacDonald, *Adela Cathcart*, 2:68.
[153] As I have already noted above, in some translations of the Lord's Prayer the Greek word 'οφελιλεμα (Matt. 6:12) is rendered as "debts" rather than "sins."
[154] MacDonald, *Adela Cathcart*, 2:60.
[155] Charles Kingsley, *The Water Babies* (Ware: Wordsworth Classics, 1994), 59.
[156] See Charles Kingsley's polemic against John Henry Newman *"What, Then, Does Dr Newman Mean?": A Reply to a Pamphlet Lately Published by Dr Newman* (London and Edinburgh: Macmillan, 1864).
[157] MacDonald, *At the Back of the North Wind*, 129–130.
[158] MacDonald, *At the Back of the North Wind*, 134.

that there will always be a "cupboard" somewhere from which the family will be able to obtain food, since "there must be a big cupboard somewhere, out of which the little cupboards are filled."[159] Diamond's mother falls silent at this, since "she had heard something at church the day before, which came back upon her—something like this, that she hadn't to eat for tomorrow as well as for to-day; and that what was not wanted couldn't be missed."[160]

MacDonald's stichomythic dialogue in this passage conveys a level of existential incomprehension comparable to Wordsworth's poem *We Are Seven*, which also recounts a dialogue between a well-meaning adult and a child whose apparent lack of understanding of what the adult is saying is shown to be rooted in a spiritual intuition which exceeds the adult's frame of reference.[161] The analogy Diamond draws between his family's situation and how birds get through the winter echoes Jesus' injunction "Behold the fowls of the air: for they sow not, neither do they reap, nor gather into barns; yet your heavenly Father feedeth them,"[162] which his mother seems to be vaguely recalling by the end of their exchange. MacDonald here defamiliarizes a well-known Biblical passage so that the full force and strangeness of Jesus' teaching can be appreciated by the reader.[163]

A similar kind of typological narrativization of the spiritual can be found in "The Light Princess," the fairytale "fitter for grown than for young children"[164] told to Adela by the narrator of *Adela Cathcart*. In this burlesque fairytale narrative, whose beginning is close in tone to Thackeray's *The Rose and the Ring*, the king forgets to invite his poor sister, Princess Makemnoit to his daughter's christening. Unfortunately, she is a witch who "beat all the wicked fairies in wickedness and all the clever ones in cleverness," and decides to attend anyway to pronounce a curse:

> LIGHT OF SPIRIT, BY MY CHARMS,
> LIGHT OF BODY, EVERY PART,

---

[159] MacDonald, *At the Back of the North Wind*, 134–6.
[160] MacDonald, *At the Back of the North Wind*, 136.
[161] Aaron Fogel, "Wordsworth's 'We Are Seven' and Crabbe's 'The Parish Register': Poetry and Anti-Census," *Studies in Romanticism* 48, no. 1 (2009): 31–2.
[162] Matt. 6:26.
[163] MacDonald's use of defamiliarization to revivify religious teaching could be compared to the recent religious apologia of Francis Spufford, where conventional religious language such as "sin" is deliberately avoided in favor of expressions such as "the human propensity to fuck things up," *Unapologetic: Why Despite Everything, Christianity Can Still Make Surprising Emotional Sense* (London: Faber, 2013), 27. Spufford continues this project in his novel *Light Perpetual*, where a character's solitary gormandizing can be interpreted as an image of damnation, though this is left unstated. Spufford, *Light Perpetual* (London: Faber, 2021), 233
[164] MacDonald, *Adela Cathcart*, 1:119.

Never weary human arms —
Only crush thy parents' heart!¹⁶⁵

The curse deprives the princess "of all her gravity"¹⁶⁶ in every sense. Not only "when the nurse began to float the baby up and down" does she fly "from her arms towards the ceiling," but she is in "constant good-humour," letting out "peals of laughter" when the servants play with her.¹⁶⁷ The princess is now "light" in multiple ways, which are explored in a dialogue early on in the story between the king and queen:

> The king could not help a sigh, which he tried to turn into a cough, saying,—
> "It is a good thing to be light-hearted, I am sure, whether she be ours or not."
> "It is a bad thing to be light-headed," answered the queen, looking, with prophetic soul, far into the future.
> " 'Tis a good thing to be light-handed," said the king.
> " 'Tis a bad thing to be light-fingered," answered the queen.
> " 'Tis a good thing to be light-footed," said the king.
> " 'Tis a bad thing," began the queen; but the king interrupted her.
> "In fact," said he, with the tone of one who concludes an argument in which he has had only imaginary opponents, and in which, therefore, he has come off triumphant—"in fact, it is a good thing altogether to be light-bodied."
> "But it is a bad thing altogether to be light-minded," retorted the queen, who was beginning to lose her temper.¹⁶⁸

The queen's attempt to have "more last words," when she screams after the retreating king "and it's a bad thing to be light-haired," which he interprets as potentially meaning "light-*heired*,"¹⁶⁹ suggests the underlying implied issue behind this dialogue, that of sexual "lightness" or infidelity, so incompatible with Victorian ideas about true womanhood.¹⁷⁰ The punning here, criticized subsequently in an interruption to the narrator's story by the visiting clergyman, at a more serious level reflects the period's preoccupation with how shifts of meaning might reveal the underlying intellectual and existential roots of words— an approach to linguistic analysis popularized in Britain by the radical thinker Horne Tooke in the late eighteenth century,¹⁷¹ and which eventually culminated in the mid-nineteenth-century founding of the project that became the *Oxford English Dictionary*.¹⁷²

---

[165] MacDonald, *Adela Cathcart*, 1:127–8.
[166] MacDonald, *Adela Cathcart*, 1:130.
[167] MacDonald, *Adela Cathcart*, 1:131, 137.
[168] MacDonald, *Adela Cathcart*, 1:139–40.
[169] MacDonald, *Adela Cathcart*, 1:141.
[170] Poovey, *Uneven Developments*, 11.
[171] John Horne Tooke, *Epea Pteroenta, or, The Diversions of Purley*, 2 vols., (1786), 1:152–4.
[172] See Richard Chevenix Trench, *On the Study of Words and English Past and Present* (London and Toronto: Dent and Dutton, n.d.), 13–16.

Being and Truthfulness

The princess' "lightness" reflects a moral deficiency, as John Smith's narration comments: "she would laugh like the very spirit of fun; only in her laugh there was something missing. [...] I think it was a certain tone, depending upon the possibility of sorrow,—*morbidezza*, perhaps."[173] The narration also suggests a remedy for this somewhat sociopathic condition in the shape of "falling in love," but highlights "a difficulty—perhaps *the* difficulty" in the shape of her lack of "gravity," which makes it impossible for her to "fall into anything."[174] Swimming turns out to provide a partial remedy for her airy insouciance, as when in the water "she seemed more sedate than usual," so that "the passion of her life was to get into the water, and she was always the better behaved and the more beautiful, the more she had of it," appearing "more modest and maidenly in the water than out of it."[175] The "witch-princess" responsible for the curse in the first place threatens this remedy for the princess' "lightness," and with it her life itself, by drying up the lake, something for which the only remedy, as revealed by a mysterious "plate of gold, covered with writing," is to stop up the hole at the bottom of the lake with "the body of a living man" who offers himself up "of his own will."[176]

A prince in disguise, who has been swimming with the princess in secret, volunteers for this slow death, on the condition that "the princess [...] shall go with me, feed me with her own hands, and look at me now and then to comfort me."[177] As the waters rise over his face, the princess begins "to feel strange," eventually giving "a shriek" and springing into the lake to save him by pulling him into her boat.[178] She carries his unconscious body to her own bed, where her "old nurse" tries everything to save him, and, finally, the prince opens his eyes. The princess' reaction is described in terms which emphasize the poetic device of "pathetic fallacy" underlying the narrative:

> The princess burst into a passion of tears, and *fell* on the floor. There she lay for an hour, and her tears never ceased. All the pent-up crying of her life was spent now. And a rain came on, such as had never been seen in that country. [...] The torrents poured from the mountains like molten gold, and if it had not been for its subterraneous outlet, the lake would have overflowed and inundated the country. It was full from shore to shore.[179]

Significantly, as the italicization of the word at the beginning of the passage shows, the princess can now fall as she is weighed down by her loving concern

---

[173] MacDonald, *Adela Cathcart*, 1:150.
[174] MacDonald, *Adela Cathcart*, 1:161.
[175] MacDonald, *Adela Cathcart*, 1:163, 187.
[176] MacDonald, *Adela Cathcart*, 1:190, 200.
[177] MacDonald, *Adela Cathcart*, 1:206.
[178] MacDonald, *Adela Cathcart*, 1:216, 217.
[179] MacDonald, *Adela Cathcart*, 1:218–19.

for the prince, and with this comes a new ability to cry, which is paralleled by the breaking of the general drought created by her aunt the witch. The narrative gives this act of self-sacrifice a typological dimension by the detail, slightly earlier, of the princess feeding the prince as the lake's waters rise over him "with bits of biscuit, and sips of wine," which recalls the Eucharistic commemoration of Christ's sacrificial death on the cross.[180] Rather than this sacrifice being interpreted as the payment of a debt, however, from MacDonald's incarnational perspective it can be seen as renewing a source of life and feeling which the princess shares with all humanity, figured in the new flow of water (we learn earlier in the narrative that the witch's spell has even resulted in "all the babies throughout the country [...] crying dreadfully,—only without tears").[181]

VITALISM AND PERSONAL RELIGION IN MACDONALD

The conclusion of "The Light Princess" typifies MacDonald's overall literary strategy of using personal forms of meaning (represented here by the apparent capriciousness of fairytale narrative) as a way of making the abstractions of theology incarnate, in order to render them as living truth instead of the "dance of Death" of the Congregationalist sermon he describes in *David Elginbrod*.[182] During the ensuing discussion among the characters who inhabit *Adela Cathcart*'s realist frame narrative, when Mrs. Cathcart asks "What is the moral of it?," the ailing Adela responds to her aunt, slightly cattily, "That you need not be afraid of ill-natured aunts, though they are witches"—an asperity explained slightly later in the narrative when we learn that the aunt's pet project is marrying Adela off to her superficial son Percy for the sake of her "very tolerable fortune."[183] The doctor, Harry Armstrong, on the other hand, whose "health and humanity" the narrator regards as having "something healing in the very presence and touch of the man," suggests in an altogether more existentially resonant way that the moral is "that no girl is worth anything till she has cried a little."[184] It is this ability to respond to the tale's typological implications that marks Harry Armstong out, for the narrator, as the possessor of the "true manhood" that will enable his love to rescue Adela from her listless wasting disease and make her "a fortunate woman indeed,"[185] despite the disparity in their social positions.

MacDonald's systematic deployment in his fiction of the vitalist medical ideas which were so generally current in nineteenth-century culture that they

---

[180] MacDonald, *Adela Cathcart*, 1:214.
[181] MacDonald, *Adela Cathcart*, 1:196.
[182] MacDonald, *David Elginbrod*, 3:100. I discuss the sermon earlier in this essay.
[183] MacDonald, *Adela Cathcart*, 1:224, 233.
[184] MacDonald, *Adela Cathcart*, 1:228, 224.
[185] MacDonald, *Adela Cathcart*, 1:232.

represent a recognizable set of Victorian narrative tropes[186] provides him with a way of articulating in narrative terms a theology of incarnation as an ongoing process of development in the Christian believer. This narrative theology of incarnation can be regarded as a religiously inflected version of the nineteenth-century preoccupation with the development of "character" which is responsible for the importance of the genre of the bildungsroman in the Victorian novel,[187] a theme for which MacDonald's "The Light Princess" can be seen as an extended narrative metaphor in its fundamental opposition between gravity and light-mindedness.

In a more literal vein, the curate's story in *Adela Cathcart* also represents this kind of bildungsroman of the developing incarnation of the transcendent in the individual life, through the way in which the curate's coming to consciousness of the spiritual dimension to life involves his gradual personal individuation from the social environment which he inhabits, as typified by the unusually late age at which he has finally taken up his clerical vocation. The condition of "moral atrophy" afflicting Adela herself can be defined as a blockage in her character's ability to embody the transcendent—a form of spiritual indigestion from which she is rescued by the medicinal "pabulum" of the various narratives offered up to her in MacDonald's book, which offer both her and the reader an easy way to get in touch with a transcendent spiritual dimension through their typological significance. In *At the Back of the North Wind*, Diamond's ability to incarnate the teaching of Jesus' Sermon on the Mount in unwitting words to his anxious mother testifies to his narrative role as an embodiment of the transcendent (though perhaps his status as a consumptive also points to the fragility and temporary status of any such typological embodiment). MacDonald's *The Princess and the Goblin*, on the other hand, presents in the goblins resolutely materialist and untranscendent bourgeois individualists, in a way which has recently been echoed in contemporary culture by the coinage of the term "goblin mode" to denote unapologetically anti-social behavior.[188]

My examination in this essay of the typological resonances of MacDonald's fiction, as outlined above, suggests the need for some critical reconceptualization of the notion of typology itself, when applied to the literature of the later nineteenth century, in a way corresponding to Carlyle's well-known invocation in

---

[186] I analyze these across a variety of genres in *Romanticism, Medicine and the Natural Supernatural*.

[187] Alan Mintz, *George Eliot and the Novel of Vocation* (Cambridge, MA: Harvard University Press, 1978).

[188] "Goblin mode," Wikipedia, February 2, 2024, https://en.wikipedia.org/wiki/Goblin_mode.

Sartor Resartus of "moveable types" as creating "a whole new democratic world."[189] Far from typology being reliant upon a static and hierarchical conception of the world antithetical to the fluidity of social modernity, as is implied, for example, in Ian Watt's classic study *The Rise of the Novel*,[190] typology as understood within an incarnational theology embodying the influence of vitalism can be seen as an evanescent aspect of particular narrative moments. Typology's religious significance becomes something to be constantly renewed in the process of living rather than being separable from lived experience, just as, at around the same time, impressionist painting reconfigures the celebration of moments of historical significance in the prestigious genre of history-painting as the artistic redemption of the mundanity of the present moment by imbuing it with a peculiar and inarticulable resonance. From this perspective, typological consciousness can be characterized as an existentially mature acceptance of life and its evanescence, rather than as an infantile rejection of reality, as it is in Leavisian secularism.[191] In Carlylean terms, the existential rejection of meaninglessness (the Everlasting No) is what enables a personal and truly human life.[192]

---

[189] Thomas Carlyle, *Sartor Resartus* (Oxford: Oxford University Press, 1987), 31.

[190] Ian Watt, *The Rise of the Novel: Studies in Defoe, Richardson, and Fielding* (London: Chatto and Windus, 1957), 27–34.

[191] For an example of this kind of dismissal, see Q. D. Leavis' description of the religious novelist Charlotte M. Yonge as "selecting the anti-Life elements in Christianity for stress and idealization." "Charlotte Yonge and Christian Discrimination," *Scrutiny* 12 (1944): 153.

[192] Carlyle, *Sartor Resartus*, 129.

UNCOMMON INTERPRETATION:
READING DANTE IN CHARLES KINGSLEY AND GEORGE MACDONALD'S FAIRYTALES[1]

Amanda B. Vernon

Dante was enormously popular in nineteenth-century Britain. Indeed, so great was his popularity that he achieved "cult" status in Victorian society.[2] As Alison Milbank demonstrates in her expansive study *Dante and the Victorians*, the Florentine poet was drawn upon to justify a variety of cultural ideas, political causes, and aesthetic ideals. Transgressive figures such as Oscar Wilde, John Henry Newman, and George Eliot identified their own physical appearances with Dante's as "a means of expressing difference and seeking justification in one gesture," while John Ruskin drew on Cary's translation of the conclusion of the *Commedia* to make a socio-cultural claim about the role women in society and the work they "must do."[3] Like many of their friends and fellow-writers, including Tennyson and the Brownings, Charles Kingsley and George MacDonald were numbered amongst the faithful. MacDonald's fiction, sermons, and essays are riddled with references to Dante whom he professes to love as a "big brother,"[4] and while the Italian poet makes fewer appearances in Kingsley's work than MacDonald's the references are no less positive. In fact, somewhat surprisingly given his notorious antagonism toward Catholicism, Kingsley even goes so far as to draw on Dante as a theological and historical authority in *Twenty-Five Village Sermons* (1849):

> There was a great poet once—Dante by name—who described most truly and wonderfully, in his own way, heaven and hell, for, indeed, he had been in both. [...] And so well did he speak of them, that the ignorant people used to point after him with awe in the streets, and whisper, There is the man who has been in hell.[5]

Kingsley's merging of Dante the character—who has travelled to hell and heaven and back—and Dante the poet was not uncommon in the nineteenth century. Milbank writes that it is precisely this elision of Dante's art and his life that gives

---
[1] Thanks to Daniel Gabelman for his incisive comments and expertise.
[2] Alison Milbank, *Dante and the Victorians* (Manchester: Manchester University Press, 1998), 1.
[3] Milbank, *Dante and the Victorians*, 2, 43.
[4] Barbara Amell, "MacDonald on Dante," *Wingfold* 49 (2005): 7–9.
[5] Charles Kingsley, *Twenty-Five Village Sermons* (Philadelphia: H. Hooker, 1854), 233.

the poet's work a theological authority that, in some cases, rivalled even the Bible.[6] This chapter traces the presence of Dante in the work of Kingsley and MacDonald, arguing that both writers appeal to Dante's cultural and theological authority in order to articulate—and even advance—their differing beliefs about revelation, interpretation, and, consequently, the nature of God. Kingsley emphasizes a faith-informed mode of scientific enquiry, one that regards the moral and natural laws as a revelation of a God characterized by both love and destruction. Alternatively, MacDonald offers an interpretive approach that champions affective engagement with the natural world and literature (including fairytales), all of which reveal a God who is not only loving, but also fundamentally creative.

Despite their intellectual and theological differences (which will become apparent throughout this chapter) the relationship between Kingsley and MacDonald was, it seems, one of great affection and respect both personally and professionally. To be sure, there is much that unites the two writers including a mutual regard for one another's work,[7] professional collaboration,[8] roles as novelists-cum-preachers, and shared discipleship under the Anglican minister Frederick Denison Maurice. Perhaps the most surprising point of commonality, however, is the fact that both writers chose to articulate some of their central theological beliefs in fairytale form. This chapter considers three of these fairytales, doing so with particular reference to the way in which each writer draws on Dante to articulate his theology of revelation: his understanding of the means by which God reveals himself and the kind of God that is thereby revealed. While much of the scholarly work on the relationship between Dante and Kingsley has been focused on questions of heaven and hell,[9] my reading will consider how Kingsley uses Dante to justify his attempts to reconcile contemporary scientific theories, moral law, and the scriptural revelation of the Christian God. It will begin by considering some of Kingsley's key ideas on the relationship between science and faith, before tracing the influence of Dante in Kingsley's natural theology in *The Water Babies* (1863). The second part of the chapter will explore how, through his Dantean depiction of a shape-shifting divinity, MacDonald contributes to nineteenth-century debates on reading and revelation while at the

---

[6] Milbank, *Dante and the Victorians*, 5.
[7] Kingsley was a supporter of MacDonald's early dramatic poem *Within and Without* (1855), while MacDonald included a few of "the poems of our honoured Charles Kingsley" in his 1868 anthology of devotional poetry *England's Antiphon*. George MacDonald, *England's Antiphon* (London: Macmillan, 1874), 324.
[8] MacDonald was editor of the periodical *Good Words for the Young* during the serialized publication of Kingsley's *Madam How and Lady Why* in 1869.
[9] For example, Milbank, *Dante and the Victorians*; Rachel Fountain Eames, "Geological Katabasis: Geology and the Christian Underworld in Kingsley's The Water Babies," *Victoriographies* 7, no. 3 (2017): 195–209; Stephen Prickett, *Victorian Fantasy* (Waco, TX: Baylor University Press, 2005).

same time communicating his own ideas on the nature of God as fundamentally creative. MacDonald understood God to reveal himself in all manner of ways (including Scripture and the natural world), but he particularly emphasized the importance of fairytales as a means of revelation. The influence of Dante on MacDonald's 1868 fairytale *At the Back of the North Wind* has been the subject of a fair amount of scholarly consideration, as has its relationship to *The Water Babies*.[10] The overt references to Dante in *North Wind*, and the fact that it was published only a few years after *The Water Babies*, explains the scholarly choice to consider the two fairytales in light of their relationship with Dante. Far less attention has been paid to *The Princess and Curdie* (1883) and "The Lost Princess: A Double Story" (1875),[11] both of which contain scenes of revelation that are, arguably, closer in language and theme to the final Canto of the *Paradiso* (and also to the revelatory scene in *The Water Babies*), than similar moments in *At the Back of the North Wind*. My close reading will, therefore, focus on these later fairytales to demonstrate the extent of MacDonald's engagement with Dante and how these tales offer a contribution to nineteenth-century debates on questions of interpretation and revelation.

The term "natural theology" is often regarded as synonymous with a particular Enlightenment version of the theology that "argues directly from the observation of nature to demonstrate the existence of God."[12] There are, however, various forms of natural theology. Amy M. King identifies a particularly nineteenth-century "altered form" of natural theology that was no longer concerned with proving God's existence but was, rather, "a kind of affective scientific argument."[13] King identifies Kingsley as one of the nineteenth-century figures whose version of natural theology falls into this category. Kingsley is well known for his interest in natural theology and for his engagement with debates on the relationship between Christian belief and scientific understandings of the natural world.[14] He was a regular correspondent with T. H. Huxley—with whom

---

[10] See John Pazdziora and Joshua Richards, "The Dantean Tradition in George MacDonald's *At the Back of the North Wind*," *VII* 29 (2013): 1–16; Milbank, *Dante and the Victorians*; Prickett, *Victorian Fantasy*; Colin Manlove, *Christian Fantasy 1200 to the Present* (Notre Dame, IN: University of Notre Dame Press, 1992).

[11] Given that the publication dates of these texts have no bearing on my readings of them, I have chosen to consider them in this order as I believe it offers greater clarity in terms of the development of my argument.

[12] Alister E. McGrath, *The Open Secret: A New Vision for Natural Theology* (Hoboken, NJ: Wiley, 2011), 4.

[13] Amy M. King, *The Divine in the Commonplace: Reverent Natural History and the Novel in Britain* (Cambridge: Cambridge University Press, 2019), 6.

[14] See John C. Hawley, "Charles Kingsley and the Book of Nature," *Anglican and Episcopal History* 60, no. 4 (1991): 461–479; Gillian Beer, *Darwin's Plots: Evolutionary Narrative in*

he developed a friendship beginning in 1855—and also with Charles Darwin. His admiration for the latter, whom he referred to as his "master," approached something akin to hero worship and Darwin himself was undoubtedly pleased to have such an advocate (and, one might venture, such an acolyte). According to Bernard Lightman, Darwin "tried to defuse religious hostility by drawing attention to Kingsley's positive response" to the *Origin of the Species*, referring to him in the second edition of the book as "a celebrated author and divine."[15] Kingsley's position as a prominent Anglican clergyman, his deep curiosity about the natural world, and his conviction about the importance of reconciling scientific and theological notions of God and nature led to his tireless attempts to bridge gaps and create understanding between those who perceived science and religion to be opposed. It also led to a life-long process of intellectual and emotional engagement with ideas of natural theology so as to find peace with the subject for himself.

Kingsley's personal—and, at times deeply agonized—wrestlings with natural theology are evident in an 1856 letter to another "dear master" of his, F. D. Maurice. In the letter, Kingsley explains that he had "long ago found out how little I can discover about God's absolute love, or absolute righteousness, from a universe in which everything is eternally *eating* everything else."[16] He goes on to write that one must, on the basis of an innate moral law, "trust against all appearances, and cry out of the lowest deep (as I have had to do)—Thou art not Siva the destroyer. Thou art not even Ahriman and Ormuzd in one. And yet, if Thou art not, why does Thy universe seem to say that Thou art? Art Thou a 'Deus quidam Deceptor,' after all?"[17] Kingsley's references to "Siva" the Hindu creator and destroyer of the universe, and "Ahriman and Ormuzd," the Evil and Good Spirits of Zoroastrianism, indicate that, for him, the natural world reveals only a struggle between destructive and creative forces—between evil and good—characteristics that Kingsley was unable to reconcile with his understanding of the Christian God as absolutely righteous. In a similar vein, Kingsley locates the idea of "Deus quidam Deceptor" ("God who is sometimes a deceiver") not in God's planting of a false fossil record to test the faithful,[18]

Darwin, George Eliot and Nineteenth-Century Fiction, (Cambridge: Cambridge University Press, 2000); Will Abberley, "Animal Cunning: Deceptive Nature and Truthful Science in Charles Kingsley's Natural Theology," *Victorian Studies* 58, no. 1 (2016): 34–56; King, *The Divine in the Commonplace*.

[15] Bernard Lightman, *Victorian Popularizers of Science: Designing Nature for New Audiences* (Chicago: University of Chicago Press, 2007), 75.

[16] *Charles Kingsley: His Letters and Memories of His Life*, ed. Frances Kingsley (London: Macmillan, 1894), 181–2.

[17] *Charles Kingsley: His Letters and Memories of His Life*, 181–2.

[18] For more on Kingsley's response to his friend Philip Henry Gosse's notion of *Deus quidam Deceptor*, see Will Abberley, "Animal Cunning."

but in the apparent falseness of God's self-revelation as absolute love in light of a distinctly unloving natural world.

The "cry out of the lowest deep" might have happened "long ago," but Kingsley's attempt to bring scientific theories and observation of the natural world together with Christian ideas of revelation was a life-long endeavor. The same can be said of his public attempts to reconcile "a wide, and as some think increasing, divorce between Science and Christianity."[19] His late[20] 1871 address to Anglican clergy at Sion College on "The Natural Theology of the Future" is, in part, an appeal to these ministers of religion to reclaim a (distinctly Anglican) heritage of Natural Theology in the footsteps of "the three greatest natural theologians:" George Berkeley, Joseph Butler, and William Paley.[21] Kingsley regarded natural theology as a "mission" to guarantee faith—a mission that is, fittingly, marked by the quality of adaptability. The mission "has to be re-filled again and again, as human thought changes and human science develops," otherwise "the God who seems to be revealed by Nature" and the God of "the then popular religion" will appear to be at odds and people will eventually cease to believe.[22] Kingsley's acknowledgement that theological, as well as scientific, theories might need to be adapted did not, however, mean that he was prepared to reject his interpretation of scriptural representations of God that were, apparently, opposed to what he referred to as "our conception of a God of love."[23] Somewhat surprisingly given the contents of his letter to Maurice in 1856, he goes on to argue that the stern, and often destructive, God of the Bible (who is, he argues, as destructive in the New Testament as in the Old), is compatible with the destructive violence of the natural world. The conclusions that Kingsley sometimes arrived at as the result of his mode of interpreting nature and scripture are arguably problematic. For example, in sermons he preached during a cholera epidemic, and which were published in 1854 under the title "Who Causes Pestilence?" he asserted "cholera to be God's judgment on the sin of living in filth."[24] Such a conclusion stands in stark contrast with MacDonald's view (which will be discussed presently), of God's creative love and justice.

Given their prominence in histories of natural theology, Kingsley's references to Paley et al. in his address are largely unsurprising. The same cannnot be said of his subsequent appeal to the work of a very different kind of authority than the

---

[19] Charles Kingsley, "The Natural Theology of the Future," 1871, www.online-literature.com/charles-kingsley/scientific/7/, n.p.
[20] Kingsley died in 1875.
[21] Kingsley, "The Natural Theology of the Future," n.p.
[22] Kingsley, "The Natural Theology of the Future," n.p.
[23] Kingsley, "The Natural Theology of the Future," n.p.
[24] Quoted in Larry Uffelman and Patrick Scott, "Kingsley's Serial Novels, II: *The Water-Babies,*" *Victorian Periodicals Review* 19, no. 4 (1986): 127.

seventeenth-century natural theologians in whose footsteps he claimed to follow: Dante Alighieri. Quoting Thomas Carlyle's commentary on Dante, Kingsley reminds his audience of ministers of the "great words about poor Francesca in the Inferno: 'Infinite pity, yet also infinite rigour of law. It is so Nature is made. It is so Dante discerned that she was made.'"[25] Carlyle's comment is made in the context of a defense of Dante's work as demonstrating his infinite rigor and infinite pity (rather than being "a poor splenetic impotent terrestrial libel" against Dante's enemies[26]), but Kingsley uses the quotation to make a theological point about these qualities. The reference to Dante at this moment in Kingsley's argument is significant for several reasons: it neatly and vividly articulates Kingsley's belief in the compatibility between the moral law and pity (or love) of God; it links his conception of a rigorous moral law with the rigorous laws of the natural world; and it draws on the cultural authority of Dante to support Kingsley's case about how best to interpret both scripture and nature. Perhaps most significantly, however, it demonstrates what I read as Kingsley's enlisting of Dante as a sort of natural theologian—one whose impact on Kingsley's work is as significant, in its own way, as the Anglican natural theologians Kingsley so admired.

At first glance it might seem odd for Kingsley to be appealing to Dante for support regarding matters of theology and science. After all, the science in Dante's *Commedia* is based upon an inaccurate Aristotelian model of the universe that is, amongst other things, geocentric. Not only that, science itself was conceived of in a markedly different way in fourteenth-century Italy than it was in Victorian Britain. Simon Gilson writes that in Dante's day "the words *scientia* and *scienzia* connoted profound knowledge of any object's nature, its causes, and its origins" and that Dante and early commentators on the *Commedia* used the terms to refer not only to "natural philosophy, arithmetic, geometry, and astrology, but also to a variety of other disciplines such as theology, grammar, dialectic, rhetoric, music, and poetry."[27] While Dante would not have made a distinction between theology and science,[28] the *Commedia* does raise "fundamental questions about the relationship between a world of natural causes that can be rationally understood and a divine order governed directly by God."[29] Grappling with similar questions in the nineteenth century, Kingsley does make a distinction between science and theology, claiming that they answer different questions about the natural

---

[25] Kingsley, "The Natural Theology of the Future," n.p.
[26] Thomas Carlyle, *On Heroes, Hero-Worship, and the Heroic in History*, ed. Henry David Gray (London: Longmans, 1906), 92.
[27] Simon Gilson, "Medieval Science in Dante's *Commedia*: Past Approaches and Future Directions," *Reading Medieval Studies* 28 (2001): 40.
[28] Theology was, after all, termed the "Queen of the Sciences" in the Middle Ages.
[29] Gilson, "Medieval Science," 53.

world: the former "how" and the latter "why."[30] Kingsley's understanding of the "mission" of natural theology, with its inherent need for adaptation on the part of both scientists and theologians, goes far to explain why he might have appealed to Dante as an authority despite scientific differences. Although he was operating with an inaccurate scientific framework, the Italian poet was, after all, delving into questions about the relationship between God and the laws of nature and morality—the very kinds of questions that preoccupied Kingsley.[31]

Dante is referenced throughout Kingsley's writings, including in his lectures on literature and in his sermons. The appeal Kingsley makes to Dante as an authority and a shaping influence for his natural theology is, however, most evident in *The Water Babies*. Before considering the ways in which Kingsley draws on Dante in his fairytale it is worth briefly unpacking his motivation for writing the story,[32] as it has bearing upon why Kingsley might have drawn on Dante so extensively in the text. *The Water Babies* was published in book form in the summer of 1863, after having been serialized in Macmillan's Magazine from August 1862 to March 1863. At the time, Kingsley was still formulating his thoughts on the relationship between evolutionary theory and natural theology—something that can be seen in a letter to Maurice from 1862, where he reminds his "dear master" "that the physical science in the book is *not* nonsense, but accurate earnest as far as I dare speak yet."[33] While Kingsley might not have dared to speak in full detail about his current ideas at this stage in his thinking, *The Water Babies* reveals a broader attempt to demonstrate the compatibility of scientific and theological interpretations of nature without needing to have the particulars nailed down. As John Hawley writes, at the time of its publication "the book was generally accepted for what it was: an imaginative endorsement of contemporary evolutionary theory which sought to leave its readers open to the possibility of divine intervention and revelation."[34] Kingsley's intention in this regard is evident in his 1862 letter to Maurice about the book, in which he explains that he has "tried, in all sorts of queer ways, to make children and grown folks understand that there is a quite miraculous and divine element underlying all physical nature, and nobody knows anything about anything, in the sense in

---

[30] Kingsley, "The Natural Theology of the Future," n.p.
[31] Unlike recent commentators, Kingsley does not, as far as I am aware, attempt to "fragment off the science in Dante and to make him into a mythologized precursor of modern scientific discoveries," Gilson, "Medieval Science," 45. As Gilson demonstrates, such an argument is tenuous at best.
[32] In addition to being motivated to fulfil a promise to write his son a book. See *Charles Kingsley: His Letters and Memories of His Life*, 245.
[33] *Charles Kingsley: His Letters and Memories of His Life*, 245.
[34] Hawley, "Charles Kingsley and The Book of Nature," 469.

which they may know God in Christ, and right and wrong."[35] While Kingsley's claim that "nobody knows anything about anything" indicates more than a touch of agnosticism regarding specific theories about the natural world, his primary intention was not to deconstruct scientific theories, but to challenge the claims of a materialist stance that regarded evolutionary theory as doing away with the possibility of divine involvement.[36] Such a materialist philosophy was threatening to those who, like Kingsley, believed in the existence of God, and the threat often resulted in a reactive rejection of contemporary scientific theories such as evolution—theories that were perceived to be handmaidens of materialism and harbingers of the loss of faith. Kingsley's intention is evident in his instruction to the young reader of *The Water Babies* to listen respectfully to "wise" and "great" men such as "Professor Owen, or Professor Sedgwick, or Professor Huxley, or Mr. Darwin," but to remember that these men do not know—no one knows—"what Nature is, or what she can do."[37] The letter to Maurice demonstrates a clear conviction that what *can* be known is "right and wrong," and Jesus as the revelation of God—points of conviction that are consistent with his letter of 1856 and which continued to form his interpretive lens when it came to his reading of the natural world. For Kingsley, it is divine revelation (via the conscience and Scripture) that offers the lens by which one interprets the presence of God in nature—by which one interprets, as Kingsley understands Dante to do, the infinite rigor and infinite pity of both nature and God.

Critics like Milbank have identified the Dantean imagery beginning in chapter one of the *The Water Babies* when the hapless chimney-sweep Tom loses his way in the woods and is "pursued by beasts (here guard-dogs)."[38] However, my own reading of Kingsley's Dantean engagement begins in chapter two, just after Tom has fallen into both the river and into the "delightful sleep" (of death)—a falling-asleep that the narrator attributes to the fact that "the fairies took him."[39] The narrator's explanation of the involvement of fairies leads to an apparent rabbit-trail considering the possibility of the existence of fairies and the futility of trying to prove that there are none. This thinly-veiled argument for the impossibility of proving that there is no divine element in the universe—one of Kingsley's attempts to make the reader see that "nobody knows anything about anything"—includes a passing (and apparently flippant) reference to the

---

[35] *Charles Kingsley: His Letters and Memories of His Life*, 245.
[36] For more on the "theistic biologists," "Christian Darwinians," Spiritualists, and others who sought to counter the materialist strand in nineteenth-century thought, see J. Jeffrey Franklin, *Spirit Matters: Occult Beliefs, Alternative Religions, and the Crisis of Faith in Victorian Britain* (Ithaca, NY: Cornell University Press, 2018), 14.
[37] Charles Kingsley, *The Water Babies* (London: Harper Press, 2011), 46.
[38] Milbank, *Dante and the Victorians*, 179.
[39] Kingsley, *The Water Babies*, 38.

possibility that "there may be fairies in the world, and they may be just what makes the world go round to the old tune of '*C'est l'amour, l'amour, l'amour / Qui fait le monde* à *la ronde:*' and yet no one may be able to see them except those whose hearts are going round to that same tune."[40] Kingsley is not just being silly here. He is, alongside the silliness, alluding to *The Divine Comedy*. On beholding the beatific vision Dante recounts that "my / desire and will were moved already—like / a wheel revolving uniformly—by / the Love that moves the sun and the other stars."[41] To compare Kingsley's argument for an interpretation of the natural world that is "crammed with heaven"[42] (or fairies), with the final lines of the *Paradiso* may seem to be a "queer way" of doing things, but such an eccentric approach was, after all, Kingsley's intention. His eccentricity is the way in which he delights, or possibly startles, his readers into looking at the natural world afresh. The implication of the allusion to Dante is that it is only those who have eyes of faith—those whose hearts are tuned to the great Love—that are able to see the presence of the divine within the natural world.

Kingsley's reference to Dante's great Love anticipates the more explicit references to Dante's beatific vision near the end of *The Water Babies*. It also prepares the reader for interpreting the moral education that ultimately enables Tom to see the connections between divine love, the moral law, and the natural world. After falling into the river, Tom goes through a sort of purgatorial state in which his knowledge of "right and wrong" is developed by Kingsley's personification of the moral law, Mrs. Bedonebyasyoudid. As Milbank has pointed out, Tom's encounter with this personification of moral law, Mrs. Bedonebyasyoudid, reflects the Dantean law of *contrapasso*, "whereby the punishment not only fits the crime but is in some way the self-creation of the sinner, rather than something being imposed from without."[43] In *The Water Babies*, this takes the form of those who have unwittingly treated children poorly being subjected to the same kinds of treatment: doctors are bled and forced to take disgusting medicines, mothers are made to wear the uncomfortable clothing that they insisted their children wear, and careless nursery-maids have pins stuck into them. For those who, like Tom's abusive former master Mr. Grimes, knew the wrong they were doing and did it anyway, the punishment in hell is more severe, but still in keeping with the law of *contrapasso* (Mr. Grimes is trapped in a sooty chimney and deprived of creature

---

[40] Kingsley, *The Water Babies*, 39.
[41] Dante Alighieri, "*Paradiso 33*," trans. Allen Mandelbaum, Digital Dante, Columbia University Libraries (2019), ll. 142–5, https://digitaldante.columbia.edu/dante/divine-comedy/paradiso/paradiso-33/.
[42] Elizabeth Barrett Browning, *Aurora Leigh*, ed. Kerry McSweeney (Oxford: Oxford University Press, 2008), 246.
[43] Milbank, *Dante and the Victorians*, 86.

comforts such as his pipe).⁴⁴ The details of these punishments echo, albeit far more humorously, the grotesque depictions of punishments in Dante's *Inferno* and *Purgatorio*—depictions such as that of Bertran de Born who suffers in the eighth circle of hell for sowing division between Henry the Young King and his father Henry II. De Born uses the term *contrapasso* (here translated "counter—penalty") to describe his punishment for severing the father/king (a "head" in more ways than one) and the son: "Because I severed those so joined, I carry— / alas—my brain dissevered from its source, / which is within my trunk. And thus, in me / one sees the law of counter—penalty."⁴⁵ While the representations of punishment in *The Water Babies* are suitably child-friendly, they do the work of depicting the relationship between natural and moral law in the particularly Dantean way that Kingsley conceives of it. As if to underscore the relationship between Kingsley's and Dante's moral law, the narrator tells us that "Tom did not quite dislike [Mrs. Bedonebyasyoudid]: but he could not help thinking her a little spiteful"⁴⁶—a charge of spite that was similarly levelled against Dante for his depictions of the souls in hell.⁴⁷ Tom, however, must learn to find Mrs. Bedonebyasyoudid beautiful, something that is a challenge for him as (unlike her sister Madam Doasyouwouldbedoneby) she is "so ugly that Tom was tempted to make faces at her."⁴⁸ What Mrs. Bedonebyasyoudid tells him, however, is that she will continue to be "the ugliest fairy in the world [...] till people behave themselves as they ought to do. And then I shall grow as handsome as my sister, who is the loveliest fairy in the world."⁴⁹ Tom, it seems, must become like the souls in Dante's Purgatory who recognize the goodness (and thus beauty) of the moral law and welcome its rigorous nature as fitting them for Paradise.

Kingsley's personification of Dante's rigorous moral law is another one of the "queer ways" in which he sought to open the eyes of his readers to the presence of the divine in nature. Mrs. Bedonebyasyoudid is the stereotype of a Victorian schoolmarm, complete with "black bonnet, and a black shawl."⁵⁰ Although she

---

⁴⁴ Unlike the lower realms, the *Empyreum* (where God dwells) does not depend on natural laws. In *Paradiso*, Dante is told that "There, near and far do not subtract or add; / for where God governs with no mediator, / no thing depends upon the laws of nature," Dante Alighieri, "*Paradiso 30*," trans. Allen Mandelbaum, Digital Dante, Columbia University Libraries (2019), ll. 30.122–3, https://digitaldante.columbia.edu/dante/divine-comedy/paradiso/paradiso-30/.

⁴⁵ Dante Alighieri, "*Inferno 28*," trans. Allen Mandelbaum, Digital Dante, Columbia University Libraries (2019), ll. 139–142, https://digitaldante.columbia.edu/dante/divine-comedy/inferno/inferno-28/.

⁴⁶ Kingsley, *The Water Babies*, 136.

⁴⁷ It is this charge that Carlyle is defending Dante from when he writes of his "infinite pity."

⁴⁸ Kingsley, *The Water Babies*, 130.

⁴⁹ Kingsley, *The Water Babies*, 133.

⁵⁰ Kingsley, *The Water Babies*, 130.

is a fairy, she is one who works "by machinery, just like an engine; and am full of wheels and springs inside; and am wound up very carefully, so that I cannot help going."[51] Mechanical necessity is, the fairy explains to Tom, the reason why "I cannot help punishing people when they do wrong. I like it no more than they do; I am often very, very sorry for them, poor things: but I cannot help it. If I tried not to do it, I should do it all the same."[52] This mechanical schoolmarm version of "infinite pity, yet also infinite rigour of law" might initially be read as Kingsley's version of the idea of the Divine Watchmaker—the (primarily Deist) theory that "God has wound up the universe like a clock" before leaving it to go on ticking without him.[53] Kingsley, however, found the theory a "shallow mechanical notion of the universe and its Creator which was too much in vogue in the eighteenth century,"[54] thus indicating that, while the moral law might be characterized by a seemingly-mechanical law of cause and effect, God continues to be present and involved with the natural world. This is evident in Tom's later encounter with the evolutionary life-force Mother Carey, who, like Mrs. Bedonebyasyoudid, is one manifestation of the divine presence Kingsley is encouraging his readers to read in the natural world.

Tom's meeting with Mother Carey comes only after he undergoes his moral education with Mrs. Bedonebyasyoudid, Madame Doasyouwouldbedoneby, and his little friend Ellie (the Beatrice figure in the tale). In this way, Kingsley underscores the primacy of moral concerns when it comes to engaging with scientific theories of the natural world. Tom sets off to complete the final stage in his moral development: to "go where [he doesn't] like, and hel[p] someone that [he doesn't] like,"[55] which takes the form of a journey to the Other-end-of-Nowhere to help his former abusive master, Grimes. Along the way he meets Mother Carey, the evolutionary force who is purported to be "always making new beasts out of old," but, Tom discovers, is actually sitting and "mak[ing] them make themselves."[56] The narrator comments that "people do not yet believe that Mother Carey is as clever as all that comes to; and they will not till they, too, go the journey to the Other-end-of-Nowhere."[57] In other words, one must, like Tom, undergo moral development to be able to read nature, and the process of evolution, rightly. Tom's crowning moment of moral development comes when, having found Grimes, Tom effectively guides him to repentance through his

---

[51] Kingsley, *The Water Babies*, 132.
[52] Kingsley, *The Water Babies*, 132.
[53] Kingsley, "The Natural Theology of the Future," n.p.
[54] Kingsley, "The Natural Theology of the Future," n.p.
[55] Kingsley, *The Water Babies*, 151.
[56] Kingsley, *The Water Babies*, 184–5.
[57] Kingsley, *The Water Babies*, 185.

forgiveness of, and compassion on, his old master.⁵⁸ Mrs. Bedonebyasyoudid, who appears during their conversation, becomes momentarily beautiful just when Grimes recognizes that he is deserving of the punishment he is suffering. However, it is only after Grimes is taken away to purgatory (to, in fitting *contrapasso* style, "sweep out the crater of Etna"⁵⁹), that the true beauty, and nature, of Mrs. Bedonebyasyoudid is revealed.

Kingsley draws on Dante throughout *The Water Babies* as a means of articulating and supporting the links he makes between the natural and moral laws, and the interpretation of divine presence in nature. However, the influence of the Florentine poet is particularly evident in the moment of Tom and Ellie's beatific vision. Having been reunited after Tom's journey, the children stand gazing at one another until their attention is demanded by Mrs. Bedonebyasyoudid:

> "look at me once more," said she.
> They looked—and both of them cried out at once, "Oh, who are you, after all?"
> "You are our dear Mrs. Doasyouwouldbedoneby."
> "No, you are good Mrs. Bedonebyasyoudid; but you are grown quite beautiful now!"
> "To you," said the fairy. "But look again."
> "You are Mother Carey," said Tom, in a very low, solemn voice; for he had found out something which made him very happy, and yet frightened him more than all that he had ever seen.
> "But you are grown quite young again."
> "To you," said the fairy. "Look again."
> "You are the Irishwoman who met me the day I went to Harthover!"
> And when they looked she was neither of them, and yet all of them at once.⁶⁰

The emphasis on sight in this final scene, and the changing appearance of Mrs. Bedonebyasyoudid, reflects the Dantean language of the beatific vision in Canto XXXIII of *Paradiso*. Dante recounts that his mind was "completely rapt, intent, / steadfast, and motionless,"⁶¹ in contemplation of the "Living Light at which I gazed,"⁶² and although he emphasizes that the Living Light is one substance he describes how, as he gazes on it, "that sole appearance, even as I altered, / seemed to be changing."⁶³ In a similar way, as the children gaze upon the personification of the moral law they discover that she is, mysteriously, also the personifications of love and the evolutionary life force, as well as the Irishwoman who watched

---

⁵⁸ For more on Grimes' post-death repentance in light of nineteenth-century debates over the existence or nature of hell see Milbank, *Dante and the Victorians*.
⁵⁹ Kingsley, *The Water Babies*, 221.
⁶⁰ Kingsley, *The Water Babies*, 225.
⁶¹ Alighieri, "*Paradiso 33*," ll. 97–8.
⁶² Alighieri, "*Paradiso 33*," l. 110.
⁶³ Alighieri, "*Paradiso 33*," ll. 113–114.

over Tom before he slipped into the river (and who, the narrator has informed the reader earlier, is Queen of the Fairies). It is not until this moment of revelation that Tom perceives the presence of the "divine" in the evolutionary process and begins to understand that the laws of nature, morality, and love are, in some ungraspable sense, one. This is significant, for it underscores Kingsley's emphasis on the necessity of revelation to read the presence of the divine element in nature.

For both Kingsley and Dante, the divine element underlying nature and morality is, of course, specifically Christian. As Dante gazes at the Living Light he perceives that the changes within it take the form of three circles of different colors: "one circle seemed reflected by the second, / as rainbow is by rainbow, and the third / seemed fire breathed equally by those two circles."[64] Seeking to find the figure of Jesus in the Trinitarian vision, Dante recounts that his "wings were far too weak for that. / But then my mind was struck by light that flashed / and, with this light, received what it had asked."[65] In other words, although he is in himself too "weak" to grasp the nature of the Trinity, he is granted a moment of revelation—although he is unable to articulate it (or even properly remember it) later. Dante is both theologically-informed and -transformed and therefore has some understanding of the Living Light he gazes upon. Not so with Tom and Ellie, however. The children's bewilderment in the face of the "divine" fairy creature they are gazing at is only increased as, having revealed the various manifestations of herself, she offers to reveal to them her name—her true identity:

> "My name is written in my eyes, if you have eyes to see it there."
> And they looked into her great, deep, soft eyes, and they changed again and again into every hue, as the light changes in a diamond.
> "Now read my name," said she, at last.
> And her eyes flashed, for one moment, clear, white, blazing light: but the children could not read her name; for they were dazzled, and hid their faces in their hands.
> "Not yet, young things, not yet," said she, smiling.[66]

As the self-reflecting rainbow circles of Dante's trinitarian vision change color, so the changing circles of the fairy's eyes shift in color like the rainbow light refracted by a diamond. While a flash of revelatory light brings Dante illumination, the children's experience of the fairy's flashing eyes dazzles them, and they are unable to "read her name." The divergence from the narrative of Dante's experience serves to emphasize the importance Kingsley placed upon moral development to do natural theology—to read nature aright. While the natural world reveals God, the beauty and goodness of the divine is, it seems, only visible to those who themselves are beautiful and good. The implication in this scene is that further

---

[64] Alighieri, "*Paradiso 33*," ll. 118–120.
[65] Alighieri, "*Paradiso 33*," ll. 139–141.
[66] Kingsley, *The Water Babies*, 225.

development is needed for the "young things" to read revelation fully. Unlike Dante, their wills seem to be slightly out of tempo with the Love *"Qui fait le monde à la ronde."*

I have claimed throughout my reading of Kingsley that he has drawn on Dante as a source of theological and cultural authority as he attempts to reconcile contemporary scientific theories, moral law, and the scriptural revelation of the Christian God. In doing so, he sought to address what he regarded as the encroaching threat of a materialist interpretation of the natural world—one that left no room for the presence of a divine love to, as it were, make the world go round. Kingsley was confident in his intention to "make" his readers see the divine element in nature even if some of the finer points of his thinking were not yet worked out. In this respect, Dante is an ideal source not only because he is dealing with questions of natural and moral law, but also, and perhaps more significantly, because while Dante's account offers profound theological insights the finer details of theory ultimately disappear in the light of revelation. Just before his description of the beatific vision Dante claims that he saw:

> ingathered
> and bound by love into one single volume—
> what, in the universe, seems separate, scattered:
> substances, accidents, and dispositions
> as if conjoined—in such a way that what
> I tell is only rudimentary.[67]

In the profundity of God's light Dante sees the seemingly-chaotic "substances, accidents, and dispositions" of human experience (including, one might venture, the apparent chaos of the natural world), bound together into one book. His attempts to describe the way in which these seemingly-disparate aspects of human existence are reconciled do no justice to the complexity of the vision he sees—to the revelatory reading of this divine "book." This vision of the all-encompassing power of love to hold together what seems separate and scattered in the universe would, in all likelihood, have appealed to Kingsley the man of faith as he himself attempted to read the natural world in light of God's love.

—

While Kingsley's interest in reading nature as the revelation of God was shared by MacDonald, their ideas on the best way to interpret nature diverged from one another in significant ways. Similarly, they both appreciated and appealed to Dante as a source of authority and yet, as we shall presently see, their different notions of God's nature led them to different interpretations of the Florentine

---

[67] Alighieri, *"Paradiso 33,"* ll. 85–90.

poet. Kingsley emphasized faith-driven scientific inquiry in his writings,[68] MacDonald's natural theology was more concerned with an aesthetic and affective appreciation of nature. MacDonald's emphasis on the affective over the scientific did not mean that he was antagonistic to science. He studied the natural sciences as an undergraduate at the University of Aberdeen and considered further studies in that field. MacDonald did, though, regard the scientific method and the knowledge produced by it as being of a lower order than the knowledge one might apprehend by attending to how nature affects a person and what this feeling or impression might indicate about God. In his sermon "The Truth" MacDonald articulates his understanding of this hierarchy of knowledge, claiming that the "idea of God is the flower; his idea is not the botany of the flower. Its botany is but a thing of ways and means—of canvas and colour and brush in relation to the picture in the painter's brain. The mere intellect can never find out that which owes its being to the heart supreme."[69] While Kingsley places Paley in his trinity of natural theologians, MacDonald finds Paley's theories inadequate, even misleading, when it comes to drawing conclusions about the nature of God. He writes that he is "not satisfied that the world should be a proof and varying indication of the intellect of God. That was how Paley viewed it. He taught us to believe there is a God from the mechanism of the world. But, allowing all the argument to be quite correct, what does it prove? A mechanical God, and nothing more."[70] MacDonald believed that the fundamental characteristic of God is not rationality but creativity—a quality that is, for him, inextricable from love. Therefore, to read God's presence in the natural world via scientific analysis is to put oneself at risk of arriving at a faulty understanding of God. MacDonald's belief that God is "the first of artists,"[71] who created all things as an imaginative expression of love, led to his conclusion that the best way of discovering God in nature is to engage with it as a work of art to be attended to and enjoyed, rather than as a mechanism to be analyzed. Significantly, MacDonald writes that even if a person, feeling the effects of nature, is unaware that there is any meaning to be apprehended, "God's thought, unrecognized as such, hold[s] communion with

---

[68] Kingsley's writings emphasize the theological value of a scientific approach to nature, but he did, at least in one instance, discourage a scientific approach to engaging with nature. In 1842 he instructed his future wife, Fanny Grenfell, not to engage with nature scientifically for it would "take an eternity to do" and "superficial science is the devil's spade, with which he loosens the roots of the trees prepared for the burning." Kingsley writes that Fanny should, rather, study and enjoy aspects of the natural world "not to classify them, but to admire them and adore God," *Charles Kingsley: His Letters and Memories of His Life*, 32–3.
[69] George MacDonald, "The Truth," in *Unspoken Sermons (Series 3)* (London: Longmans, Green, and Co., 1889), 65.
[70] George MacDonald, "Wordsworth's Poetry," in *A Dish of Orts: Chiefly Papers on the Imagination, and on Shakspere* (London: Sampson Low, Marston, 1895), 246.
[71] MacDonald, "Wordsworth's Poetry," 246.

her."[72] In other words, a person may "meet" God in nature—and even benefit spiritually and emotionally from that meeting—while yet remaining unconscious of the fact that she has come into contact with the divine. For MacDonald, these experiences of beatitude will eventually waken meanings within the person to give her an even clearer revelation of God.

MacDonald's emphasis on reading nature as a work of art, and his confidence in nature's capacity to awaken its reader spiritually, is echoed in his ideas on reading fairytales. In his essay on "The Fantastic Imagination" he offers advice on how to read fairytales—advice that heavily emphasizes the affective impact of a well-written tale.[73] Fairytales are, like nature, not to be analyzed but experienced and enjoyed. Just as "Nature is mood-engendering, thought-provoking; such ought the sonata, such ought the fairytale to be."[74] Unlike a work that seeks to persuade by logic, fairytales, like nature, aim to "move by suggestion, to cause to imagine."[75] MacDonald is, in most things, primarily concerned with a person's spiritual state and for this reason he writes that, apart from appealing to a person's sense of right and wrong, the best thing one can do for him is not to get him *thinking*, but to get him *feeling*—"to wake things up that are in him."[76] For MacDonald, to awaken meaning within a person is a form of divine encounter. As a product of the mind of God, the natural world is layered with sacred meanings and because human writers necessarily draw on the world around them their work carries within it meanings of which they are unaware. The reader will, therefore, inevitably find (spiritual) meanings within the text that the writer did not intend. For MacDonald, this is particularly the case with fairytales, the "playful form" which, Daniel Gabelman writes, "lightly fertilizes the mind of a reader and initiates a dynamic imaginative exchange that proliferates signification."[77] Furthermore, it is not only the reader and text that are participants in this dynamic imaginative exchange, but God himself. For MacDonald, a "wise imagination […] is the presence of the spirit of God" and "the best guide that man or woman can have,"[78] a claim that not only asserts

---

[72] MacDonald, "Justice," 66.
[73] MacDonald refuses to offer a definition of a fairytale, for he would "as soon think of describing the abstract human face, or state what must go to constitute a human being," George MacDonald, "The Fantastic Imagination," in *The Complete Fairy Tales*, ed. U. C. Knoepflmacher (London: Penguin Books, 1999), 5. For him a fairytale is, like a human being, unique and multi-faceted and cannot be produced by a formula or reduced to an abstract set of criteria.
[74] MacDonald, "The Fantastic Imagination," 9.
[75] MacDonald, "The Fantastic Imagination," 10.
[76] MacDonald, "The Fantastic Imagination," 9.
[77] Daniel Gabelman, *George MacDonald: Divine Carelessness and Fairytale Levity* (Waco, TX: Baylor University Press, 2013), 96.
[78] George MacDonald, "The Imagination: Its Functions and Its Culture," in *A Dish of Orts:*

the intrinsically theological nature of the imagination,[79] but also indicates the guiding—revelatory—presence of God.

One of the most striking aspects of MacDonald's thought on the theological nature of fairytales is his refusal to attempt to control interpretation, whether the interpretation of a fairytale or the natural world. This refusal is due, in part, to his understanding of the dynamic nature of language, but it is also the result of his trust in the unhurried working of God's spirit to reveal God in the timing and in the meanings that will speak best to each person. The idea that God might reveal himself in a piece of music, in a fairytale, or indeed even in nature was a contested one for many religious believers in the nineteenth century. MacDonald's novels are filled with representations of Calvinist evangelicals who, while well-intentioned, are more worried about falling into theological or moral error through self-delusion than in enjoying the beauty of nature, music, or literature. Mr. Osbourne, for instance, who features in MacDonald's 1871 novel *Wilfrid Cumbermede*, is an "Evangelical of the most pure, honest, and narrow type" who offers "a solemn admonishment on the danger of being led astray by what men called the beauties of Nature—for the heart was so desperately wicked that, even of the things God had made *to show his power*, it would make snares for our destruction."[80] While not all evangelicals were so cautious,[81] many did believe that the sinful fallenness of humanity distorted a person's perception so much that the safest kind of reading material was overtly religious and consistent with Calvinist theology.[82] Indeed, MacDonald's theological views on reading

---

Chiefly Papers on the Imagination, and on Shakspere (London: Sampson Low, Marston, 1895), 28.

[79] As with nature, even for those who do not have a "wise" imagination, or even acknowledge God's existence, the imagination still serves as "the voice of God himself," MacDonald, "The Imagination," 32.

[80] George MacDonald, *Wilfrid Cumbermede: An Autobiographical Story* (London: George Routledge & Sons, 1911), 134. Kingsley also refers to this attitude toward nature in "The Natural Theology of the Future."

[81] See Mark Knight, *Good Words: Evangelicalism and the Victorian Novel* (Columbus, OH: Ohio State University Press, 2019). It should also be noted that nineteenth-century concerns over claims about the revelatory potential of literature were not limited to evangelicalism. This can be seen in the Anglo-Catholic John Keble's ideas on the revelatory potential of Pagan literature discussed below. Similarly to MacDonald, Keble found it necessary to defend himself against the accusation "that men have corrupted Truth divinely entrusted to them by an over-zealous devotion to literature," John Keble, *Keble's Lectures on Poetry: 1832–1841*. Vol. 2, trans. Edward Kershaw Francis (Oxford: Clarendon Press, 1912), 471.

[82] MacDonald's own upbringing in a stringently-Calvinist environment where many would have held such views, goes far to explain why he repeatedly addresses the question of whether (and how) literature might reveal the Christian God if "in words there is nothing Christian," George MacDonald, *Adela Cathcart*, 3 vols. (London: Hurst and Blackett, 1864), 2: 262.

and revelation brought him under fire from critics like the evangelical Samuel Law Wilson, who criticizes MacDonald's fiction because "undue emphasis is laid on the part played by natural influences in the process of man's salvation, and regenerating efficacy, which we had thought belonged exclusively to the Spirit of God, is freely attributed to such things as fiddles, kites, scenery, music, and the memorials of departed friends."[83] While Wilson and other who shared his beliefs maintained the need for explicitly Christian language in order for readers to know exactly how they should interpret the process of spiritual conversion as coming about, MacDonald would have read the "regenerating efficacy" of nature, fairytales, and other aesthetic forms as evidence of the Spirit's work. Indeed, the freedom to find one's own meanings within a text or the natural world, and the act of interpretation itself, is, for MacDonald, a vital part of the way that the Spirit reveals God to each person individually. In MacDonald's mind, each person has been made to receive a particular revelation of God and to share that revelation with others, thus broadening the universal understanding of a God who is beyond human comprehension. The act of interpretation thus becomes a participation in the divine life as the Spirit reveals God to each person in the particular meanings that speak to her and she, in turn, offers that revelation to others.

Given how often Dante was appealed to as an authority for various causes in the nineteenth century it is, perhaps, unsurprising that writers turned to him in debates on interpretation and revelation. Milbank points out that thinkers such as Macauley and Ruskin read Dante's poetry as if it "were some sort of biblical commentary," while nineteenth-century liberal theologians prioritized Dante's *Commedia* over "biblical verification" when it came to debates about the credibility of heaven and hell.[84] Several decades before the publication of MacDonald's fairytales John Keble gave his "Lectures on Poetry" (1832–1841) in which he justifies a claim about pagan poets serving as unconscious revealers of divine truth by pointing out that Dante chose Virgil as his guide through the first two stages of his journey and "openly declare[s] that his Master Virgil, among all the writers of antiquity known in his own times, best prepared the way for the seekers after truth."[85] In appealing to Dante as an authority Keble is picking up on an idea articulated in Cantos XXI-II of the *Purgatorio* when Dante and Virgil encounter the poet Statius who tells them that he actually converted to Christianity by reading Virgil's poetry.[86] It is difficult to say whether

---

[83] Samuel Law Wilson, *The Theology of Modern Literature*, (Edinburgh: T&T Clark, 1899), 284.

[84] Milbank, *Dante and the Victorians*, 29, 5.

[85] Keble, *Keble's Lectures*, 472.

[86] In the medieval world Virgil was actually "looked upon as having been an unconscious prophet of Christianity," Dorothy L. Sayers, Introduction to *The Comedy of Dante Alighieri*

Keble would have been willing to draw on Dante to extend his defense of the revelatory potential of poetry to the genre of fairytales (I suspect not, as I doubt he would have placed fairytales alongside such a "high" art form as poetry). Even Kingsley, with his Dantean depiction of revelation in *The Water Babies*, would likely have drawn the line at actually claiming that a fairytale might itself perform a revelatory function. His use of "seeming Tomfooleries" in writing his "parable" was to make his message more palatable to his readers—something he likened to sugaring a pill.[87] Not only does Kingsley regard his message as distinct from the fairytale form, but he sees it as the thing of real substance and benefit. His is an instrumental attitude toward the fairytale.[88] But while the fairytale was largely a means to an end for Kingsley, it operated as a means of revelation for MacDonald.[89] Rather than regarding it as an instrument to serve his own purpose, he saw the fairytale as a live thing "that now flashes, now is dark, but may flash again."[90] These flashes of light—of revelatory meaning—are not engineered by the author, but are the result of the form's revelatory function.

Both Kingsley and MacDonald are not only interested in Dante,[91] but also in the moral development of their protagonists. Their depictions of how this development takes place are bound up in their relative understandings of the ways and means by which God reveals himself. While Tom's development comes about as the result of his interactions with the embodiment of the moral law and his meeting with the evolutionary life force, Curdie's development in *The Princess and Curdie* begins with an experience of nature that underscores the affective over the analytical. His subsequent experiences of magically-produced music lead him to several moments of revelation, both revelation of his own moral state

---

the Florentine: Cantica II, Purgatory, trans. Dorothy L. Sayers (London: Penguin, 1955), 67.

[87] *Charles Kingsley: His Letters and Memories of His Life*, 245.

[88] And a view that, as Daniel Gabelman points out, reveals an anxiety about the fear of the fairytale being misinterpreted. See "Organised Innocence: MacDonald, Lewis and Literature For the Childlike," in *Informing the Inklings: George MacDonald and the Victorian Roots of Modern Fantasy*, ed. Kirstin Jeffrey Johnson and Michael Partridge (Hamden, CT: Winged Lion, 2018), 81.

[89] Even without reference to revelation, MacDonald's ideas about finding individual meanings within fairytales is widely divergent from Kingsley's views on the matter. Writing to his wife in 1842, Kingsley warns her not to "be too solicitous to find deep meanings in men's words. Most men do, and all men ought to mean only what is evident at first sight in their books (unless they be inspired or write for a private eye). This is the great danger of such men as Novalis, that you never know much he means," *Charles Kingsley: His Letters and Memories of His Life*, 33. MacDonald, of course, admired Novalis at least as much as he did Dante.

[90] MacDonald, "The Fantastic Imagination," 10.

[91] Dante's *Divine Comedy* was a favorite lecture topic for MacDonald, who often gave a three-part series of lectures (one on each part of the poem) over the course of as many days. He lectured in cities from Belfast to Glasgow to London, as well as in his home in Bordighera Italy.

and of the shape-shifting princess (the divine being in the story). By and large, MacDonald tends to emphasize the positive, aesthetic impact of nature, but the stirring-up of less positive feelings has its place in provoking thought as well. In this case, Curdie's interpretation of the natural world is colored by feelings of guilt and shame for he has needlessly shot down one of the white pigeons belonging to the "grand old princess" with an arrow. Assaulted by guilt, Curdie feels that suddenly "everything round about him seemed against him. The red sunset stung him; the rocks frowned at him; the sweet wind that had been laving his face as he walked up the hill dropped—as if he wasn't fit to be kissed any more. Was the whole world going to cast him out?"[92] MacDonald's claims about the "mood-engendering, thought-provoking" power of nature—a power that speaks to each person as he has need—is here illustrated in the effect that nature has in "rousing [the] conscience" of Curdie.[93] Unlike the biblical murderer Cain, though, Curdie is not destined to be cast out to wander the earth. As he stands uncertain of what to do with the newly-roused feelings of dissatisfaction with himself, or indeed with the dying pigeon in his hand, Curdie sees a great light shining from the castle nearby. The light turns out to be the old princess' moon lamp—a symbol of divine guidance and revelatory light both here and in *The Princess and the Goblin*.[94] Curdie follows the light but is uncertain of where exactly to find the old princess once he is inside the castle. In his search for her he knocks on a door and "heard no answer. He was answered nevertheless; for the door gently opened."[95] This allusion to Christ's assurance in the gospel of Matthew that the door to God will be opened to those who knock[96] not only hints that Curdie is being guided by the princess in some mysterious way, but also underscores the revelatory nature of his subsequent meeting with her.

Curdie has been brought into the princess' castle by way of nature and by the guiding light of her moon lamp. It is, however, through the revelatory power of music that he first comes face-to-face with the old princess. As he stands in a

---

[92] George MacDonald, *The Princess and the Goblin and The Princess and Curdie*, (Oxford: Oxford University Press, 1990), 182.
[93] MacDonald, "The Fantastic Imagination," 9.
[94] The revelatory nature of the moon-lamp is particularly evident in *The Princess and the Goblin* when the old princess tells her great-granddaughter Irene that without it Irene "would fancy [her]self lying in a bare garret, on a heap of old straw, and would not see one of the pleasant things round about [her]," MacDonald, *The Princess and the Goblin and The Princess and Curdie*, 65. This is precisely how Curdie sees the grandmother's room in *The Princess and the Goblin*, for, it seems, he is not yet ready the revelation he has of her in *The Princess and Curdie*.
[95] MacDonald, *The Princess and the Goblin and The Princess and Curdie*, 185–6.
[96] "Ask, and it shall be given you; seek, and ye shall find; knock, and it shall be opened unto you: For every one that asketh receiveth; and he that seeketh findeth; and to him that knocketh it shall be opened," Matt. 7:7, KJV.

corridor with two doors, uncertain as to which he should knock at, he hears the sound of a spinning wheel which he recognizes instantly "because his mother's spinning wheel had been his governess long ago, and still taught him things. It was the spinning wheel that first taught him to make verses, and to sing, and to think whether all was right inside him."[97] It is music and not a rigorous moral law of cause and effect that forms Curdie's sense of right and wrong and continues to act as his spiritual guide. This mentorship is, significantly, both spiritual and creative for it has not only informed Curdie's spiritual development but his growth as a poet and singer as well. It is not, however, only music that has acted as Curdie's guide. As he listens, the thought-provoking power of the wheel's music draws him into a trance, "spinning in his brain songs and tales and rhymes."[98] In keeping with MacDonald's capacious understanding of the means by which God reveals himself, music, poetry, and (fairy)tales are all here associated with Curdie's moral sense and development. Furthermore, there are several moments in Curdie's subsequent conversations with the old princess where the music of her spinning wheel and her own voice are either indistinguishable from one another or join together to convey something to him. The second time Curdie visits the princess in her room she asks him to tell her what the music is saying:

> "It is singing," answered Curdie.
> "What is it singing?"
> Curdie tried to make out, but thought he could not; for no sooner had he got a hold of something than it vanished again. Yet he listened, and listened, entranced with delight.[99]

The music resists intellectual comprehension and precise linguistic description (characteristics that MacDonald also applies to language in "The Fantastic Imagination"), but consistent with MacDonald's ideas about the power of nature, music, and fairytales to reveal divine meanings, Curdie has apprehended more than he realizes. To help him realize how much he has actually grasped the princess plays her wheel and sings a song that, the narrator tells the reader, "would make you weep if I were able to tell you what that was like, it was so beautiful and true and lovely."[100] The merging of voice and music once again highlights both the revelatory power of the creative art and the artistically-creative nature of the divine being. Furthermore, the narrator's inability to articulate what the song was like indicates ineffability, thus gesturing toward the mystical function of music and language. Upon finishing her song, she extends an invitation: "Come now, Curdie, to this side of my wheel, and you will find me."[101] Until now the

---

[97] MacDonald, *The Princess and the Goblin and The Princess and Curdie*, 186.
[98] MacDonald, *The Princess and the Goblin and The Princess and Curdie*, 186.
[99] MacDonald, *The Princess and the Goblin and The Princess and Curdie*, 216.
[100] MacDonald, *The Princess and the Goblin and The Princess and Curdie*, 216–17.
[101] MacDonald, *The Princess and the Goblin and The Princess and Curdie*, 217.

princess had been hidden behind the "great revolving wheel in the sky," but now, after teaching him how to understand, or interpret, her music, she invites him to experience a fuller revelation.[102]

In addition to highlighting the old princess' creativity and representing Curdie's moral education as taking place through an aesthetic medium, I read MacDonald's representation of the divine figure as offering a subtle corrective to the notion of divine justice that underwrites Tom's moral education in *The Water Babies* and the punishment meted out in Dante's *Inferno*. Unlike Kingsley's interpretation of Dante's tortured souls as evidence of the pity and rigor of the moral and natural law (and thus of God), MacDonald read Dante's attitude as a demonstration of how "Pity and truth had abandoned [Dante] together,"[103] and argued that "God is not God as He is represented" in Dante's hell.[104] MacDonald's critique of this representation of justice is evident in the treatment Curdie receives from the old princess. Having knocked at the door from which the music proceeds, and having been answered, Curdie enters the room to find "a small withered creature" spinning away at a wheel that is as delicate as "a spider's web in a hedge."[105] He is initially amused by the princess' less-than-impressive appearance, but then "the little lady leaned forward into the moonlight, and Curdie caught a glimpse of her eyes, and all the laugh went out of him."[106] Curdie's reaction at seeing the princess' eyes—the one aspect of her that never changes—is one of awe. This is because, as in *The Water Babies*, it is the princess' eyes that most clearly reveal her divine nature. Curdie shows this figure of divine authority the injured bird and, having seen that he did not mean any harm, she tells him that although "whoever does not mean good is always in danger of harm," she does her best "to give everybody fair play; and those that are in the wrong are in far more need of it always than those who are in the right: they can afford to do without it."[107] Unlike Mrs. Bedonebyasyoudid, who cannot help punishing even if the culprit did not intend any harm, the old princess operates on the moral principle of "fair play," which takes into account the variety of factors at play in the operation of justice.

For many in the nineteenth century, the growing understanding of the effect of heredity and environment upon a person, and the increasing influence of theories that emphasized the reformation of criminal behavior over

---

[102] MacDonald, *The Princess and the Goblin and The Princess and Curdie*, 216.
[103] George MacDonald, *The Seaboard Parish* (Philadelphia: David McKay, 1911), 472.
[104] George MacDonald, "Dante's Inferno," *The Shields Daily News* (May 20, 1890): 11.
[105] MacDonald, *The Princess and the Goblin and The Princess and Curdie*, 186.
[106] MacDonald, *The Princess and the Goblin and The Princess and Curdie*, 188.
[107] MacDonald, *The Princess and the Goblin and The Princess and Curdie*, 188.

simple punishment, made a Dantean notion of hell (and justice) untenable.[108] MacDonald's "fair play" not only takes human complexity into account, but also emphasizes that the point of justice is not punishment but the refining and restoration of the individual. This conception of justice is echoed in one of his lectures on Dante (and in his references to Dante in his sermons on justice), in which he articulates his main critique of Dante that, "tied down as he was with the low poverty-stricken notion of what justice was, [he] thought it meant tit-for-tat" whereas the justice of God means "that He gives every creature He has made fair play."[109] While this cutting reference to Dante's notion of justice as "tit-for-tat" might seem to reduce a weighty theological topic to the realm of schoolyard slang MacDonald uses such language to cut through a theological discourse that, for him, only serves to mask injustice. "Tit-for-tat" offers an appropriate contrast to "fair play"—a phrase that he acknowledges as "boyish" but which he uses because it is "the best the language will now afford me because of misuse."[110] Turning back to *Curdie* we find that, unlike Dante's tit-for-tat (which does not refine or restore the sinners in hell), or the mechanistic law of punishment and reward through which Tom receives his moral education, it is the princess' practice of "fair play" and her spinning-wheel song that awaken Curdie's conscience and lead to an even fuller revelation of the princess.

Unlike the *The Water Babies*, which culminates in a final scene of Dantean revelation, Curdie experiences several moments of increasing revelation as he gets to know the princess. However, the revelation scene that is most Dantean in language, and which most closely parallels the one found in *The Water-Babies*, takes place as Curdie and his father see a light deep in the mines where they are working. The light grows, and, echoing the Dantean focus on vision, the two miners see a "dark and yet luminous face" looking at them with "living eyes":

> Curdie felt a great awe swell up in his heart, for he thought he had seen those eyes before.
> "I see you know me, Curdie," said a voice.
> "If your eyes are you, ma'm, then I know you," said Curdie.[111]

As they watch, a lady is revealed whose appearance is as young and beautiful as it was old and crooked upon Curdie's last meeting with her. As she reveals herself in her full form the natural world around them is also transformed: the underground cavern is filled with light that comes "streaming, sparkling, and shooting from stones of many colours in the sides and roof and floor."[112] The

---

[108] See Geoffrey Rowell, *Hell and the Victorians* (Oxford: Oxford University Press, 1974), 13.
[109] George MacDonald, "Dante's Divine Comedy," ed. Barbara Amell, *Wingfold* 49 (2005): 20–21.
[110] MacDonald, "Justice," 115.
[111] MacDonald, *The Princess and the Goblin and The Princess and Curdie*, 203.
[112] MacDonald, *The Princess and the Goblin and The Princess and Curdie*, 204.

reflected rainbow light evokes Dante's Trinitarian vision, especially when Curdie's gaze shifts from contemplating the gemstones and "all the beauty of the cavern" to the lady herself—for "all he knew of the whole creation, seemed gathered in one centre of harmony and loveliness in the person of the ancient lady who stood before him in the very summer of beauty and strength."[113] Eternal in her ancient youth, the princess is referred to in this passage as the "Mother of Light" and the "Lady of Light"—feminized versions of the biblical "Father of Lights" and the "Eternal Light" that Dante gazes upon in *Paradiso*'s Canto XXXIII.[114]

Even with the revelation he is given, Curdie remains uncertain as to how he should interpret the nature and identity of the ancient princess. In a manner echoing Dante's attempts to understand the presence of Christ in the dynamic movement of the Trinity, Curdie attempts to find out the real "name" of the creative divinity who has revealed herself to him in various forms. Upon asking her if she is the "Lady of the Silver Moon," she responds in the affirmative before adding that he may call her what he likes for "[w]hat it means is true."[115] MacDonald's ideas about the multiplicity of meanings to be found in fairytales, and the freedom of interpretation to name those meanings as they present themselves, are here applied to the revelation of the dynamic and creative princess. The association MacDonald makes here between the individual's interpretation of fairytales and her experience of divine revelation is reflected in his unspoken sermon "The New Name," which claims that each person has a particular revelation of God—indeed that there is, in a sense, "a chamber in God himself, into which none can enter but the one, the individual, the peculiar man,—out of which chamber that man has to bring revelation and strength for his brethren. This is that for which he was made—to reveal the secret things of the Father."[116] The princess goes on to say that she "could give you twenty names more to call me, Curdie, and not one of them would be a false one. What does it matter how many names if the person is one?"[117] The important thing is, then, not to know

---

[113] MacDonald, *The Princess and the Goblin and The Princess and Curdie*, 204. Like Kingsley, MacDonald draws on both the Dantean imagery of the beatific vision and on that used to describe Beatrice.

[114] These feminized titles might initially be read as references to the Virgin Mary, especially given the princess' possession of a purifying fire of burning roses (roses are a typical symbol of Mary and one that Dante draws on to depict the place of her heavenly residence in *Paradiso*'s Canto XXXI). Despite these associations, however, and despite his high regard for the mother of Jesus, MacDonald does not seem to have Mary in mind. His lectures on Dante make clear that he regards her elevation in the *Paradiso* as an act that replaces Christ, and that such a replacement indicates a sign of spiritual weakness: out of fear of Christ people (including Dante, apparently) "took refuge with His mother," MacDonald, "Dante's Divine Comedy," 20–21.

[115] MacDonald, *The Princess and the Goblin and The Princess and Curdie*, 208–9.

[116] George MacDonald, "The New Name," in *Unspoken Sermons* (London: Strahan, 1867), 112.

[117] MacDonald, *The Princess and the Goblin and The Princess and Curdie*, 208–9.

the princess' name but to know the princess herself. When Curdie worries that he will be unable to recognize her the next time she appears to him in a different form and asks "could you not give me some sign, or tell me something about you that never changes—or some other way to know you, or thing to know you by?" she responds by telling him that that would be "but to know the sign of Me—not to know me myself."[118] There is, in other words, a constant need for her continued revelation, and Curdie's interpretation, in order for him to know not just the sign or the form but the dynamic person herself.

Turning briefly to consider the scene of revelation in "The Lost Princess: A Double Story" we find the same cluster of ideas being played out in similarly Dantean language, but with an even more overt reference to fairytales as the revelatory medium. Near the end of the story the princess Rosamond is set a series of trials by the wise woman all of which take place in a "mood-chamber"—a room that transports Rosamond to another world and has similarly "mood-engendering, thought-provoking" properties to MacDonald's definition of a fairytale. For the third and most crucial trial Rosamond enters a world where flowers grow by magic, a winged pony makes an appearance, and she converses with a "goddess-child." It is, in other words, a fairytale world. Rosamund passes a series of tests in this fairy world, before, standing before the goddess-child, an interchange occurs that is striking in its resemblance to the language and structure of Kingsley's Dantean revelation scene:

> "Did you never see me before, Rosamond?" [the child] asked.
> "No, never," answered the princess. "I never saw any thing half so lovely."
> "Look at me," said the child.
> And as Rosamond looked, the child began [...] to grow larger. Quickly through every gradation of growth she passed, until she stood before her a woman perfectly beautiful, neither old nor young; for hers was the old age of everlasting youth.
> Rosamond was utterly enchanted, and stood gazing without word or movement until she could endure no more delight.[119]

Lost in the contemplation of this beatific vision whose everlasting youth and old age reflect the eternal nature of the Trinity, Rosamond is, like Dante, eventually overwhelmed. Her "mind collapse[s]" and she finds herself back in the wise woman's cottage with the goddess-child still before her.[120] As with Dante, the force of Rosamond's "high fantasy"[121] has failed, but the work of the wise woman (who is, of course, also the goddess-child and the beautiful lady) has succeeded—

---

[118] MacDonald, *The Princess and the Goblin and The Princess and Curdie*, 210.
[119] George MacDonald, "The Wise Woman, or The Lost Princess: A Double Story," in *The Complete Fairytales*, ed. U. C. Knoepflmacher (London: Penguin Classics, 1999), 293.
[120] MacDonald, "The Wise Woman, or The Lost Princess: A Double Story," 293.
[121] Alighieri, "*Paradiso 33*," l. 142.

Rosamond's will has begun to align with that of divine love. The wise woman warns Rosamund not to dismiss the revelation she has seen in the fairytale world: "Do not think [...] that the things you have seen in my house are mere empty shows. You do not know, you cannot yet think, how living and true they are."[122] The tendency to elide the worlds and experiences of the historical Dante (the poet) and the fictional Dante (the pilgrim), and thus to find in it a theological resource, is here productively reflected in Rosamund's experience in the wise woman's fairytale world. The fairytale, like Dante's *Commedia*, is not an "empty show" but is in many ways both "living and true" and may thus act as a guide as she continues to develop morally. The wise woman's warning is also, however, a reminder to the reader that the tale she is reading is, like the worlds of Dante and of Rosamund, one that is alive with divine meanings.

It seems fitting that in the sermon quoted at the start of this chapter Kingsley claims that Dante "described most truly and wonderfully, in his own way, heaven and hell." Kingsley's characterization of what critics such as Colin Manlove have described as one of the earliest, if not *the* earliest, works of Christian fantasy,[123] happily echoes MacDonald's characterization of fairytales as "living and true." While Kingsley and MacDonald differed in aspects of their interpretations of Dante, their shared appeal to his work demonstrates not only the rich aesthetic, cultural, and theological resources of the *Commedia*, but the creativity of the Victorian writers in drawing on these resources in order to participate in debates about interpretation, revelation, and the nature of God. Kingsley's commitment to scientific and theological adaptation is reflected in his appeal to Dante—a natural theologian who, although operating within a different scientific framework, continued to offer resources for the development, and the fantastical depiction, of nineteenth-century natural theology. Drawing on the Dantean beatific vision in *The Water Babies*, Kingsley reveals the divine presence that informs the natural and moral laws that he—and in his mind Dante— understood to be fundamentally connected. In reading Dante as he does, and in drawing on Dante's cultural authority to combat the threat of materialism, Kingsley enlists the Florentine poet to help him point the reader outside of the text to arrive at a "right reading" of nature. Like Kingsley, MacDonald adapts the representation of Dante's beatific vision to articulate his ideas about how to read revelation. However, instead of pointing the reader outside to nature MacDonald invites her deeper into the fairytale to read her own meanings, and the presence of the divine, within the text. In doing so, he offers an affective

---

[122] MacDonald, "The Wise Woman, or The Lost Princess: A Double Story," 294.
[123] Manlove, *Christian Fantasy*, 21.

form of natural theology that goes beyond the scientific enquiry of nature to interpret various forms of art as revelatory. Unlike Kingsley's focus on the moral law as educative, MacDonald depicts music and the literary arts as performing a spiritually-pedagogic function. His depiction echoes Dante's choice of Virgil the pagan poet as teacher and guide on his journey toward heavenly revelation and represents MacDonald's own theological emphasis on God's creativity. For both Kingsley and MacDonald, Dante's *Commedia* offered not only cultural authority as they weighed in on nineteenth-century theological debates, but also a fantasy that inspired their imaginations as they sought to articulate their own visions of the divine.

Part III
MacDonald and Theology

PHANTASTES AS THEOLOGICAL CRITIQUE OF E. T. A. HOFFMANN'S *THE GOLDEN POT*[1]

Charles Beaucham

In his sermon, "Life," MacDonald laments the commonplace state of humanity:

> The condition of most men and women seems to me a life in death, an abode in unwhited sepulchres, a possession of withering forms by spirits that slumber, and babble in their dreams. That they do not feel it so, is nothing. The sow wallowing in the mire may rightly assert it her way of being clean, but theirs is not the life of the God-born.[2]

Yet these men and women are not distressed by their condition. Rather, they are quite comfortable and even pleased with it. In *Miracles of Our Lord*, MacDonald describes a "destroying spirit, who works in the commonplace," and "is ever covering the deep and clouding the high." The deep and high things of God are made commonplace for these people who "cannot see them, for in themselves they do not aspire."[3] MacDonald views it as the Christian's ever-present task to resist this spirit of the commonplace, that is, to "believe in God our strength in the face of all seeming denial, to believe in him out of the heart of weakness and unbelief, in spite of numbness and weariness and lethargy; to believe in the wide-awake real, through all the stupefying, enervating, distorting dream."[4] When our vision of God is dimmed and our deepest longings are obscured, we are most vulnerable to succumbing to the comfort of the commonplace. The commonplace is easily accessible, it does not stir up any frustratingly unattainable longings, and it demands nothing of us morally. The "sow wallowing in the mire" is perfectly contented and any aspiration for a higher life would ruin that contentment. By contrast, the Incarnation of Christ is an invasion of the commonplace. Christ's presence in the commonplace disrupts the easy comfort of the spiritually numb and confronts them with divine reality. It also sacralizes the commonplace, revealing it as a gateway to the divine rather than an end point in itself. For

---

[1] This chapter is a substantially revised and expanded version of an article of the same title published in *North Wind: A Journal of George MacDonald Studies* 38 (2019): 95–104.
[2] George MacDonald, "Life," in *Unspoken Sermons* (Whitehorn, CA: Johannesen, 2004), 308.
[3] George MacDonald, *Miracles of Our Lord* (Whitehorn, CA: Johannesen, 2000), 245–6.
[4] MacDonald, "Life," 305.

MacDonald, the Incarnation was essential to his artistic attempts to redeem the commonplace.

In *George MacDonald in the Age of Miracles*, Timothy Larsen draws on the work of Boyd Hilton to trace the theological shift in the Victorian church from an emphasis on the Atonement to an emphasis on the Incarnation. Larsen argues that MacDonald "is a fine representative of the Age of Incarnation in terms of theological themes that he stressed throughout his life, work, sermons, and ministry."[5] The centrality of the Incarnation to MacDonald's theology becomes especially clear when it is isolated as a differentiating factor between *Phantastes* (1858) and one of its primary literary antecedents, E. T. A. Hoffmann's *The Golden Pot* (1814).

In a letter to his wife written in 1856 (two years before MacDonald began *Phantastes*), MacDonald shared that he was reading *The Golden Pot* "again" and found it "delightful."[6] Greville MacDonald speculates that "it made an arresting impression on him," and goes on to mark the many ways it likely influenced *Phantastes*, highlighting the "faculty of bi-local existing" in both stories— that is, the coexistence of different worlds in one physical space. Stephen Prickett notes that *The Golden Pot* has "regularly been cited as a probable model for *Phantastes*;" however, he argues that "any structural resemblance" between the two texts "is very slight."[7] Prickett's assessment may seem correct if one merely compares the linear sequence and external trappings of each novel. However, what Prickett misses is that the plot of *Phantastes* is an inversion of the plot of *The Golden Pot*—an engagement with *The Golden Pot* that demonstrates the significance of its influence on the structure and themes of *Phantastes*.

The Golden Pot is almost entirely set in the commonplace world with the ideal world miraculously breaking into it in the form of Serpentina, the green snake. In *Phantastes*, however, the opposite is true. Anodos spends nearly all his time in the realm of Fairy Land (where ideal beauty resides), while the mundane world occasionally breaks through in the form of the shadow's disenchanting effect on Anodos' perception. Furthermore, while Anselmus leaves the world of men behind forever, Anodos returns to it. These divergent endings articulate equally divergent theological conceptions of the spiritual journey and man's relationship both to common and to ultimate reality. In *The Golden Pot*, the goal of the spiritual journey is to escape the common world in a Platonic flight to ultimate reality. In *Phantastes*, the goal (or, perhaps, a goal) of the spiritual journey

---

[5] Timothy Larsen, *George MacDonald in the Ages of Miracles* (Downers Grove, IL: IVP Academic, 2018), 28.

[6] Greville MacDonald, *George MacDonald and His Wife* (London: George Allen & Unwin, 1924), 298.

[7] Stephen Prickett, *Victorian Fantasy* (Waco, TX: Baylor University Press, 2005), 182.

is to discover the divine inherent in the common and to contribute selflessly to the redemption of the common from the "degrading spirit of the commonplace." Although Platonic philosophy is integral to *Phantastes*, MacDonald ultimately breaks with Hoffmann's purely Platonic worldview by inverting Hoffmann's plot. In this regard, *Phantastes* may be read as offering a theological critique of *The Golden Pot*. Moreover, by reading *Phantastes* in this way, we can see which aspects of Platonic philosophy MacDonald affirms and which aspects he rejects in favor of the Christian doctrine of the Incarnation.

Though separated by over fifty years, both MacDonald and Hoffmann are attempting to subvert the same pernicious social and economic forces unleashed by the Enlightenment and the Industrial Revolution, forces which desacralized human life in the pursuit of profit and efficiency. MacDonald pays homage to Hoffmann by incorporating much of *The Golden Pot* into *Phantastes*, but his inversion serves not only to critique Hoffmann's *Weltanschauung* in the abstract, but also to overcome its theological inadequacy in challenging the harmful forces of political economy dominant in nineteenth-century Europe. While it is unclear to what extent MacDonald consciously intended *Phantastes* as a critique of *The Golden Pot*, I will argue that when put in dialogue with Hoffmann's text MacDonald's incarnational theology emerges as a confrontational aspect of *Phantastes*.

MISENCHANTMENT

To varying degrees, both MacDonald and Hoffman draw on a Platonic model of reality to represent the same conflict between the commonplace and the ideal. Their protagonists have visions of otherworldly bliss, but the vision is fragile and easily obscured by worldly influence. Through these plots, MacDonald and Hoffman, like the Romantics, are attempting to work out a resolution to a larger spiritual crisis that had overtaken nineteenth-century Europe in Hoffmann's lifetime and continued to develop as MacDonald began writing. The enchanted, sacramental world of Medieval Christendom had passed. A new scientific understanding of the world had disenchanted it. "Political economy" or capitalism, as represented by Adam Smith's *The Wealth of Nations* (1776), had emerged, redefining both social progress and individual virtue in terms of the self-interested pursuit of wealth.

In *The Enchantments of Mammon*, Eugene McCarraher traces the dramatic shift in worldview brought about by Enlightenment thinkers and Protestant theologians. McCarraher's claim is that, rather than disenchanting the world as Weber famously argued, political economy cast its own competing form of enchantment as the sacramental universe of medieval Christendom was dismantled. This "reformation of enchantment" produced a "new metaphysical imagination," out of which arose "a cosmology of matter and spirit conducive to industrial exploitation."[8] Protestant theology, especially Calvinist theology, destroyed "the Catholic sacramental architecture that sacralized medieval society," which resulted in the upending of traditional values in favor of capitalist enchantment. Furthermore, "by commencing the desacralization of nature— the denial of any sacramental character in matter—Protestants set the stage for pecuniary enchantment, the unwitting metaphysics of capital."[9] According to McCarraher, once the "Catholic sacramental architecture" was dismantled by Protestant theologians and Enlightenment thinkers, work, motivated by the self-interested desire for individual wealth and status, was exalted to the preeminent ideal of human flourishing. This seemingly godless pursuit of wealth, however, was integrated into a warped theological vision in which economic productivity, rather than sacramental adoration and humble service to the poor, became the means of glorifying God. McCarraher points to the writings of Anglican pastor and economist Thomas Malthus as offering one influential articulation of this emerging ideology:

> Departing from the mainstream of Christian theology since Augustine, Malthus argued that moral evils and natural calamities were "absolutely necessary to the production of moral excellence [...] instruments employed by the Deity" to spur industriousness and ingenuity [...]. Malthus wrote in the 1826 edition [of *Essay on the Principle of Population*], "we should facilitate, instead of foolishly and vainly endeavoring to impede, the operations of nature in producing this mortality"—i.e., the death of the poor.[10]

According to Malthus, the free market was ordained by God to produce virtue and discourage vice. In conflating the market with divine purpose, Malthus defines virtue as behaviors and dispositions that lead to success in the market. Wealth takes on a teleological significance, resulting in the sanctification of work, a type of work motivated by pecuniary self-interest rather than a desire to contribute to the common good. Rather than considering political economy as a separate and secular realm of human life, British evangelicals viewed it as an integral part of their religion. One British evangelical praised "the harmony and beauty, the symmetry and order of that system, which God and nature have established in the world."[11] To these evangelical economists, "the laws of the market, discernible by science, were the edicts of an active and ever-present Almighty." This fusion

---

[8] Eugene McCarraher, *The Enchantments of Mammon: How Capitalism Became the Religion of Modernity* (Cambridge, MA: Harvard University Press, 2019), 23.
[9] McCarraher, *The Enchantments of Mammon*, 29.
[10] McCarraher, *The Enchantments of Mammon*, 52–3.
[11] Quoted in McCarraher, *The Enchantments of Mammon*, 50.

of religious sentiment with economics resulted in "the theology of capitalist misenchantment."[12]

Rather than disenchanting a sacramental universe, capitalism became a competing form of enchantment that in some cases appropriated the language of Protestant theology to achieve a deification of market forces, pecuniary self-interest, and general economic utility. These evangelical economists imbued a secular economic theory with ultimate theological significance using the sacral language of Christian liturgy. This religious branding of the science of self-interest conveniently justified and sacralized the pursuit of profit in the minds of businessmen who served Mammon in the name of God. What McCarraher calls the "theology of capitalist misenchantment" stood in direct opposition to the ideals and values of orthodox Christianity as represented in scripture and Catholic tradition, meriting the negative term "misenchantment."

Although neither MacDonald nor Hoffmann was Catholic, they would likely agree with much of McCarraher's diagnosis of Europe's increasingly "mammon-worshiping" culture as being under the spell of "capitalist misenchantment." Both MacDonald and Hoffmann despised the pursuit of wealth and resented the extent to which they were forced to compromise their artistic vocations to make a living. Both were so devoted to aesthetic and spiritual pursuits that they resented having to engage with the more practical-minded bourgeois, on whom they were dependent for their living. According to Peter Bruning, Hoffmann abandoned:

> the relatively secure and respectable civil service to which his legal education commended him—"die Staatskrippe" as he termed it [… and] temporarily slid into the bohemian life of a poverty-ridden private tutor of piano and voice. Under these circumstances he found himself entirely at the mercy of the well-to-do bourgeois from whose ranks he had alienated himself.[13]

Hoffmann despised the "middle-class dilettantes–people with whom he had nothing in common, and whom in reality he resented."[14] In his introduction to Hoffman's *Fantasiestucke in Callots Manier*, Jean Paul remarks that Hoffmann was prone to "hate humanity out of a love of art."[15]

MacDonald's experience as a young man pursuing his artistic vocation was similar to Hoffmann's. Larsen notes that, as a young pastor, MacDonald "haughtily assumed that those in trade or business were worldly, greedy, vulgar,

---

[12] McCarraher, *The Enchantments of Mammon*, 50.
[13] Peter Bruning, "E. T. A. Hoffmann and the Philistine," *The German Quarterly* 28, no. 2 (1955): 112.
[14] Bruning, "Hoffmann and the Philistine," 112.
[15] My translation of "aus Künstliebe in Menschenhass geraten." Quoted in Bruning, "Hoffmann and the Philistine," 112.

and dishonest, and therefore he did not respect his deacons."[16] MacDonald did not last long as a pastor and was forced out of his position after just two years. Larsen suspects "that MacDonald might even have been unconsciously sabotaging his own ministry. His real dream was to be a poet."[17] MacDonald and Hoffmann both, somewhat reluctantly, found a degree of commercial success as novelists. Hoffmann thought of himself first and foremost as a musician, viewing music as the purest of arts. Under the necessity of supporting his large family, MacDonald turned from writing poetry and Romance to the realistic fiction novels preferred by the market. Personally and professionally, MacDonald and Hoffmann's devotion to the ideal was tested by a world under capitalist misenchantment, and we can see this struggle reflected in their writings.

This chapter argues that MacDonald offers a distinctly Christian response to capitalist misenchantment as opposed to Hoffmann's purely Platonic response. However, before I demonstrate how incarnational theology differentiates *Phantastes* from *The Golden Pot*, I will first consider the extent to which both stories embody Platonic philosophy.

TRUE BEAUTY IN *PHANTASTES* AND *THE GOLDEN POT*

In *Phantastes*, Fairy Land is literally an other-worldly realm filled with beings, forms, and tangible realities that correspond to humanity's deepest desires, as well as its existential dreads. The novel's second and longest epigraph, a quotation from Novalis, offers insight into MacDonald's creative vision of Fairy Land and its function in the novel. In a true *Märchen*, writes Novalis, "the whole of nature must be wondrously blended with the whole world of the Spirit" and "the world of the fairy story is that world which is opposed throughout to the world of rational truth."[18] In the "world of rational truth," as Novalis terms the everyday world, one's deepest longings are muted and obscured, but in the world of Fairy, the realm of spiritual longing assumes the form of tangible reality.

Anodos is first introduced to Fairy Land by his fairy-grandmother, whose beauty partakes of Fairy Land's transcendence. As he looks into her eyes, "they [fill him] with an unknown longing," and Anodos feels as if those eyes contained a vast sea in whose waters he would gladly sink.[19] When Anodos comes out of his reverie, he realizes that he is only looking at a "low bog burnished by the moon," and declares, with hopeful longing, that "surely there must be such a

---

[16] Larsen, *George MacDonald in the Age of Miracles*, 99.
[17] Larsen, *George MacDonald in the Age of Miracles*, 97.
[18] George MacDonald, *Phantastes*, ed. John Pennington and Roderick McGillis (Hamden, CT: Winged Lion, 2017), 198.
[19] George MacDonald, *Phantastes: A Faerie Romance for Men and Women* (Whitehorn, CA: Johannesen, 2000), 19. All subsequent references to this text come from this edition.

sea somewhere!" In "a low sweet voice," Anodos hears his grandmother reply, "in Fairy Land, Anodos."[20] Although Anodos will never find the ocean he longs for in the world of men, such an ocean does exist in Fairy Land, a world in which poetic reality takes definite shape. In the novel's first chapter, Fairy Land is defined as a realm in which the ideal can transcend the commonplace. Just as Anodos' grandmother teaches him that the sea he longs for is in Fairy Land, Diotima, in Plato's *Symposium,* teaches Socrates that he will find true beauty by gazing "not at beauty in a single example [… but by turning] to the great sea of beauty." This "great sea of beauty," continues Diotima, "is not anywhere in another thing, as in an animal or in earth, or in heaven, or in anything else, but itself by itself with itself, it is always one in form; and all the other beautiful things share in that."[21] The "low bog burnished by the moon" that momentarily captivates Anodos merely partakes of that "great sea of beauty" that actually exists in its ideal form in Fairy Land. MacDonald's Fairy Land clearly does not always correspond to Plato's ideal realm: there are terrors and deceptions in Fairy Land as well as beauty, but it seems that in Fairy Land it is possible to experience ideal beauty.

Anodos encounters the most perfect form of Fairy Land's other-worldly beauty in the Marble Lady: "What I did see appeared to me perfectly lovely; more near the face that had been born with me in my soul than anything I had seen before in nature or art."[22] The Platonic overtones, first signaled by his grandmother in her description of Fairy Land, are striking in Anodos' description of the Marble Lady. Anodos remarks that the white, delicate marble from which she is hewn is "destined to become an ideal woman in the arms of the sculptor."[23] She is "perfectly lovely," with a face and form that are beyond "nature or art." Anodos' desire for the Marble Lady clearly transcends the physical—it is his soul that thirsts for her beauty because it "had been born with [him] in [his] soul." This Marble Lady, then, functions as a Platonic form in the inner life of Anodos. Although the Platonic form of beauty is, according to Diotima in Plato's *Symposium,* "absolute, pure, unmixed, not polluted by human flesh or colors or any other great nonsense of mortality," MacDonald must necessarily represent the ideal in concrete rather than abstract terms in a work of fantasy.[24] His purpose is not to philosophize about ultimate beauty in the abstract but to suggest it. However, MacDonald is careful to emphasize that the Marble Lady's

---

[20] MacDonald, *Phantastes,* 19.
[21] Plato, *Symposium,* trans. Alexander Nehamas and Paul Woodruff (Cambridge, MA: Hackett Publishing Company, 1997), 211b.
[22] MacDonald, *Phantastes,* 67–8.
[23] MacDonald, *Phantastes,* 67.
[24] Plato, *Symposium,* 211e.

beauty transcends both art and nature, corresponding to the pure beauty of Platonic philosophy.

Considering MacDonald's well documented love of the *The Golden Pot*, it seems plausible that MacDonald used Hoffmann's portrayal of a character caught between the pull of the commonplace and ideal worlds as a model for *Phantastes*. Like Anodos, Anselmus' longings for true beauty are awakened by and meet their object in an other-worldly female, albeit at first in the form of a green snake with "a pair of glorious dark-blue eyes" that looked "at him with unspeakable longing; and an unknown feeling of the highest blessedness and deepest sorrow [that] was like to rend his heart asunder."[25] The otherworldly beauty of the green snake contrasts sharply with the bourgeois citizens of Dresden and Anselmus' conventional pursuit of wealth and status through the position of Court Counselor. Shortly after his encounter with the green snake, a strange magician named Lindhorst hires Anselmus to copy manuscripts. He gradually learns that Lindhorst is actually an otherworldly being, the salamander or Elemental Spirit of Fire from the ideal realm of Atlantis, who has been banished to the commonplace realm of men until he finds husbands for his three snake daughters. The beautiful green snake that awakened Anselmus' longing turns out to be Lindhorst's daughter, Serpentina. Serpentina functions as a Platonic form of true beauty, originating from the ideal realm of Atlantis, but breaking into the commonplace world of Dresden. Like Anodos, Anselmus becomes obsessed with possessing true beauty in female form, and just as the Marble Lady dwells in the otherworldly realm of Fairy Land, Serpentina comes from the ideal realm of Atlantis. MacDonald maintains the same character dynamic between male protagonist and ideal female, and also emulates Hoffmann by grounding this relationship in Plato's philosophy of ideal beauty.

Anselmus and Anodos also encounter the same challenge in their pursuit of true beauty. In *Phantastes*, much of Anodos' education revolves around his ability to perceive and recognize the ideal. Anodos' first great failure in Fairy Land is his inability to distinguish the true Marble Lady from the deceptions of the Maid of the Alder-tree. This maid claims to be the white Marble Lady, and in the "gathering darkness," Anodos is unable to see that she is lying. He does, however, have a faint premonition that something is not right:

> Yet, if I would have confessed it, there was something either in the sound of the voice, although it seemed sweetness itself, or else in this yielding which awaited no gradation of gentle approaches, that did not vibrate harmoniously with the beat of my inward music. And likewise, when, taking her hand in mine, I drew closer to her, looking for the beauty of her face, which, indeed,

---

[25] E. T. A. Hoffmann, "The Golden Pot" in *German Romance*, trans. Thomas Carlyle (New York: Charles Scribner's Sons, 1898), 28.

I found too plenteously, a cold shiver ran through me; but "it is the marble," I said to myself, and heeded it not.[26]

Anodos' desperate desire to find his white lady compromises his ability to discriminate between the true and the false and, rejecting his intuition, he lets his rash, undisciplined longing get the best of him. The Maid of the Alder-tree craftily delivers Anodos up to the monstrous Ash-tree, and he is only saved by the heroics of the knight. The mistake nearly costs him his life and serves as a painful means of sensitizing and disciplining his sense of true beauty which, according to Plato's Diotima, is the source of virtue. Diotima teaches Socrates that only when one can recognize pure beauty "will it become possible for him to give birth not to images of virtue (because he's in touch with no images), but to true virtue (because he is in touch with true Beauty)."[27] Anodos' first moral failing in Fairy Land is a result of his confusing the image of beauty with true beauty. Only a vision of true beauty can rightly guide his decision, thus making and engendering virtuous action. His next moral challenge is to keep his faith in the otherworldly beauty of Fairy Land even when he temporarily loses touch with it.

Even after experiencing the most beautiful and terrifying aspects of Fairy Land, Anodos succumbs to the materialistic influence of a farmer who lives on the outskirts of Fairy Land. This encounter momentarily causes him to cease to believe in Fairy Land's very existence. Anodos' next challenge is to maintain his belief in the ideal beauty of Fairy Land when its reality is not immediately evident to him. Even after he has encountered his ideal woman in the Marble Lady and pure terror in the form of the Ash, he is lulled into a malaise of unbelief when he flees to the more mundane outskirts of the fairy forest. A "kind-looking, matronly woman" provides a refuge for Anodos in her home after his near-fatal encounter with the Maid of the Alder-tree and helps him make sense of the deception he has fallen for.[28] The woman, however, begs Anodos "not to say a word about these things" to her husband due to his inability to perceive Fairy Land and his annoyance with those who acknowledge its existence:

> He thinks me even half crazy for believing anything of the sort. But I must believe my senses, as he cannot believe beyond his, which give him no intimations of this kind. I think he could spend the whole Midsummer-eve in the wood and come back with the report that he saw nothing worse than himself.[29]

When the farmer, the lady's husband, walks in and speaks, his "kind and jovial" voice "seemed to disrobe the room of the strange look which all new places

---

[26] MacDonald, *Phantastes*, 80.
[27] Plato, *Symposium*, 212a.
[28] MacDonald, *Phantastes*, 89.
[29] MacDonald, *Phantastes*, 89–90.

wear—to disenchant it out of the realm of the ideal into that of the actual."³⁰ The farmer's limited, materialistic mode of perception gradually rubs off on Anodos: "In the morning I awoke refreshed, after a profound and dreamless sleep. [...] I did not believe in Fairy Land."³¹ The influence of the lady's daughter, who perceives Fairy Land quite clearly, eventually awakens Anodos' belief again. When he looks out of the window of her room, he says that "a gush of wonderment and longing flowed over my soul like the tide of a great sea. Fairy Land lay before me, and drew me towards it with an irresistible attraction."³² The rhythms of everyday life and its practical focus on material concerns make Anodos view his longings as foolish and his recent experiences in Fairy Land as delusions. The power of the commonplace temporarily overwhelms him. However, once awakened, his desire for the ideal beauty and terror of Fairy Land again holds sway.

Like Anodos, Anselmus experiences fluctuations in his belief in true beauty. The entire plot of *The Golden Pot* revolves around Anselmus' struggle to maintain his belief in, and love for, Serpentina despite the numbing influence of bourgeois Dresden society. His encounters with Serpentina are infrequent enough to make him vulnerable to the seductive lure of a comfortable, respectable life as Court Counselor with the charming, but superficial, Veronika as his wife. Even after he declares his love for Serpentina to be "eternal" and asserts that "before [he] would leave her, [he] would die altogether," Anselmus still finds himself doubting Serpentina's reality:

> And now Anselmus felt as if a battle were beginning in his soul: thoughts, images flashed out—Archivarius Lindhorst,—Serpentina,—the green Snake—at last the tumult abated, and all this chaos arranged and shaped itself into distinct consciousness. It was now clear to him that he had always thought of Veronica alone [...]. He could not but laugh heartily at the mad whim of falling in love with a little green Snake; and taking a well-fed Privy Archivarius for a Salamander.³³

Immersed in the world of bourgeois Dresden, Anselmus temporarily succumbs to its more accessible—even if less captivating—charms due to their immediate and persistent influence. Like Anodos, Anselmus finds himself overpowered by the commonplace. The rest of the story is a battle between the influence of the otherworldly Serpentina and the bourgeois Veronica over Anselmus' mind, as well as battle between Anselmus' intentions to stay true to Serpentina and the alluring comforts of bourgeois life that tempt him to forget her.

---

³⁰ MacDonald, *Phantastes*, 92.
³¹ MacDonald, *Phantastes*, 97.
³² MacDonald, *Phantastes*, 99.
³³ Hoffman, "The Golden Pot," 69, 88.

Both MacDonald and Hoffmann situate their respective protagonists in a conflict that is best understood in terms of Platonic philosophy. Like Anodos, Anselmus at times fails to distinguish between the true female embodiment of the ideal and a counterfeit. And, like Anodos, Anselmus has moments in which his longings for and belief in the ideal world seem ridiculous. Both protagonists are young men struggling to maintain a fleeting vision of the true Beauty Diotima speaks of in Plato's *Symposium*. In both stories, true beauty and ultimate reality are synonymous, and each protagonist struggles to discern true beauty from a mere likeness. Of "someone who believes in beautiful things, but doesn't believe in the beautiful itself," Socrates asks Glaucon, "Don't you think he is living in a dream rather than in a wakened state? Isn't this dreaming: whether asleep or awake, to think that a likeness is not a likeness but rather the thing itself that it is like?"[34] Anodos and Anselmus have moments of clear, ecstatic perception of true beauty, but when that true beauty is no longer present, they can no longer discern "the thing itself" from "a likeness," and are more like dreamers in sleep rather than one who is wide awake to reality. The Maid of the Alder-tree and Veronika are a likeness to The Marble Lady and Serpentina, so that Anodos and Anselmus are vulnerable to their charms when they momentarily lack the capacity to perceive true beauty.

Anodos' ability to perceive the beauty of Fairy Land is most hindered by his shadow, whom he meets shortly after leaving the farmer's house and who becomes his near constant companion until near the end of his time in Fairy Land. In Chapter IX, we learn how exactly the shadow affects his experience of Fairy Land. Anodos meets a "lovely fairy child," whom Anodos looks at with "wonder and delight," but as soon as the child steps into Anodos' shadow, "straightway he was a commonplace boy, with a rough broad-brimmed straw hat."[35] MacDonald presents the "lovely fairy" aspect of the child as being completely antithetical to the "commonplace," which is the absence of "wonder and delight." Throughout Anodos' time in Fairy Land, the shadow continues to rob Fairy Land of its sublime and beautiful qualities. Prickett sums up Anodos' experience of his shadow:

> Anodos is both frightened and disgusted by the dark menacing presence of the shadow, always with him: it insidiously destroys all sense of beauty and wonder in the world around him as he travels, imprisoning him into something like Blake's "cavern'd man" lit only by the fragmented evidence of the five senses as Locke imagined them to be.[36]

On the very outskirts of Fairy Land, the shadow warps Anodos' perception into that of the farmer, who cannot perceive the existence of Fairy Land, despite the

---

[34] Plato, *Republic*, 476c.
[35] MacDonald, *Phantastes*, 110.
[36] Prickett, *Victorian Fantasy*, 177.

fact that he lives on its threshold. Even though Anodos is in Fairy Land, where ideals are more immediately apparent, he is still unable, at times, to see its beauty due to the aesthetically-nullifying effects of his shadow.

Misenchantment is arguably a far more accurate term than *disenchantment* to describe what Anodos contends with in his shadow. The word "enchantment" implies an augmentation of, or even a departure from, reality via magic, yet MacDonald represents the "enchanted" worlds of Fairy Land as being more real than the commonplace world, and so more deserving of Anodos' faith and allegiance. Hence McCarraher's concept of capitalist misenchantment serves as an enlightening interpretive tool for making sense of the antagonistic forces that Anodos encounters. Just as advocates of political economy dispensed with the sacramental Catholic worldview in order to discern the more practical market forces of capitalism, Anodos is tempted to view his shadow as a positive means of disenchanting Fairy Land, that is, granting him a reliable vision of bare, unidealized reality:

> I began to be rather vain of my attendant, saying to myself, "In a land like this, with so many illusions everywhere, I need his aid to disenchant the things around me. He does away with all appearances, and shows me things in their true colour and form. And I am not one to be fooled with the vanities of the common crowd. I will not see beauty where there is none. I will dare to behold things as they are. And if I live in a waste instead of a paradise, I will live knowing where I live."[37]

But if, as Anodos asserts in the next chapter, "deepest truth must be deepest joy," then the shadow is actually misenchanting Anodos' perception of the highest reality embodied in Fairy Land, obscuring his vision of deepest truth so that he cannot experience deepest joy.[38] The shadow's misenchantment lies in the seduction of egotistically believing oneself to know the truth of things through a purely rationalistic perspective devoid of aesthetic or sacramental appreciation. In contrast, the enchantment of Fairy Land is not an artificial enhancement of aesthetic experience that improves upon an otherwise commonplace reality, but rather a revelation of deepest truth and deepest joy that necessarily are one and the same.

Just as the shadow's negation of true beauty clears the way for the seductive power of egotism, it also makes Anodos susceptible to the commonplace mindset of the farmer, whose voice, although "kind and jovial, seemed to disrobe the strange look which all new places wear—to disenchant it out of the realm of the ideal into the actual."[39] The farmer tells his daughter to feed the pigs who

---

[37] MacDonald, *Phantastes*, 112.
[38] MacDonald, *Phantastes*, 126.
[39] MacDonald, *Phantastes*, 92.

"are of no use but to get fat. Ha! Ha! Ha!" He goes on to joke that "gluttony is not forbidden in their commandments. Ha! Ha! Ha!" It is the farmer's jovial, contented tone with which he speaks of practical farm work which "disrobe[s]" the room of its strangeness. Anodos sees that the farmer is perfectly "jovial" viewing the world in a purely practical way. The farmer is content with the commonplace, which makes Anodos feel as if there were no Fairy Land to long for, as if the commonplace were perfectly satisfactory in itself. The inferior yet comfortably muted beauty of the Farmer's lands outside the border of Fairy Land embody the farmer's commonplace mindset. The Farmer has physically altered and cultivated the land to suit his commonplace values. Once Anodos' intensity of desire and clarity of vision have been muted by the farmer's influence, Anodos becomes numb, yet content, as he surveys the pleasantly commonplace scene. If we reconsider the scene's effect on Anodos in light of misenchantment, we see that Anodos is not bravely embracing disenchantment, but fearfully giving into misenchantment:

> The sun was high, when I looked out of the window, shining over a wide, undulating, cultivated country. Various garden-vegetables were growing beneath my window. Everything was radiant with clear sunlight. The dew drops were sparkling their busiest; the cows in a near-by field were eating as if they had not been at it all day yesterday; the maids were singing at their work as they passed to and fro between the out-houses: I did not believe in Fairy Land.[40]

This land is not wild like Fairy Land, but "cultivated" by a farmer who repurposes its beauty for his materialistic concerns. In the sober "clear sunlight" of day, Anodos perceives the dew drops to be "sparkling their busiest," as though they too were earnestly working and had no time for leisure. The cows, who "were eating as if they had not been at it all day yesterday," are entirely engrossed in satisfying their physical desires. And though the maids sing, they too are busily at work. This image of contented industriousness amidst a pleasantly commonplace setting leads Anodos to no longer desire or believe in Fairy Land as his formerly intense longings are replaced by a charming malaise. Anodos' vision of true beauty is not merely disenchanted, but replaced by a misenchanted vision of the commonplace which makes up for its comparative lack of intensity with an easy sense of satisfaction that makes no exacting demands on the spirit.

The farmer's daughter, who is criticized by her father for reading and believing in fairy tales, reawakens Anodos' longing for and belief in Fairy Land. As he longingly gazes into the forest, he sees the "trees bath[ing] their heads in the waves of the morning while their roots were planted deep in gloom."[41]

---

[40] MacDonald, *Phantastes*, 97.
[41] MacDonald, *Phantastes*, 99.

In his enlightened state of belief, Anodos personifies the trees, describing them as mysterious and beautiful beings. Anodos' perception of the forest contrasts sharply with that of the Farmer, who, although having lived on its borders all his life, has been "too busy to make journeys of discovery into it." Not only that, but he is also doubtful that there is anything worth discovering there since "[i]t is only trees and trees, till one is sick of them."[42] The farmer's industrious focus on the practical and commonplace shield him from the intense longings that the forest of Fairy Land could awaken. As long as he keeps himself "busy" and uninterested in the forest, his contentment in the commonplace will not be threatened by a longing for the ideal. His jovial mockery of his wife and daughter's interest in fairy tales and belief in Fairy Land, along with his dogged attentiveness to practical affairs, are his unconscious attempts to misenchant himself and Anodos. The Farmer's misenchantment is powerful and temporarily successful in its effects on Anodos, but the daughter's belief in the reality of Fairy Land is eventually able to break the spell and return Anodos to his belief in Fairy Land.

In *The Golden Pot*, as in *Phantastes*, true reality is found in the otherworldly, and each protagonist must battle against the misenchantment of this-worldly forces. The commonplace, bourgeois world of capitalist misenchantment becomes Plato's cave of illusion while Fairy Land and Atlantis are the light of ultimate reality. In *The Golden Pot*, Veronica enlists the help of the old crone Liese to literally enchant Anselmus on her behalf with magic. Liese's enchantment actually misenchants Anselmus, obscuring his vision of the higher reality he has experienced through Serpentina and Lindhorst. Anselmus feels "as if a foreign power, suddenly breaking in on his mind, were drawing him with resistless force to the forgotten Veronica," and he dreams that "Veronica was actually beside him, complaining with an expression of keen sorrow, which pierced through his inmost soul, that he should sacrifice her deep true love to fantastic visions, which only the distemper of his mind called into being, and which, moreover, would at last prove his ruin."[43] Veronica's attraction to Anselmus seems to lie mostly in his likely promotion to Hofrath and the resulting social and material benefits afforded by the marriage—something that is evident in her daydream of her hypothetical marriage with Anselmus. In her dreams as "Mrs. Hofrath, Frau Hofräthin, […] she occupied a fine house in the Schlossgasse, or in the Neumarkt, or in the Moritzstrasse; her fashionable hat, her new Turkish shawl, became her admirably." She imagines Hofrat Anselmus coming home "dressed in the top of the mode" with "his gold watch," "draw[ing] from his waistcoat pocket a pair of beautiful earrings, fashioned in the newest style."[44] Veronica herself is clearly in

---

[42] MacDonald, *Phantastes*, 95.
[43] Hoffman, "The Golden Pot," 29.
[44] Hoffman, "The Golden Pot," 14.

the grips of materialistic misenchantment, and Anselmus must resist this same misenchantment even as its power is augmented by the magic of old Liese.

DIVERGING RESPONSES TO CAPITALIST MISENCHANTMENT

Thus far in each story, the protagonists experience essentially the same conflict: Anodos and Anselmus both find themselves in the grips of capitalist misenchantment as they struggle to perceive true beauty. While MacDonald and Hoffmann both see capitalist misenchantment as the primary obstacle to the perception of reality, they oppose it in two distinct ways. Hoffmann uses a purely Platonic model as his weapon of choice in the fight against capitalist misenchantment, while MacDonald uses incarnational theology. Hoffmann scholar Hewett-Thayer remarks that the "biographies and special monographs as a rule do not raise the question [of Hoffmann's religiosity] or state that religion played no role in his life."[45] According to Bruning, it was the composer Franz Schubert rather than the Christian tradition who provided Hoffmann with the ontological structure of *The Golden Pot*:

> According to Schubert, the harmony of both the empirical and spiritual words, exhibited in a primeval period of the history of mankind, has been turned in our era into a clashing dualism. In the first epoch, the primeval paradise, man still lived "in der ersten heiligen Harmonie mit der Natur, ohne eigenen Willen, erfüllt von dem göttlichen Instinkt der Weissagung und Dichtkunst." Then he awakes to consciousness, "das klare Selbstbewusstsein, die Reflection," so that the gift of pure perception inherent in him is destroyed. An identical cosmogony forms the substratum of *Der golden Topf*.[46]

For Schubert and Hoffmann, holiness is defined as the ability to perceive beauty. In analyzing how Hoffmann describes the ideal world in *The Golden Pot*, Bruning goes on to argue that, rather than adhering to traditional Christianity, Hoffmann embraced an unsystematic religion of art and beauty. Hoffmann's names for the other-worldly Atlantis ("das paradiesische Wunder-reich," "das Geisterreich Atlantic," "das Leben in der Poesie") "signify a metaphysical world which remains remarkably constant throughout his life, as is best demonstrated by his aesthetic writings about music, particularly Beethoven's Instrumentalmusik, 1813."[47] For Hoffmann, this otherworldly realm was identified as the realm of music.

Hoffmann's equivalent term for the Christian *sinner* is *Musikfeinde* (enemy of music): someone who listens to music for mere entertainment rather than as

---

[45] Harvey Hewett-Thayer, "E. T. A. Hoffmann and Religious Faith," *Germanic Review* 13 (1938): 274.
[46] Bruning, "Hoffmann and the Philistine," 114.
[47] Bruning, "Hoffmann and the Philistine," 114.

an act of aesthetic worship. To approach the holy music of Beethoven casually would be sacrilege to Hoffmann. In Hoffmann's religion of beauty, sin is not defined primarily as failure to love thy neighbor, but as the failure to discern true beauty from bourgeois beauty and the failure to remain faithful to a vision of true beauty. Hoffmann's vision of reality has much more in common with Plato than St. Paul. Schelling provided the foundation for much of Schubert's thinking, and, according to Bruning, Hoffmann was fascinated by "Schelling's concept of the 'Intellectual Anschaung,' the intuitive knowledge of the absolute in nature, which, according to Schelling, only artists could possess."[48] The contrast between Hoffmann's Platonism and MacDonald's Christian theological vision becomes apparent as one examines the endings of *The Golden Pot* and *Phantastes*.

At the end of *The Golden Pot*, Anselmus, after resisting the forces of capitalist misenchantment and proving his loyalty to Serpentina, quenches his thirst for ideal Beauty in union with her:

> Serpentina! Belief in thee, Love of thee has unfolded to my soul the inmost spirit of Nature! Thou hast brought me the Lily, which sprung from Gold, from the primeval Force of the world, before Phosphorus had kindled the spark of Thought; this Lily is Knowledge of the sacred Harmony of all Beings; and in this do I live in highest blessedness for evermore.[49]

Not only does Anselmus possess his beloved Serpentina, but in her he has access to "the sacred Harmony of all Beings" and lives "in highest blessedness forevermore." The completion of Anselmus' Platonic flight to ultimate reality is also represented by Anselmus joining her in the ideal realm of Atlantis, leaving the commonplace world of bourgeois Dresden behind forever. The narrator, who turns out to be a character within the story, is permitted by Serpentina's father to see a vision of the happy couple in Atlantis, and with envy exclaims, "[a]h, happy Anselmus, who has cast away the burden of week-day life, who in the love of thy kind Serpentina fliest with bold pinion, and now livest in rapture and joy on thy Freehold in Atlantis!"[50] He goes on to lament that "enthralled among the pettiness of necessitous existence, my heart and my sight are so bedimmed with thousand mischiefs, as with thick fog, that the fair Lily will never, never be beheld by me."[51] It is precisely this "alltäglich" or commonplace world of Dresden, in which one's heart and sight are "bedimmed" by the "pettiness of necessitous existence," that Anselmus is abandoning forever to live in the mystical realm of Atlantis, where the "sacred harmony of all beings" is completely unobscured by mortal concerns and capitalist misenchantment. In

---

[48] Bruning, "Hoffmann and the Philistine," 114.
[49] Hoffmann, "The Golden Pot," 113.
[50] Hoffmann, "The Golden Pot," 113.
[51] Hoffmann, "The Golden Pot," 114.

The Golden Pot, the "alltäglich," commonplace world, in which work and the pursuit of wealth dominates, is portrayed as something that needs escaping from because it limits man's perception of and communion with the world of ultimate beauty. Hoffman depicts a Platonic flight from the commonplace and material to the ideal that seems to echo Plato's *Symposium* in which "one goes always upwards for the sake of [...] Beauty, starting out from beautiful things and using them like rising stairs."[52] Anselmus learns to agree with Socrates statement in Plato's *Theaetetus* that "a man should make all haste to escape from earth to heaven."[53] In his portrayal of Anselmus' abandonment of the commonplace in pursuit of the ideal at the end of *The Golden Pot*, Hoffman maintains a striking adherence to Platonic philosophy.

Considering the stories' many similarities, the ending of Anodos' journey is markedly different from Anselmus'. It is in this difference that MacDonald breaks with Hoffman's Platonism. Long before his sacrificial death in Fairy Land, Anodos gives up on possessing the Marble Lady when he learns that she loves the knight. Upon his death, Anodos realizes "that it is by loving, and not by being loved, that one can come nearest the soul of another; yea, that, where two love, it is the loving of each other, and not the being loved by each other, that originates and perfects and assures their blessedness."[54] Anodos achieves "blessedness" without possessing the Marble Lady through the disinterested purity of his love for her. Anselmus, on the other hand, achieves blessedness through marriage with Serpentina in Atlantis. While Anselmus spends most of the story attempting to break free from the commonplace world into the ideal realm of Atlantis, Anodos spends most of his time in Fairy Land only to return to the commonplace world. MacDonald's inversion of Hoffmann's plot is essential in conveying his distinct response to capitalist misenchantment. When Anodos returns to the mundane world, he wonders: "Could I translate the experience of my travels [in Fairy Land], into common life? This was the question. Or must I live it all over again, and learn it all over again, in the other forms that belong to the world of men, whose experience yet runs parallel to that of Fairy Land."[55] In the very asking of the question, it is clear that Anodos' perception of "the world of men" has changed in that he now realizes that it "runs parallel to that of Fairy Land." The common life of man is not limited to the commonplace or separate from the spiritual reality embodied by Fairy Land. He has an unshakable feeling that these two worlds are not two separate, antithetical realms as Anselmus' Dresden is to Atlantis: "Nor

---

[52] Plato, *Symposium*, 211c.
[53] Plato, *Theaetetus*, trans. M. J. Levett (Cambridge, MA: Hackett Publishing Company, 1997), 176b.
[54] MacDonald, *Phantastes*, 313.
[55] MacDonald, *Phantastes*, 317–18.

could I yet feel quite secure in my new experiences. When, at night, I lay down once more in my own bed I did not feel at all sure that when I awoke, I should not find myself in some mysterious region of Fairy Land."⁵⁶ Now that Anodos has experienced Fairy Land, the commonplace world feels shaky and insubstantial, as if it could easily merge with and be sublimated into the realm of Fairy Land. The blending of the two worlds becomes even more obvious when Anodos lays beneath a great, ancient beech-tree, listening to the sound of its leaves:

> At first, they made sweet inarticulate music alone; but, by-and-by, the sound seemed to begin to take shape, and to be gradually moulding itself into words; till, at last, I seemed able to distinguish these, half-dissolved in a little ocean of circumfluent tones: "A great good is coming—is coming—is coming to thee, Anodos;" and so over and over again. I fancied that the sound reminded me of the voice of the ancient woman, in the cottage that was four-square. I opened my eyes, and, for a moment, almost believed that I saw her face, with its many wrinkles and its young eyes, looking at me from between two hoary branches of the beech overhead.⁵⁷

Not only does Anodos begin to see the images and hear the sounds of one world in the other, but he is now able to receive spiritual messages and mystical insight through the commonplace world because, to him, it is no longer quite so commonplace or separate from the ideal realm of Fairy Land. The commonplace is no longer a wall limiting his perception, but a window through which the divine is manifested. Anodos' time in Fairy Land has reoriented him to the inherent divinity of the commonplace.

MacDonald's Theology

An examination of MacDonald's theological orientation and influences will serve to elucidate the theological implications of *Phantastes* and MacDonald's complicated relationship with Platonism. In Christianity, MacDonald found a *via media* between Platonic idealism and pantheism that could challenge the worldview emerging out of the Industrial Revolution economy that viewed the material world merely as a means to economic ends. As Gisela Kreglinger points out, MacDonald "understands the world to be created by God, and any correspondence between the physical and spiritual dimension exists because God placed it in his creation."⁵⁸ For MacDonald, the material world was not merely a ladder, as Plato argues in the *Symposium*, to the ideal. Breaking from a purely Platonic understanding of the material world, MacDonald "sought to recover a theological understanding of the material world in the face of the

---

⁵⁶ MacDonald, *Phantastes*, 317.
⁵⁷ MacDonald, *Phantastes*, 319.
⁵⁸ Gisela Kreglinger, *Storied Revelations: Parables, Imagination, and George MacDonald's Christian Fiction* (Eugene, OR: Pickwick, 2013), 94.

dangers that came with the Industrial Revolution. MacDonald saw, in a rather prophetic way, a worldview emerging that was purely empirical and void of any sense of wonder and awe."[59] Neither pantheist nor Platonic idealist, MacDonald seeks to articulate a view of creation that sanctifies it without deifying it, in an attempt to avoid the devastating consequences—experienced in our own age of Climate Crisis—of the spiritual devaluation and disenchantment of the material world. Kerry Dearborn expresses MacDonald's theological nuance concisely: "Here is immanence without pantheism, and harmony without loss of God's transcendence."[60] Referring to "the Kantian tendency to abstract aesthetic experience from physical reality," Dearborn asserts that "MacDonald would contend against this [Kantian] tradition," and object "that the imagination and the Christian faith offer a way to integrate aesthetic experience and physical reality."[61] More specifically, it is through the Christian doctrine of the Incarnation that MacDonald successfully integrates "aesthetic experience and physical reality," the spiritual and the material, the holy and the mundane.

The closest MacDonald came to systematic theological writing was in his sermons, although his purpose, as always, is to waken the soul rather than build a system. In his sermon, "The Inheritance," we see a direct attempt to articulate his incarnational theology, that is, his belief in the sanctity and sacral nature of the material world. MacDonald asserts that he would not be content to believe merely that "the loveliness of the world has its origin in the making will of God," rather, he believes that "the very loveliness of [the world] is the loveliness of God, for its loveliness is his own lovely thought, and must be a revelation of that which dwells and moves in himself."[62] For MacDonald, the world is not merely an imperfect representation of God's loveliness, but, for those with eyes to see, a revelation of God's perfect loveliness. In the same sermon, MacDonald admits that "never has [the world] shown me things lovely or grand enough to satisfy [him]," but goes on to speculate that "it may be that [his] unsatisfaction comes from not having eyes open enough, or keen enough, to see and understand what [God] has given." "All that is needed to set the world right enough for me," he concludes, "is that my will and desires keep time and harmony with [God's] music."[63] For MacDonald, the material world is a sacramental incarnation of the divine, whether we perceive it as so or not. MacDonald's friend, mentor, and priest, F. D. Maurice, wrote that the sacraments are "a perfectly transparent medium, through

---

[59] Kreglinger, *Storied Revelations*, 136.
[60] Kerry Dearborn, *Baptized Imagination: The Theology of George MacDonald* (Aldershot: Ashgate, 2006), 75.
[61] Dearborn, *Baptized Imagination*, 26.
[62] MacDonald, "Self-Denial," in *Unspoken Sermons*, 381.
[63] MacDonald, "The Truth in Jesus," in *Unspoken Sermons*, 386.

which His glory may be manifested." And according to Maurice, "the world is full of sacraments. Morning and evening, the kind looks and parting words of friends, the laugh of childhood, daily bread, sickness and death; all have a holy sacramental meaning, and should as such be viewed by us."[64] According to the incarnational theology of Maurice and MacDonald, the human world (material and social) is inherently sacramental and, therefore, serves as a medium for the divine. The everyday world of men is not a burden to be cast off or an inferior realm to be escaped from as Hoffmann depicts in *The Golden Pot*. Such a purely Platonic understanding of the world fails to appreciate the revelatory power of creation and human activity.

In *Phantastes*, MacDonald uses lines from Coleridge's "Dejection: An Ode" as an epigraph to Chapter 9—the chapter in which the shadow misenchants Anodos' perception of Fairy Land. Anodos cannot see the beauty of Fairy Land or its people because, as Coleridge writes, "we receive but what we give / and in our life alone does nature live." Like Coleridge, MacDonald believes that it is the moral quality of our hearts and minds that determines our ability to perceive the divine. Whether in Fairy Land or the world of men, it is Anodos' perception that ultimately determines his quality of experience. The Platonic binary between Fairy Land and the world of men established in the first few chapters turns out to be merely a matter of perception in Anodos' subjective consciousness. Just as Anodos' shadow can misenchant Fairy Land, his clarified moral vision allows him to see the enchantment of Fairy Land in the world of men.

The result of Anodos' spiritual growth is that he can now perceive the sacramental meaning of the world of men. Now that he is no longer under the spell of misenchantment, Anodos recognizes that what he formerly considered commonplace is actually a "perfectly transparent medium" through which the true beauty and divine reality are manifested. In other words, he perceives the true enchantment (divine incarnation) of God's sacramental universe now that the spell of capitalist misenchantment has been broken. Because Anodos now sees the commonplace, material world as a "perfectly transparent medium," his return to the world of men is not a sorrowful one. Anselmus must initially escape from the commonplace world to achieve his happy ending, but because Anodos now sees the "translucence of the mundane," his return is accompanied by a profound sense of hope and peace communicated to him through what he once might have perceived as merely commonplace.

---

[64] F. D. Maurice, *The Kingdom of Christ* (London: J. M. Dent & Co., 1907), 328.

An Objection

James Beitler challenges an incarnational interpretation of *Phantastes* in his response to Larsen's argument in *George MacDonald and the Age of Miracles*. While Beitler concedes that "Larsen's argument illuminates a great deal about MacDonald's work," he also argues that incarnational theology is not necessarily relevant to *Phantastes*.[65] Beitler points out that the climactic moment of Anodos' journey is his sacrificial death leading to a disembodied experience of bliss: "His development as a character would seem to move us in the opposite direction of incarnation, and it is not for nothing that Stephen Pricket calls MacDonald a 'temperamental Plantonist.'"[66] Beitler is correct that, in a literal sense, Anodos' journey in Fairy Land climaxes in a seemingly Platonic moment of disembodied bliss. However, I would argue that Anodos' disembodiment is incidental rather than essential to the plot. Of far more thematic significance is that Anodos selflessly sacrifices his own life for the sake of the knight. Anodos' literal death in Fairy Land symbolizes his death to self, and MacDonald presents this death to self as the gateway to ultimate bliss.

In *Phantastes*, MacDonald does represent Anodos' death as being experienced as pure consciousness in the absence of a body, but the cause of the bliss is not the absence of materiality, but the moral act of death to self. A literal reading of Anodos' disembodiment could understandably, but mistakenly, attribute the cause of his bliss to the absence of the body. Anodos does literally emphasize the purity of his disembodied consciousness as ultra real compared to his bodily experience:

> The hot fever of life had gone by, and I breathed the clear mountain-air of the land of Death. I had never dreamed of such blessedness. It was not that I had in any way ceased to be what I had been. The very fact that anything can die, implies the existence of something that cannot die; which must either take to itself another form, as when the seed that is sown dies, and arises again; or, in conscious existence, may, perhaps, continue to lead a purely spiritual life.[67]

While MacDonald briefly lapses into tangential speculation as he imagines what a literal disembodied state would be like, this speculation is merely tangential. The more thematically significant aspect of MacDonald's description is the way in which death is characterized as a means to pure bliss. Just as Anodos' physical death is symbolic of his death to self, so his experience of pure consciousness is symbolic of the pure bliss of selflessness. The "clear mountain-air of the land

---

[65] James Edward Beitler III, "Response," in Timothy Larsen, *George MacDonald in the Age of Miracles* (Downers Grove, IL: IVP Academic, 2018), 40.
[66] Beitler, "Response," 40.
[67] MacDonald, *Phantastes*, 310.

of Death" is pure primarily because Anodos has fully died to self. For most of his journey in Fairy Land, Anodos had been in pursuit of the Marble Lady, the object of his deepest longing. Anodos' great moral challenge is to love the Marble Lady selflessly rather than possessively. He begins to learn this lesson when he reluctantly accepts that the Marble Lady loves the knight rather than him and acknowledges that the knight is far more worthy of her than him. In sacrificing his life for the knight, his rival for the Marble Lady's love, Anodos' moral transformation is complete, as he experiences the pure bliss of selfless love: "I knew now, that it is by loving, and not by being loved, that one can come nearest the soul of another; yea, that, where two love, it is the loving of each other, and not the being loved by each other, that originates and perfects and assures their blessedness."[68] Anodos is not intentionally fleeing from the material world to an otherworldly Platonic realm. Rather, his temporary disembodiment is incidental to MacDonald's primary purpose of using Anodos' physical death symbolically. This interpretation of Anodos' physical death is consistent with other instances of MacDonald using physical death to represent death-to-self such as in *Lilith* where Mr. Raven cryptically explains to Mr. Vane: "you will be dead, so long as you refuse to die."[69] Likewise, in *Phantastes*, death is primarily symbolic and of moral significance. It is Anodos' moral state, rather than literal disembodiment, that primarily brings him bliss.

My purpose in comparing *Phantastes* to *The Golden Pot* is to highlight the centrality of incarnational theology in *Phantastes* in contrast to the pure Platonism of *The Golden Pot*, and the contrast between Anodos and Anselmus at this point is especially useful in responding to Beitler's skepticism. While Anodos is required to sacrifice his physical body and his desire to possess his ideal woman, no such moral demand is made of Anselmus, who ascends to the perfectly beautiful realm of Atlantis in complete possession of his ideal woman, Serpentina. Anselmus ascends to ideal reality by intentionally leaving behind the misenchanted commonplace world, while Anodos' momentary experience of disembodiment is merely incidental to his morally transformative death in an act of self-sacrifice.

And, in contrast to Anselmus who flees materiality, Anodos delights in lingering within the material world even in his state of disembodied consciousness: "Now that I lay in her bosom, the whole earth, and each of her many births, was as a body to me, at my will. I seemed to feel the great heart of the mother beating into mine, and feeding me with her own life, her own essential being and

---

[68] MacDonald, *Phantastes*, 313.
[69] George MacDonald, *Lilith* (Whitehorn, CA: Johannesen, 2001), 224.

nature."⁷⁰ Anodos' bliss is not diminished, but rather enhanced or at least capable of being embodied in union with nature. The incarnational overtones become even more striking as Anodos' consciousness fuses with the form of a primrose: "I felt that I could manifest myself in the primrose; that it said a part of what I wanted to say; just as in the old time, I had used to betake myself to a song for the same end." Anodos uses this primrose as he would a song to communicate his pure love to the Marble Lady, who kisses it and places it lovingly in her bosom. Anodos considers this "the first kiss she had ever given [him]."⁷¹ The primrose successfully embodies Anodos' spiritual essence to the extent that he considers the kiss to be given to *him* and not merely to the rose. Materiality and embodiment are portrayed as essential for intimacy. There is no reluctance on Anodos' part to embrace the material world, just as there is no sign that he is compromising his experience of pure love by taking material form.

DIVERGENT ENDINGS

The distinctively Christian element in *Phantastes* is all the more striking when one contrasts the ending of *Phantastes* with that of *The Golden Pot* and considers the social implications of each ending. Both MacDonald and Hoffmann portray their protagonists as having achieved an enlightened perspective by the end of each novel; however, Anodos and Anselmus end up with completely divergent attitudes toward the commonplace world of men. While Anselmus shows absolutely no concern for those whom he leaves behind, Anodos' experience of bliss in Fairy Land, after his bodily death, engenders a deeply compassionate desire to serve and comfort those who live lives of suffering in the commonplace world:

> "How many hopeless cries," thought I, "and how many mad shouts go to make up the tumult, here so faint where I float in eternal peace, knowing that they will one day be stilled in the surrounding calm, and that despair dies into infinite hope, and the seeming impossible there, is law here! But, O pale-faced women, and gloomy-browed men, and forgotten children, how I will wait on you, and minister to you, and, putting my arms about you in the dark, think hope into your hearts, when you fancy no one is near!"⁷²

Anodos is filled with a profound sense of mission, and imagines fulfilling this mission by "putting [his] arms" about those suffering in the physical realm. Even as a supposedly disembodied spirit, Anodos intends to minister to the sufferers with a physical body. And even from his position in the purely spiritual realm of "eternal peace," he considers the suffering of others and desires to minister

---

⁷⁰ MacDonald, *Phantastes*, 312.
⁷¹ MacDonald, *Phantastes*, 312–13.
⁷² MacDonald, *Phantastes*, 314.

to them. In having Anodos, from his blissful state, desire to minister to those in the commonplace world of men, MacDonald conveys the social aspect of incarnational theology. The world of men is sacramental, but it is also filled with suffering. Because Anodos has learned to see the inherent divinity in the commonplace, he believes that it is worth redeeming, and longs to participate in the process of its redemption, just as God's love for humanity resulted in the Incarnation of Christ for the redemption of humanity. And just as Christ took on human flesh to carry out his divine mission, so Anodos imagines himself taking on bodily form to carry out his own mission.

MacDonald Christianizes Hoffman's Platonic flight to ultimate reality by insisting on the need for his enlightened hero to participate in the redemption of the commonplace world and reorient himself to its inherent divinity. Read as a reaction to, and critique of, *The Golden Pot*, *Phantastes* serves as an artistic embodiment of MacDonald's understanding of the Incarnation and its centrality to his theology. When these two narratives are contrasted, the moral and social implications of their underlying worldviews become clear. As noted above, Jean Paul once commented that Hoffmann could "hate humanity out of a love of art."[73] This attitude of hatred toward humanity is evident in Anselmus' enthusiastic abandonment of the commonplace world and in his Platonic flight to the perfectly beautiful realm of Atlantis. MacDonald's incarnational theology as represented in his inversion of Hoffmann's plot serves as not only a theological critique, but as a moral corrective to Hoffmann's narrative.

Conclusion

Although there are significant similarities between *The Golden Pot* and *Phantastes* both thematically and structurally, MacDonald significantly inverts the plot of *The Golden Pot* in *Phantastes* and, in doing so, defines the relationship between the commonplace and the ideal in a way that is theologically opposed to the relationship portrayed in *The Golden Pot*. While Anselmus' spiritual fulfillment is represented as leaving the commonplace world behind forever to be united with Serpentina in the mystical kingdom of Atlantis, Anodos returns to the everyday, commonplace world with a refined perception of its inherent spiritual realities and a newly found sense of mission. Anodos learns to see the commonplace with new eyes: not as a muting and obscuring of the divine, but as a "perfectly transparent medium" revealing the divine. Anselmus, in contrast, can only achieve satisfaction by learning to scorn and ultimately fleeing from the commonplace to the otherworldly realm of Atlantis.

---

[73] Bruning, "Hoffmann and the Philistine," 111.

Without the Incarnation, without the Divine's sanctifying and redeeming presence, humanity and nature are merely disappointments to be abandoned in search of true beauty. With the incarnation, humanity is redeemed, dignified, and exalted; nature and the commonplace occurrences of daily life are a revelation of, rather than a hindrance to, knowledge of the Divine. Hoffmann's purely Platonic response to capitalist misenchantment proves inadequate in that Hoffmann's narrative condemns the misenchantment but serves up the world to the enemy. In contrast, MacDonald's incarnational theology has the power to resist capitalist misenchantment and reclaim the world for truth, and it is only incarnational theology that can protect nature and human dignity from the desacralizing forces of capitalism. According to MacDonald, humanity—ugly as it is—has been judged capable and worthy of union with the Divine, for the Lord of the Universe, of his own loving initiative, came down from heaven to us and became one with us when we were powerless to ascend to Him. The original Incarnation narrative of the New Testament is, in a way, even more of an inversion of Hoffmann's plot: Anselmus flees the mortal realm and ascends to the Divine, whereas Christ leaves the heavenly realm and condescends to take on human flesh. At the end of *Phantastes*, when Anodos has returned to the world of men after his adventures in Fairy Land, the leaves of the beech tree seem to speak to him: "A great good is coming—is coming—is coming to thee, Anodos."[74] MacDonald believed that God, the great good of existence, is ever and always coming to us right where we are.

---

[74] MacDonald, *Phantastes*, 319.

ANOTHER SERVING OF ORTS:
ISSUES THEOLOGICAL, LITERARY, AND POETIC IN THE THOUGHT OF GEORGE MACDONALD, F. D. MAURICE, AND THOMAS ERSKINE[1]

Trevor Hart

The story of theology in the modern age, it has been suggested, may helpfully be traced by paying attention to a series of shifts in emphasis from one pole to the other of a seeming paradox within the doctrine of God: namely, between what theologians are wont to call God's transcendence with respect to the world on the one hand, and God's radical immanence or presence to the world on the other.

So, for instance, Stanley Grenz and Roger Olsen adopt this dialectic device in their careful chronicling of theology in the twentieth century.[2] Articulated typically in terms of the spatial metaphors embedded inescapably in religious language—and perhaps misled by a failure to grasp the essentially poetic logic of such language—the religious and theological truths at stake, they suggest, are often misconstrued as matched in a sort of zero-sum game. God must either properly be pictured as "up there," "high above" the created cosmos, or else be identified "down here" with us, "in" the midst of the world and sharing fully in its processes and events. In the nature of the case, absent due sensitivity to the way metaphor works, paying Paul is bound to involve robbing Peter ("up" and "down" being literal and logical opposites) and initiatives laying stress on the radical transcendence of God tend, sooner or later, to provoke a vigorous swing back in the other direction in order to safeguard the concerns bound up with affirming of God's immanence. Rather than resulting either in equilibrium (except of a very unstable and provisional sort) or the heroic achievement of a Hegelian "higher synthesis," the story is instead one of wearying ebb and flow, retreat and advance, exile and restoration, with no significant theological ground ever really being made.

---

[1] Since the preparation and delivery of this material as a paper at the 2016 conference of the George MacDonald Society the larger part of it has already been revised and published as "Ups and Downs of Nineteenth-Century Theology: Issues Theological, Literary and Poetic," in *The End of the Church? Conversations with the Work of David Jasper*, ed. Bridget Nichols and Nicholas Taylor (Durham: Sacristy Press, 2022), 176–196.

[2] Stanley J. Grenz and Roger E. Olsen, *Twentieth Century Theology: God and the World in a Transitional Age* (Downers Grove, IL: InterVarsity Press, 1992).

Almost exactly one hundred years earlier, looking back across the decades of the nineteenth century to its roots in the late eighteenth, the liberal Anglo-Catholic theologian Aubrey Moore (1848–1890) traced more or less the same dialectic. The story of theology in this era, too, he suggested, flip-flopped identifiably between insistence upon a remote transcendence the more extreme forms of which threatened to banish God altogether from the cosmos, and radical versions of immanence which tended instead to reduce God to the dimensions afforded by the cosmos itself, either containable by or identifiable with it in whole or in part.[3] The Bible on the other hand, Moore observed, appears remarkably unconcerned by any such antagonism or contest, and is able to move easily from picturing God as exalted over all things in the highest heaven to finding God intimately and closely involved in the minutiae of natural processes, historical events and the fabric of individual lives.

It might be suggested by some, no doubt, that this is due to a degree of intellectual naivety or lack of sophistication on the part of biblical authors and the religious cultures they represent. Perhaps. Or, perhaps the shoe is on the other foot, and theirs was a culture with an intuitive grasp of the essentially imaginative and poetic nature of our patterns of speech and thought about God, happy to permit metaphors (up and down, here and there, inside and outside) to conflict and cross-fertilize creatively as useful fictions when the truth of an apprehension seemed to require it. In any event, unworried by such dialectical categories as "transcendence" and "immanence," the biblical texts resound with images intended to convey God's radical *otherness from* the world God has created, while yet (and at the same time) managing to portray God as radically *present to and involved in* the world. Indeed, if we would follow biblical intuitions, then we would perhaps have to say that it is precisely *because* God as Creator is radically other than his creature that God is so close to it and to us—closer to us even, we might say, than we are to ourselves. If spatial metaphor connotes anything, then we are bound to say that, far from being remote from us this God, having created "all things, visible and invisible," now "sustains in being all that is" not by some exercise of divine fiat across unimaginable distance, but by holding the cosmos and each of us in his loving embrace from first to last, and, as George MacDonald notes in one of his *Unspoken Sermons*, can never withdraw from us without us ceasing to be.[4] Far from compromising or being secured only

---

[3] Charles Gore, ed., *Lux Mundi: A Series of Studies in the Religion of the Incarnation*, 9th ed. (London: John Murray, 1889).

[4] George MacDonald, "The Consuming Fire," in *Unspoken Sermons* (Whitehorn, CA: Johannesen, 1997), 31. For a reliable account of MacDonald's wider theology see Kerry Dearborn, *Baptized Imagination: The Theology of George MacDonald* (Aldershot: Ashgate, 2006).

despite God's "transcendence" or unbridgeable "otherness" from the world, in other words, on this account God's closeness and involvement look very different, being in effect a function, mode or expression of it.

Moore's essay, taking in a wide historical sweep, suggests that this biblical apprehension of God as uniquely present to all created times and places precisely because, as Creator, God transcends them and grants them their being, finds its first intellectually robust articulation with the careful formulation of the Christian doctrine of God as trinity during the fourth century. For here, the Greek notion of "Logos" as the overarching rational unity in which the world coheres, already appropriated by the Gospel of John and by some early Christian theologians such as Clement of Alexandria, is now formally drawn into the scope of the language used in liturgy and theology to identify God's presence and activity, fusing the creaturely and the divine by identifying the orderliness and meaning of the former with something that exists as *a distinct mode of God's own being*— the divine Logos or Word, who was in the beginning and by and through whom all things were made, and who holds or binds all things together in himself. Logos, in other words, is something God and God's creation have in common, but this is not the whole story about God who, as Father, remains distinct from his Logos or Word, and transcendent with respect to the creaturely sphere. By its failure to acknowledge such a distinction in God, Moore notes, Unitarianism (a dissenting theological tradition far more prominent in the nineteenth than since) is incapable of affirming the radical immanence of God without constant risk of collapsing into pantheism, its whole God, as it were, being sucked down into the order and "logic" of the processes of nature and history without effective remainder.[5]

It is at this point that Moore's account of the matter goes awry, taking a theological turn which provides a convenient foil to the thought of two of his near contemporaries, F. D. Maurice (1805–1872) and George MacDonald (1824–1905). Maurice is chiefly remembered now as an Anglican theologian, having held chairs both in Divinity at King's College London and Moral Philosophy at Cambridge. It should also be recalled, though, that he had previously been instrumental, together with his mentor and friend A. J. Scott, in establishing the emergent academic discipline of English Literature, having been only the second appointee to one of the first chairs in that subject (also at King's College) as early as 1840[6] when, as literary historian Franklin E. Court observes, Matthew Arnold was still only fourteen years old and the recognition of English Literature as a

---

[5] Gore, *Lux Mundi*, 102.
[6] He moved to the Chair of Divinity in 1846. Scott was appointed Professor of English Literature and Language at the relatively juvenile University College London (founded in 1828) in 1848.

worthy academic subject by the University of Cambridge thirty-eight long years away yet.[7] For his part, MacDonald is usually classified miscellaneously as an author, poet and preacher, all of which he undoubtedly was, but he, too, as a close friend, confidant and intellectual disciple of both Scott and Maurice, duly found his main source of gainful employment in the teaching of English Literature and in literary criticism, including eight years as Professor of English Literature at Bedford College for Women[8] from 1859 to 1867, and as an itinerant lecturer in this *avant garde* discipline to audiences ranging from the "working men" attending educational institutes established by the spirit of Christian Socialism in London and Manchester, to the well-heeled Anglican undergraduates in the lecture halls of King's College on The Strand.[9] Since A. J. Scott was himself both ordained and a considerable theologian (another intellectual emigré from north of the border cast out by his refusal to subscribe to certain austere Calvinist dogmas officially endorsed by his national church), it is worth noting in passing that the roots of English Literature and literary criticism are entangled from the outset with theology, though not yet of the sort that is later to be found at particularly low ebb on the sands of Dover Beach. It is to the theology of these pioneers in that fruitful inter-disciplinary relationship that we now return.

The vulnerability of Aubrey Moore's reading of the classic trinitarian tradition is that it effectively *identifies* the distinction between the Father and the Son or Logos in God with that other distinction between God's transcendence and God's immanence or presence in the world (whether in creation or, subsequently, incarnation), a view which is, stated thus, rather more Hegelian than Christian. While the patristic writers certainly held that God's Word was closely bound up with God's *relationes ad extra* (that is to say God's relatedness to the created order) from the beginning, they also insisted that the distinctions identifiable *within* God between Father, Son or Word, and Spirit *pre-exist* the act of creation; thus, while there is clearly a positive relationship between the "logos" or ratio

---

[7] Literary historian Franklin E. Court refers to Scott and Maurice as primary movers in the birth and shaping of the new discipline and "academic precursors of modern literary studies." Franklin E. Court, *Institutionalizing English Literature: the Culture and Politics of Literary Study, 1750–1900* (Stanford: Stanford University Press, 1992), 122. On Arnold and Cambridge: 117, 38.

[8] Established in 1849 by Elizabeth Jesser Reid to provide education for women identifiable as religious "dissenters" whether by virtue of birth or personal conviction. Scott, a Presbyterian Scot from Greenock, had himself held this position a decade earlier.

[9] The elision of this larger part of MacDonald's intellectual contribution in popular portrayals of the man and his work is both striking and unfortunate. See Chapter 5 ("Servants of All" by Kirstin Jeffrey Johnson) for a vital corrective to this aspect of MacDonald's life and work as well as her doctoral dissertation: "Rooted in All Its Story, More is Meant than Meets the Ear: A Study of the Relational and Revelational Nature of George MacDonald's Mythopoeic Art" (University of St Andrews, 2010).

of the world and the Word or Logos in God, the two are not simply identical, as though God's going out of himself to create *is* the point at which the divine Logos assumes a distinct existence or *hypostasis*. The Logos is already present, immanent in God, and there should be no suggestion that God's investment of creation with order and meaning and value lays bare its substance, let alone exhausts it. On the contrary, it is out of its inexhaustible fullness that creation is born, a point which MacDonald makes provocatively by referring us not to the logos but instead to the *imagination* of God.[10] The relationship, he suggests, is one analogous to the way in which an artist or poet brings to expression something born in their imagination, granting it form and order as well as mere concrete existence. And although the order must first in some sense have been in the poet's own mind's eye, it does not exhaust the possibilities of the creative impulse, and, once made, has its own integrity and freedom over against it. It is precisely the grace or gift of *existence* (and otherness from itself) which the poetic imagination bestows upon it. The analogy has its distinct limits, of course, which is why MacDonald typically eschews the use of the language of "creating" in connection with any human acts of *poesis*, reserving that term for the incomparable aspects of the divine circumstance.[11] But the analogy holds good at this point at least: the orderliness of creation is a natural expression of the divine artist's capacity first to imagine and then to fashion it, and thus is a gift or grace bestowed upon the world together with its existence. But the divine Logos himself wholly transcends this particular "cosmos," rather than being bound up—let alone confined—within it.

Another feature of MacDonald's own characteristic way of referring to God's action in calling a world to exist alongside himself is his occasional insistence that God does not really, as the tradition has it, create *ex nihilo* ("out of nothing") but "out of the divine nature,"[12] as the "flowing forth of his heart,"[13] language which at first blush suggests some Neo-Platonic emanation that holds the world itself to be divine, born or summoned forth out of divine "stuff." But this does not appear to be what MacDonald intends at all. On the contrary, he is ever mindful, he tells us, of the "unsurpassable gulf which distinguishes [...] all that is God's from all that is man's," part of which is precisely the fact that, whereas every human artist

---

[10] George MacDonald, "The Imagination: Its Functions and Its Culture," in *A Dish of Orts* (Whitehorn, CA: Johannesen, 1996), 3.

[11] MacDonald, "The Imagination," 2, 20. See also George MacDonald, "The Creation in Christ," in *Unspoken Sermons*, 418–19.

[12] MacDonald, "The Creation in Christ," 424. See also *Weighed and Wanting* (Whitehorn, CA: Johannesen, 1996), 362: "I repent me of the ignorance wherein I ever said that God made man out of nothing: there is no nothing out of which to make anything; God is all in all, and he made us out of himself. He who is parted from God has no original nothingness with which to take refuge." The worry about the "ex nihilo" formula seems greater in MacDonald's later writings than his earlier ones.

[13] MacDonald, "Wordsworth's Poetry," in *A Dish of Orts*, 247.

begins with something already given to him or her, in a vital sense the world is indeed called or summoned forth to exist by God and alongside God where once there was nothing except God himself.[14] MacDonald is mindful too that it is the very purpose of God in creation and redemption to bestow "divine life" as a gift upon creatures who are themselves finite and free, and must choose to receive it.[15] His worry about the formula *ex nihilo*, though, is its possible suggestion of divine caprice, as though God might not have created at all, as though creating were not, as we might say, something that "comes naturally" to God. Nothing could be further from the truth than this MacDonald insists. "The being of God is love," he writes in a contracted syllogism, "therefore creation."[16] Again, therefore, creation is to be understood not merely as the work of God's hands, but "as the flowing forth of his love of us, making us blessed in the union of his heart and ours." And, underpinning this, MacDonald himself resorts to Trinitarian categories, not now appealing to the language of the Logos, but to the more mainstream biblical and credal language of Father and Son, whose mutual love for one another in the Spirit is the music of eternity, a relational fullness which nonetheless always tends to overflow, and would always have others share in its joy. "Speaking after our poor human fashions of thought—the only fashions possible to us—," he writes, "I imagine that God has never been contented to be alone even with the Son of his love, [...] but that he has from the first willed and labored to give existence to other creatures who should be blessed with his blessedness."[17]

Here, then, is the final reason for resisting any theological scheme which would apportion and limit immanence to the peculiar remit of the second person of the trinity in order supposedly to preserve the transcendence of the first (a zero-sum approach which is needless to the extent that biblical patterns are permitted to shape our imagining of the circumstance, and more akin to the impulses of Arianism than those of what duly became trinitarian orthodoxy[18]).

---

[14] MacDonald, "The Imagination," 2, 3. Hence, while rejecting what he takes to be the unhelpful connotations of the traditional formula, MacDonald can nonetheless concede that there is a proper sense in which what arises in the divine imagination is "out of nothing"—i.e. nothing other than God himself. See "The Imagination," 3.

[15] George MacDonald, "Life," in *Unspoken Sermons*, 301.

[16] MacDonald, "Life," 299.

[17] MacDonald, "Life," 299.

[18] Scholarly readings of Arianism tend nowadays to present its founder not so much as a theological radical driven by adherence to philosophical rather than theological convictions, but instead as a theological conservative whose arguments were grounded in what was at times a rather arthritic exegesis of biblical texts. Nonetheless, the habits of exegesis most likely to have formed Arius were those associated with the tradition of the Catechetical School in Alexandria, heavily influenced in its turn by the religious philosophy of Plotinus whose unswerving emphasis on the radical transcendence of The One it brought to bear on the biblical text in ways comparable to the "Hellenic Judaism" of

For MacDonald and for Maurice (by whom MacDonald was undoubtedly influenced in this respect), *salvation*, the partaking in divine life for which we were created and to which God now calls us, consists in our sharing in the eternal relation or bond of love between Father and Son; and this not in any abstract way, but very concretely—in the down to earth realities of our life in the world, in discovering that the God and Father of Jesus is our Father too, in realizing that at the heart and root of *all* things is a divine reality the most fitting analogy for which is a human parent's goodness and love for a child; and in relating to God as Father from moment to moment as Jesus himself did, driven by nothing more than a desire to obey him and so to be made ever more fully like him. To know God as Father, to know the Father to be closer to us than we are even to ourselves and to be holding us even (perhaps most especially) when we walk through life's darkest and most painful experiences, this, for MacDonald and for Maurice, is of the essence of eternal life itself. But it is just this that Unitarianism and Moore's neo-Arianism alike are unable to permit. Each in its way projects the divine Father into a remote transcendence, leaving him far-removed from any creaturely concerns and experience rather than embracing these and drawing them into the very life of God itself, making them unequivocally God's own in the flesh and blood of the Son who is *homoousios* with the Father (shares fully in the "being" of God) eternally. While from one perspective, therefore, the incarnation might indeed look like a "going out" of God to become "not God," as Karl Barth puts it provocatively,[19] the insistence of Christological orthodoxy is that it must also be acknowledged as a radical "drawing in" of what is indeed not God (the creature) nevertheless to share in its proper creaturely fashion in the dynamics of that same life and love in which God's being eternally consists. The point of the distinction between Father and Son in God, therefore, Maurice and MacDonald held, was not that the Father was transcendent and the Son immanent, but simply that the Father is not the Son and the Son not the Father, the relation between them being that love or communion in which their shared "being" eternally consists.

F. D. Maurice was in fact raised as a Unitarian, eventually receiving baptism in the Church of England in his twenty-sixth year and to the great distress of his father—a Unitarian minister who had already seen his wife and daughters make the same ecclesiastical transition. Michael Maurice was of good dissenting stock, a man with liberal principles, a strong conviction in love and justice as

---

Philo. The impulse of Arian theology, in other words, was almost certainly not, as typically supposed, a concern to diminish the status of the Son of God, but instead to secure the transcendence of the Father, of whom Jesus himself had said "The Father is greater than I" (John 14:28, ESV). For a judicious account see Rowan Williams, *Arius: Heresy and Tradition* (London: Darton, Longman and Todd, 1987).

[19] Karl Barth, *The Göttingen Dogmatics: Instruction in Christian Religion,* vol. 1 (Edinburgh: T & T Clark, 1991), 136.

the key attributes of the God in whom he believed, and an equal aversion to the doctrines of Evangelicalism which, he held, compromised precisely those qualities in its teaching about God and the heart of God's dealings with humankind. Frederick Denison clearly soaked up the characterization of God as loving and just from first to last, and it shaped his later theology from top to bottom. But the Unitarian God he found rather too abstract, too remote from the world and its messy complexities ever to be the pulse of a living faith. As his biographer Florence Higham writes,

> [Maurice] had always believed in a God of Love in theory, but [...] gradually he came to feel that only if men could contemplate God in a human form and could believe that His Spirit was still potent to remove from the human heart the selfishness that shut him out, only then would God become real and truly significant. So, he professed faith in God the creator, God manifest in Christ, God guiding men by the light of his Holy Spirit.[20]

Maurice wanted a God whose love was active in the world, active in the lives of men and women, available to all who would avail themselves of it, and powerful in its impact. And, under the impact of the mature Coleridge (who, courtesy of his own personal struggles with sin and brokenness, had finally exchanged his earlier dalliances with the pantheistic leanings of German Idealism for a more orthodox trinitarianism[21]) and the writings of another Scot, Thomas Erskine of Linlathen (1788–1870) (close friend of A. J. Scott and, duly, of both Maurice and MacDonald),[22] he gradually found himself, as Higham puts it, "in a new atmosphere, as if [...] he had emerged from a dark tunnel into a land diffused with the light of God's presence."[23]

It was precisely this, an apprehension of God's immediacy and God's threefold invitation to the human creature to commune with himself that Maurice found in the trinitarian faith of Anglican orthodoxy, a faith which increasingly burned itself into his heart, rather than simply lodging inertly in his head as the sort of arithmetical conundrum to which regular rehearsal of the so-called "Athanasian Creed" at Mattins and Evensong threatened to reduce it. In the terms eventually coined by his direct contemporary John Henry Newman (1801–1890), what Maurice sought and found here was an account of the God of the gospel to which he could grant "real" rather than merely "notional" assent.[24]

---

[20] Florence Higham, *Frederick Denison Maurice* (London: SCM Press Ltd, 1947), 27.
[21] See further Trevor Hart, "Who am I: Coleridge, Imagination and the God of *Biographia Literaria*," *The Coleridge Bulletin*, New Series 38 (Winter 2011): 53–66.
[22] For a valuable account see Don Horrocks, *Laws of the Spiritual Order: Innovation and Reconstruction in the Soteriology of Thomas Erskine of Linlathen* (Milton Keynes: Paternoster, 2004).
[23] Higham, *Frederick Denison Maurice*, 30.
[24] John Henry Newman, *An Essay in Aid of a Grammar of Assent* (London: Burns, Oates, &

The desire for actual communion with God, to know God "not in a vague, loose sense, but actually to know Him as a friend" was, he suggested to his father in a letter dated February 1832, what the human heart craved most deeply, even when that craving was, as it often was even in himself, obscure to itself and overlaid by sin. It was, at root, the craving of our very human creatureliness, that *for which* we were made, and it was in satisfying this same demand of the heart (the "real test" of any doctrine of God Maurice insisted) that he discovered the truth of trinitarianism.[25] God was no longer remote, but close at hand; no longer one aloof from the trials of existence in the world, but one who had borne them fully himself, and revealed himself most fully precisely in the manner of his doing so; the world no longer a disenchanted place, but the theatre of God's glory and God's action in drawing people back to himself and, in the Johannine language which Maurice himself so loved, giving them "power to become sons and daughters of God."[26]

A similar emphasis on the reality and immediacy of God to the receptive soul is to be found in MacDonald's writing, not least in what is sometimes referred to as his "sacramentalism," under which heading I think we might include two distinct sorts of things. First there is his love of Nature, dating back to his early years spent in the Scottish countryside, and nurtured by his love for poetry, especially that of the Romantics with their grasp of Nature as haunted by the presence of God himself. In his essay "A Sketch of Individual Development"[27] MacDonald presents a sense of wonder, curiosity, mystery in the face of Nature as a normal part of human development, before exposure to the ideology so often attendant upon the teaching of the natural sciences squeezes that sense of wonder out of us, leaving in Nature's place only quantitative analysis and a law-regulated mechanism cold in its indifference to humankind.[28] MacDonald was no overly enchanted opponent of the right of natural science to demand a hearing for its discovery of the regular patterns and processes of the material world. He had himself trained as a chemist, and held (again, as did both Scott and Maurice) that all genuine truth must be God's truth, and therefore to be welcomed wherever it was to be found. But precisely as someone with a hands-on knowledge of science's dealings with the world at its coal face, MacDonald was more aware, too, than many of his Christian peers of those proper limits within which science could respectfully claim any authority, and utterly impatient of the imperialistic

---

Co., 1870).
[25] Frederick Maurice, ed., *The Life of Frederick Denison Maurice Chiefly Told in His Own Letters*, vol. 1 (London: Macmillan, 1884), 133.
[26] John 1:12.
[27] George MacDonald, "A Sketch of Individual Development," in *A Dish of Orts*, 43–76. The essay dates from 1880.
[28] MacDonald, "A Sketch of Individual Development," 51–2.

tendencies (still with us, alas) which would grant it unquestioning deference well outside those proper bounds. "Madam Science," he insists, shows no antagonism whatever "to Lady Poetry; but the atmosphere and plan on which alone they can meet as friends who understand each other, is the mind and heart of the sage, not of the boy."[29]

In any case, having achieved what I suppose today might be called a "secondary naivety" or post-critical perspective in this regard, for MacDonald as for some of his poetic forebears, Nature was without doubt "charged with the grandeur of God,"[30] a "place full of a presence" as Margaret Elginbrod describes it in the opening pages of MacDonald's first novel. Indeed, she tells Hugh Sutherland (who, while she has been contemplating the pulsing depth of the fir wood, has instead been quarrying its surfaces in a much more instrumental manner for images with which to supply his own verse, being ironically oblivious to that which would transfigure his poetry into liturgy) "I canna richtly say ma prayers in ony ither place."[31] Nature was a place which might provoke a response not just to its own beauty, but to God himself, where one might "read the word of God in his own handwriting; or rather, [...] pore upon that expression of the face of God, which, however little a man may think of it, yet sinks so deeply into his nature, and moulds it towards its own likeness."[32] These are strong statements, and clearly testify to MacDonald's sense that God might give his beauty, goodness and holiness to be known (and does give them to be known) sometimes more fully, directly and clearly through a soul's immersion in the unalloyed encounter with nature than in the constipated, tortured and (he believed) all too often disloyal mis-characterizations of God to be heard raining down from pulpits across the land.

MacDonald, like Erskine, Scott and Maurice before him, anguished over the theological schemes into which, he believed, Scripture had been tortured and forced in the churches, all but obliterating the true character of the God portrayed in it, and leading to all manner of pastoral and spiritual malformations. His response, like theirs, was certainly not to set Scripture aside, but to immerse himself in it ever more thoroughly, seeking an interpretation of it which was consonant in its particulars with an overarching characterization of God as a loving father determined to deliver his sons and daughters from their sins so that they might enjoy life in all its fullness. But MacDonald felt no need to limit God's unwavering pursuit of his creatures to the church's handling of its scriptural inheritance. According to Erskine, the "spiritual order" as he called it

---

[29] MacDonald, "A Sketch of Individual Development," 51.
[30] From the poem "God's Grandeur" by Gerard Manley Hopkins.
[31] George MacDonald, *David Elginbrod* (London: Hurst & Blackett Ltd., 1863), 33–4.
[32] MacDonald, *David Elginbrod*, 40.

was shot through the material order like leaven in the lump, and the "spiritual eye, and ear, and heart [...] might see, and hear, and love God in everything—in every object of nature, in every event of time, in every duty, every difficulty, every sorrow, every joy."[33] I see no reason to suppose that, if pressed, MacDonald would or could have challenged the broad catholicity of this vision, but more than his friends (and perhaps it was his own poetic gift which influenced him here) MacDonald followed the Romantics in finding God more fully present and more likely to be apprehended (and with sanctifying effect) in, with and under the glories of Nature (both pastoral and sublime) than anywhere elsewhere in the world.

MacDonald himself refers to this conviction as he finds it palpable in Wordsworth's poetry, for instance, as "Christian Pantheism."[34] The description is deliberately playful and provocative, but while it may send someone seeking a PhD topic back excitedly with shibboleths to discern the color of Wordsworth's orthodoxy, we should be in no doubt about MacDonald's own. He was *not* advocating pantheism (the identification of God with nature, and thus the deifying of nature). The conviction that God is close to creation rather than far removed from it is, as we have already seen, an ordinary observation of biblical faith, no matter how shocking it might have been to those still emerging from the Deism of the eighteenth century. For the apostle Paul, the more shocking realization was that God himself, in the person of the Spirit of Christ, dwells *in* us, tabernacling in each of us, just as the divine Son tabernacles in our flesh as the man Jesus, thereby making it his own. In fact, for Erskine and Maurice and MacDonald in their wake, the incarnation was a moment which changed history for good; for by uniting himself with our humanity, they held, Christ, the eternal Son of the Father had united himself to every human being in such a way that his own life (the life of God taking appropriate creaturely form) might flow from him into them as the sap flows through the vine, with transfiguring, sanctifying effect. This was the ancient claim of many of the church fathers in their wrestling with Scripture, sometimes sniffily rejected by more modern theologians on the basis that it seems to presuppose a metaphysic borrowed from Platonism or some other philosophical system long past its sell-by date.

Two things may be said about this: First, the suggestion that because Plato (or whomever among the intellectual giants of history) offered something to the world, any theological ideas contingent on it should be treated with inherent suspicion is not one MacDonald or his friends would have had much time for

---

[33] William Hanna, ed., *Letters of Thomas Erskine of Linlathen From 1800 Till 1840* (Edinburgh: David Douglas, 1877), 74.

[34] See MacDonald, *David Elginbrod*, 34. Cf. MacDonald, "Wordsworth's Poetry" in *A Dish of Orts*, 244–63.

as such. Each of them, as I have said, held that truth, whatever its source, if it commends itself to the human heart, conscience and intellect, should be welcomed and reckoned with. But in any case, we risk mistaking the intellectual scaffolding for the substance of the building (to borrow one of MacDonald's own favorite metaphors) if, without further ado, we identify the idea of God uniting himself to humankind with redemptive effect as an obvious product of Platonism. It's not. It finds expression in all sorts of biblical categories and institutions ranging across both testaments, and is presented by some of its patristic advocates as little more than an inference of the claim that in Christ, the Creator of the world himself (in whom we live and move and have our being) has made himself one of us, and is now intimately related to each of us no longer as our Creator alone, but now as our brother, one with whom we share (as the Reformer John Calvin puts it) a "fraternal alliance" by virtue of having creaturely "flesh" in common.[35] Such a claim, insisting as it does that what God now shares with us is not limited to a spiritual participation in the realm of nonmaterial universals or Forms (the *kosmos noetos*) but extends all the way down to the messy exigencies of particular flesh and blood lives lived, is one any self-respecting Platonist will be inclined to baulk at rather than encourage, let alone endorse.[36]

To return, though, from this fleeting digression: MacDonald's discovery of God close at hand in nature, finding the face of God impressed upon nature, is not Pantheism in any textbook meaning of that word. It is simply the sensibility of the Psalms, which acknowledges God's presence to be found even in the depths of *Sheol* and ascribes to the hills and the trees their own peculiar liturgical calling and capacity to sound forth God's praise—an image on which MacDonald offers a delightful riff in his description of "a noisy stream, that obstinately refused to keep Scotch Sabbath, praising the Lord after its own fashion."[37]

Where MacDonald's "sacramentalism" is concerned, the other thing to mention briefly, perhaps, is his related (but I think distinct) suggestion that God has made the world to be the sort of place where there are direct correspondences between things we find to be true in the material order, and the realities of our inner lives (our minds, our hearts, our imaginations) such that the one provides a natural language in terms of which to speak of the other.[38] I say this is a

---

[35] The incarnation itself, Calvin argues in his commentary on Psalm 22, establishes a "true fellowship of the flesh" by virtue of which all humans possess a *ius fraternae coniunctionis* with Christ, although "the true enjoyment thereof belongs to genuine believers alone." John Calvin, *Commentary on the Book of Psalms*, trans. Rev. James Anderson, vol. 1 (Edinburgh: Calvin Translation Society, 1845), 379; cf. *Corpus Reformatorum* 31:231.

[36] See further, Trevor Hart, *In Him Was Life: The Person and Work of Christ* (Waco, TX: Baylor University Press, 2019), 55–115.

[37] MacDonald, *David Elginbrod*, 36.

[38] See MacDonald, "The Imagination," 9–18.

distinct suggestion from MacDonald's claims about Nature, because the relevant "spiritual" realities which he has in mind, while hardly divorced from the reality of God (since nothing creaturely *is* finally divorceable from the reality of God), are themselves purely and properly creaturely realities—thoughts, feelings, mental actions, apprehensions of beauty, and so on. Our humanity, he understands, immerses us awkwardly in two distinct dimensions of reality at once. Our bodies key us into a world of material objects and processes, but there is another aspect to us which we know will not be reduced to or confined by materiality alone— the soul, mind, spirit, imagination or whatever else we may choose to call it, and the order of meanings, values, persons and other things unavailable to any empirical science for inspection, dissection or classification. The circumstance is a challenging one, MacDonald suggests, not least because as citizens of both dimensions we are called upon to hold them together rather than allowing them to drift apart, and constantly to interpret each in terms belonging rightly to the other. Among other things, he notes, this means that our language is originally and inexorably *metaphorical*, driven as we are to borrow terms used first to denote physical conditions, actions, relations and the like now to suggest non-material states, actions, and relations. Thus, the acting of paying attention (lat. *attentio*) to something is a "stretching towards" it so as to "grasp" its importance more fully; an argument "goes back and forth" in its consideration of an issue "from all sorts of different angles"; our heart is "chilled" by some piece of bad news; and so on and so forth.

The constitution of our "species being" itself, in other words, makes *poetic* ventures inevitable. This observation itself was not new, and MacDonald borrows it openly from Carlyle. He does with it, though, what Carlyle does not; namely, grounds linguistics or poetics within an unashamedly *theological* vision of creation, and of the human creature in particular. Such connections or correspondences, MacDonald insists, are neither accidental nor arbitrary, but are part of the fabric which holds reality together as a single coherent whole. The material forms that resonate naturally with immaterial things, that is to say, lie already to hand, put there by God for our eventual discovery and enjoyment in use. The simplest bodily gesture expressive of an inner state thus lies on the same plane (albeit at a different point on it) as the most lofty instance of poetry. What is common to both is that command of metaphor to which Aristotle refers as, in its most exalted mode, the mark of genius.[39] It is the eye for detecting identity in difference, oblique yet profound correspondences most of which still remain hidden, but which, when we grasp them and tease them out, strike us at once as exuding that "air of rightness" of which Paul Ricoeur speaks in his own

---

[39] Aristotle, *Poetics* 1459a.

discussion of metaphor,[40] distinguishing them at once from the merely fanciful or clumsily conventional, and granting us revelatory glimpses of the mesh around which the world is woven.

Characteristically, but at odds with the wider habit of his own century, MacDonald demurs on theological grounds from all easy talk of genius or of the "creative" power of the poetic imagination. Only God truly creates, he insists, and the distinction between God's artistry and ours is one we must keep clearly in view. Again, no sooner do we reckon with themes such as presence and sacramentality than we find ourselves hard up against the utter difference and incomparability of the God who is constantly present and close to the world he has made.[41] In a sense, he avers, we are not even poets or "makers" but merely *trouvères*, "finders" engaged in a constant heuristic play, stumbling across and uncovering a deeper connectivity forged in the creation of the world itself, that it might be a habitation fit for the flourishing of human beings, those most imaginative of creatures.[42] This is how MacDonald understood it—a world crying out for imaginative response, because already laden with a surplus or excess of symbolic significance. A world, furthermore, teeming with further meaning as yet to be discovered or given birth. For here, again, in the sphere of imaginative response, MacDonald recognized, there is a paradoxical interplay between the heuristic and the creative,[43] even our most daring trespasses beyond what the world already has to offer frequently feeling as though the new creative thought or vision itself is one in some sense already "out there" placing us under obligation, revealing itself to us, waiting to be uncovered or given voice, rather than sheerly summoned into being by the artistic imagination.[44]

And in some sense, of course, it is always thus. No artist or writer or composer ever begins *de novo*, but draws more or less consciously on fragments, samples

---

[40] Paul Ricoeur, *The Rule of Metaphor: Multidisciplinary Studies of the Creation of Meaning in Language* (Toronto: Toronto University Press, 1977), 239.

[41] Thus "We must not forget […] that between creator and poet lies the one unpassable gulf which distinguishes […] all that is God's from all that is man's; […] It is better to keep the word creation for that calling out of nothing which is the imagination of God." MacDonald, "The Imagination," 2–3.

[42] MacDonald, "The Imagination," 8.

[43] "The man who cannot invent will never discover." MacDonald, "The Imagination," 13.

[44] See, for example, MacDonald, "The Imagination," 24–5. MacDonald addresses directly the then current (and today still common) speculation that would push the relevant creative mechanism into the shadows of the unconscious (individual or corporate). He sees no reason to deny this, but every reason to offer a solidly theological account of the matter: "From that unknown region we grant they come, but not by its own blind working. […] God sits in that chamber of our being in which the candle of consciousness goes out in darkness, and sends forth from thence wonderful gifts into the light of that understanding which is His candle. Our hope lies in no most perfect mechanism even of the spirit, but in the wisdom wherein we live and move and have our being."

of experience which he then reconfigures into something new. But MacDonald insists upon a theological and religious rather than a merely sociological or psychological account of the matter. God, he suggests, has hidden things—meanings, imaginative possibilities, works and worlds of art—in the depths of the world that he has made. And even in our most creative ventures, therefore, we are in truth "following and finding out" what God has already imagined and given to the world as part of its developmental potential,[45] and in poetry as well as in science (albeit often in a different mode) the chief role of imagination is "to inquire into what God has made."[46]

All this is sometimes referred to as MacDonald's Platonism, and Stephen Prickett (erstwhile President of the George MacDonald Society) has referred suggestively to him as a "temperamental Platonist."[47] At the end of the day, though, I am not sure about the helpfulness of the category, or the need to resort to it in order to account for this aspect of MacDonald's thought. As already indicated, I have no necessary aversion to Platonism as a source of helpful philosophical tools, and no particular desire to absolve MacDonald from his entanglements with the thought of one of the world's greatest philosophical minds. But the eschewal of materialistic naturalism is not yet Platonism, and acknowledgment that creation consists in things both "visible and invisible" (as the creed has it), and thoughtful recognition of ourselves as creatures with a foot in both those categories, compels intelligent theological reflection about how those two dimensions might be related to one another. Such reflection has been conducted in recent years, for example, by philosopher Nicholas Wolterstorff, whose discussion of "cross-modal correspondences" in human experience touches upon the very same phenomenon,[48] and something similar lies at the heart of Iain McGilchrist's recent work on the impact of the bi-hemispheric structure of the human brain in structuring our distinctly human ways of experiencing the world.[49] Neither are Platonists of any sort that I can easily identify, but both, significantly, while offering their accounts solely from within the remit and scope of their respective disciplines, does so from a perspective more than sympathetic to the sorts of theological claims MacDonald makes.

One final note of caution where MacDonald's sacramentalism is concerned: while he holds that material realities of all sorts, but especially our experiences of

---

[45] MacDonald, "The Imagination," 41–2.
[46] MacDonald, "The Imagination," 2.
[47] Stephen Prickett, *Victorian Fantasy* (Waco, TX: Baylor University Press, 2005), 170.
[48] See, for example, Nicholas Wolterstorff, *Art in Action: Toward a Christian Aesthetic* (Carlisle, UK: Solway, 1997), 96–121.
[49] Iain McGilchrist, *The Master and his Emissary: The Divided Brain and the Making of the Western World* (New Haven and London: Yale University Press, 2009).

Nature, can be the means in, with and under which God may engage us, and offer himself for our apprehension and engagement in turn, he by no means sees this as an automatic or even a probable occurrence in every case. In his first venture into the form of the novel, as we have already seen, Margaret Elginbrod's rapture in the fir wood at dawn is matched by Hugh Sutherland's relative indifference, the wonder of the holy place leaving him virtually unscathed, for the time being at least.[50] Worse than this, far from being sacramental, translucent with respect to the spiritual order, the things of this world (even the things of nature) can become opaque, occluding our vision rather than enabling it, and, as we seek to grasp them for their own sake, drag us down into a material tyranny from which we must be delivered. So, MacDonald writes,

> no man who has not the Father so as to be eternally content in him alone, can possess a sunset or a field of grass or a mine of gold or the love of a fellow-creature according to its nature—as God would have him possess it—in the eternal way of inheriting, having and holding. He who has God, has all things, after the fashion in which he who made them has them.[51]

The spiritual condition of the one who encounters (or is encountered by) the objects and events of this world is just as relevant to the epiphanic nature of the encounter as whatever presence we may suppose is there to be apprehended. Theologically, for MacDonald and for Maurice (for whom, Florence Higham suggests, "*every* activity of life was sacramental"[52]) it was always and at best a matter of the God who is *with* us, close to us, seeking to draw us to himself in, with and under the whole of the creaturely world in which, by body and soul, we are immersed, calling out and soliciting resonance from the God who is in us, the Christ who, by virtue of the incarnation, is now joined to us and present by his Spirit in the depths of our innermost being. But that resonance may be, and all too often is, drowned out by the cacophony of sin and the curving in of the self upon itself (and away from God and from truth) in which sin consists. Maurice urges his readers:

> There is a light within you, close to you. Do you know it? Are you coming to it? Are you desiring that it should penetrate you through and through? Oh, turn to it! [...] It will reveal yourself to you! It will reveal the world to you! [...] When I say Repent: I say, Turn and confess His presence. You have always had it with you. You have been unmindful of it.[53]

"The spirit of God," writes MacDonald, "lies all about a man like a mighty sea, ready to rush in at the smallest chink in the walls that shut him out from his

---

[50] MacDonald, *David Elginbrod*, 33–4. See n.29 above.
[51] George MacDonald, "The Hardness of the Way," in *Unspoken Sermons*, 201.
[52] Higham, *Frederick Denison Maurice*, 115.
[53] Maurice, *Theological Essays*, 101.

own,"⁵⁴ seeking opportunities to strengthen what is good, and to burn out what is evil. For, organic and oceanic metaphors aside, redemption is a matter of the heart and the will, and, if God's purpose is that his creatures should share in his own life and joy, become partakers in the divine nature, then what this means humanly is the conformity of heart, mind and will to the Father's own. "Because we are come out of the divine nature," MacDonald writes, "we must choose to be divine, to be of God, to be one with God, loving and living as he loves and lives, and so be partakers of the divine nature, or we perish."⁵⁵ The "unsurpassable gulf" between creator and creature, the intimate presence of creator to creation, and the radical participation into which the one is invited and drawn by the other prove, at the last, to be matters grasped more in terms of the moral than the metaphysical, and they are manifest nowhere more completely than in the realm of the human imagination, which lives and moves and has its being entirely as the creative offspring of God's own.

This brings me, finally, to attempt some brief account of how Erskine, Maurice, and MacDonald understood the doctrine of the atonement; for it seems to me that they all understood it in much the same way, that this was probably due (more obviously than anywhere else in their theology) to the influence first of Erskine on Maurice (it is, with little significant modification, the doctrine unfolded in Erskine's two seminal works *The Brazen Serpent* and *The Doctrine of Election*, published in 1831 and 1837 respectively), and then of Maurice (and others influenced by Erskine such as A. J. Scott) on MacDonald, and that their account is distinctive and important in its own right within the history of that doctrine's development. It is also easily misconstrued. And I want to take as my starting point one such mis-characterization, offered by Philip Davis in his otherwise excellent book on Victorian literature and culture.⁵⁶ Writing of Maurice's involvement in the initiatives of Christian Socialism, Davis suggests that they represent the practical outworking of a wider theological shift from concentration on "the love offered in the Incarnation, rather than the pain suffered in the Atonement."⁵⁷ If there is truth in this way of putting things (which there is) it is nonetheless buried too deep beneath the surface for anyone unfamiliar with Maurice's thought not to be misled. Let me state my main point here tersely, and then seek to unpack it. For Erskine, for Maurice, and for MacDonald there is and can be no choosing between incarnation and atonement, nor between love and suffering; there cannot even be any helpful prioritizing of one over the other,

---

⁵⁴ George MacDonald, *Robert Falconer* (London: Hurst & Blackett Ltd., 1868), 181.
⁵⁵ MacDonald, "The Creation in Christ," 424.
⁵⁶ Philip Davis, *The Victorians* (Oxford: Oxford University Press, 2002).
⁵⁷ Davis, *The Victorians*, 139.

because *God's love, made concrete in the incarnation, is from first to last an atoning love, and it works from first to last through suffering and finally through death.*

For all three figures the matter is perhaps most concretely summed up in the claim that Christ lived and died *to deliver us from our sins*. The way that this was interpreted in the theologies with which each was familiar and felt obliged to part company was that such deliverance consisted in the purchasing of a pardon or securing of an amnesty, so that we might not incur the punishment attendant on our guilt, this punishment having been borne instead by Christ, an innocent third party, in our stead, his suffering and death being the precondition of our forgiveness. This, our three detractors each insisted, was a dreadful distortion as well as a thin and weak rendering of the true meaning of the words. To begin with, it is the Father's love and forgiveness which precedes and provides the atonement, being the very ground of the salvation which seeks us out and makes us his own. Christ is God himself, bearing the full cost of his own decision to create, a decision which he always knew would involve him in a long, messy, and costly struggle, ending in his own coming to be one of us and to share in the darkness of our nature so that he could redeem it and, finally, raise it up into new and eternal life. The whole history of God's dealings with creation, MacDonald writes,

> is a divine agony to give divine life to creatures. The outcome of that agony, the victory of that creative and again creative energy, will be radiant life, whereof joy unspeakable is the flower. Every child will look in the eyes of the Father, and the eyes of the Father will receive the child with an infinite embrace.[58]

So, Maurice insists, it is not punishment but *sin*, the work of the devil in our hearts and minds and bodies, from which we need and should most desire to be delivered.[59] He enquires,

> What is it to assure [men] that transgressions are forgiven by a bare act of amnesty, unless the sin of the heart and will, the separation from God which is the root of these transgressions, is at an end? How can you ever persuade them that it is at an end unless God himself has removed it? How can God have removed a separation unless there is some One in whom we are bound more closely to Him than our evils have put us asunder?[60]

It is precisely here that the word atonement finds its most direct application. In Christ, God has bound us closely to himself by taking our humanity upon himself, drawing it and us into his own life, and infusing his life into us by taking up a new residency in each human soul. Thus, MacDonald explodes: "I believe

---

[58] George MacDonald, "Life," 301.
[59] Maurice, *Theological Essays*, 389.
[60] Maurice, *Theological Essays*, 120.

that Jesus Christ is our atonement; that through him we are reconciled to, made one with God. There is not one word in the New Testament about reconciling God to us," he continues; "it is we that have to be reconciled to God."[61] And this is it: in Christ God has taken our broken, fallen nature and reconciled it, rendered it at-one with himself, so that it is perfectly and freely conformed to his own character and able to share the joy of his own life. But this takes place through the obedience of Jesus, an obedience which involves him in dreadful struggle and suffering, being faithful to his Father despite being immersed in the dark web of sin and evil and its consequences, remaining true even as the final and most awful consequence of sin—a death which threatens to separate sin finally from God—breaks over him; suffering it all, not less, but much *more* intensely than we ever could, precisely because his spirit is one which feels things as God feels them, and which flourishes only in unalloyed communion with his Father.

But here's the thing, the thing which turns more familiar notions of the relationship between atonement, suffering, and death upside down: "Did he not," MacDonald enquires of his reader, "thus lay down his life persuading us to lay down ours at the feet of the Father? Has not his very life by which he died passed into those who have received him, and re-created theirs, so that now they live with the life which alone is life? [...] Verily he made atonement!"[62] Erskine draws out the implication more fully: Christ, he insists, suffers and dies in the process of making our nature anew, refashioning it from within the conditions of its fallen and corrupt and alienated state, and so realigning it with his Father's will and its own intended participation in the image and the likeness and the life and the joy of God. And he did all this for us. But he did not suffer and die *instead of* us, so that we might not have to. Endless empirical evidence quickly puts paid to any such silly suggestion. No—he came to suffer and to die "to change the character of our suffering, from an unsanctified and unsanctifying suffering to a sanctified and sanctifying suffering" and death, as his own new life at work in us grants us the power to bear it as the will and the means of our loving Father at work, destroying the taint of death, "the work of the devil," that is in us.[63] For this, MacDonald insists, is what God is always bound by his nature to do; not, as some theologies have suggested, bound to punish by some abstract code of law; but, far more radical and more salvific—to destroy utterly sin and death so that they may no longer despoil his good creation.[64] And this is not the work of

---

[61] George MacDonald, "Justice," in *Unspoken Sermons*, 536.
[62] MacDonald, "Justice," 537.
[63] Thomas Erskine of Linlathen, *The Brazen Serpent, Or, Life Coming Through Death* (Edinburgh: Waugh & Innes, 1831), 39.
[64] MacDonald, "Justice," 511.

law, but precisely the work of love. "God," he writes simply, "is life, and all that is not God is death. Life is the destruction of death, of all that kills, of all that is of death's kind."[65]

What, then, are we to say of punishment? Once again, according to Erskine, we must say that God in Christ bore the punishment of human sin because he suffered the consequences of human sin, including death itself, when he became one of us. But his manner of bearing it transformed it, and so transformed our manner of bearing it. "There is something to be done by penal suffering," he writes, "which cannot be done without it. It is not a ceremony, it belongs to the eternal constitution of things. It is the refiner's fire, without which the refining cannot take place."[66] "The notion that the salvation of Jesus is a salvation from the consequences of our sins," MacDonald concurs, "is a false, mean, low notion. The salvation of Christ is salvation from the smallest tendency or leaning to sin. It is deliverance into the pure air of God's ways of thinking and feeling."[67] Suffering is the only way, Erskine avers, by which "human nature, fallen as it is, can be delivered from the bondage of corruption, and fitted for communion with God, and for participation in his glorious blessedness."[68] Through Christ at work in us through his Spirit, Maurice insists, we learn to endure the wrath or punishment of our sins as that which comes to us precisely from the love of the Father, burning the sin out of us, and in our endurance of it we vindicate his judgment upon our sin, and pray that it may not be quenched until it has effected its full loving purpose.[69] For punishment in and of itself has no purpose: it is no equipoise to sin; it makes nothing good. And it has nothing to do with pardon of forgiveness. These are entirely a matter of the personal relationship with the one wronged by our sin, and can be made good only by our reconciliation to him, as he seals his logically prior forgiveness of us into the state of forgiven-ness in us.[70] This, the bearing of the consequences of sin—our own and that of others in the world we share together—is fitted to accomplish in God's hands, as the life of Christ secures an ever more secure hold upon our will, our heart and mind. Thus, MacDonald insists in a statement as theologically provocative as it is profound—"Jesus, our propitiation, our atonement [...] could not do it without us, but he leads us up to the Father's knee: he makes us make atonement."[71]

---

[65] George MacDonald, "The Fear of God," in *Unspoken Sermons*, 320.
[66] Erskine, *The Brazen Serpent*, 41.
[67] MacDonald, "Justice," in *Unspoken Sermons*, 518 (italics added).
[68] Erskine, *The Brazen Serpent*, 34.
[69] Maurice, *Theological Essays*, 121.
[70] Maurice, *Theological Essays*, 118–9.
[71] MacDonald, "Justice," 538.

If there is a character in MacDonald's fiction in whose narration this theological recasting of the salvific relationships between God's love, suffering, death, and redemption is most fully enfleshed, then it seems to me to be Leopold, the brother of Helen in *Thomas Wingfold, Curate*,[72] a soul all but lost to darkness, whose return to the light is excoriating, entailing as it does and must the full psychological, spiritual, and physical consequences of his moral state, and who is spared no suffering until, at the last, he is able to embrace death in effect as an offering of himself and all that he is into the hands of the God he has discovered to be for him rather than against him, vindicating the righteousness of his judgment, and entrusting himself to his love. MacDonald is not optimistic, it must be said, about this pattern being completed or even very much advanced within the three score years and ten (or in his day more often considerably less) of our time on the earth. "The condition of most men and women," he admits, "seems to me a life in death, an abode in unwhited sepulchers, a possession of withering forms by spirits that slumber."[73] A horrid counterfeit, then, of that life for which God has created them, and for the enjoyment of which Christ has reconciled and prepared their nature, and now longs to work out in and through them. It is for this reason that Erskine, MacDonald, and Maurice respectively all baulk at the Reformation's dogmatic abandonment of the ancient doctrine of a purgatorial state. Erskine writes to a correspondent in 1864,

> When I think of God making a creature [capable of participation in His own blessedness], it seems to me almost blasphemous to me to suppose that He will throw it from Him into everlasting darkness, because it has resisted his gracious purposes towards it for the natural period of human life. No; He who waited so long for the formation of a piece of old red sandstone will surely wait with much long-suffering for the perfecting of a human spirit.[74]

If that is God's purpose—the formation of human persons into his sons and daughters, fitted to share in his eternal blessedness—then for Erskine it was as intolerable to suppose that an arbitrary temporal limit be placed on this, as unthinkable that God would not take all the time available to him, all the time necessary, to secure his purposes, as Maurice found the notion that God might dispatch unrepentant souls to unending punishment—punishment to be endured for its own sake, with no redemptive efficacy.

We tread here on the threshold of things better spoken of gently and in a spirit of hope, rather than dogmatically. But those whose concern is for the character of the God spoken of in Christian Scripture to be allowed to shine

---

[72] George MacDonald, *Thomas Wingfold, Curate* (Whitehorn, CA: Johannesen, 1996).
[73] George MacDonald, "Life," 308.
[74] William Hanna, ed., *Letters of Thomas Erskine of Linlathen*, 4th ed. (Edinburgh: David Douglas, 1884), 427.

through the systematizings and theologizings of its human interpreters will need nonetheless to say something. So, in the interests of that I close with some words from Maurice, and the final fateful contribution to his *Theological Essays* of 1853, on the theme of "Eternal Life and Eternal Death":

> I ask no one to pronounce, for I dare not myself pronounce, what are the possibilities of resistance in a human being to the loving will of God. There are times when they seem to me—thinking of myself more than others—almost infinite. But I know that there is something which *must* be infinite. I am obliged to believe in an abyss of love which is deeper than the abyss of death: I dare not lose faith in that love. I sink into death, eternal death, if I do. I must feel that this love is compassing the universe. More about it I cannot know. But God knows. I leave myself and all to Him.[75]

---

[75] Maurice, *Theological Essays*, 405–6.

Ἔπεα Ἄπτερα
CHILDREN IN THE MIDST:
A DEADLY PLAYDATE WITH MACDONALD AND DERRIDA
AN UNSPOKEN TALK[1]

Daniel Gabelman

Hors-Texte or Horse Text?
THIS IS A HORSE
THERE IS NO HORS-TEXTE

I think MacDonald and Derrida[2] would have been friends. Their caricatured difference (theism/atheism) seems logically insurmountable, but a playful coup d'état might be possible to dissolve this "spoken" difference via Derrida's "unspoken" *différance* or what MacDonald might call the child in the midst.

Some (Un)Ground Rules
Thus to be playfellows with God in this game
When one prays, one is always a child

MacDonald's apparent affinity with Derrida has long fascinated me. Or perhaps I should say it has disturbed me into thought—both would like that, even if neither would necessarily like what I am attempting in this chapter: that is, puzzling through MacDonald's various hints and cryptic comments to piece together some fragments of his theory of language (which turns out, I think, to be something like a triadic grammatology) and its parallels with Derrida. I will begin with an extended consideration of the title page and dedication of *Unspoken Sermons* (1867) followed by an uncomfortably close reading of "The Child in the Midst," the first and most dangerously seminal sermon.

I am conscious of the irony of trying to "fix" meanings that MacDonald seemed content to leave unfixed so will attempt to follow Roland Barthes'

---

[1] I spoke a paper at the Cambridge conference, but it was not this one. Those winged words have been unwinged and winged their way elsewhere (Daniel Gabelman, "Celestial Nonsense: George MacDonald's Apophatic Play," *Literature and Theology* 36, no. 3 (September 2022): 273–297). So, I offer these unspoken words as a supplement.

[2] Jacques Derrida is the founder of a mode of criticism called "deconstruction" and one of the most prominent continental philosophers of the last century. He is often (unjustly in my view) held up as a scarecrow of the dangers of postmodernism and irreligiosity.

recommendation that "in the multiplicity of writing, everything is to be *disentangled*, nothing *deciphered*" along with Derrida's: "the reading or writing supplement must be rigorously prescribed, but by the necessities of a *game*, by the logic of *play*."[3] Some of my unspoken words, therefore, will inevitably be *play*ful—writing about play in an unplayful mode is like humorlessly analyzing humor. The medium may not be the message, but it is at least part of the mediation of meaning. If my unspoken talk needs forgiveness, I can only plead like a playground child: Derrida made me do it.[4]

I will also play by a couple of (un)ground rules. First, I feel dared by John Patrick Pazdziora who in his recent *Haunted Childhoods in George MacDonald* gently chides me and others for drawing uncritically on "The Fantastic Imagination" (1893) because it is MacDonald's "final word" on the imagination which "belongs firmly to MacDonald's late phase, and functions as a retrospective, repackaging his work into a single whole."[5] Pazdziora's chosen method, therefore, is to focus "on texts for which there is clear evidence of influence during the composition." I will accept this wager and even raise the stakes: all my MacDonald quotations will come from works first published in 1867 (the year the first series of *Unspoken Sermons* was published).[6] I do this not because I think that the historical-critical method is always superior to other methods, but because I think it will be a fun, fecund game. But this game is almost too easy (1867 is probably the most prolific and profound single year of MacDonald's publishing career) so I will double dare myself to quote from each work at least once.[7] For Derrida, as ever, there

---

[3] Roland Barthes, "The Death of the Author," in *Image, Music, Text*, trans. Stephen. Heath (London: Fontana, 1977), 147; Jacques Derrida, *Dissemination*, trans. Barbara Johnson (Chicago: Chicago University Press, 1981), 64.

[4] I also invoke Jean-Luc Marion's words: "theological discourse offers its strange jubilation only to the strict extent that it permits and, dangerously demands of its workman that he speak beyond his means. [...] One must obtain forgiveness for every essay in theology. In all senses." *God Without Being*, trans. Thomas Carlson (Chicago: Chicago University Press, 1991), 2.

[5] John Patrick Pazdziora, *Haunted Childhoods in George MacDonald* (Leiden & Boston: Brill, 2020), 23. In addition to accepting his dare, I also would like to thank John Patrick Pazdziora for reading and commenting on this chapter during the initial composition phase. There are Derridean traces of his suggestions sprinkled throughout. Likewise, my thanks are also due to my co-editor, Amanda Vernon, for reigning in my playful excesses.

[6] And by "published," I mean according to their title pages—which creates an originary historical-critical problem for my game (and Pazdziora's?) because *Unspoken Sermons* actually came out in December 1866 (a common Victorian white lie) and most of the other works arrived later in the year—so clearly after the "during composition" phase of "The Child in the Midst"—not to mention that MacDonald seems to have preached a version of "The Child in the Midst" at least as far back as 1855. So, what is the *arche* and what the *telos*?

[7] In addition to the first series of *Unspoken Sermons*, 1867 includes *Dealings with the Fairies* (with the first publication of "The Golden Key"), "Luther the Singer," "The Imagination:

are no rules—he will haunt this "talk" as he pleases. And for the "audience" I have a game of whose epigraph is whose: two unattributed quotations for each section, one from MacDonald and one from Derrida. Master them all and find the surprise within![8]

Pre-ludic: Title Page—Innocent as a Winged Dove or Wise as a Wingless Serpent?

> *Where more is meant than meets the ear*
> *A text is not a text unless it hides from the first comer*

Derrida would have enjoyed the title page of *Unspoken Sermons*: it prefigures the unresolved textual tensions between speech and writing, origins and supplements, rule and play, authority and subversion, certainty and the precariousness of hope. It is also beautiful, "unspeakably beautiful."[9]

On its surface, as several early reviews comment, "the title of the book explains itself."[10] According to the *Illustrated Times*, "the discourses have never been preached; they were written down on 'broken' Sundays," while the review in the *Pall Mall Gazette* is titled "Sermons Never Preached."[11] Yet, as early as 1855, MacDonald seems to have preached a version of "The Child in the Midst" in Huntly.[12] Christmas variants of the sermon were also "thought" by Julian in *Within and Without* (1855) and "preached" in *Adela Cathcart* (1864) by the fictional curate Mr. Armstrong.[13] Indeed, the ideas of "A Child in the Midst" (and all the sermons) can be found throughout MacDonald's works from the 1860s,[14]

Its Functions and Its Culture," the serialization of all of *Guild Court* most of *Robert Falconer* (not chapters 1–6) and some of *The Seaboard Parish* (chapters 1–14), the conclusion of "The Carosoyn" and *The Disciple and Other Poems*. Clearly, 1867 displays MacDonald's incredible range, depth, and breadth in a striking way.

[8] "There is always a surprise in store for the anatomy or physiology of any criticism that might think it had mastered the game, surveyed all the threads at once, deluding itself, too, in wanting to look at the text without touching it, without risking—which is the only chance of entering into the game, by getting a few fingers caught." Derrida, *Dissemination*, 63.

[9] This was Ruskin's comment on reading the book, discussed later in the chapter.

[10] Anonymous, "Unspoken Sermons," in *The Illustrated London News* (Mar. 23, 1867): 287.

[11] Anonymous, "Sermons Never Preached," in *Pall Mall Gazette* (Jan. 5, 1867): 68.

[12] Letter to His Wife, 28 July 1855, in *An Expression of Character: The Letters of George MacDonald*, ed. Glenn Edward Sadler (Grand Rapids, MI: Eerdmans, 1994), 97. Pazdziora has an extended discussion of this journey to Huntly and its relationship to MacDonald's view of the childlike, 60–65.

[13] The 1867-game prevents me from quoting, but I will secretly point you to where the earlier Gabelman discusses this: "The Day of all the Year: MacDonald's Christmas Aesthetic," *North Wind: A Journal of George MacDonald Studies* 29 (2010): 11–23.

[14] To take an example almost at random, here is MacDonald in *Guild Court* (another 1867 work): "Christ [...] is present in the soul of such a child, as certainly as in the Church, or in the spirit of a saint. [...] He can be present in the weakest child's heart [...] in an infinitely

and it is hard to believe that MacDonald would have intentionally excluded these sermons from his guest preaching engagements. Even if they were never preached aloud in this precise form, why advertise them as such? Is it a veiled criticism of the typical quality of "spoken" sermons—a way of promising that his readers will not be as bored as they normally are on Sundays as *The Glasgow Herald* review implies?[15] If so, is MacDonald suggesting that the written word is in some sense superior to the spoken word?

Whatever MacDonald meant, he could hardly have been ignorant of the paradoxical potential hidden on the surface: "sermon" is from the Latin *sermo* meaning talk or speech (without religious connotations), so the title glossed could be "not spoken speeches" or "unsaid talks." If all he meant was "something I wrote but never said," there is a more straightforward word for this: "essays." F. D. Maurice's *Theological Essays* (1853), for example, has significant similarities in content and method to *Unspoken Sermons* with a less ambiguous title. If MacDonald preferred the spiritual or didactic connotations of "sermons" to "essays," there was no need to include "unspoken" as the sermon was also a well-recognized written genre. Coleridge notably published some of his essays under the title *Lay Sermons* (1817).

Moreover, the signification of the words is slippery. "Unspoken" could mean "not uttered," but it could also mean "not spoken of" as in a phrase like "unspoken rules," that which is forbidden or secret. "Unspoken Sermons" might, therefore, be "taboo sermons," like the secret messages that naughty pupils circulate behind the backs of their teachers, perhaps encoded just in case they are intercepted. "Unspoken" might also mean "words taken back or negated" as when in *Macbeth* Malcom renounces what he has previously said to MacDuff ("I put myself to thy direction, and / Unspeak mine own detraction").[16] MacDonald frequently unsays things in his sermons, so there is a sense in which they are self-deconstructing discourses. He also unsays many of the commonplace, oppressive doctrines of his day; thus, there is a further sense in which the sermons that are "unspoken" might not be MacDonald's but those of hegemonic religious leaders—unspeaking the sermons of Victorian Pharisees.

This last reading (unsaying onerous religious commonplaces) is supported by the central epigraph ("Comfort ye, Comfort ye my people") which implies

---

deeper way than those." *Guild Court* (Whitehorn, CA: Johannesen, 1999), 161.

[15] "Most people somehow believe they get enough of that 'sort of thing' served up to them on Sundays [...]. Compositions which may fairly pass muster in the pulpit, and are good enough as 'spoken' productions, may come, and very often do come, far short of the requisites of tolerably good readable matter." Anonymous, "Unspoken Sermons," in *Glasgow Daily Herald* (Dec. 29, 1866), 2.

[16] *Macbeth*, Act 4 Scene 3, ll. 141–2.

some affliction from which the people desire to be liberated. In the context of Isaiah 40, God is speaking to the Israelites living in captivity in Babylon. In alluring red lettering that anticipates red-lettered Bibles and the illusion of God speaking unmediated to the reader, MacDonald suggests that his readership is in some sort of spiritual bondage and that what follows is an attempt to loosen or "unspeak" those bonds. "Comfort" might be an evocation of the Holy Spirit as "the Comforter" who inspires and uplifts the individual, giving them the courage and good cheer necessary to trust what is unseen and unspoken even in the face of opposition from religious authority. "Comfort" also implies a particular mode and tone of communication: not logical dialectic but poetic rhetoric, not cold argumentation to convince the head but warm words to encourage the heart. There is a promise of pleasure or at least the release of some psychic anxiety-causing tension, and, as Derrida points out, deconstructing rigid logocentric structures "has the effect, if not the mission, of liberating forbidden *jouissance*."[17]

MacDonald further suggests a deconstructive impulse in his dedication:

> These Ears of Corn,
> gathered and rubbed in my hands
> upon broken Sabbaths,
> I offer first to my Wife,
> and then to my other Friends.

As quoted above, several early readers seem to have taken these lines innocently to mean that MacDonald wrote these sermons exclusively on Sundays. Whether or not this is true (and it seems unlikely), it does not make sense of the lines, for even the harshest Scottish covenanter could not say that reading and writing about scripture was breaking the sabbath. The dedication is an allusion to Luke 6:1–5 in which Jesus' hungry disciples pluck ears of corn while walking through a field on the sabbath. When Pharisees confront Jesus claiming the disciples have broken the law, Jesus responds by reinterpreting Old Testament scripture and saying that "the Son of Man is Lord also of the sabbath." MacDonald frames himself as one of Jesus' disciples breaking the law to satisfy hunger, liberating forbidden pleasure through his transgression. Even the image of the ears of corn being "gathered and rubbed" evokes the idea of something delectable being released from a dead entrapping husk through an effort of disintegration. The lifeless shell must be removed before the kernel can be enjoyed.

In addition, MacDonald seems to anticipate pharisaic criticisms of his book and imply a riposte: Jesus, the Lord of the sabbath, came to liberate the divine joy that had become entangled in laws and doctrines, and MacDonald is merely

---

[17] Jacques Derrida, "This Strange Institution Called Literature," in *Acts of Literature*, trans. Derek Attridge (London: Routledge, 1992), 56.

imitating his teacher's method. He also mimics Jesus' mode of imaginatively reading scripture into new contexts. Jesus claims the story of David taking consecrated bread from the temple (from 1 Samuel 21) and applies it to the current situation—an imaginative hermeneutic maneuver that the Pharisees likely would have disputed—and MacDonald follows Jesus' unconventional method in the sermons that follow, sweeping away accrued doctrines and "mummies of prose" to reimagine and revivify the words of the Bible.[18]

MacDonald's method was, in fact, the biggest cause of concern for Victorian readers. With the exception of one Glasgow review which claimed that parts of the book were "like the drivel of an idiot or a man drunk" (an eerie echo of the scoffers at Pentecost[19]) early reviews were highly laudatory of the aesthetics and sentiment: "we have never read sermons as beautiful as these" wrote the reviewer in *The Illustrated Times*, while *The Glasgow Daily Herald* praised "the felicity in illustration" and the "independence and freshness of thought," and the *Pall Mall Gazette* said they held "a very large amount of true and beautiful thought, musically and eloquently expressed."[20] John Ruskin wrote to MacDonald that "if ever sermons did good, these will," and that certain passages were "very beautiful—unspeakably beautiful [...] if they were but true."[21] Despite his heart's earnest longing for goodness and beauty, Ruskin ultimately subordinated his heart to his head and an Enlightenment conception of truth as manifested in rational methodologies. Ruskin seems to be punning on "unspoken" in his phrase "unspeakably beautiful." Is it "unspeakable" for Ruskin because beauty is ultimately silenced by the dominant Enlightenment discourse? Later in the letter, Ruskin evokes both Feuerbach's higher criticism and Darwin's evolutionary materialism[22] when he continues that "I feel so strongly it is only the image of your own mind that you see in the sky" and that the hand that made MacDonald's mind was "the same hand that made the adder's ear—and the tiger's heart." Surprisingly for the most famous art critic of the nineteenth century and a champion of certain aspects of medievalism, Ruskin ultimately privileges a rationalistic version of "truth" shorn of its associations with other transcendentals (goodness and beauty): he lets his head silence his heart.

---

[18] George MacDonald, "The Imagination: Its Functions and Its Culture," in *A Dish of Orts* (Whitehorn, CA: Johannesen, 1996), 9.
[19] Acts 2:13 (AV): "Others mocking said, 'These men are full of new wine.'"
[20] *Greenock Telegraph* (Feb. 16, 1867); *Illustrated Times*; *Glasgow Daily Herald*.
[21] Greville MacDonald, *George MacDonald and His Wife* (London: George Allen & Unwin, 1924), 337.
[22] Feuerbach's *The Essences of Christianity* (1841 but translated into English by George Eliot in 1854) argued that God's real origin is in the mind of humans while Darwin's *On the Origin of Species* (1859) hinted that all living things had a material origin.

Ruskin would perhaps have agreed with the *Pall Mall Gazette* that "the method of Mr. MacDonald's mind cannot be applied to the purpose of bringing out the meaning of any writings considered as authoritative" and that he lacks "textual control of every kind and degree" because the texts are not "approached with simple dramatic intelligence," "historical knowledge" or "textual criticism." Linking MacDonald with F. D. Maurice, it claims that "Mr. Maurice [uses] the same method" but when reading both "one is yet torn with the painful conflict between love and reverence for a beautiful spirit, and dissatisfaction with the working of its method." The review then concludes by citing William Paley and arguing that only "once the plain textual meaning is fixed" should one make spiritual inferences. The invocation of Paley—the eighteenth-century apologist for the joyless marriage of Enlightenment rationality and Christianity—accentuates the reviewer's typically modern hermeneutic anxieties: a nervous longing to pin down or "fix" the "plain textual meaning" to the original saying, a desperate desire for certainty and a quavering fear of uncertainty, compensated for by an overconfidence in the historical-critical method's ability to distill and fix "plain textual meaning."

The reviewer in *The Illustrated Times* similarly worries about "Mr. MacDonald's methods […] of textual elucidation in general" and complains that his treatment of the text is "as unhappy as anything can possibly be" because he treats "words spoken centuries ago, with special applications of their own, just as if they had dropped from the skies yesterday." MacDonald finds "'infinite depths of meaning' with a vengeance," but this violates the laws of interpretation:

> Where a symbolic meaning is founded upon a "literal" meaning, the law is, that the higher meaning shall be *inferable* from the lower, and vice versa. When this rule is not observed, an infinite-depths-of-meaning system only leads […] to infinite depths of confusion.

MacDonald is accused of rampant (or at least incipient) relativism: he has unmoored meaning from its fixed rational anchor. Though the reviewer agrees with most of the spiritual "truths," the methodological failures unnerve him: they violate his "law" of interpretation; meaning is not properly "founded," and "rules" are "not observed" such that "textual authority" is threatened with an "infinite depth of confusion." In other words, MacDonald is too (pre)postmodern for the reviewer's jittery faith in hermeneutics—MacDonald's Isaiah-like "comfort" is discomforting; he has rubbed the ears wrong and broken the reviewer's sabbath.

Derrida, who also was frequently criticized for his "muddled" method,[23] would probably have diagnosed both reviewers (and Ruskin) as afflicted by

---

[23] Notably by John Searle in "The World Turned Upside Down," *The New York Review* (Oct. 27, 1983).

logocentricism—a "nostalgia for origins, an ethic of archaic and natural innocence, of a purity of presence and self-presence in speech," a turn "towards the lost or impossible presence of the absent origin."[24] Were he in a prescribing mood, he would have offered them a *pharmakon*, a deconstructive medicine/drug to cure/kill their idolatrous devotion to the *logos* of philosophy, criticism and theology.[25] MacDonald's version of the *pharmakon* might seem more palatable or even harmless, but, as we will see, it too is ultimately playful and perilous.

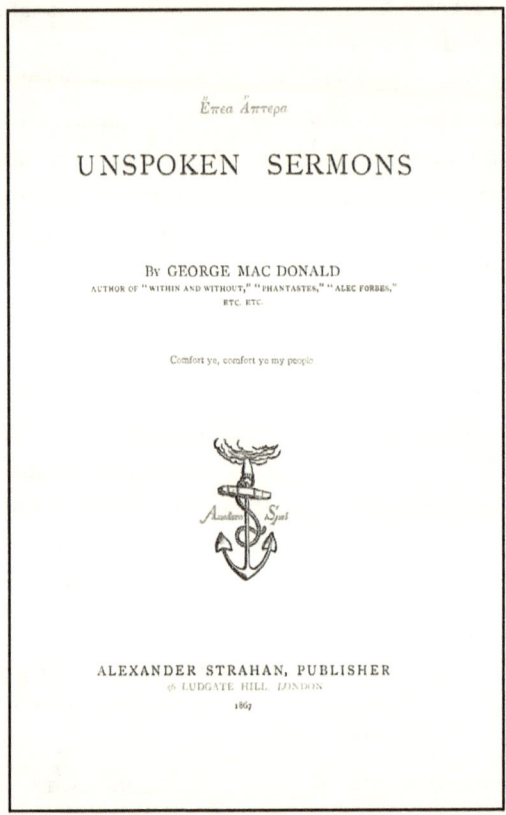

TITLE PAGE OF *UNSPOKEN SERMONS* (1867). IMAGE COURTESY OF JOHN FLYNN

Some final paratextual hints of this perilous play appear in the two Greek phrases on the title page. The first appears as part of the publisher's device: an anchor, with its rope dangling, held in suspension by a mysterious hand which itself is held or shrouded by a cloud. Inked in striking red, the phrase *Anchora Spei* (anchor of hope) is divided by the anchor. This was Alexander Strahan's personal device, a reference to Hebrews 6:19 ("which hope we have as an anchor of the soul") that emphasized his initials (AS) through capitalization. Like MacDonald,

---

[24] Jacques Derrida, *Writing and Difference*, trans. Alan Bass (London and New York: Routledge, 2009), 369.
[25] See Derrida, "Plato's Pharmacy" in *Dissemination*, 61–156.

Strahan was an expatriated Scot living in England. The two became close in the mid-1860s, sharing many friends and theological sympathies, particularly F. D. Maurice and his Broad Church theology. It was Strahan that in 1872 brought the news of Maurice's death to the MacDonalds.[26] Strahan's biographer notes how "the *Anchora Spei* appeared on nearly every volume written by George MacDonald" but Strahan made only "occasional use" of it elsewhere. It was, for instance, markedly absent from his less explicitly religious periodicals like the *Argosy* and the *Contemporary Review*.[27] Thus, though not directly of MacDonald's making, the device's appearance on the title page is at least partially authorial—he must have approved of it to have it on all his works when Strahan also frequently used a simpler device (just his initials) or no device at all.

Like the other titular paratexts, the device is more of an irresolvable riddle than an anchoring clarification. The paradox begins with the biblical text, for in what sense is hope an anchor? Hope, as Jurgen Möltmann, notes "is forward looking and forward moving and therefore also revolutionizing and transforming the present."[28] An anchor, meanwhile, is all about restraining movement, remaining fixed and stationary through turbulence and uncertainty. Hope focuses on the futural *not yet*: the desire which is not yet manifest, the dream which is not yet real, the beautiful which is not yet true. Hope is light and mobile; anchors are weighty and immobile. Strahan's image of the suspended anchor intensifies this paradoxical tension: is the hand lifting the anchor or is the anchor pulling the hand down out of the cloud? Which force is uppermost—gravity or levity? Either way is problematic, for if the hand is levitating the anchor, then its function and *telos* as an anchor is negated, while if the anchor is pulling the hand back down to earth, then hope is paralyzed into despair. To use a nautical phrase, the anchor has been weighed—but does this mean up or down? The paradoxical device is like John Henry Newman's comment about logic: it "hangs loose at both ends."[29] Unlike logical ratiocination, though, it does not hide the fact but emblazons it on title pages. There is, thus, real peril and real play in the device. On the one hand, it hopes that anchors will be unanchored—somehow transforming gravity's attraction to the fixed center into levity's longing for the open sky. On the other hand, however, it might turn out that hope is hopeless—that gravity's black hole is, indeed, inevitably drawing all things toward motionless death.

---

[26] Greville MacDonald, *George MacDonald and His Wife*, 415.
[27] Patricia Thomas Srebrnik, *Alexander Strahan: Victorian Publisher* (Ann Arbor, MI: University of Michigan Press, 1986), 70.
[28] Jurgen Möltmann, *Theology of Hope* (London: SCM, 1974), 16.
[29] John Henry Newman, *An Essay in Aid of a Grammar of Assent* (London: The Catholic Publication Society, 1870), 272.

Eerily hovering above the title, the Greek epigraph Ἔπεα Ἄπτερα (*Epea Aptera*) similarly plays precariously with the presence and absence of meaning. The phrase is a pun on one of the most frequent Homeric formulas ἔπεα πτερόντα (*epea pteroenta*), typically translated as "winged words" but functioning somewhat like the tag "he said" before and after dialogue in the *Illiad* and *Oddyssey*. The addition of the negative prefix *(a-ptera)* inverts the meaning to "wingless words," "unwinged words," or "words without wings." Though the phrase poses as a proper epigraph or motto—like Isaiah 40, an evocative quotation from an authoritative source—it is, as far as I can tell, original to MacDonald.[30] Ironically, then, the epigraph pretends to mythical origins and classical authority but is itself "unwinged words," a never-before-spoken formulation, MacDonald masquerading in writing as an epic oral poet, his own (and only?) Greek composition. The two words Ἔπεα Ἄπτερα seem balanced and paired (though reversed) with the two words *Unspoken Sermons*, as if one is claiming to be a translation and elucidation of the other. But which is the translation and which the original in this game of supplementation? What meaning gap or *aporia* is filled through this play with a fictional authority? Is Ἄπτερα a gloss for "unspoken," and if so, is MacDonald debasing writing and elevating speech through the symbol of it being "wingless" or "without wings"? Are "sermons" equated with Ἔπεα, and if so, what classical connotations are evoked in this comparison? Liddell-Scott notes, for example, that after Homer the plural of *epos* ("word") often meant "epic" as in Plato's *Republic* when Socrates says that we should always attribute "the true quality of God [...] to him whether we compose in epic [*epesin*], lyric or tragic verse."[31] Ἔπεα could also mean "hymns" or "songs" (Homer's epics were sung), so Ἔπεα Ἄπτερα might also be translated "unwinged epic" or "unsung hymns." MacDonald seems at least partially aware of these meanings in another work from 1867, "The Imagination: Its Functions and Culture," when he writes,

> Thousands of words which were originally poetic words owing their existence to the imagination, lose their vitality, and harden into mummies of prose. [...] No poetry comes by the elevation of prose; but the half of prose comes by the "massing into the common clay" of thousands of winged words.[32]

Here the phrase "winged words" is clearly linked to poetry, though in *The Seaboard Parish* (serialization begun in 1867[33]) it is also linked with the Bible:

---

[30] The 1855 *Liddell & Scott Greek-English Lexicon* notes that *apteros* in Homer occurs exclusively in the phrase τῇ δ' ἄπτερος ἔπλετο μῦθος, translated "the speech was to her without wings" and meaning "settled in her mind, sank into her heart."
[31] Plato, The *Republic*, 379a.
[32] MacDonald, "The Imagination," 9.
[33] It seems more than coincidental that MacDonald's only two uses of "winged words" also appeared in such chronological proximity to *Unspoken Sermons*.

"But certain words of the apostle kept coming again and again into my mind; for they were winged words those, and even when they did not enter they fluttered their wings at my window."[34]

Both poetry and the Bible are "winged" because of their primal "vitality:" they are living things that keep "coming again and again" into our minds and thus have a kind of active agency; they have at least the semblance of dynamism. Hence Joseph Johnson speculates that MacDonald "called his sermons 'wingless words,' possibly because they were not uttered, and perhaps because his poems were his 'winged words.'"[35] But is MacDonald's elaborate paratextual play merely facile? A way of telling his readers what is immediately obvious: that he is *writing prose* rather than *speaking poetry* (like writing "THIS IS A HORSE" under a drawing of a horse)?[36] Is MacDonald just being an innocent dove or is he also being wise as a serpent?

Perhaps the most widely known usage of ἔπεα πτερόντα in nineteenth-century Britain outside of Homer was John Horne Tooke's *Epea Pteroenta or The Diversions of Purley* (1786–1805), a philological treatise promulgating an etymological method capable of clarifying all philosophical perplexities. For Tooke, words are not ideas but things (objects and sensations in a Lockean sense), such that language is primarily about *conveyance* of thought, not thinking itself. For thoughts to be conveyed quickly (rather than laboriously or painfully dragged) they need to be condensed or abbreviated ("Abbreviations are the *wheels* of language, the *wings* of Mercury"), but abbreviation is a form of concealment, and we are deceived when "supposing all words to be *immediately* either the signs of things or the signs of ideas."[37] In this way "the artificial wings of Mercury" cheat the eyes of philosophy by hiding the true origin of words. Etymology, for Tooke, solves this problem by following the chain of signification back to the *arche* of a word in a thing, thus providing a sure foundation for communication and philosophy (Derrida would thus clearly place Tooke as an "onto-theologian" nostalgically longing for "the lost or impossible presence of the absent origin"). According to Stephen Prickett, the book "dominated sections of English philology"

---

[34] George MacDonald, *The Seaboard Parish* (Whitehorn, CA: Johannesen, 1995), 496.
[35] Joseph Johnson, *George MacDonald: A Biographical and Critical Appreciation* (London: Sir Isaac Pitman & Sons, 1906), 282.
[36] The reader will have spotted the quotation from the banned 1893 text "The Fantastic Imagination" (*A Dish of Orts*, 321); however, I am allowing it on a technicality since MacDonald refused (in writing) to write these words, so their ontological (or hauntological as Derrida would say) status is uncertain. The phrase was intended figuratively to represent MacDonald's unwillingness to provide an explanatory supplement to his texts, instead trusting to the internal play of the text to reveal itself (or not).
[37] John Horne Tooke, *Epea Pteroenta or The Diversions of Purely* (London: William Tegg, 1860), 13.

for over fifty years and included admirers such as Ralph Waldo Emerson, James Mill and William Hazlitt.[38] It also significantly impacted Coleridge who initially adopted Tooke's etymological method somewhat uncritically, but, according to H. T. Jackson, ultimately radically transformed it, seeking for the origins of words "increasingly in intangibles, in actions rather than in names for things" and affirming not the constancy but "the flux and constant change of language."[39] In the end Coleridge found Tooke's theory of language too fixed and static; words were "living Things:" they were mobile and continually developing.

Might MacDonald be ironically alluding to Tooke in his autographic epigraph? As we will see, in *Unspoken Sermons* he clearly rejects fixing words to stable sources and embraces something much closer to Coleridgean flux. If so, *Epea Aptera* could signal this flux, could be an invocation of something like Derrida's *trace*, the marking of an absence, an erasure of the philosophical stability to be found in totalizing methodologies. Coleridge himself might have been satirizing Tooke when in *Omniana* (1812—the year Tooke died) he translated ἔπεα πτερόντα as "hasty words."[40] Thus, MacDonald's Ἔπεα Ἄπτερα might suggest "slow words," "deep words,"[41] or "considered words:" words that MacDonald has mulled ("gathered and rubbed") over many years; words not extemporized but carefully meditated; words about other words, signifiers of other signifiers, always already caught in the web of signification and unable to wing away the problem of interpretation. As much as one might want to be innocent as a winged dove, one cannot help being wise as a wingless serpent.

Derrida reminds us that "writing is the name of two absences:" the absence of the "signatory" and the absence of the "referent."[42] There is a general longing for speech over writing because speech is conceived as a double "presence:" the presence of the speaker and the presence of the sound of the words. Louisa MacDonald conveys this typical desire for the presence of speech over the absence of writing when in a letter to MacDonald while he is away speaking at a Broadland's conference (Aug. 2, 1877) she says, "I keep picturing you to myself under the beeches comforting and inspiring other people—and I am not to hear

---

[38] Stephen Prickett, *Words and the Word* (Cambridge: Cambridge University Press, 1986), 136.
[39] H. T. Jackson, "Coleridge, Etymology and Etymologic," *Journal of the History of Ideas* 44, no. 1 (1983): 80; Prickett, *Words and the Word*, 136.
[40] Samuel Taylor Coleridge, *Omniana* (London: Longman, Hurst, Rees, Orme, and Brown, 1812), 228.
[41] "Deep words" is also suggested by the Liddell & Scott definition of *apteros* cited above: "settled in her mind, sank into her heart."
[42] Jacques Derrida, *Of Grammatology*, trans. Gayatri Chakravorty Spivak (Delhi: Motilal Banarsidass, 2002), 40–1.

your winged words."[43] But according to Derrida, writing is not a corrupted, lesser form of speech because speech itself is not "innocent language" and does not represent "a simple origin." Instead "language is first writing," and the "humbling of writing beneath a speech dreaming its plenitude" is just the "gesture required by an onto-theology" which desires "the subordination of the trace to the full presence summed up in the logos."[44] In other words, all language—including speech—is writing in the sense that meaning is *never* fully present, rather meaning is perpetually deferred or differed in "traces," the absent part of all signs. By "onto-theology" Derrida means the history of Western metaphysics that tries to unite philosophy (ontology is the study of "being" or "presence") and theology (study of God) into one all-mastering discourse that contains and controls all knowledge and experience in one system of thought. By self-consciously calling attention to his sermons as "unspoken" and his words as "unwinged," MacDonald might just be overly exaggerating the humble gestures required by the dominant system of onto-theology (though as is well-known, MacDonald was no lover of systems[45]). Maybe he is—as most readers seem to have thought—just innocently pointing out the obvious that he has never preached these sermons in person to a live audience ("unspoken") and that his words in the text that follows are just prose and not nearly as beautiful or powerful as poetry or scripture ("unwinged").

Or maybe something serpentine is simultaneously happening. Maybe "unspoken" is not a denigration of writing, but a denial of the myth of pure presence in speech, a recognition that speech does not elude the taint of the trace and that all language is writing (derivative, responsive, mediated) and therefore cut off from the innocent origin. Writing is not secondary but primary. MacDonald seems to indicate something like this in two other 1867 paratexts from *Dealings with the Fairies*. In his dedicatory letter to his children, he says: "you know I do not tell you stories as some papas do. Therefore, I give you a book of stories." Even with "telling" his own children his own stories, MacDonald prioritized writing over speech (or so he says—in writing). Meanwhile, the epigraph, taken from Milton's "Il Penseroso" commenting on Chaucer's *Canterbury Tales* (thus already an inextricably entwined chain of signification), is "where more is meant than meets the ear," suggesting that his stories are playfully "textual" in Derrida's sense: "a text is not a text unless it hides from the first comer, from the first glance, the

---

[43] Greville MacDonald, *George MacDonald and His Wife*, 473. Here Louisa's "winged words" gestures to how MacDonald rarely preached from a prepared manuscript, yet, although she highly valued his extemporaneous speeches, it would be odd if she were simultaneously denigrating his "wingless words."

[44] Derrida, *Of Grammatology*, 37, 71.

[45] In "It Shall Not Be Forgiven," for example, MacDonald says mockingly, "How, then must the truth fare with those who, having neither glow nor insight, will build intellectual systems upon the words of our Lord?" *Unspoken Sermons*, 46.

law of its composition and the rules of its game."⁴⁶ In this way, "unspoken" might also be the textual "within"—interior, hidden, ineffable, forbidden, apophatic—*tracing* the sermons' surface "without"—exterior, revealed, articulate, dutiful, cataphatic.⁴⁷ Moreover, like MacDonald's anonymous "Homeric" epigraph, the quotation from Isaiah ("Comfort, Comfort ye my people") is also an "unspoken sermon," composed by an anonymous sixth-century (BC) exile in Babylon (called "Deutero-Isaiah" by Biblical scholars) and ventriloquized into the mouth of an eighth-century (BC) prophet.⁴⁸ Assisted by the vibrant red-lettering, the words purport to be *immediately* spoken by God, but they arrive always already textually mediated beyond hope of deciphering the origin of pure presence. They come to us mediated by MacDonald's epi*graph* via the Authorized *Version* as *translated* from the Masoretic *text* as *transcribed* for two millennia as *written* by an anonymous writer imaginatively *rewriting* Isaiah hearing the voice of God (and none of this dismays MacDonald). So too Jesus' *spoken* reply (evoked in the dedication) to the Pharisees (defending sabbath breaking by citing the text of 1 Samuel) is nevertheless inextricably already writing in Derrida's sense—even *The Word* descends into the web of unwinged words. Maybe, therefore, in advertising this double absence (shouting about his muteness ("unspoken") and inventing a new Homeric symbol (*Epea Aptera*) to debase his work as derivative) MacDonald is playing with us—and along with Derrida.

Ludic: A Triadic Grammatology, or MacDonald's Not-Quite-Platonic, Sort-of-Triune Semiotics

The infinite mediator, mediates between all hopes and all positions; between the most debased actual and the loftiest ideal
We are all mediators, translators.

There are two recurrent questions about MacDonald that I have long mulled: 1) to what extent was he Platonic? and 2) to what extent did he believe in the Trinity (particularly the Holy Spirit)? I was asked both questions in my doctoral *Viva Voce*, and I stuttered out some apparently passable answers.⁴⁹ I was not,

---

⁴⁶ Derrida, *Dissemination*, 63.

⁴⁷ For the sake of the 1867-game, I deny that this is an allusion to *Within and Without* (1855), though this might be uppermost in some readers' minds. It is an allusion to Derrida's famous phrase "il n'y a pas de hors-texte," which I translate (never having studied French) "there is no without-text." A hors-texte is a blank page in a book (so not a horse). This phrase occurs in his discussion of a "surprise" (prise = within) "being held within" Rousseau's writing about "mother nature," as a deconstruction of the idea of the "blank slate" or innocent origin; *Of Grammatology*, 158. Here is your surprise:⁵ we're all **MaD** here.

⁴⁸ Although he never comments on it one way or another, MacDonald likely knew the theory of Deutero-Isaiah, first formulated by Johann Döderlein in his *Esaias* (1775).

⁴⁹ One must pass the Viva before a PhD is awarded. *Viva Voce* is Latin for "living voice" where spoken words defend unspoken ones, a tradition which implies the superiority of speech

however, satisfied with my replies, so subsequently those spoken questions became unspoken ones in much of my thinking and research on MacDonald. They are also questions which have provoked much debate and discussion in MacDonald criticism more generally (including in this volume), suggesting to me they cannot be answered simply or straightforwardly by normal critical methods. So, in this section I will venture a more playful approach, open to the risk (as all play must be) that it might fail spectacularly, though hopefully at least in an entertaining and instructive way.

Moreover, I now think the two questions are related, or perhaps even that they are the same "unspoken" question. My unspeakable-word-symbol answer is ~~KING~~FATHER$_{play}$*father*. My expanded "unspoken" reply is: MacDonald was grammatologically triune, such that his Plato was surprised to find that Heraclitus' flux-child had assassinated Parmenides' Monadic *Being* with a simile-dagger. But perhaps I should explain.

MacDonald's triadic semiotics is hiding in plain sight in *Unspoken Sermons*. To take a blunt example from "The Higher Faith:"

> [The Bible] nowhere lays claim to be regarded as *the* Word, *the* Way, *the* Truth. The Bible leads us to Jesus, the inexhaustible, the ever unfolding Revelation of God. It is Christ "in whom are hid all the treasures of wisdom and knowledge," not the Bible, save as leading to him. And why are we told that these treasures are *hid* in him who is the *Revelation* of God? [...] Is not their hiding in him the mediatorial step toward their unfolding in us?[50]

There are three levels of meaning exchange here, each of which roughly relates to traditional semiotic categories (referent, signified, signifier) and one person of the Trinity (Father, Son, Holy Spirit). MacDonald deconstructs the widespread doctrine of the Bible as "*the* Word of God" by taking the Bible at its word: Jesus is "*the* Word" and "the *Revelation* of God." The Bible is debased to just words about the Word, who himself is prepositionally ("of") distanced from God. This is a grammatological maneuver: anticipating Saussure[51] and Derrida, MacDonald dilates the sign into three parts—signifier, signified and referent—thereby exposing to view what is normally semantically occluded in the condensed, dualist form, "the Word of God." Fundamentalists, therefore, could be said to be shuttling Jesus haphazardly (never playfully) from one side of this dyadic structure to the other depending on whether accentuating his distance from God (**Word** of God) or his distance from humanity (Word of **God**—though in this

---

over writing.

[50] George MacDonald, "The Higher Faith," in *Unspoken Sermons*, 36.

[51] "We propose to keep the term sign to designate the whole, but to replace concept and sound pattern respectively by signification and signal." Ferdinand de Saussure, *Course in General Linguistics*, trans. Roy Harris (London: Bloomsbury, 2013).

version, Jesus is almost entirely erased). But MacDonald unveils their grammar game and insists that Jesus should have his own semantic space to play. The Bible is just the signifier of Jesus the signified who in turn signals God the Father (the referent—sort of, more on this below). The Spirit, meanwhile, seems to be what makes this game of hide and seek possible, the play between the parts of the sign (particularly between the signifier and the signified), the oily lubricant that prevents the sign from seizing up and becoming motionless (fixed to the "plain textual meaning"). Indeed, shutting down the play of the spirit is the only "unforgiveable sin" for MacDonald as he reveals in "It Shall Not Be Forgiven," which is why he regularly exposes the tripartite structure of "The Word of God" to view (Bible-Jesus-God) and rails against literalism.

Clearly, MacDonald was by no means the first to emphasize that Jesus, not the Bible, was "the Word of God." MacDonald traces the idea to its textual source in the opening chapter of the gospel of John (though the *trace* of the *logos* goes back further via Philo, Plato, Heraclitus, etc.). More immediately, MacDonald was likely influenced by F. D. Maurice on this point, who in *The Gospel of John* (1857) wrote,

> Those who will not have the Word of God abiding in them, must shut out the invisible world, must become the slaves of the visible world. They may not have idols of wood and stone; but they must have idols. [...] Their religious men will fall into worship of letters. The letters of the book which testify of a living God, will receive the homage which the only God claims in this book for himself.[52]

Maurice makes the same grammatological point, but not quite as bluntly as MacDonald. There is enough distance (roughly five clauses) between his "Word of God" (meaning Jesus) and his "letters of the book" (the Bible) that a "dull disciple" could still miss the semiotic point. MacDonald has taken Maurice's grammatological clue and shoved it into his reader's face (he makes this same point manifest in nearly every *Unspoken Sermon*). Moreover, Maurice's comments are a gentle hand slap compared to MacDonald's exuberant unsaying of the doctrines of verbal and plenary inspiration of the Bible so popular in Victorian times (as today). He says, "I have seen nothing breed [arrogance] faster or in more offensive forms than the worship of the letter," and he repeatedly mocks "the dull disciple" for whom "revelation has ceased with and been buried in the Bible, to be with difficulty exhumed, and, with much questioning of the decayed form, re-united into a rigid skeleton of metaphysical and legal contrivance."[53] Reviewers might claim MacDonald's methods lead to "infinite depths of confusion," but he has already rebutted how their methods (historical-critical or fundamentalist)

---

[52] F. D. Maurice, *The Gospel of John* (London: Macmillan, 1888), 168.
[53] MacDonald, "The Higher Faith," 35.

lead to the depths of arrogance, dullness and death. In place of their dull, deadening method, MacDonald offers something like Derridean play, a triune grammatology that liberates Jesus from the Bible as "the Word" (via its own words) "to play in ten thousand places" within his own semiotic playground.[54] But it is in "The Child in the Midst" that MacDonald fully liberates the play within the name of God.

Every unspoken sermon begins with a biblical epigraph, which functions as the "winged words" to MacDonald's "unwinged words," the words of the Bible (spoken signifier) from which MacDonald plays (via the Spirit) to get at something like "Jesus The Word of God" (unspoken signified) and even—hesitantly, precariously—God the Father (un-unspoken referent). Here the epigraph is from Mark 9:33–37. Much like the red-lettering on the title page, the extreme indentation and smaller italic font evoke an intimate effect, garbing the well-worn[55] words in the soft glow of the innocent past, hiding the tears of textual transmission, and making it seem as if the reader has been transported back to the moment when they were first spoken.[56] And yet MacDonald's first written words draw attention to the textuality of the words of the Bible: "Of this passage in the life of our Lord, the account given by St Mark is the more complete. But it may be enriched and its lesson rendered yet more evident from the record of St Matthew."[57] The words given as immediate are immediately unspoken as mediated, and the reader is offered a supplement from Matthew to fill up what is lacking in the source (Luke also is supplemented later). After the Matthew quotation, MacDonald continues,

> These passages record a lesson our Lord gave his disciples against ambition, against emulation. It is not for the sake of setting forth this lesson that I write these words of our Lord, but for the sake of a truth, a revelation about God, in which his great argument reaches its height.[58]

MacDonald gives the "plain textual meaning" of the passage in one sentence ("against ambition"), and in the next sentence says this is not his subject. He admits it is the "fixed" meaning—what everyone agrees this text signifies—but then makes the same triune grammatological maneuver that we have already seen: he explodes the sign into three parts and lightly skips past the first level

---

[54] A line from Gerard Manley Hopkins' poem "As Kingfishers Catch Fire."
[55] Derrida uses the metaphor "wear and tear" to discuss the phenomenon of dead metaphors in "White Mythology: Metaphor in the Text of Philosophy," *New Literary History* 6, no. 1 (1974): 6.
[56] Italic type is based on calligraphic handwriting (hence the slanting) and was originally intended to suggest informality or greater intimacy because of its closer similarity to medieval manuscripts.
[57] George MacDonald, "The Child in the Midst," in *Unspoken Sermons*, 1.
[58] MacDonald, "The Child in the Midst," 2.

(signifier) for the sake of the signified and ultimately the referent, to reach for "its height." To play MacDonald's joker-card, I think this is what he most means by "unspoken sermons" (though I suspect he would have also delighted in the phrase's slipperiness as a space for the Spirit to play): the sermons that Jesus, The Word of God, did not directly speak but nevertheless meant. Not the immediate and obvious signifiers showing themselves to even the "dull disciple" on the surface, but the signified playing[59] in the midst of the dull disciple's nearly-dead signifiers.

After asserting that the child Jesus chose must have had a "childlike countenance and bearing" and "confess[ing] that there are children who are not childlike" he continues,

> One of the saddest and not least common sights in the world is the face of a child whose mind is so brimful of worldly wisdom that the human childishness has vanished from it, as well as the divine childlikeness. For the *childlike* is the divine and the very word "marshals me the way that I was going."[60]

MacDonald is throwing a grammatological party here, once again distending a sign (child) into its semiotic parts and holding it in semantic tension for us to attend to. The "face" of the commonplace child is the signifier from which MacDonald traces a double absence: the lack of the signified (human childishness) and the lack of the referent (divine childlikeness). Yet there is a not-quite-total absence of both traces in this child's face for they have only "vanished" (not never existed), suggesting that there is some ghostly presence of both still somehow haunting the face. It is "worldly wisdom" that drives both "childishness" and "childlikeness" out of the child's signifying face. Both levels are in agonistic tension with "worldly wisdom." Perhaps unsurprisingly, MacDonald never fixes the definition of "worldly wisdom,"[61] but there are enough hints to get a good picture (our unfriendly "dull disciple"), and it looks remarkably like the "logocentric" reviewers who complain about MacDonald's playful method leading to "infinite depths of confusion." Working backwards, therefore, at least one of the resonances of *childlikeness* (if not the uppermost) is as an antonym or unsaying of logocentricism—the systems of the "onto-theologians" that seek to control language and interpretation.

Having expanded the child-sign as far as possible (for now), MacDonald then collapses it down into *childlike*, but he leaves a trace of his triadic grammatological fingers on the surface of his symbol in the suffix "like." He could have favored

---

[59] In classical Greek, as we will see, the word for play is the same as child: *paidia*.
[60] MacDonald, "The Child in the Midst," 3.
[61] This is perhaps an allusion to Mr. Worldly Wiseman from *Pilgrims Progress*, but to follow that trace would be to digress and maybe even to regress.

"childness" as the abbreviation of "childlikeness" or created a personal neologism like "child-essence;" instead, he trumpets the simile, specifically by inscribing or enshrining the copula, the intermediary, the liminal linking space between two terms. "Childness" would have been a more essentialist choice, perhaps we might say a more purely Platonic choice, a choice that connected two semantic worlds immediately, like a Platonic rapture from shadow to essence that veiled or erased the mediatorial term. Daring, then, "to climb the height of [MacDonald's] truth"[62] in this symbol, we might finally suggest that MacDonald's erasure of "ness" from the fully triune "child-like-ness," as well as being more rhetorically beautiful, might also be a kind of apophatic hesitancy about essentialist claims or the precariousness of ever transgressing the distance from the signifier to the referent, the riskiness of traversing the space between the first term and the last of a simile, particularly as it relates to God. Inscribing and concluding the grapheme *childlike* with the mediator *like* could be evoking something of this fragility and hesitancy when speaking about the divine.

If this seems extreme, the final sentence ("the *childlike* is the divine and the very word 'marshals me the way that I was going'") goes even further—presaging the death of something like Derrida's onto-logocentric God. MacDonald's "spoken" meaning is straightforward: God is like a child, and this simile is what MacDonald is going to explain in the rest of the sermon. The "unspoken" meaning, meanwhile, is worthy of Nietzsche's *Zarathustra*, only more subtle—like a knife, or rather a dagger. Italicizing the word *childlike*, MacDonald claims that there is something about "the very word" that is ushering him toward some *telos*. "Very" tends to mean "actual" in common usage and as such normally just functions as an intensifier, but here MacDonald invokes the older meaning of "true" or "faithful:" the word *childlike* is MacDonald's paradoxical vision, his ecstatic revelation of a true sign (a true and faithful union of signifier-signified-referent *in the midst* of mostly dead or dying signifiers). Having had this revelation unveiled to him (partially, never fully), it "marshals" him, possessing or haunting him like a ghost and leading him to some martial act, summoning him to kill the God of the dull disciple.

Tracing MacDonald's Shakespearean reference, we discover that it is from Macbeth's famous soliloquy in Act 2 Scene 1:

> Is this a dagger which I see before me,
> The handle toward my hand? Come, let me clutch thee.
> I have thee not, and yet I see thee still.
> Art thou not, fatal vision, sensible
> To feeling as to sight? or art thou but
> A dagger of the mind, a false creation,

---

[62] MacDonald, "The Child in the Midst," 20.

> Proceeding from the heat-oppressed brain?
> I see thee yet, in form as palpable
> As this which now I draw.
> Thou marshall'st me the way that I was going.

The "winged words" ("marshals me...") that MacDonald invokes from this soliloquy are innocent on their surface, but they are not rhetorically striking enough for MacDonald to have chosen them just for what meets the ear: I hear an unspoken serpent, and this is a particularly sinister serpent. Macbeth speaks these lines on the threshold of murdering King Duncan while having a phantasmal vision of a hovering dagger. Hence, MacDonald suggest that the "very word" *childlike* is like a floating dagger in his mind, utterly real to his imagination even though he cannot touch it and cannot prove to the satisfaction of the ontotheologians that it is not a fancy of his "heat-oppressed brain," a spectral dagger haunting him toward some fatal act of regicide. Moreover, MacDonald has just told us that "worldly wisdom" is the antagonist of the childlike, so we have a "very" clue where this dagger is leading.

After this veiled assassination-assignation, MacDonald, like a good dramatist, leaves the reader of his "unspoken" plot in suspense ("But I must delay my ascent to the final argument") for roughly five pages to argue the finer points of why Jesus' unspoken meaning was "not in the humanity but in the childhood of the child."[63] He gestures to the murderous subplot again with his first usage of the word "kingdom:"

> The Lord wanted to show them that such a dispute had nothing whatever to do with the way things went in his kingdom. Therefore, as a specimen of his subjects, he took a child and set him before them. [...] For the idea of ruling was excluded where childlikeness was the one essential quality. It was to be no more who should rule, but who should serve; no more who should look down upon his fellows from the conquered heights of authority—even sacred authority.[64]

The rebellion is brewing in this passage with the unsaying of "ruling," "authority" and "sacred authority," but so far it is still just a rumor, the unheard sound of marshalling in the distance: the "King" is still in "kingdom." MacDonald's coup d'état is not yet ready to spring; he still needs to muster the full strength of his *childlike*. To do this, he needs more grammatological aid:

> For it is *In my name*. This means *as representing me*; and, therefore, *as being like me*. [...] *In my name* does not mean *because I will it*. An arbitrary utterance of the will of our Lord would certainly find ten thousand to obey it, even to suffering, for one that will be able to receive such a vital truth of

---

[63] MacDonald, "The Child in the Midst," 3.
[64] MacDonald, "The Child in the Midst," 8–9.

> his character as is contained in the words. [...] *In my name*, if we take all we can find in it [...] involves a revelation from resemblance, from fitness to represent and so reveal. He who receives a child, then, in the name of Jesus, does so, perceiving wherein Jesus and the child are one.[65]

MacDonald forces his readers past the surface signification of "in my name," beyond the "plain textual meaning" which is something like "because I tell you to" or "because I love everyone, even and especially the low and marginal." Instead, he delves into the unspoken meaning of "name" treating it as a meta-signifier, a signifier about the nature of signification. He explains this idea more fully in "The New Name" when he writes,

> a name of the ordinary kind in this world, has nothing essential in it. It is but a label by which one man and a scrap of his external history may be known from another man and a scrap of his history. The only names which have significance are those which the popular judgement or prejudice or humour bestows, either for ridicule or honour, upon a few out of the many. [...] As far as they go, these are real names, for, in some poor measure, they express individuality. The true name is one which expresses the character, the nature, the being, the *meaning* of the person who bears it. It is the man's own symbol,—his soul's picture, in a word,—the sign which belongs to him and to no one else. Who can give a man this, his own name? God alone.[66]

The triadic structure is becoming more familiar now, so it is easier to see his three levels of names: one that is a mere arbitrary signifier ("a name of the ordinary kind"), one that touches somewhat on the signified ("real names") and one fully resonant with the referent that only God knows ("the true name"). Thus, when MacDonald emphasizes Jesus' phrase "*in my name*" he is thrusting his reader beneath (or beyond) the semantic surface. Jesus, "The Word of God," could not use words haphazardly, could not just mean the "ordinary"—and therefore arbitrary—plain meaning; he must be meaning something further up the chain of signification. In MacDonald's view, Jesus' semiotic exchanges of meaning must always be fuller, indeed almost excessive, as he says in *Luther the Singer*: "I believe that there must be more meaning in the simplest word of our Saviour than we have yet found—probably than we shall ever find out."[67] The more we attend to the very words, the more meaning emerges. In this case, "in my name" is Jesus' way of saying this *childlike* child is a true symbol of me (not just an "arbitrary" signifier). MacDonald admits that probably only one in ten-thousand people will see this meaning—that most are mindlessly content to obey the surface meaning (receive children) without receiving the "vital truth of his character" that "Jesus

---

[65] MacDonald, "The Child in the Midst," 10–11.
[66] George MacDonald, "The New Name," in *Unspoken Sermons*, 105–6.
[67] George MacDonald, "Luther the Singer," *Sunday Magazine* (1867): 255.

and the child are one"—but this does not dissuade him. In fact, he wants to go further:

> But the argument as to the meaning of our Lord's words, *in my name*, is incomplete, until we follow our Lord's enunciation to its second and higher stage: "He that receiveth me, recieveth him that sent me." It will be allowed that the connection between the first and second link of the chain will probably be the same as the connection between the second and the third. I do not say it is necessarily so; for I aim at no logical certainty. I aim at showing, rather than at proving, to my reader, by means of my sequences, the idea to which I am approaching. For it, once he beholds it, he cannot receive it, if it does not shew itself to him to be true, there would not only be little use in convincing him by logic, but I allow that he can easily suggest other possible connections in the chain, though, I assert, none so symmetrical.[68]

This is the method that appalled his logocentric reviewers (and still does[69]). Having levitated the *childlike* from the signifier (words of the Bible) to the signified (Jesus) via "showing" rather than "logic," MacDonald attempts the final leap from the signified (Jesus) to the referent (God). His method, however, is not Aristotelian or Enlightenment rationality or textual criticism but what he calls "showing," something closer to rhetoric or aesthetics, and he is unconcerned that the "logic" might be flawed or that someone else might come up with another chain of "possible connections" (he almost seems to welcome it). Nevertheless, he thinks he has found the most "symmetrical" chain; in other words, he thinks it is "unspeakably beautiful," and he trusts not to the historical-critical method but to some unspoken, fragile force (the play of the Spirit) to help individuals "receive it." There is no rational guarantee at any stage in this meaning exchange, none of William Paley's *Evidences of Christianity* (1794). Rather this "unspeakably beautiful" simile (*childlike*) is a kind of aesthetic catalyst working itself up the divine semiotic chain, but also like a daggered assassin sneaking up on a monadic monarch.

So, "to receive the child is to receive God himself," but MacDonald "traces" Jesus' "golden thread" even deeper "through the shining web of his golden words:"

> What is the kingdom of Christ? A rule of love, of truth—a rule of service. The king is the chief servant in it. […] The great Workman is the great King, labouring for his own. […] no rule of force, as of one kind over another kind.

---

[68] MacDonald, "The Child in the Midst," 12–13.
[69] In a 2013 YouTube video, two well-known evangelicals, John Piper and Tim Keller, scathingly describe MacDonald's *Unspoken Sermons* as "Pelagian," "awful stuff" and how they "turned with loathing" from them (reusing MacDonald's phrase for his reaction to "the God of Jonathan Edwards"). They further express bafflement that C. S. Lewis (their idol) was so impacted by MacDonald, and they laughingly dismiss MacDonald as "not a Christian," "disappointing," and only "filled with common grace." https://www.youtube.com/watch?v=uqiZJaDeM6Y&ab_channel=DesiringGod

It is the rule of *kind*, of *nature*, of deepest nature—of *God*. If, then, to enter this kingdom, we must become children, the spirit of children must be its pervading spirit throughout, from lowly subject to lowliest king. [...] This is the sign of the kingdom between them. This is the all-pervading revelation of the kingdom.[70]

MacDonald's *childlike* has plunged an unspoken dagger into the onto-logocentric King: he has snuck a Derridean *pharmakon*[71] into the King's cup, though it will take the King a few more pages to die fully (this is a Shakespearean play, after all). Perhaps now—while we wait for the King's death-throes—is a good moment for some light entertainment: a philosophical parable about Heraclitus, Parmenides, and Plato.

INTER-LUDIC: A PLAY WITHIN THE PLATO

Plato is not the father of Western philosophy as is sometimes dyadically suggested. He is not a pure source, not a perfect spring from which to drink the untainted waters of metaphysical thought, nor a virgin binary: just the *a priori* dualist pointing to the realm of forms to Aristotle's *a posteriori* monism pointing to earth as Raphael's *School of Athens* would have us believe. Like the Old Testament was to Jesus, so the pre-Socratics were to Plato, particularly Parmenides and Heraclitus. To sum up briefly, Parmenides claimed that *Being* was monadic, changeless, and static while Heraclitus argued that opposites coincided into a higher unity and, hence, everything seemed in flux. Most Platonists see Plato as somewhat reconciling the two by subordinating Heraclitus' *flux* to Parmenides' *Being*. But MacDonald seems to push his Plato away from Parmenides and toward Heraclitus, giving the playful flux of things greater heft and significance.

To my knowledge, MacDonald never mentions Heraclitus by name,[72] but the concatenation of three famous Heraclitan fragments with the "Old Man of the Fire" from "The Golden Key" (1867) is, at the very least, highly suggestive:

> B52: αἰὼν παῖς ἐστι παίζων, πεττεύων·παιδὸς ἡ βασιληίη [Eternity is a child playing draughts, the kingship is the child's]
>
> B12: ποταμοῖσι τοῖσιν αὐτοῖσιν ἐμβαίνουσιν ἕτερα καὶ ἕτερα ὕδατα ἐπιρρεῖ [You cannot step twice into the same river; for fresh waters are ever

---

[70] MacDonald, "The Child in the Midst," 14–15.
[71] MacDonald fictionalizes something very like Derrida's *pharmakon* in "The Carosoyn" (concluded in 1867). Carosoyn is a tripartite substance made from dreaming "three days without sleeping" followed by working "three days without dreaming" and finally working and dreaming "three days together." It also turns out to be poisonous to tyrannical monarchs, for the fairy queen loses her power after drinking it.
[72] Though in another 1867 work he does mention Pythagoras, another key pre-Socratic figure: "Pythagoras had taught about the stars moving in their orbits with sounds of awful harmony." George MacDonald, *Robert Falcolner* (Whitehorn, CA: Johannesen, 2005), 127.

flowing in upon you]

B30: κόσμον τόνδε [...] ἦν ἀεὶ καὶ ἔστιν καὶ ἔσται πῦρ ἀείζωον, ἁπτόμενον μέτρα καὶ ἀποσβεννύμενον μέτρα [this world was ever, is and will be an ever-living fire, with measures of it kindling, and measures going out]

Compare this to how Tangle must throw herself into a river and then pass through scorching heat to reach the Old Man of the Fire who is "a little naked child [...] playing with balls of various colors and sizes, which he disposed in strange figures upon the floor beside him." It is only here that she glimpses how "everything meant the same thing, though she could not put it into words again."[73] Also note the triadic structure of the old men (Sea-Earth-Fire) and the suggestive "mirror of something like silver" belonging to the second (dyadic) "Old Man of the Earth" who sees "shadows sometimes in [his] mirror" of the land whence the shadows fall. Could this be the Plato to the Old Man of the Fire's Heraclitus? If so, Platonism, for MacDonald, is not a pure origin but tainted (in a Derridean sense) by Heraclitus. Plato is not the Father of this topsy-turvy Platonism, but himself the offspring of Heraclitus' fiery play-child.

Patricide was the comic relief: now back to regicide.

LIBERATING DIVINE PLAY

In case the dull disciple missed MacDonald slipping a dagger in the middle of their King-God, he finally climaxes his "unspoken" play with his tripartite simile slaying the onto-theologians' monadic God:

> How terribly, then, have the theologians misrepresented God [...]! Nearly all of them represent him as a great King on a grand throne, thinking how grand he is, and making it the business of his being and the end of his universe to keep up his glory, wielding the bolts of Jupiter against them that take his name in vain. [...] The simplest peasant who love his children and his sheep were—no, not a truer, for the other is false, but—a true type of our God beside that monstrosity of a monarch.[74]

The God-King, that "monstrosity of a monarch," is dead, long live the *childlike* un-king. There are no half measures here. This is one of the rare times that MacDonald denies any truth content ("not a truer, for the other is false") to a well-attested biblical revelation (God "as a great King on a grand throne"). The divine hierarchy has been turned on its head: the *childlike* has thrown the *arche* (which means both "source" and "rule") into anarchy. Moreover, MacDonald has supplanted the King-God (monarchy) not with a lesser *arche* like Father-God (patriarchy), but with the playful antithesis to *arche* itself, for a child is an origin-less origin and an authority-less authority.

---

[73] George MacDonald, *Dealings with the Fairies* (London: Alexander Strahan, 1867), 139.
[74] MacDonald, "The Child in the Midst," 22–3.

Nevertheless, regicide does have a surprising trickle-down anarchic effect:

> we praise and magnify and laud his name in itself, saying *Our Father*. [...] For it is his childlikeness that makes him our God and Father.[75]

Blink and you miss it, but MacDonald just committed patricide as well, slipping the fully triune *childlikeness* dagger into the dyadic *Our Father*. Here MacDonald momentarily reveals his deepest "unspoken sermon:" that as we ascend the pinnacle of revelation (or traverse the semantic gaps from signifier-signified-referent) God correspondingly descends his symbolic manifestation (King-Father-child). God at his highest is at his lowest: not King and not Father but child. Thus, when MacDonald "speaks" of the dyadic (Platonic) *Our Father* (here and throughout his oeuvre), I suspect it is a concession to the "ten thousand" who cannot receive this highest/lowest revelation. Meanwhile, his "unspoken" meaning is always something like "Our ~~KING~~ F̶A̶T̶H̶E̶R̶$_{child}$*father*." But God is only "Father" because he is first "child." Wordsworth's dictum (beloved by MacDonald) that "the child is father of the man" also applies to God: the divine child is father of *Our Father*.

Moreover, the word for "child" in this New Testament pericope is παιδιά, which as Liddell-Scott notes also means "childish play, sport," or "game."[76] In this way, MacDonald's insemination of childlikeness into the very name of God, disseminates something remarkably like Derridean play:

> *Either* play is *nothing* (and that is its only *chance*); either it can give place to no activity, to no discourse worthy of the name—that is, one charged with truth or at least with meaning—and then it is *alogos* or *atopos*. Or else play begins to *be* something and its very presence lays it open to some sort of dialectical confiscation. It takes on meaning and works in the service of seriousness, truth and ontology. [... It] cannot, in classical affirmation, be affirmed without being negated.[77]

Derrida's "play" seems to resonate with the *via negativia* of negative theology, the apophatic method of unsaying whatever is affirmed about God so as not to trap God in words and fool oneself into thinking one has mastered the Godgame ("dialectical confiscation"). But I think Derrida and MacDonald are doing something even more radical than just piously protecting what we say about God (or play). In deconstructing the divine sign both seem to aim at liberating the forbidden *jouissance* hidden within the name of God itself, the play that playfully plays itself into play. MacDonald is not anxiously buttressing the crumbling edifice of God with rationalistic or onto-theological arguments about his existence, but ruthlessly removing these arguments as impediments that normally obstruct our

---

[75] MacDonald, "The Child in the Midst," 24.
[76] Henry Liddell and Robert Scott, *A Greek-English Lexicon* (Oxford: Oxford University Press, 1855), 1079.
[77] Derrida, *Dissemination*, 157.

vision of the beauty within the name of God. God is not a King, if by king you mean powerful, "monstrous monarch:" in fact, God is almost exactly the opposite of King, his rule is the rule-less love, his strength is the "weakness" of sacrificial service. God is not a Father, if by father you mean masculine family dictator: there is no patriarchy in God (neither "father-rule" nor "father-origin"), which is what frees MacDonald fearlessly to create simulacrum of God as grandmothers, fairies, and fire-children in his fantasies. παιδιά is a neutral noun whose presence in the referent-of-God gap (for ~~God~~ is always within and without signification) deconstructs the gendered construct of the name of God even as it liberates the play of God within ~~him~~~~her~~itself, the world, and those "playfellows" willing to play along with his Spirit.

Perhaps MacDonald's relative silence and ambiguity about the Holy Spirit could, therefore, be a playful grammatological game. The Spirit is the player that teaches (παιδώγωγός) us to play through the semantic gaps: first from signifier to signified (dyadic) but then, as we learn how to be "playfellows with God in this game," even through the hermeneutic, philosophical chasm that separates the signified from the referent. There is a risky courage in this paradoxical play that is absent from the monadic, maniacal faith of the fundamentalist, as well as the delusional objectivity of the dyadic rationalist. To conc*lud*e[78] this section how MacDonald conc*lud*es "The Disciple" (and conc*lud*e my 1867-game):

> Even of thy truth, both in and out,
> That so I question free:
> The man that feareth, Lord, to doubt,
> In that fear doubteth thee.[79]

Concludic: Monstrous play?

The childlike is the divine, and the very word "marshals me the way that I was going" [… to kill] that monstrosity of a monarch.

Monsters cannot be announced […] without immediately turning the monsters into pets.

I once considered Derrida a fiend; it was MacDonald who convinced me he might be a friend. Derrida, meanwhile, keeps revealing to me that MacDonald is not a friendly dovelike pet but a serpentine fiend of the dull disciple's monarchical God and patriarchal Father.

So, when MacDonald dedicated his *Unspoken Sermons* "first to [his] wife and then to [his] other Friends," I like to think that he was pre-posterously

---

[78] The OED traces the etymology of "conclude" to Latin concludere "to shut up closely;" nevertheless, it hosts a play-surprise, suggesting that endings might not be as final as they pretend.

[79] George MacDonald, *The Disciple and Other Poems* (London: Alexander Strahan, 1867), 49.

including Derrida within the "unspoken" *hors-texte*, foreseeing and rewriting the erasure that seems to separate them, the *surprise* that could transform a fiend into a friend.

Be warned: in reading MacDonald you might think you are stroking a winged dove, but a wingless serpent might inject you with a *pharmakon*. On the other hand, Derrida might not just be a snake in the garden; he might also surprise you into making room for the flight of a playful dove.

MacDonald's ~~King~~ ~~Father~~$_{play}$ does not comfort like a cuddly toy. When one "prays for comfort" to this player-God "the answer may come in dismay and terror." The innocuous child in the midst might—like Derrida's play ("the formless, mute, infant, and terrifying form of monstrosity")—"for love's sake turn [his] countenance away from that which is not lovely" and unveil himself "awful and glorious" as *"a consuming fire."*[80]

But that is another unspoken talk.

---

[80] MacDonald, "The Child in the Midst," 26.

LIST OF CONTRIBUTORS

Charles Beaucham received his B.A. in religion and philosophy from Berry College and his M.A.T. in English Education from Georgia State University. He teaches in the humanities department at Culver Academies in Culver, Indiana, and previously taught English literature at Korea International School and Darlington School. His work has been published in *North Wind*.

Gavin Budge is an honorary research fellow in the School of Humanities and Social Sciences, Anglia Ruskin University. He is the author of *Romanticism, Medicine and Natural Supernatural: Transcendent Vision and Bodily Spectres, 1789–1852* (Palgrave, 2013) and *Charlotte M Yonge: Religion, Feminism and Realism in the Victorian Novel* (Lang, 2007).

Kerry Dearborn is Emerita Professor of Theology at Seattle Pacific University where she taught for 20 years. She also taught at Sheldon Jackson College, Alaska; Fuller Theological Seminary extension, Seattle; Regent College, Vancouver, Canada; and World Vision International staff trainings in Kenya and the UK. She completed her PhD at the University of Aberdeen, Scotland, and has authored two books, *Drinking from the Wells of New Creation*, and *Baptized Imagination: The Theology of George MacDonald*, along with numerous journal articles and chapters in edited books. She enjoys life with her husband, Tim, and their three daughters and families, including 8 grandchildren.

Daniel Gabelman (PhD, University of St Andrews) is Head of English at King's Ely in Cambridge. He is the academic representative of the George MacDonald Society, and the author of *George MacDonald: Divine Carelessness and Fairytale Levity* (Baylor UP, Mythopoeic Award Finalist). He has also published on G. K. Chesterton, Lord Byron, C. S. Lewis, Lewis Carroll, J. M. Barrie, Max Beerbohm, and William Blake. He has co-written two books on literary doodling forthcoming with Cambridge University Press (*Genre and Theory of Literary Doodling* and *History and Contexts of Literary Doodling*), and he is currently co-editing the *Cambridge Companion to George MacDonald* (Cambridge UP, 2026).

Trevor Hart is Rector of Saint Andrew's Episcopal Church, St Andrews and Canon Theologian of St Ninian's Cathedral, Perth. He was formerly Professor of Divinity and founding Director of the Institute for Theology, Imagination and the Arts in the University of St Andrews. Trevor has lectured internationally and published widely on the importance of imagination for Christian faith, ministry, and theology. His publications include *Between the Image and the Word* (Ashgate, 2013), *Making Good: Creation, Creativity and Artistry* (Baylor, 2014), *Faith Thinking: The Dynamics of Christian Theology* (Wipf & Stock, 2020) and most recently *Confessing and Believing: The Apostles' Creed as Script for the Christian Life* (Fortress, 2022).

Elisabeth Jay is Professor Emerita of English Literature at Oxford Brookes University where she was Director of the Institute for Historical and Cultural Research. She has written widely on the fiction, prose and poetry of the nineteenth and early twentieth centuries, with a particular focus on women's writing. Her recent work includes *British Writers and Paris, 1830–1875* (2016) and editions of three novels in a 25-volume series devoted to Margaret Oliphant, for which she was joint general editor. Her other major interest lies in the interdisciplinary area of literature and theology where she continues to review and publish.

Kirstin Jeffrey Johnson (PhD, University of St Andrews) publishes and lectures internationally on George MacDonald, nineteenth-century Britain, the Inklings, faith and the arts, and ecology and community. She is on the advisory board of the Inklings journal *VII* and *North Wind: the Journal of George MacDonald Studies*, a founding board member of *C. S. Lewis & Kindreds Society of Eastern & Central Europe*, and co-chair of the George MacDonald Society. Kirstin directs *Windstone Farm Linlathen*, a nonprofit that seeks to facilitate and encourage community through "Theology, Ecology, & the Arts" in the Ottawa Valley, Canada.

Franziska E. Kohlt is a Leverhulme Research Fellow in History of Science at the University of Leeds and Inaugural Carrollian Fellow at the University of Southern California. She holds a doctorate from the University of Oxford where her DPhil explored the shared histories of Victorian Psychology and Fantastic Literature. Her research interests include science communication and its history, the role of narrative and metaphor in it, the history and historiographies of science and religion, of nature writing, especially entomology. She has published widely on the life and works of Lewis Carroll. Fran is also broadcaster, curator, and former translator for Marvel Comics.

Stephen Prickett was Regius Professor Emeritus of English Language and Literature at the University of Glasgow and honorary Professor of English at the University of Kent, Canterbury. He taught at the University of Sussex, The Australian National University of Canberra, Duke University, North Carolina, and Baylor University. He was President of the George MacDonald Society, a Fellow of the Australian Academy of the Humanities, Chairman of the U. K. Higher Education Foundation, and President of the European Society for the Study of Literature and Theology. He published two novels, nine monographs, ten edited volumes, and over a hundred articles on Romanticism, Victorian Studies and literature and theology. He died in 2020. He will be sorely missed in MacDonald studies.

Amanda B. Vernon received her PhD from Lancaster University where she researched the relationship between theology and literary form in George MacDonald's writing. In 2019 Amanda held a short-term fellowship at Yale's Institute of Sacred Music, where she undertook work on the George MacDonald Collection at the Beinecke Library. She has taught at Lancaster and Anglia Ruskin Universities, and her work has been published in *Victorian Review* and *Among Winter Cranes*. She is currently writing a monograph, *Reading with the Trinity: Theology and Literary Form in George MacDonald* (Manchester UP, 2026), and is a contributor to the forthcoming *Cambridge Companion to George MacDonald* (co-edited by Daniel Gabelman and John Patrick Pazdziora).

THE GEORGE MACDONALD SOCIETY

The importance of George MacDonald's life, work, and influence is increasingly being rediscovered, and the George MacDonald Society is at the forefront of the efforts to further interest in this un-commonplace writer. Established in 1981 by many of the figures to whom this book is dedicated, the Society publishes a respected annual journal, *North Wind*, which carries articles related to MacDonald, reviews of new books, and other publications relevant to MacDonald studies. A newsletter, *Orts*, is also produced to provide news of events, meetings, conferences, lectures, and any other information of interest to our members. For more information and to become a member, visit our website **www.george-macdonald.com**.

INDEX

Aberdeen, University of, 12, 18, 27, 46–51, 56, 61n74, 62, 175
Adela Cathcart, 5–6, 13, 98n5, 138–39, 142–47, 150–59, 177n83, 241
Anglicanism (Anglican), 11–12, 19, 21, 22, 23, 24, 27–41, 162, 164, 165, 166, 194, 219, 220, 224
Broad Church Anglicanism, 22, 29, 34n17, 247
apophasis, 9
Arnold, Matthew, 103n17, 149, 219, 220n7
Arthurian revival: see Medieval revival
At the Back of the North Wind, 13, 48n21, 75–76, 132, 134, 136–37, 154–55, 159, 163
atonement, 11, 13, 14, 129, 131n22, 133, 138, 150, 154, 192, 233–36
Aubrey Moore, 218, 220

Beattie, James, 48n20, 56n50, 57, 64, 128n3, 5, 7, 129n9, 134n39, 40
Beaucham, Charles, 139
Bedford College for Women, 104n19, 220
Beecher Stowe, Harriet, 79
Bible, 5, 12, 17, 38, 39, 40, 69, 99, 111, 137, 141–42, 152, 155, 162, 165, 180, 184, 218, 243, 244, 248–49, 253–55, 260, 262; scholarship/interpretation, 33, 70, 137, 141, 178, 218, 219, 222, 227, 228, 247, 252
Bodichon, Barbara, 34, 123n83
Brewster, David, 55, 56
Brontë, Charlotte, 20; *Jane Eyre*, 127, 146n112
Browning, Robert, 24, 28, 161
"Browning's 'Christmas–Eve'," 8–9

Brunonian medicine, 13, 139–40, 144–47
Bunyan, John, 111–12

Calvinism, 27, 129, 133, 177, 194, 220, 228
Cambridge Apostles, 10, 11, 17–18, 21–23, 25, 102, 106, 108
capitalism (capitalist), 13, 23, 149, 193, 194n8, 194–96, 202, 204, 205–07, 210, 214–15
Carlyle, Thomas, 18, 20, 23, 30–31, 33, 103n16, 105, 106, 150n133, 159, 160, 166, 170n57, 229
Carroll, Lewis, 22, 46, 55, 63,
Chalmers, Thomas, 99
Chaucer, Geoffrey, 100, 101, 112, 251
Chesterton, G. K., 34, 119
childlike (unchildlike, childlikeness), 10, 14, 83, 241n12, 256–65
Chopin, Frédéric, 99
Christ (Christlike, Jesus), 9, 68, 72, 87–88, 90–93, 129, 131, 135, 138, 142, 144, 155, 157, 159, 168, 173, 180, 184, 191, 214, 215, 221n11, 221n12, 223–24, 227, 228, 232, 234–37, 241n14, 243–44, 252–61
Christian Socialism, 11, 23–25, 97n3, 104, 220, 233
Christmas, 5, 8, 38, 109n34, 138–40, 142–43, 241
Coleridge, Samuel Taylor, 17–18, 20–23, 25, 103n16, 133, 135, 137, 138, 139, 140, 150, 210, 224, 242, 249–50
Collins, Wilkie, 30, 33, 148
commonplace, 5–14, 68, 71, 80, 88, 90, 112, 152, 191–93, 197–208, 212, 213–14, 242, 256

273

Congregationalism (Congregational church), 20, 27, 34, 129, 130, 147, 158

Dante Alighieri, 13, 24, 28, 52, 55n48, 98n4, 104n19, 112, 119, 121, 123, 161–64, 166–70, 172–74, 178–79, 182–87
Darwin, Charles (Darwinism), 22–23, 30, 52, 67, 81, 82, 87, 99, 132, 164, 168, 244; Social Darwinism, 67, 82, 132
Darwin, Erasmus, 99, 139–40
Dearborn, Kerry, 132–33, 135, 209
Deconstruct (Deconstruction) 14, 77, 80, 82, 84, 168, 242, 243, 253, 263, 264
Derrida, Jacques, 14, 239–43, 245–46, 249, 250–53, 255n55, 257, 261n71, 263–65
Dickens, Charles, 30, 31, 33, 93, 140, 141, 146
Disestablishment (Anglican), 12, 36, 37, 39, 41
Donne, John, 32
doubt (religious), 27, 29, 69, 89, 123, 131, 151, 264
dreams (dreamer, daydreams), 6–7, 12, 43–44, 46, 52–64, 71–72, 112, 191, 200–01, 204, 211, 247, 250, 261n71

education, 5, 24–25, 28, 36, 38, 39, 40, 44, 46, 48n18, 62, 65, 67, 68, 77, 81, 82, 83, 92, 97n3, 98–100, 103, 106, 107, 111, 114–16, 119, 122, 123n83, 124, 128, 133, 134, 143, 145, 169, 171, 182, 183, 198, 220n8
Elginbrod, David, 48n21, 92n136, 147–48, 158, 226, 227, 228, 232
Eliot, George, 30, 35n21, 37, 130, 161, 244n22,
England's Antiphon, 18, 97, 101n13, 110n39, 112, 123, 162n7
English literature, discipline of, 97–98, 104, 219–20
Erskine, Thomas, 13–14, 97n3, 103n16, 217, 224, 226–27, 233, 235–37
Essays and Reviews (Temple, Williams, Powell, Wilson, Goodwin, Pattison, Jowett), 32
Eucharist (Communion), 29, 39, 73, 139, 157
eugenics, 68, 77, 81, 87, 93
Evangelicalism, 22, 29, 32, 36n27, 127, 137, 138, 146–48, 177–79, 181, 184–86, 194–95, 203–4, 224, 260n69
evolution, 55, 68, 71, 80, 83, 86, 167–68, 171–73, 179, 244

fairytales, 5, 13, 59, 112, 113n48, 143, 148–49, 155, 158, 161–63, 176–79, 181, 184–86
"Fantastic Imagination, The," 43, 176, 179n91, 180n94, 181, 240, 249n36
fantasy (fantastic, fantastical), 12, 21, 22, 43–6, 52, 58, 59–65, 110, 112, 113n49, 119, 124, 128, 135, 186–87, 197
Faraday, Michael, 61–62
Freud, Sigmund, 6, 53
Froude, James Anthony, 31, 33, 34n17, 140n75
Furnivall, Frederick James, 24, 105, 106, 107, 109
Gabelman, Daniel, 55n48, 98n5, 104n19, 111n42, 130, 141, 176, 179n89
Gaskell, Elizabeth, 99, 106, 123n83
Gladstone, William, 29, 36
Goethe, Johann Wolfgang von, 19,

20–21, 50, 57, 101
"Golden Key, The," 261
Golden Pot, The, see Hoffmann, E. T. A.
Good Words (periodical), 32, 109n36, 162n8,
Great Disruption (Scotland), 35–36

Haeckel, Ernst, 87
Hardy, Thomas, 24, 130
Hare, Julius, 18–21, 22, 25, 99, 103n16
Hazlitt, William, 249
heaven (heavenly), 69, 72, 76, 80, 127, 155, 161, 162, 169, 178, 184n115, 186, 187, 197, 207, 215, 218
Hegel, Georg Wilhelm Friedrich (Hegelian), 50, 59, 217, 220
Hein, Rolland, 10n23, 45n9, 132n26
Hell, 60, 161, 162, 169–70, 172n58, 178, 182–83, 186
Herbert, George, 32, 39
Heraclitus, 253, 254, 261, 262
Hilton, Boyd, 129n10, 131n22, 138, 150, 192
Hoffmann, E. T. A., 195–96; *Golden Pot, The*, 13, 191–93, 196–98, 200, 204–07, 210, 212–24
Holland, Henry, 53, 54, 56, 58
Holy Spirit (Spirit, Holy Ghost), 89, 224, 232, 243, 252, 253, 264
Homer (Homeric), 101, 247–49, 251–52
Hooker, Richard, 32, 39
Hopkins, Gerard Manley, 226n30, 254n54
Horne Tooke, John, 156, 249
Hughes, Arthur, 10, 54, 107, 120, 122
Hunt, Holman, 153
Huxley, Thomas Henry, 52, 163, 168
Hypocrisy (religious), 127, 146, 147, 150

Hymns, 8, 41, 98n6, 250

Imagination, 6, 7, 11, 12, 13, 14, 18, 43, 44, 51, 55, 59, 62–63, 64–65, 68n6, 84, 93, 94, 133, 138, 140, 143, 146, 176–77, 181, 187, 193, 209, 221, 222n14, 228, 229, 230, 231, 233, 240, 248, 258
immanence (of God), 13, 135, 209, 217–23
Incarnation, 11, 13, 102n14, 129, 131, 133, 135, 137–39, 142, 144, 146–47, 150, 15–54, 158–59, 191–93, 196, 205, 209–15, 220, 223, 227, 228n35, 232–34
Industrialization (industrialism, Industrial Revolution), 18, 99, 100n9, 104n18, 107, 149, 193, 194, 208
Irving, Edward 35, 36n26

Johnson, Kirstin Jeffrey, 68n6, 220n9
Justice (injustice), 10, 13, 32, 83, 91, 165, 174, 182–83, 223

Kant, Immanuel (Kantian), 20, 131n23, 209
Keats, John, 18
Keble, John, 24, 141–42, 177n82, 178–79
Kemble, Fanny, 99
Kemble, John, 106
Kierkegaard, Søren, 131n23
King's College School, 28
Kingsley, Charles, 10, 11, 13, 22–24, 28, 30, 46, 55, 63, 99, 120n69, 154, 161–75, 177n81, 179, 182, 184n114, 185–87; *The Water Babies*, 13, 23, 162–63, 167–74, 179, 182–83, 186

Lewis, C. S., 34, 111, 112n45, 136,

260n69
Liddell & Scott Greek–English Lexicon, 248, 250n41, 263
"Light Princess, The," 132, 155–59
Lilith, 48, 50, 52, 55n48, 57, 61n74, 71–2, 86, 89–90, 113n49, 128, 135, 212
"Lost Princess, The" ("The Wise Woman"), 13, 163, 185–6
Logocentrism (logocentric), 243, 245, 256–57, 260, 261
love (divine) 8, 69, 87, 91, 92, 137, 162, 164–65, 166, 169, 173–75, 186, 209, 222–25, 233–34, 236–38, 265
   Luther the Singer, 240fn7, 259

MacDonald, Greville, 20, 28, 31–2, 35, 50, 90, 97n2, 98n4, 102n14, 192,
MacDonald, Louisa, 120, 250
MacDonald, Mary Josephine, 10, 120n71,
MacLeod, Norman, 32
Malcolm, 7, 91n132, 117n60
Marquis of Lossie, 5, 7–8
Marsh, Herbert, 20
Mary (mother of Jesus), 40, 184n115
Materialism (materialist), 23, 47, 51, 53, 58, 64, 140, 159, 168, 174, 186, 199, 203–04, 231, 244
Maurice, Frederick Denison, 11, 13–14, 18–19, 21–24, 29, 35–36, 40–41, 97–98, 101–10, 113, 120, 122, 124, 139, 162, 164, 165, 167, 168, 209–10, 219–20, 223–27, 232–34, 236–38, 242, 245, 247, 254; *The Kingdom of Christ*, 21–22, 29
McGillis, Roderick, 58n61, 129n10
Medieval revival 98, 105–13, 124
Metaphor (metaphorical), 44, 46, 53, 55, 58, 61–62, 63–65, 68, 141, 147n116, 159, 217–18, 228–30, 233, 255n55
Mill, James, 20, 249
Mill, John Stuart, 20, 25, 30
Milton, John, 18, 39, 100, 112, 251
Misenchantment, 13, 193–96, 202–07, 210, 214–15
Morris, William, 21, 105, 107, 109n34
Möltmann, Jurgen, 247

natural law (laws of nature), 13, 162, 164, 166, 167, 169–74, 182, 186
natural theology, 47, 51, 162–67, 173, 175, 186, 187
Nature (natural world), 13, 14, 40, 47, 51, 55, 57, 58, 81, 89, 91, 131, 135n41, 138, 142, 143, 163, 164–68, 170–81, 186–87, 194, 196, 197, 206, 210, 212, 214, 215, 219, 225–29, 232, 252n47
Neoplatonism (also see Plato), 221
Newman, Francis, 34n17, 99, 106
Newman, John Henry, 22, 140, 154n156, 161, 224, 247
Novalis (George Philipp Friedrich Freiherr von Hardenberg), 21, 50, 179n90, 196

Oliphant, Margaret, 35–36, 37
Oxford Movement, see Tractarianism

Paley, William, 51, 127, 165, 175, 245, 260
Paradox, 44–45, 130, 142, 217, 230, 242, 247, 257, 264
Parkes, Bessie Rayner, 34
Paul, St., 99n8, 206, 217, 227
Pazdziora, John Patrick, 163n10, 240, 241n12
Pennington, John, 44n7
Phantastes, 12, 13, 23, 43, 44, 46, 54–62, 63, 64–65, 74–75, 98, 104,

109–19, 120, 123, 124, 192–215,
Philo, 254
Plato (Platonic, Platonism), 11, 13, 18, 113n49, 139, 192–93, 196–214, 227–28, 231, 248, 252–53, 254, 256, 261–62, 263; *Republic, The*, 113, 201, 248
play, 14, 63, 98, 102, 130, 141, 156, 176, 227, 230, 239–41, 246–65; fair play, 182–83
polarity, Coleridge's principle of, 134
postmodern, 141n77, 245
postsecular, 130
prayer, 7–8, 39, 72, 99n6, 131n19, 154n153, 226; prayer book, 38n27, 39, 146n107
Pre-Raphaelite, 24, 105–07, 120, 122
Prickett, Stephen, 162n9, 163n10, 192, 201, 231, 249, 250n39
Princess and Curdie, The, 88, 89, 91, 149–50, 163, 179–86
Princess and the Goblin, The, 13, 48, 68n6, 88, 89, 130, 148, 159, 180n95
Providence, 83, 154
Psychology, 46, 48, 56, 59, 60, 62, 63
Purgatory, 153, 154, 170, 172, 178

Race (racial, racism), 5, 11, 12, 67, 70, 78–80, 82–3, 86–7, 91, 106n23, 108n30
Ragged Schools, 100
Reid, Thomas, 128, 133–35
Revelation (divine), 13, 51, 131, 135n41, 142, 162–3, 165 167, 168, 173–74, 176, 178–79, 180n95, 182–87, 202, 209, 214, 253–55, 257, 258, 260, 262–63
Robert Falconer, 97n2, 233–34, 240n7
Romantic (Romanticism), 131, 140, 193, 227; English Romanticism, 18, 103, 112, 131, 140, 225; German Romanticism, 3, 13, 19, 20, 59, 112
Rossetti, Dante Gabriel, 24, 28
Ruskin, John, 24, 30, 97n2, 99, 105, 106, 107, 119, 120, 121, 131, 141, 149, 161, 178, 241n9, 244–45; *Modern Painters*, 105n21, 119, 120, 121

Sabbath, 228, 243, 245, 252
Sacramentalism (sacraments), 14, 29, 33, 38, 91, 193–95, 202, 209–10, 213, 225, 228, 230–32
Saussure, Ferdinand de, 253
Schubert, Franz, 205–06
Science (Natural Philosophy), 5, 7, 12, 14, 30, 43–53, 57–9, 61–65, 67n3, 68, 86n113, 87, 100, 101, 162, 164, 165–67, 175, 194–95, 225, 226, 229, 231
Scotland, 7, 32, 34, 35, 99, 100
Scott, A. J., 97–110, 113, 124, 219–20, 224, 225, 226, 233
Scott, Sir Walter, 98n4
Seaboard Parish, The, 6, 12, 37, 39, 97, 98, 104, 107, 110, 111, 112, 119–21, 123, 124, 241n7, 248
Sectarian, 40, 41,
Semiotics, 252–60
Shakespeare, William, 18, 100, 101, 107, 109, 112, 257, 261
Shelley, Mary, 21
Shelley, Percy Bysshe, 18, 24, 55
Shields, Frederic, 99
Sidney, Sir Philip, 39, 108, 112
Sin (sinful, sinner), 27, 60, 61, 111, 138, 155n164, 165, 177, 183, 205, 224, 225, 232, 234, 235, 236, 254
Sir Gibbie, 6, 76, 87–88, 90–91, 93
Smith, Adam, *The Wealth of Nations*, 193
Spencer, Herbert, 23, 30, 52, 57,

82–84
Spenser, Edmund, 18, 59, 109, 111, 122, *The Faerie Queene*, 58, 112, 114n50, 117n61
Socrates, 197, 199, 201, 207, 248
Stephen, Leslie, 29
Sterling, John, 19, 21, 103n16
Strahan, Alexander, 246–47
Sunday Magazine (periodical), 31–32, 120
Symbolist Movement, 131
Suffering (long-suffering), 5, 76, 83, 86, 88, 99, 139, 146, 150, 170, 172, 213, 233–37, 258

Tennyson, Alfred Lord, 18, 21, 29, 105–07, 109, 120n69, 124, 130, 161
Thackeray, William Makepeace, 30, 31, 33, 99, 106, 155
Thomas Wingfold, Curate, 41, 69, 76, 88–89, 91n132, 92, 237
Tolkien, J. R. R., 21, 64, 104, 111, 112n45
Tractarianism (Oxford Movement, Anglo-Catholicism), 22, 33, 130n13, 131, 140–41, 177n82, 218
Transcendence (of God), 13, 135, 196, 209, 217–18, 220, 222–23
Trinity (Trinitarian), 13, 21, 29, 101, 102, 173, 183–84, 185, 219, 220, 222–25, 252, 253
Trollope, Anthony, 32–33
Tyndall, John, 62–63, 65
typology, 142–43, 157–60

unconscious, the, 52–53, 54–58, 60, 62, 63, 64, 230n44
Unitarian (Unitarianism), 21, 28n5, 29, 34, 102, 219, 223–24
Universalism, 130
unsaying (unspoken), 8–9, 239, 240, 242, 243, 244, 248, 251–65
Unspoken Sermons, 9–10, 14, 127, 142, 143, 184, 219, 239–44, 246, 248, 250–55, 257, 260n69, 263–64

Vernon, Amanda, 104n19, 131
Victorian medievalism: see Medieval revival
Virgil, 178, 187

Wigan, Arthur Ladbroke, 53, 56, 57, 58
Wilde, Oscar, 5, 135, 161
Within and Without, 162n7, 241, 251n47
Wordsworth, William, 18, 38, 50, 51, 58, 136, 143, 155, 227, 263
"Wise Woman, The," see "Lost Princess, The"

Yonge, Charlotte, 105n21, 127, 130n13, 141n77, 160n192

Zoroastrianism, 164

OTHER GEORGE MACDONALD SCHOLARSHIP

Phantastes by George MacDonald: Annotated Edition
John Pennington and Roderick McGillis, Editors

Phantastes was a groundbreaking book in 1858 and continues to be a seminal example of great fantasy literature. Its elusive meaning is both alluring and perplexing, inviting readers to experience a range of deep feelings and a sense of profound truth. This annotated edition, by two renowned MacDonald scholars, provides a wealth of information to better understand and enjoy this masterpiece.

Crossing a Great Frontier: Essays on George MacDonald's Phantastes
John Pennington, Editor

> "This is the first collection of scholarly essays on George MacDonald's seminal romance Phantastes. Appropriately to the age of its hero Anodos, here we have twenty-one of the best essays written on Phantastes from 1972 onwards, in which straightforward literary analysis works together with contextual, psychological, metaphysical, alchemical and scientific approaches to the elucidation of this moving and elusive work."
> Colin Manlove, author of *Scotland's Forgotten Treasure: The Visionary Novels of George MacDonald*

Lilith by George MacDonald: Annotated Scholarly Edition
John Pennington & Roderick McGillis, Editors

Following the acclaim of their scholarly edition of MacDonald's *Phantastes*, these editors combine their expertise to create a foundational resource to enjoy *Lilith*, a masterpiece of fantasy literature. Over 500 footnotes, seven appendices, reviews, and more. [forthcoming publication]

Behind the Back of the North Wind:
Essays on George MacDonald's Classic Book
Edited and Introduction by John Pennington and Roderick McGillis

The unique blend of fairy tale atmosphere and social realism in this novel laid the groundwork for modern fantasy literature. Sixteen essays by various authors are accompanied by an instructive introduction, extensive index, and beautiful illustrations.

Through the Year with George MacDonald: 366 Daily Readings
Rolland Hein, editor

These page-length excerpts from sermons, novels and letters are given an appropriate theme/heading and a complementary Scripture passage for daily reading. An inspiring introduction to the artistic soul and Christian vision of George MacDonald.

Diary of an Old Soul & The White Page Poems
George MacDonald and Betty Aberlin

The first edition of George MacDonald's book of daily poems included a blank page opposite each page of poems. Readers were invited to write their own reflections on the "white page." Betty Aberlin responded to MacDonald's invitation with daily poems of her own.

> *Betty Aberlin's close readings of George MacDonald's verses and her thoughtful responses to them speak clearly of her poetic gifts and spiritual intelligence.*
> Luci Shaw, poet

George MacDonald: Literary Heritage and Heirs
Roderick McGillis, editor

This latest collection of 14 essays sets a new standard that will influence MacDonald studies for many more years. George MacDonald experts are increasingly evaluating his entire corpus within the nineteenth century context.

> *This comprehensive collection represents the best of contemporary scholarship on George MacDonald.*
> Rolland Hein, author of *George MacDonald: Victorian Mythmaker*

In the Near Loss of Everything: George MacDonald's Son in America
Dale Wayne Slusser

In the summer of 1887, George MacDonald's son Ronald, newly engaged to artist Louise Blandy, sailed from England to America to teach school. The next summer he returned to England to marry Louise and bring her back to America. On August 27, 1890, Louise died leaving him with an infant daughter. Ronald once described losing a beloved spouse as "the near loss of everything". Dale Wayne Slusser unfolds this poignant story with unpublished letters and photos that give readers a glimpse into the close-knit MacDonald family. Also included is Ronald's essay about his father, *George MacDonald: A Personal Note,* plus a selection from Ronald's 1922 fable, *The Laughing Elf,* about the necessity of both sorrow and joy in life.

Shadows and Chivalry:
C. S. Lewis and George MacDonald on Suffering, Evil, and Death
Jeff McInnis

Shadows and Chivalry studies the influence of George MacDonald upon one of the most influential writers of modern times, C. S. Lewis—the creator of Narnia, literary critic, and best-selling apologist. Without ever ceasing to be a story of one man's influence upon another, the study also serves as an exploration of each writer's thought on, and literary visions of, good and evil.

The Downstretched Hand:
Individual Development in MacDonald's Major Fantasies for Children
Lesley Willis Smith

Smith demonstrates that MacDonald is fully aware of the need to integrate the unconscious into the conscious in order to achieve mature individuation. However, for MacDonald, true maturity and fulfillment can only be gained through a relationship with God. By exploring MacDonald's major biblical themes into his own myth, Smith reveals his literary genius and profound understanding of the human psyche. Smith interacts with other leading scholarship and in the context of other works by MacDonald, especially those written during the same time period.

A Novel Pulpit: Sermons From George MacDonald's Fiction
David L. Neuhouser

Each of the sermons has an introduction giving some explanation of the setting of the sermon or of the plot. *"MacDonald's novels are both stimulating and thought-provoking. This collection of sermons from ten novels serve to bring out the 'freshness and brilliance' of MacDonald's message."from the author's introduction*

www.ingramcontent.com/pod-product-compliance
Lightning Source LLC
LaVergne TN
LVHW040042080526
838202LV00045B/3453